Acoustic Properties of Absorbing Materials

Acoustic Properties of Absorbing Materials

If the book has a subtitle add it here

Editors

Edoardo Alessio Piana
Paolo Bonfiglio
Monika Rychtarikova

MDPI • Basel • Beijing • Wuhan • Barcelona • Belgrade • Manchester • Tokyo • Cluj • Tianjin

Editors
Edoardo Alessio Piana
University of Brescia
Italy

Paolo Bonfiglio
Spin-off of the University of Ferrara
Italy

Monika Rychtarikova
KU Leuven
Belgium

Editorial Office
MDPI
St. Alban-Anlage 66
4052 Basel, Switzerland

This is a reprint of articles from the Special Issue published online in the open access journal *Applied Sciences* (ISSN 2076-3417) (available at: https://www.mdpi.com/journal/applsci/special_issues/Acoustic_Properties_Absorbing_Materials).

For citation purposes, cite each article independently as indicated on the article page online and as indicated below:

LastName, A.A.; LastName, B.B.; LastName, C.C. Article Title. *Journal Name* **Year**, *Volume Number*, Page Range.

ISBN 978-3-0365-4607-0 (Hbk)
ISBN 978-3-0365-4608-7 (PDF)

© 2022 by the authors. Articles in this book are Open Access and distributed under the Creative Commons Attribution (CC BY) license, which allows users to download, copy and build upon published articles, as long as the author and publisher are properly credited, which ensures maximum dissemination and a wider impact of our publications.
The book as a whole is distributed by MDPI under the terms and conditions of the Creative Commons license CC BY-NC-ND.

Contents

About the Editors vii

Preface to "Acoustic Properties of Absorbing Materials" ix

Edoardo Alessio Piana, Paolo Bonfiglio and Monika Rychtarikova
Acoustic Properties of Absorbing Material
Reprinted from: *Applsci* 2022, 12, 4446, doi:10.3390/app12094446 1

Dengke Li, Zhongcheng Jiang, Lin Li, Xiaobo Liu, Xianfeng Wang and Mu He
Investigation of Acoustic Properties on Wideband Sound-Absorber Composed of Hollow Perforated Spherical Structure with Extended Tubes and Porous Materials
Reprinted from: *Applsci* 2020, 10, 8978, doi:10.3390/app10248978 5

Yaw-Shyan Tsay, Jui-Yen Lin and Faxin Ma
Development of a Panel Membrane Resonant Absorber
Reprinted from: *Applsci* 2021, 11, 1893, doi:10.3390/app11041893 17

Hasina Begum and Kirill V. Horoshenkov
Acoustical Properties of Fiberglass Blankets Impregnated with Silica Aerogel
Reprinted from: *Applsci* 2021, 11, 4593, doi:10.3390/app11104593 31

Louena Shtrepi, Arianna Astolfi, Elena Badino, Giovanni Volpatti and Davide Zampini
More Than Just Concrete: Acoustically Efficient Porous Concrete with Different Aggregate Shape and Gradation
Reprinted from: *Applsci* 2021, 11, 4835, doi:10.3390/app11114835 43

Manuela Neri, Elisa Levi, Eva Cuerva, Francesc Pardo-Bosch, Alfredo Guardo Zabaleta and Pablo Pujadas
Sound Absorbing and Insulating Low-Cost Panels from End-of-Life Household Materials for the Development of Vulnerable Contexts in Circular Economy Perspective
Reprinted from: *Applsci* 2021, 11, 5372, doi:10.3390/app11125372 63

Zihao Li, Xin Li and Bilong Liu
Optimization of Shunted Loudspeaker for Sound Absorption by Fully Exhaustive and Backtracking Algorithm
Reprinted from: *Applsci* 2021, 11, 5574, doi:10.3390/app11125574 83

Elisa Levi, Simona Sgarbi and Edoardo Alessio Piana
Acoustic Characterization of Some Steel Industry Waste Materials
Reprinted from: *Applsci* 2021, 11, 5924, doi:10.3390/app11135924 97

Federica Bettarello, Andrea Gasparella and Marco Caniato
The Influence of Floor Layering on Airborne Sound Insulation and Impact Noise Reduction: A Study on Cross Laminated Timber (CLT) Structures
Reprinted from: *Applsci* 2021, 11, 5938, doi:10.3390/app11135938 117

Xin Li, Bilong Liu and Chong Qin
A Perforated Plate with Stepwise Apertures for Low Frequency Sound Absorption
Reprinted from: *Applsci* 2021, 11, 6180, doi:10.3390/app11136180 135

Daniel Urbán, N. B. Roozen, Vojtech Jandák, Marek Brothánek and Ondřej Jiřiček
On the Determination of Acoustic Properties of Membrane Type Structural Skin Elements by Means of Surface Displacements
Reprinted from: *Applsci* 2021, 11, 10357, doi:10.3390/app112110357 149

Lamberto Tronchin, Angelo Farina, Antonella Bevilacqua, Francesca Merli and Pietro Fiumana
Comparison Failure and Successful Methodologies for Diffusion Measurements Undertaken inside Two Different Testing Rooms
Reprinted from: *Applsci* **2021**, *11*, 10523, doi:10.3390/app112210523 . . . . **173**

Hasina Begum and Kirill V. Horoshenkov
Correction: Begum, H.; Horoshenkov, K.V. Acoustical Properties of Fiberglass Blankets Impregnated with Silica Aerogel. *Appl. Sci.* 2021, *11*, 4593
Reprinted from: *Applsci* **2021**, *11*, 2834, doi:10.3390/app12062834 . . . . **191**

About the Editors

Edoardo Alessio Piana

Edoardo Alessio Piana is an associate professor at the Department of Mechanical and Industrial Engineering (University of Brescia). He studied Mechanical Engineering at University of Brescia. He received his Ph.D. degree in Energetics at Politecnico of Milan. During her research stays, he visited the Mercus Wallenberg Laboratory (KTH – Stockholm) and Belgian the Laboratory for Acoustics (KU Leuven). He founded the Laboratory for Acoustics (University of Brescia). Since 2005 he has been active in different fields of acoustics in general and in particular: acoustic modelling and characterisation of materials, noise from high-voltage power lines and electrical infrastructures, noise propagation in ducts, design of innovative instrumentation for acoustic measurements.

Paolo Bonfiglio

Paolo Bonfiglio is vice president of Materiacustica srl (spin-off company of the University of Ferrara). He got the Degree in Physics at the University of Catania in 2003 and in 2007 he received the Ph.D. degree in Civil Engineering and the European Doctorate in Sound and Vibration Studies (EDSVS) at the University of Ferrara. Part of the Ph.D. has been carried out at The Marcus Wallenberg Laboratory in Stockholm (Sweden). From 2007 to 2017 has been assistant professor at the University of Ferrara. His main research activities have been devoted to vibro-acoustics characterization of porous materials and experimental technique for their determination, numerical modelling for the study of acoustical radiation and noise and vibration control, active noise control in industrial and automotive fields.

Monika Rychtáriková

Monika Rychtáriková is a full professor at the Faculty of Architecture (KU Leuven). She studied architecture and building constructions at the Faculty of Civil Engineering at STU Bratislava, where she graduated, received her Ph.D. degree and become a full professor. During her research stays, she has visited TU Wien, TU Delft, RWTH Aachen, TU Zagreb and Belgian Building Research Institute. For more than 10 years she has been working in the Laboratory for Acoustics (KU Leuven) on different topics related to architectural acoustics. Since 2002 she has been active in different fields of building physics in general and building and room acoustics, environmental and virtual acoustics and perception of sound in particular. During the years 2011-2017 she has been a chair of Technical committee of Room and Building Acoustics of European Acoustic Association. In 2016 she has received an award "Female Scientist of the year 2015". Since 2017 she has been the president of Slovak Acoustic Society.

Preface to "Acoustic Properties of Absorbing Materials"

Thanks to the progress made in materials research and to the introduction of innovative manufacturing technologies, a wide range of sound-absorbing elements are currently available to adjust the acoustic features of an environment. Nowadays, performance is only one of the required specifications, together with environmental compatibility, longevity, and affordable cost. This book collects the most recent advances in the broad-spectrum characterization of sound-absorbing materials used in civil, industrial, and tertiary applications, by means of experimental, numerical, or theoretical studies.

Edoardo Alessio Piana, Paolo Bonfiglio, and Monika Rychtarikova
Editors

Editorial

Acoustic Properties of Absorbing Material

Edoardo Alessio Piana [1,*], Paolo Bonfiglio [2] and Monika Rychtarikova [3]

1. Applied Acoustics Laboratory, University of Brescia, 25123 Brescia, Italy
2. Materiacustica Srl, Spin-Off of the University of Ferrara, 44121 Ferrara, Italy; paolo.bonfiglio@materiacustica.it
3. Faculty of Architecture, Katholieke Universiteit Leuven, 3000 Leuven, Belgium; monika.rychtarikova@kuleuven.be
* Correspondence: edoardo.piana@unibs.it

Overview of the Articles in This Special Issue

Thanks to the progress made in materials research and to the introduction of innovative manufacturing technologies, a wide range of sound-absorbing elements are currently available to adjust the acoustic features of an environment. Nowadays, performance is only one of the required specifications, together with environmental compatibility, longevity, and affordable cost. The Special Issue, "Acoustic Properties of Sound-Absorbing Materials", collected the most recent advances in the broad-spectrum characterization of sound-absorbing materials used in civil, industrial, and tertiary applications, by means of experimental, numerical, or theoretical studies. Among many submissions, 11 articles were accepted and published.

The first published paper is an investigation by Dengke Li et al. [1] about the improvement of the sound absorption characteristics of a porous material coupled with a spherical structure. The aim was to improve the sound absorption of a specimen at relatively low frequencies, without increasing its thickness and keeping a good mid- to high-frequency sound absorption. Such behavior was obtained introducing a hollow perforated spherical structure, featuring extended tubes in a foam. The overall thickness of the specimen was less than 1/28 of the wavelength. Good agreements were observed between the simulated and the experimental results. The second paper, by Yaw-Shyan Tsay et al. [2], concerns the development of a resonant membrane panel absorber. The study focused on the improvement in acoustic quality parameters for auditoria, and showed how it is possible to manufacture a prototype, which proved to be particularly effective below 800 Hz. The tests were carried out during an experimental campaign, carried out in the Ge-Chi Hall of the National Cheng Kung University. The third paper, authored by Hasina Begum and Kirill Horoshenkov [3], studied the acoustical properties of fiberglass blankets impregnated with silica aerogel. The use of aerogel with fibrous blankets allows one to improve both acoustic absorption and thermal insulation performances. Since the mechanism influencing the acoustic performance of aerogel-impregnated blankets is still unclear and there is a lack of studies attempting to explain the measured absorption properties with a valid mathematical model, this paper contributed to this knowledge gap through a simulation that predicts the measured complex acoustic reflection coefficient of aerogel blankets with different filling ratios. The fourth contribution to the Special Issue, by Shtrepi et al. [4], is an experimental characterization of the sound absorption performances of "normal weight" and "lightweight" porous concrete aggregates. For each concrete type, three panel thicknesses were tested. Moreover, different mounting conditions were investigated, considering the combination of single panels in multiple layers, adding an air gap between the panel and the backing structure, and inserting a layer of rock wool in the air gap. The results show weighted absorption coefficients in the range of 0.30 to 0.75, depending on the thickness and mounting conditions. In the context of recycling materials that reached their end of life, but can still be used for other applications, Neri et al. [5] studied the sound absorption characteristics of low-cost insulating elements made of non-conventional materials. Given

Citation: Piana, E.A.; Bonfiglio, P.; Rychtarikova, M. Acoustic Properties of Absorbing Materials. *Appl. Sci.* **2022**, *12*, 4446. https://doi.org/10.3390/app12094446

Received: 11 March 2022
Accepted: 26 April 2022
Published: 28 April 2022

Publisher's Note: MDPI stays neutral with regard to jurisdictional claims in published maps and institutional affiliations.

Copyright: © 2022 by the authors. Licensee MDPI, Basel, Switzerland. This article is an open access article distributed under the terms and conditions of the Creative Commons Attribution (CC BY) license (https://creativecommons.org/licenses/by/4.0/).

that household materials at their end of life (EoLHM) are free of costs and available also to the more disadvantaged population, they can be used to build acoustic panels for such contexts. The acoustic properties of EoLHM, such as cardboard, egg cartons, clothes, metal elements and combinations of them, are investigated by means of a four-microphones impedance tube. The measured sound absorption coefficient and transmission loss showed that EoLHM can be used for manufacturing acoustic panels. However, since none of the analyzed materials show good absorbing and insulating properties at the same time, EoLHM must be wisely selected. The sixth article is authored by Zihao Li et al. [6] and proposes the application of a technique based on semi-active structure of a shunted loudspeaker and a fully exhaustive backtracking algorithm, in order to obtain an optimized sound absorption in a specific frequency range. In the seventh article, Levi et al. [7] investigated the acoustic and non-acoustic properties of steelwork by-products. The inverse method adopted in the paper is founded on the Johnson–Champoux–Allard (JCA) model and uses a standard minimization procedure, based on the difference between the experimentally obtained sound absorption coefficients and the absorption coefficients predicted by the JCA model. The eighth paper, by Bettarello et al. [8], investigates the sound insulation properties of timber floors. Such structures must be properly designed in order to meet the requirements of indoor comfort and comply with current building regulations. This work presents the results obtained by in-field measurements developed using different sound sources on Cross-Laminated Timber floors (tapping machine, impact rubber ball, and airborne dodecahedral speaker), changing different sound insulation layering conditions (suspended ceiling and floating floors). The results clearly show that there is no available analytical model able to correctly predict the acoustic performances of Cross-Laminated Timber floors. In the ninth paper, Xin Li et al. [9] studied the low-frequency sound absorption of a Perforated Plate with Stepwise Apertures. Such panels can match the acoustic resistance of air and moderately increase the acoustic mass, especially at low frequencies. Some prototypes made by 3D printing technology were tested in an impedance tube. The measured results agree well with the predictions. The tenth paper, by Urban et al. [10], focuses on the determination of the acoustic properties (sound absorption and transmission coefficients) of membrane types of specimens. The characterization was made by means of a combination of incident plane wave sound pressure and membrane surface displacement information, measuring the sound pressure with a microphone and the membrane displacement by means of a laser Doppler vibrometer. The proposed method was compared with the conventional methods for sound transmission loss and absorption measurements in an impedance tube, both numerically and experimentally. Subsequently, the proposed method was tested in a laboratory environment. The last paper in the Special Issue is authored by Lamberto Tronchin et al. [11], and compares different methodologies that can be applied for the evaluation of the sound diffusion inside a room. This article considers the surface-scattering effects and the diffusion phenomena related to some types of MDF and plywood panels, tested by disposing the wells horizontally and vertically. The test results, undertaken inside a semi-reverberant room and inside a large reverberant room, were compared to highlight the success and the failure of the different measuring methodologies adopted.

Author Contributions: Conceptualization, E.A.P., P.B. and M.R.; writing—original draft preparation, E.A.P., P.B. and M.R.; writing—review and editing, E.A.P., P.B. and M.R. All authors have read and agreed to the published version of the manuscript.

Funding: This research received no external funding.

Acknowledgments: We gratefully thank all authors, who made this Special Issue a success.

Conflicts of Interest: The authors declare no conflict of interest.

References

1. Li, D.; Jiang, Z.; Li, L.; Liu, X.; Wang, X.; He, M. Investigation of Acoustic Properties on Wideband Sound-Absorber Composed of Hollow Perforated Spherical Structure with Extended Tubes and Porous Materials. *Appl. Sci.* **2020**, *10*, 8978. [CrossRef]
2. Tsay, Y.-S.; Lin, J.-Y.; Ma, F. Development of a Panel Membrane Resonant Absorber. *Appl. Sci.* **2021**, *11*, 1893. [CrossRef]
3. Begum, H.; Horoshenkov, K.V. Acoustical Properties of Fiberglass Blankets Impregnated with Silica Aerogel. *Appl. Sci.* **2021**, *11*, 4593. [CrossRef]
4. Shtrepi, L.; Astolfi, A.; Badino, E.; Volpatti, G.; Zampini, D. More Than Just Concrete: Acoustically Efficient Porous Concrete with Different Aggregate Shape and Gradation. *Appl. Sci.* **2021**, *11*, 4835. [CrossRef]
5. Neri, M.; Levi, E.; Cuerva, E.; Pardo-Bosch, F.; Zabaleta, A.G.; Pujadas, P. Sound Absorbing and Insulating Low-Cost Panels from End-of-Life Household Materials for the Development of Vulnerable Contexts in Circular Economy Perspective. *Appl. Sci.* **2021**, *11*, 5372. [CrossRef]
6. Li, Z.; Li, X.; Liu, B. Optimization of Shunted Loudspeaker for Sound Absorption by Fully Exhaustive and Backtracking Algorithm. *Appl. Sci.* **2021**, *11*, 5574. [CrossRef]
7. Levi, E.; Sgarbi, S.; Piana, E.A. Acoustic Characterization of Some Steel Industry Waste Materials. *Appl. Sci.* **2021**, *11*, 5924. [CrossRef]
8. Bettarello, F.; Gasparella, A.; Caniato, M. The Influence of Floor Layering on Airborne Sound Insulation and Impact Noise Reduction: A Study on Cross Laminated Timber (CLT) Structures. *Appl. Sci.* **2021**, *11*, 5938. [CrossRef]
9. Li, X.; Liu, B.; Qin, C. A Perforated Plate with Stepwise Apertures for Low Frequency Sound Absorption. *Appl. Sci.* **2021**, *11*, 6180. [CrossRef]
10. Urbán, D.; Roozen, N.B.; Jandák, V.; Brothánek, M.; Jiříček, O. On the Determination of Acoustic Properties of Membrane Type Structural Skin Elements by Means of Surface Displacements. *Appl. Sci.* **2021**, *11*, 10357. [CrossRef]
11. Tronchin, L.; Farina, A.; Bevilacqua, A.; Merli, F.; Fiumana, P. Comparison Failure and Successful Methodologies for Diffusion Measurements Undertaken inside Two Different Testing Rooms. *Appl. Sci.* **2021**, *11*, 10523. [CrossRef]

Article

Investigation of Acoustic Properties on Wideband Sound-Absorber Composed of Hollow Perforated Spherical Structure with Extended Tubes and Porous Materials

Dengke Li [1,2,*], Zhongcheng Jiang [2], Lin Li [3], Xiaobo Liu [2], Xianfeng Wang [2] and Mu He [4]

1. Train and Track Research Institute, State Key Laboratory of Traction Power, Southwest Jiaotong University, Chengdu 610031, China
2. The State Key Laboratory of Heavy Duty AC Drive Electric Locomotive Systems Integration, Zhuzhou 412001, China; Jiangzhongcheng.zz@crrcgc.cc (Z.J.); Liuxiaobo.zz@crrcgc.cc (X.L.); Wangxianfeng.zz@crrcgc.cc (X.W.)
3. National Innovation Center of Advanced Rail Transit Equipment, Zhuzhou 412001, China; Lilin.zz@crrcgc.cc
4. Green Building, Energy Saving and Noise Reduction Research Center, Department of Urban Construction, City College, Wuhan University of Science and Technology, Wuhan 430083, China; mu.he@wic.edu.cn
* Correspondence: ldk@mail.ioa.ac.cn or lidengke.zz@crrcgc.cc

Received: 4 November 2020; Accepted: 11 December 2020; Published: 16 December 2020

Abstract: Traditional porous media such as melamine foam absorb sound due to their three-dimensional porous struts. However, the acoustic properties at low frequencies are greatly related to its thickness. In this paper, a novel type of thin and lightweight sound absorber composed of melamine foam and hollow perforated spherical structure with extended tubes (HPSET) is introduced to enhance the sound absorption performance at low frequencies. A theoretical model for the normal absorption coefficient of the HPSET with melamine foam is established. Good agreements are observed between the simulated and the experimental results. Compared with the virgin melamine foam, the proposed absorber can greatly improve the low-frequency sound absorption and retain the mid- to high-frequency sound absorption, while the thickness of the proposed absorber is less than 1/28 of the wavelength.

Keywords: hollow perforated spherical structure with extended tubes; low frequency sound absorption; melamine foam; wideband sound absorber

---

1. Introduction

Melamine foams are porous materials widely used in the transport and civil engineering industries for their remarkable properties of sound absorption and special abilities to withstand extreme environments (such as heat insulation, fire protection and environmental protection). At present, the research on this type of foam material has produced a series of papers, and the manufacturing process is protected by a large family of patents [1,2]. However, in practical noise applications, such as rail locomotive vehicles, the internal noise of the vehicle is mainly dominant in the low-frequency noise of 100–1000 Hz. If a single layer of melamine foam is used to absorb the low frequency noise inside the cab, the foam materials usually require a relatively large space and material thickness [3]. Many researches focused on the optimization of the pore size of porous foams, since the sound energy dissipation mechanism of porous materials originates from the visco-thermal dissipation of micropores. Perrot [4] studied the sound absorption properties of the open-cell foam metal structure based on the Kelvin structure. He pointed out that the pore size directly determines the flow resistivity of the material. When the pore size is small, the flow resistivity of the material increases, and the sound wave is not easy to enter the material; when the pore structure is large, the flow resistivity is very small, and the large-size micropores cannot provide sufficient damping for the incident sound waves. Later, Trinhet et al. [5] studied the sound absorption of polyurethane foam with membrane in the pore network, and their results show that decreasing the openness of the membrane could enhance sound absorption performances of the material in low frequency ranges. Park et al. [6,7] built a multiscale numerical model to optimize the sound absorption properties of PU foams, they found that the acoustic damping at low frequencies could be improved with an optimum mean cell size and cell openness.

Optimization of the geometrical parameters of the porous structure could improve the sound absorption of the porous foams to some extent; however, their first sound absorption peak frequency is still determined by its quarter wavelength resonance frequency. In recent years, much attention has been paid on developing meta-acoustic materials to enhance the low frequency absorbing performance. Kidner and Fuller experimentally investigated the use of heterogeneous (HG) acoustic materials to improve low frequency insertion loss of blankets [8]. An active-passive method, which, based on FOAM-PVDF structure, was also introduced by Fuller to enhance the transmission loss of foam materials [9]. Fuller and his colleagues further [10] used meta-materials that are composed of small masses and poro-elastic media to improve the sound absorption of the porous materials at low frequencies. Based on numerical analyses of the finite element method, Groby et al. [11,12] conducted several studies on periodic inclusions embedded in the porous layer to improve the sound absorption bandwidth. However, their effective sound absorption bandwidth of the composite absorber still lies in the mid-or high-frequency range (>1000 Hz).

Relying on the multi-layer resonance system, the sound absorption bandwidth of porous media could be significantly broadened by using the perforated plates. Lin [13] studied the structure of the sound-absorbing material behind the micro-perforated plate, and their results revealed that, when the sound-absorbing material occupied the entire cavity, the combined structure had a broader sound absorption band. Li et al. [14] studied theoretically and experimentally the sound absorption coefficient of sound-absorbing materials combined with micro-perforated plates by using the transfer matrix method. They analyzed influences of different placement of sound-absorbing materials on the sound absorptive performance for the composite absorber, and proposed a wideband sound-absorbing configuration in which the sound-absorbing material was placed in front of the micro-perforated plate. However, the composite absorber still requires a large installation space.

More recent work has laid foundations of improving the low frequency sound absorption performance by using extended tube resonators [15–19]. Li et al. [16–18] presented a kind of multiple extended tube resonators to enhance the low frequency range from 100 to 1600 Hz in a constrained space of 100 mm. In order to further improve the low frequency sound absorption of a thin layer melamine foam below 500 Hz, a new type of resonant absorber comprised of hollow perforated spherical structure with extended tubes is introduced in the present work. Hence we theoretically and experimentally investigated the low sound absorption performance of the combined absorber, and found that the coupling between the Helmholtz resonance and the quarter wavelength resonance shows a great potential to ameliorate sound absorptive performance of a traditional porous foam at low- and mid- frequencies. Meanwhile, the sound absorption in low frequency range could be greatly enhanced by tuning the tube parameters. Our proposed sound absorber reaches the same sound absorption performance of PPETs-PSAM [17,18], while it is more practical in noise control application since this device is simply made of a thin and lightweight hollow perforated spherical structure, and could be easily combined with porous foams. In what follows, we firstly conduct a theoretical analysis of the performance of combined absorber in Section 2, and then focus on parametric studies in Section 3. Section 4 is aimed at experimental verifications by impedance tube. Finally, Section 5 draws some conclusions.

2. Theoretical Analyses

2.1. Impedance Model of Melamine Foam

Following the well-known JCAL model proposed by Johnson et al. [20] and Lafarge et al. [21], the equivalent density $\rho_{eq}(\omega)$ and modulus $K_{eq}(\omega)$ of the porous fluid are

$$\rho_{eq}(\omega) = \frac{\alpha_\infty \rho_0}{\phi} \left[1 - j\frac{\sigma\phi}{\omega\rho_0\alpha_\infty} \sqrt{1 + j\frac{4\alpha_\infty^2 \eta \rho_0 \omega}{\sigma^2 \Lambda^2 \phi^2}} \right] \tag{1}$$

$$K_{eq}(\omega) = \frac{\gamma P_0/\phi}{\gamma - (\gamma-1)\left[1 - j\frac{\phi\eta}{k_0' N_{pr} \rho_0 \omega} \sqrt{1 + j\frac{4k_0'^2 N_{pr} \rho_0 \omega}{\eta \Lambda'^2 \phi^2}}\right]^{-1}} \tag{2}$$

where ω is the angular frequency, ρ_0 is the density of the air, η is the viscosity of the air, σ is the airflow resistivity, P_0 is the mean ambient pressure, ϕ is the porosity of the material considered, N_{pr} is the Prandtl number of the air, and $\gamma = C_p/C_v$ is the specific heat ratio, in which C_p and C_v are the specific heat capacities at constant pressure and at constant volume respectively. The JCAL model involves six characteristic parameters: the static viscous permeability k_0, the porosity ϕ, the tortuosity α_∞, the viscous characteristic length Λ, the static thermal permeability k_0' and the thermal characteristic length Λ'.

According to formula (1) and formula (2), the wave number k_s and characteristic impedance Z_s of the equivalent fluid medium is

$$Z_s(\omega) = \sqrt{\rho_{eq}(\omega) K_{eq}(\omega)}, \text{ and} \tag{3}$$

$$k_s(\omega) = \omega \sqrt{\rho_{eq}(\omega)/K_{eq}(\omega)} \tag{4}$$

For the melamine foam with a thickness of H, the surface impedance at $x = H$ of the sample backed by a rigid wall (see Figure 1) is given by

$$Z_{PM}(\omega) = \frac{-jZ_s(\omega) \cot(k_s(\omega)H)}{\phi} \tag{5}$$

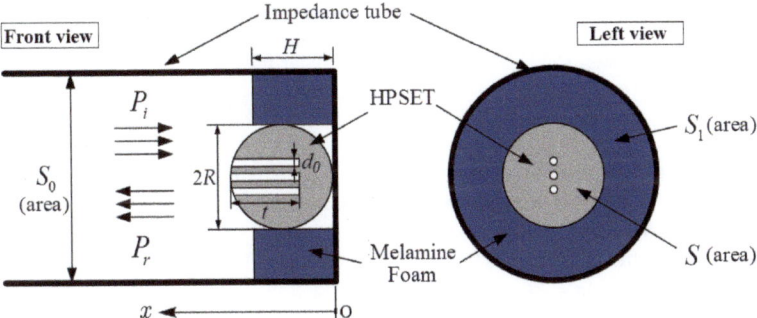

Figure 1. Illustration of HPSET and melamine foam installed at an impedance tube. The thickness of the foam is H, and the inner diameter of the HPSET is $2R$. The diameters and the maximum length of the extended tubes are d_0 and t. All extended tubes inlets are shaped to follow the sphere curvature. The cross-sectional areas of HPSET and impedance tube are S and S_0.

In this paper, an experimental characterization approach, which requires direct measurements of ϕ and k_0 and an impedance tube technique [22–24], is adopted to characterize the transport parameters of melamine foam [25,26]. Parameters of the melamine foam are listed in Table 1. The porosity ϕ is measured by a porosimeter, the air-flow resistivity σ is directly measured by resistivimeter, and the remaining four transport parameters ($\alpha_\infty, \Lambda, \Lambda', k_0'$) are determined by the inverse characterization techniques using a three-microphone impedance tube [24]. We use a commercially available software RokCell (v3.0, MATELYS, Lyon, France) [27] to automatically obtain the estimations of the parameters.

Table 1. Parameters of the melamine foam.

Parameters	σ (Pa·s/m^2)	ϕ	α_∞	Λ (μm)	Λ' (μm)	k_0' (×10^{-10} m^2)
Melamine foam	9354 ± 390	0.993 ± 0.001	1.04 ± 0.02	107 ± 5	223 ± 23	23 ± 2

2.2. Impedance Model of the Hollow Perforated Spherical Structure with Extended Tubes (HPSET)

Figure 1 illustrates the placement of the HPSET and melamine foam in an impedance tube. According to the well-known Maa model [28,29], the acoustic impedance of a single extended tube can be expressed as

$$Z = \frac{\Delta P}{\bar{u}} = j\omega\rho_0(t + 0.85d_0)\left[1 - \frac{2}{x\sqrt{-j}}\frac{J_1(x\sqrt{-j})}{J_0(x\sqrt{-j})}\right]^{-1} + \frac{\sqrt{2\omega\rho_0\eta}}{4} \quad (6)$$

where $x = d_0\sqrt{\omega\rho_0/(4\eta)}$ is the ratio between the perforation radius and the viscous boundary layer thickness inside the tube of the perforations (also named "perforation constant"), d_0 is the inner diameter of the extended tubes, t is the maximum length of the tubes, η is the viscosity of the air, ω denotes the angular frequency, $j = \sqrt{-1}$ represents the imaginary unit, ρ_0 is the mass density of the air, and J_0, J_1 are Bessel's functions of zero and first order.

The normalized impedance of the spherical resonating cavity is $Z_D = -j\cot\left(\frac{\omega}{c}\frac{(V-V_{tubes})}{S}\right)$, then the normalized impedance of HPSET absorber is given as

$$Z_{HPSET} = \frac{Z}{\varphi_p\rho_0 c} + Z_D = r_p + j\omega m_p - j\cot\left(\frac{\omega}{c}\frac{(V-V_{tubes})}{S}\right) \quad (7)$$

with

$$r_p = \frac{32\eta t}{\varphi_p\rho_0 c d_0^2}\left(\left(1 + \frac{x^2}{32}\right)^{1/2} + \frac{\sqrt{2}xd_0}{64t}\right) \quad (8)$$

$$\omega m_p = \frac{\omega t}{\varphi_p c}\left(1 + \left(9 + \frac{x^2}{2}\right)^{-1/2} + 0.85\frac{d_0}{t}\right) \quad (9)$$

where $\rho_0 c$ denotes the characteristic impedance of the air, c is the sound speed in the air (m/s), $\phi_p = NA_0/S$ corresponds to the perforation ratio of the HPSET (N denotes the number of extended tubes, $A_0 = \pi d_0^2/4$ denotes to the inner cross-sectional area of the extended tubes, $S = \pi R^2$ is the cross-sectional area of the HPSET. d_0 is the inner diameter of the extension tubes and R is the inner radius of the HPSET). $V = 4\pi R^3/3$ and $V_{tubes} = \pi t N d_0^2/4$ are the volume of the perforated ball and the extended tubes, respectively.

2.3. Normal Incidence Sound Absorption of HPSET with a Melamine Foam

Considering the sound waves impinges vertically on the composite absorber as illustrated in Figure 1. As the HPSET is embedded within the melamine foam, the equivalent impedance is the parallel of the HPSET and the melamine. Based on the impedance transfer formula [30], the specific acoustic impedance of the melamine foam at the surface of the composite absorber can be calculated as

$$Z'_{PM} = \frac{Z_{PM}(\omega) + j\rho_0 c \tan(k_s(\omega)(R-H))}{\rho_0 c + j Z_{PM}(\omega) \tan(k_s(\omega)(R-H))} \quad (10)$$

Then, the characteristic impedance of the composed absorber is given as

$$Z' = \left(\frac{1-\varphi_b}{Z'_{PM}} + \frac{\varphi_b}{Z_{HPSET}}\right) \quad (11)$$

where $\varphi_b = S/S_0$, and S_0 denotes the cross-sectional area of the impedance tube, S denotes the cross-sectional area of the HPEST. The normal incidence sound absorption coefficient of HPSET combined with melamine foam installed at an impedance tube is calculated as

$$\alpha = \frac{4\text{Real}(Z')}{(1+\text{Real}(Z')^2) + \text{Imag}(Z')^2} \quad (12)$$

3. Simulation Results and Discussion

3.1. Analytical Study of Normal Incidence Sound Absorption Coefficient of the HPSET with a Melamine Foam

Figure 2 illustrates the analytical results of the normal incidence sound absorption coefficient of the HPSET with a melamine foam obtained from Equation (12), in which the sound absorption of HPSET and a single layer melamine foam are also shown for a comparison. In the following simulations, the inner diameter of the HPSET is $2R = 65$ mm, the number of perforations is $N = 2$, the diameters and lengths of the extended tubes are $d_0 = 4.9$ mm and $t = 10$ mm, respectively. The Helmholtz resonance absorption peak of the HPSET is found at 380 Hz and the anti-resonance frequency of this combined absorber is observed at 500 Hz, while the quarter wavelength resonance frequency of the porous material is around 1500 Hz. It is shown in Figure 2a that the sound absorption of the composite absorber is superior to the single layer melamine foam and HPSET. It is clear that the sound absorption of a single layer porous foam is less than 0.5 below 500 Hz. While the composite absorber reaches a wideband sound absorption (greater than 0.5) in the frequency range from 350 Hz to 2000 Hz, hence combination of HPSET with melamine foam could greatly enhance the low frequency sound absorptive performance of the melamine foam.

It is revealed from Figure 2b that the relative resistance of single layer melamine foam and HPSET are less than 1, which is less than the combined absorber in the frequency range from 360 Hz to 2000 Hz. Hence, the present absorber could improve the acoustic resistance and enhance the sound absorption. Meanwhile, the relative acoustic reactance of this combination is nearly zero at the resonance frequency of 380 Hz and 1500 Hz, which ensures the wideband absorptive performance of the proposed absorber. The low frequency sound absorptive performance could be further enhanced by combining multiple HPSETs with different resonance frequency.

3.2. Parametric Study of the Sound Absorption Coefficient of HPSET with a Melamine Foam

Since the sound absorption of HPSET-Melamine foam absorber is influenced by many parameters, we take the same analytical process and investigate the main parameters in this section. The resistivity of the melamine foam is a key factor which dominates the sound absorption. It is demonstrated in Figure 3a that the resistivity of the melamine foam will greatly influence sound absorption both at the anti-resonance frequency and the quarter wavelength resonance frequency. When increasing the resistivity of the melamine foam, the sound absorption at the anti-resonance frequency is enhanced, while the sound absorption at the quarter wavelength resonance frequency is firstly increased and then decreased. The absorption peak at Helmholtz resonance frequency decreases slightly with the increase in resistivity. Hence, a reasonable resistivity is required to match the specific resistance of the incident sound waves for the composite absorber.

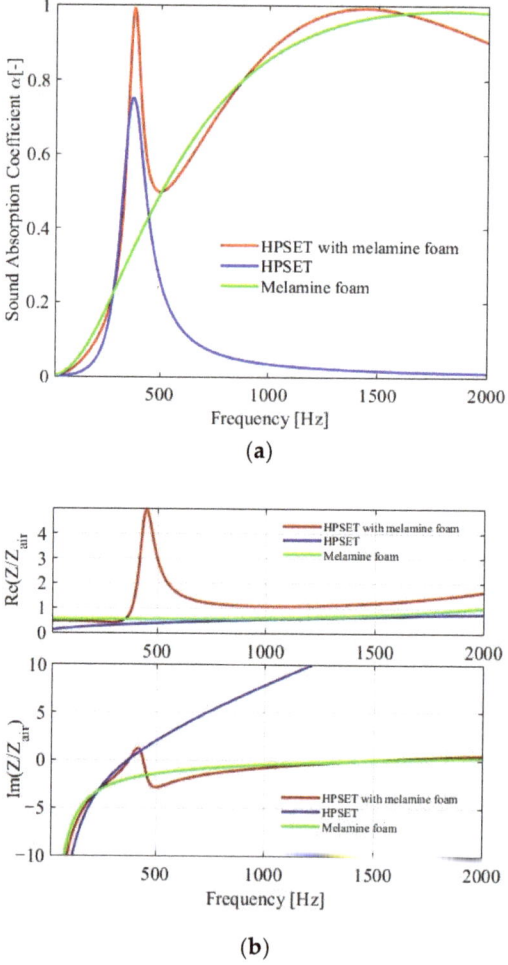

Figure 2. Analytical results of normal incidence sound absorption of HPSET with melamine foam. (a) Normal incidence sound absorption coefficient; (b) Characteristic acoustic resistance and reactance.

Figure 3b demonstrates the variation of the diameter of extended tubes on the overall sound absorption of the present absorber. The tube diameter is a critical factor which controls the sound absorption performance of the sound absorption of HPSET. When the tube diameter is too large, the relative resistance is less than 1, and the sound absorption is decreased. On the opposite, a small-diameter will induce overlarge acoustic resistance which will also decrease the sound absorption.

As illustrated in Figure 3c,d, the low frequency sound absorption peak of the combined absorber is greatly shifted to lower frequencies by decreasing the tube number or increasing the tube length, while the high sound absorption peak remains the same. It is noted that the low frequency sound absorption of the HPSET is due to the increase in mass reactance, and the resonance frequency could be tuned via optimizing the tube parameters.

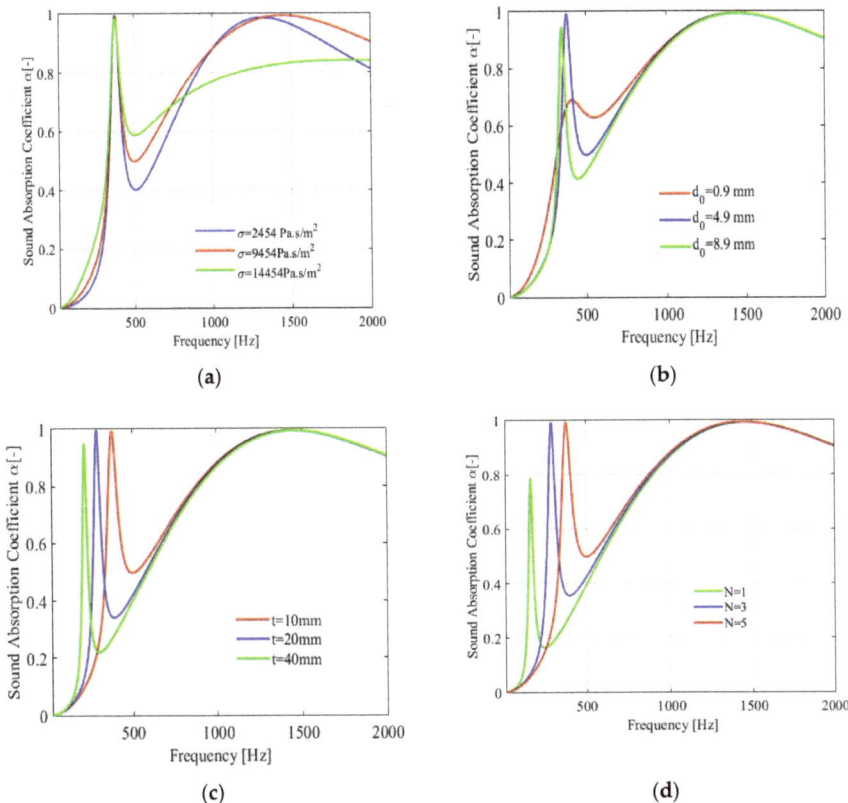

Figure 3. Comparison of the normal incidence sound absorption of composite absorber with different parameters. (**a**) The resistivity of melamine foam; (**b**) The diameter of extended tubes; (**c**) The length of extended tubes; (**d**) The number of extended tubes.

4. Experimental Validation

The normal-incidence sound absorption coefficient of the HPSET with melamine foam is measured by an impedance tube (B&K 4206, see Figure 4) based on the transfer function method. The measurements are manipulated according to the ISO 10534-2 standard [31], and the experiment set up is shown in Figure 4. The distance between the two microphones is 50 mm and the measured frequency range is from 0 to 1600 Hz. The inner diameter of the impedance tube is 100 mm. The room temperature is 17.5 °C, the atmosphere pressure is 1.01×10^5 Pa, and the relative humidity is 66.4%. The hollow perforated spherical structure used in the experiments is made of plastic, and the extended tubes are made of copper. Parameters for the HPSETs are shown in Table 2. Thickness of hollow perforated spherical structure and extended tubes is 0.5 mm. The thickness of the foam is 50 mm, and the average densities of the HPSET with foam are 47.1 kg/m^3.

Table 2. Parameters of the tested samples of HPSETs.

Parameters	d_0 (mm)	t (mm)	N	2R (mm)
HPSET$_1$	4.9	10	2	65
HPSET$_2$	4.9	10	5	65

Figure 5 shows the comparison of the experimental result and the calculation result for the sound absorption coefficient of the melamine foam. The calculation result uses the inverse characterization techniques described in Section 2.1 (inversion method-based parameters are listed in Table 1). It is shown that the calculation result is highly consistent with the actual experimental result, which verifies the reliability of this inversion characterization method.

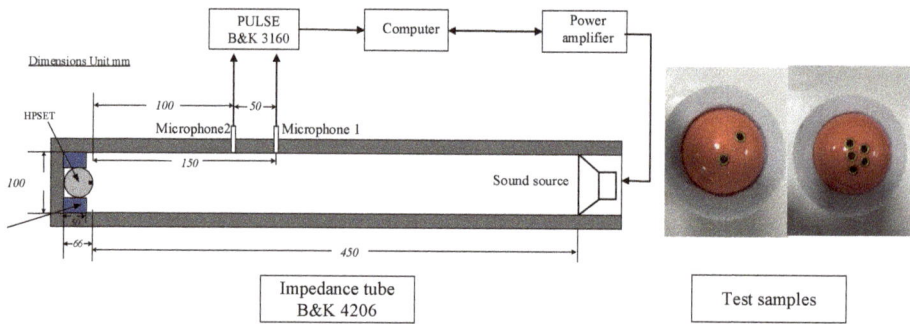

Figure 4. Experiment set up.

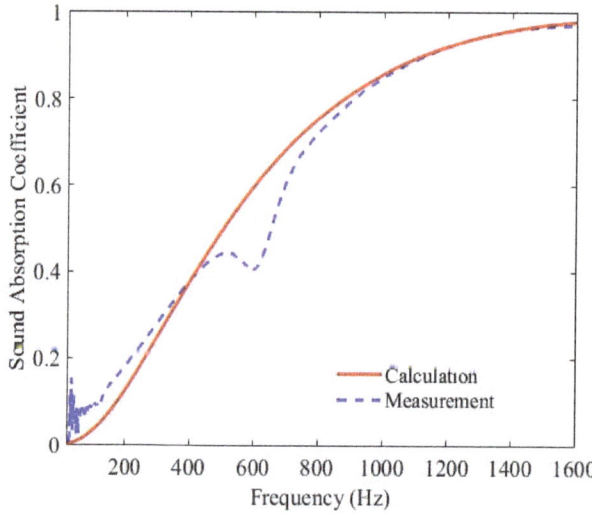

Figure 5. Sound absorption coefficient of the melamine foam. The red solid line and blue dashed line represent the calculated results by inversion method and directly measured results, respectively.

The measured and calculated sound absorption coefficient curves of HPSET with melamine foam are shown in Figure 6. Good agreement is observed between the measurement and calculation. The HPSET combined with a porous foam in a limited thickness of 65 mm reaches a good sound absorption property in the frequency range from 200 to 1600 Hz. The thickness of the porous material is only 1/28 of the sound wavelength, which realizes the purpose of controlling the large wavelength with thin layer materials.

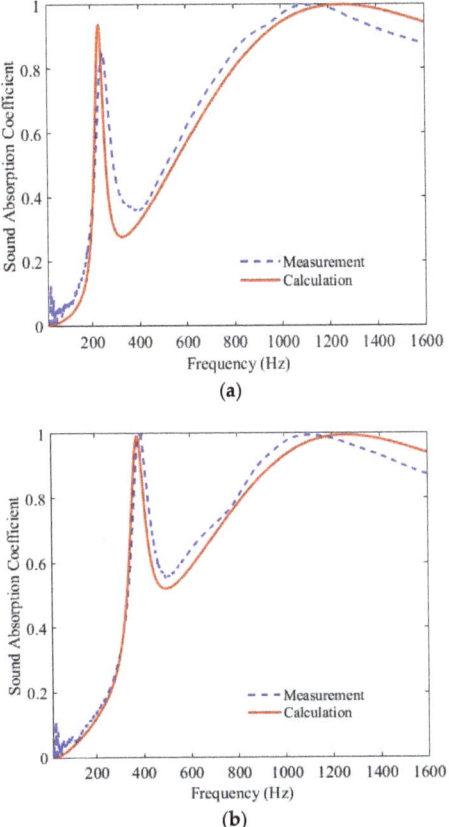

Figure 6. Sound absorption coefficient of the composite absorber for (**a**) HPSET$_1$ and (**b**) HPSET$_2$ (see Table 2). Red solid line: calculation by inversion method; Blue dashed line: direct measurement.

5. Conclusions

A thin and lightweight sound absorber is presented to improve the acoustic properties at low frequencies of melamine foams. The absorption performance of the compound absorber is validated experimentally by using an impedance tube, and the measured results are consistent with the calculation results. Our research implies that the tube diameter and the resistivity are critical factors controlling the absorption performance. When decreasing the tube number or increasing the tube length, the resonance frequency is greatly shifted to lower frequencies. Both theoretical and measured results show that the HPSET combined with a melamine foam can keep good sound absorptive performance in the frequency range from 200–1600 Hz in a limited thickness. Compared with conventional absorbers, the proposed absorber is practical in noise control applications such as in domains of rail vehicles, aircrafts cabin and automobiles.

Author Contributions: Conceptualization, L.L.; Methodology, D.L.; Software, M.H.; Formal Analysis, L.L. and Z.J.; Investigation, D.L. and M.H.; Data Curation, X.L. and X.W.; Writing—Original Draft Preparation, D.L.; Writing—Review and Editing, M.H. and Z.J.; Visualization, L.L. and D.L. All authors have read and agreed to the published version of the manuscript.

Funding: The first author would like to acknowledge the support from the project of China Postdoctoral Science Foundation (Grant No. 256069).

Conflicts of Interest: The authors declare no conflict of interest.

References

1. Imashiro, Y.; Hasegawa, S.; Matsumoto, T. Melamine Resin Foam. U.S. Patent No. 5,413,853, 9 May 1995.
2. Thom, A. Melamine Resin Foam. U.S. Patent No. 6,350,511, 26 February 2002.
3. Fuchs, H. Alternative fibreless absorbers—New tools and materials for noise control and acoustic comfort. *Acta. Acoust.* **2001**, *87*, 414–422.
4. Perrot, C.; Chevillotte, F.; Panneton, R. Dynamic viscous permeability of an open-cell aluminum foam: Computations vs experiments. *J. Appl. Phys.* **2008**, *103*, 024909. [CrossRef]
5. Trinh, V.H.; Hoang, M.T.; Perrot, C.; Langlois, V.; Khidas, Y.; Pitois, O. A systematic link between microstructure and acoustic properties of foam: A detailed study on the effects of membranes. In Proceedings of the 6th Biot Conference of Poromechanics, Paris, France, 9–13 June 2017.
6. Park, J.H.; Minn, K.S.; Lee, H.R.; Yang, S.H.; Yu, C.B.; Pak, S.Y.; Oh, C.S.; Song, Y.S.; Kang, Y.J.; Youn, J.R. Cell openness manipulation of low density polyurethane foam for efficient sound absorption. *J. Sound Vib.* **2017**, *406*, 224–236. [CrossRef]
7. Park, J.H.; Yang, S.H.; Lee, H.R.; Yu, C.B.; Pak, S.Y.; Oh, C.S.; Kang, Y.J.; Youn, J.R. Optimization of low frequency sound absorption by cell size control and multiscale poroacoustics modeling. *J. Sound Vib.* **2017**, *397*, 17–30. [CrossRef]
8. Kidner, M.; Gardner, B.; Fuller, C. Improvements in Low Frequency Insertion Loss Blankets: Experimental Investigation. *J. Sound Vib.* **2006**, *294*, 466–472. [CrossRef]
9. Fuller, C.; Kidner, M.; Li, X.; Hansen, C. Active-Passive Heterogeneous for Control of Vibration and Sound Radiation. In Proceedings of the 2004 International Symposium on Active Control of Sound and Vibration, Williamsburg, VA, USA, 20–22 September 2004.
10. Fuller, C. Sound absorption using acoustic meta materials. In Proceedings of the Inter-Noise 2012, New York, NY, USA, 19–22 August 2012.
11. Groby, J.P.; Lagarrigue, C.; Brouard, B.; Dazel, O.; Tournat, V.; Nennig, B. Enhancing the absorption properties of acoustic porous plates by periodically embedding Helmholtz resonators. *J. Acout. Soc. Am.* **2015**, *137*, 273–280. [CrossRef] [PubMed]
12. Groby, J.P.; Lagarrigue, C.; Brouard, B.; Dazel, O.; Tournat, V.; Nennig, B. Using simple shape three-dimensional rigid inclusions to enhance porous layer absorption. *J. Acout. Soc. Am.* **2014**, *136*, 1139–1148. [CrossRef] [PubMed]
13. Lin, L.; Wang, Z.; Jiang, Z. Effect of sound-absorbing material on a micro-perforated absorbing construction. *Acta. Acust.* **2010**, *35*, 385–391.
14. Li, D.; Chang, D.; Liu, B.; Tian, J. Improving the sound absorption bandwidth of micro-perforated panel by adding porous sound absorbing materials. In Proceedings of the Internoise 2014, Melbourne, Australia, 16–19 November 2014.
15. Lu, Y.; Li, X.; Tian, J.; Wei, W. The perforated panel resonator with flexible tube bundle and its acoustical measurements. In Proceedings of the Internoise 2001, The Hague, The Netherlands, 27–30 August 2001.
16. Li, D.; Chang, D.; Liu, B. Enhancing the low frequency sound absorption of a perforated panel by parallel-arranged extended tubes. *Appl. Acoust.* **2016**, *102*, 126–132. [CrossRef]
17. Li, D.; Chang, D.; Liu, B. Enhanced low- to mid-frequency sound absorption using parallel-arranged perforated plates with extended tubes and porous material. *Appl. Acoust.* **2017**, *127*, 316–323. [CrossRef]
18. Li, D.; Chang, D.; Liu, B. Diffuse sound absorptive properties of parallel-arranged perforated plates with extended tubes and porous materials. *Materials* **2020**, *13*, 1091. [CrossRef]
19. Simon, F. Long Elastic Open Neck Acoustic Resonator for low frequency absorption. *J. Sound Vib.* **2018**, *421*, 1–16. [CrossRef]
20. Johnson, D.L.; Koplik, J.; Dashen, R. Theory of dynamic permeability and tortuosity in fluid-saturated porous media. *J. Fluid Mech.* **1987**, *176*, 379–402. [CrossRef]
21. Lafarge, D.; Lemarinier, P.; Allard, J.F.; Tarnow, V. Dynamic compressibility of air in porous structures and audible frequencies. *J. Acout. Soc. Am.* **1997**, *102*, 1995–2006. [CrossRef]
22. Stinson, R.; Daigle, G. Electronic system for the measurement of flow resistance. *J. Acout. Soc. Am.* **1988**, *83*, 2422–2428. [CrossRef]

23. Iwase, T.; Izumi, Y.; Kawabata, R. A New Measuring Method for Sound Propagation by Using Sound Tube without Any Air Spaces. In Proceedings of the 1998 International Congress on Noise Control Engineering, Christchurch, New Zealand, 16–18 November 1998.
24. Salissou, Y.; Panneton, R. Wideband characterization of the complex wave and characteristic impedance of sound absorbers. *J. Acout. Soc. Am.* **2010**, *128*, 2868–2876. [CrossRef] [PubMed]
25. Panneton, R.; Olny, X. Acoustical determination of the governing viscous dissipation in porous media. *J. Acout. Soc. Am.* **2006**, *119*, 2027–2040. [CrossRef]
26. Olny, X.; Panneton, R. Acoustical determination of the governing thermal dissipation in porous media. *J. Acout. Soc. Am.* **2008**, *123*, 814–824. [CrossRef]
27. Available online: https://rokcell.matelys.com/ (accessed on 4 December 2020).
28. Maa, D.Y. Theory and design of micro-perforated sound absorbing constructions. *Sci. Sin.* **1975**, *18*, 55–71.
29. Maa, D.Y. Microperforated-panel wideband absorbers. *Noise Control Eng. J.* **1987**, *29*, 77–84. [CrossRef]
30. Allard, J.; Atalla, N. *Propagation of Sound in Porous Media: Modelling Sound Absorbing Materials*, 2nd ed.; Wiley and Sons: London, UK, 2009; Chapter 2.
31. ISO 10524-2. *Acoustics—Determination of Sound Absorption Coefficient and Impedance in Impedance Tubes—Part 2: Transfer Function Method*; ISO: Geneva, Switzerlad, 1998.

Publisher's Note: MDPI stays neutral with regard to jurisdictional claims in published maps and institutional affiliations.

© 2020 by the authors. Licensee MDPI, Basel, Switzerland. This article is an open access article distributed under the terms and conditions of the Creative Commons Attribution (CC BY) license (http://creativecommons.org/licenses/by/4.0/).

Article

Development of a Panel Membrane Resonant Absorber

Yaw-Shyan Tsay *, Jui-Yen Lin and Faxin Ma

Department of Architecture, National Cheng Kung University, Tainan 701, Taiwan; N78031132@mail.ncku.edu.tw (J.-Y.L.); N76073031@mail.ncku.edu.tw (F.M.)
* Correspondence: tsayys@mail.ncku.edu.tw; Tel.: +886-6-2757575 (ext. 54155)

Abstract: The bass ratio describes the relationship between the reverberation energy in the low frequency region and that of the middle frequency. An appropriate bass ratio can create a warm sound; however, too much bass can influence speech clarity (C_{50}) and work efficiency and can even cause listeners to feel tired or exhausted. Using perforated plate resonance theory and membrane resonance theory, this research developed the panel membrane resonant absorber (PMRA), which not only provides an outstanding continuous absorption spectrum in the broadband range of 100–800 Hz but also presents an aesthetic appearance at a low cost. We divided this study into two parts: (1) PMRA development and experiment and (2) field application and measurement to confirm the sound absorption performance of the PMRA. In part 1, PMRA was developed by combining different materials and thicknesses of the air cavity. In the field study of part 2, the PMRA with the appropriate sound-absorbing curve was installed in a small auditorium, where we conducted field measurements for reverberation time (RT) and speech clarity (C_{50}). According to the experimental results, the PMRA had great absorption performance at a low frequency. In the field validation, the PMRA was found to effectively decrease the low-frequency RT while also maintaining the RT of middle-high frequency. The C_{50} of the auditorium was also improved.

Keywords: speech clarity; bass ratio; sound absorption; reverberation time

Citation: Tsay, Y.-S.; Lin, J.-Y.; Ma, F. Development of a Panel Membrane Resonant Absorber. *Appl. Sci.* **2021**, *11*, 1893. https://doi.org/10.3390/app11041893

Academic Editor: Edoardo Piana

Received: 6 January 2021
Accepted: 17 February 2021
Published: 21 February 2021

Publisher's Note: MDPI stays neutral with regard to jurisdictional claims in published maps and institutional affiliations.

Copyright: © 2021 by the authors. Licensee MDPI, Basel, Switzerland. This article is an open access article distributed under the terms and conditions of the Creative Commons Attribution (CC BY) license (https://creativecommons.org/licenses/by/4.0/).

1. Introduction

At the beginning of the 20th century, Sabine proposed the famous reverberation time (RT) theory, which brought room acoustics into the scientific realm. However, many acousticians have proposed different methods to inspect the pros and cons of room acoustics. Knudsen and Harris [1] believe that a RT below 500 Hz used in the field of music should be higher than the middle frequency. Ehmer [2] experimented with 250 Hz and found that when the masking sound is 20 dB, the 250 Hz threshold of the same frequency is increased by about 10 dB, the masking sound is 80 dB, and the 250 Hz test signal threshold is raised by about 50 dB. Beranek [3] proposed the bass ratio (BR) indicator and believed that in the acoustic design of a hall, the RT for low frequencies (125–250 Hz) should be increased by 20% compared to intermediate frequencies (500–1000 Hz), suggesting that a concert hall could be even up to 50%, which can make the sound warm and brilliant. Therefore, while low frequency is of considerable importance in a space, too much low-frequency energy will have the opposite effect. Fuchs and Zha [4] proposed that both language and music have non-negligible energy in the low frequency, which may generate standing waves in space, indirectly strengthen the low-frequency sound field energy, and shield the middle and high frequencies that are extremely important for clarity, thus affecting speech clarity (C_{50}).

Furthermore, in addition to the feedback on the physical level of the low-frequency sound, the psychological impact is also an important factor. Vasudevan and Gordon [5] found that low-frequency noise mainly occurs in indoor environments, while Leventhall [6] considered the low-frequency noise band to be 10–200 Hz and pointed out that LAeq underestimated low-frequency noise most of the time. Alimohammadi et al. [7] found that low-frequency noise caused users to feel annoyed, whereas Waye and Rylander [8] proposed that the low-frequency noise of ventilation equipment was prone to higher levels of psychosocial symptoms, sleep disturbance, and headaches for people who are annoyed. Caniato [9] found that underestimating the interference caused by LAeq can affect sleep conditions, and Falourd et al. [10] found that low-frequency background noise causes reduced speech intelligibility and users feel stressed and fatigued. Abbasi et al. [11] conducted a noise test with 35 young males aged 20 to 30 years old and found that noise between 65 dB and 75 dB obviously caused psychological fatigue, increased heart rate, and reduced working memory. Therefore, in order to reduce the likelihood of generated low-frequency sound, some researchers have proposed the sound absorption method.

Common sound absorption systems on the market, such as Helmholtz resonance, perforated panel resonance (PPR), micro-perforated panel (MPP), and membranous vibration (MV), each have sound absorption characteristics at a different frequency. Helmholtz resonance is for mid-low frequency, but the frequency band is narrow. PPR is also for mid-low frequency but is wider than that of Helmholtz. The MPP has better sound absorption performance than PPR, but the manufacturing cost is higher. MV is the only one that can facilitate artistic creation with sound absorption ability at mid-low frequency. Since this research is focused on low frequency, we adopted the PPR and MV systems. As a result, in this paper, we took advantage of the sound absorption characteristics of PPR and MV to reach better performance at a low frequency.

A bass trap is normally used to solve the problem of acoustics at a low frequency. Some people will create a bass trap by themselves since they are expensive and enormous, but such DIY products are without measurements to confirm the sound absorption performance. Therefore, this research designed an absorbent material for low frequency (125 and 250 Hz). Common methods for improving sound absorption on building walls include installation of curtains, wood panels, porous cotton materials with perforated panels, and sandwich structure. Considering price, porous cotton materials with perforated panels have been commonly adopted in interior renovations but have not shown outstanding sound absorption performance at low frequency. Čudina et al. [12] designed a sound absorber by hanging a painting to reduce the RT and found that canvas without an oil color layer and different air layer behind had a low performance of sound absorption coefficient at low frequency. The result showed the sound absorption coefficients at 125 and 250 Hz were under 0.1. Considering the influence of sound absorption performance via canvas surface tension, Zainulabidin et al. [13] found that surface tension has no significant effect on sound absorption properties.

Traditional absorbers such as porous materials necessitate a thick absorbing material when working at a low-frequency range [14]. Hybrid materials have been proposed for broadband of low-frequency absorption with a thinner structure. Zhao et al. [15] proposed a double porosity material (DPM) that combined the micro-pore from the porous layer and the meso-pore made by the labyrinthine channel to absorb low-frequency sound. Dupont et al. [16] proposed a multi-pancake material that connected perforated materials to provide a collection of periodically spaced materials as resonant absorbers of low frequency. Liu et al. [17] proposed a perforated composite Helmholtz resonator (PCHR) that combined separating plates with a Helmholtz resonator and provided a continuous absorption spectrum in the broadband range of 450–1360 Hz. Furthermore, Zhu et al. [18] combined periodic acoustic metamaterial resonators (AMRs) with a porous layer and provided a broadband absorption of the audible sound wave at the low frequency of 180–550 Hz. Tang et al. [19] proposed a perforated honeycomb-corrugation hybrid (PHCH) model that combined a lightweight sandwich panel with a perforated honeycomb-corrugation core, providing outstanding sound absorption over a broadband low-frequency range. However, most of these hybrid materials are still in the research and development stage, their prices are relatively high, and they have not yet been verified in the field.

In general, historical buildings are usually decorated with smooth, hard, and high-reflex skin materials, such as glass, concrete, and wood, which result in long RT. On the other hand, according to Taiwan's Cultural Assets Protection Law, decoration can only be carried out after being approved regarding its configuration, shape, color, and style, thus placing restrictions on decoration. As described above, sound absorption performance has to be improved at low frequency. Therefore, for this paper, we designed public art with two sound absorption systems in order to study panel membrane resonant absorber (PMRA) sound absorption performance at low frequency.

The theory of sound absorption of PPR combined with sound absorption of MV was adopted in this research. The former has better sound absorption performance at middle frequency, while the latter has better performance at low frequencies. Therefore, the specimens, including different combinations that consisted of expanded metal mesh (EMM) and canvas, were tested to develop the PMRA with better absorption performance. This study had two parts—PMRA development and field verification. First, the PMRA was developed with different combinations of EMM and canvas; then, the sound absorption performances of the materials and PMRA were tested using ISO 354 [20]. Last, the PMRA with the best performance at 125 Hz was installed in a historic building, and its performance in the field was measured and verified. The field verification was focused on room acoustics of long RT at low frequency.

2. PMRA Development and Prototyping

2.1. Specimens

The development process of the PMRA included two stages. In stage 1, the sound absorption performances of single materials (EMM and canvas, as shown in Figure 1) with different air cavities were measured. Then, in stage 2, different air thicknesses in the PMRA composed of EMM and canvas were measured. The size of each PMRA was 1.8 × 1.2 m. The thickness and density of EMM were 1.2 mm and 2.25 kg/m³, respectively, while the density of the canvas was 0.36 kg/m³. Group A consisted of a 10 cm high wooden frame, canvas covered the surface and fixed the periphery as a membrane structure, and EMM was installed inside as a resonator, which was collocated at different heights to study sound absorption performance. Group B used a 20 cm high wooden frame and the same installation method as Group A. The detailed information of the materials and specimens are provided in Tables 1 and 2, and Figures 2–5.

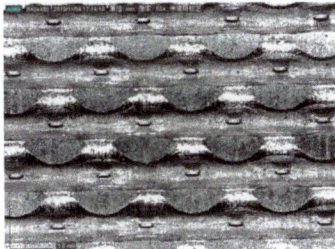 

(a) Expanded metal mesh   (b) Canvas

Figure 1. Materials.

Table 1. Detailed thickness of stage 1 specimens.

No.	Surface Texture	Air Layer (cm)	Height (cm)
1	EMM	3	3
2		20	20
3	Canvas	10	10
4		20	20

Table 2. Detailed thickness of stage 2 specimens.

Group	No.	Air Layer Behind the Material (cm)		Height (cm)
		Canvas	EMM	
A	A1	5.8	3	10
	A2	3.8	5	
	A3	1.3	7.5	
	A4	None	10	
B	B1	15.8	3	20
	B2	8.8	10	
	B3	3.8	15	
	B4	None	20	

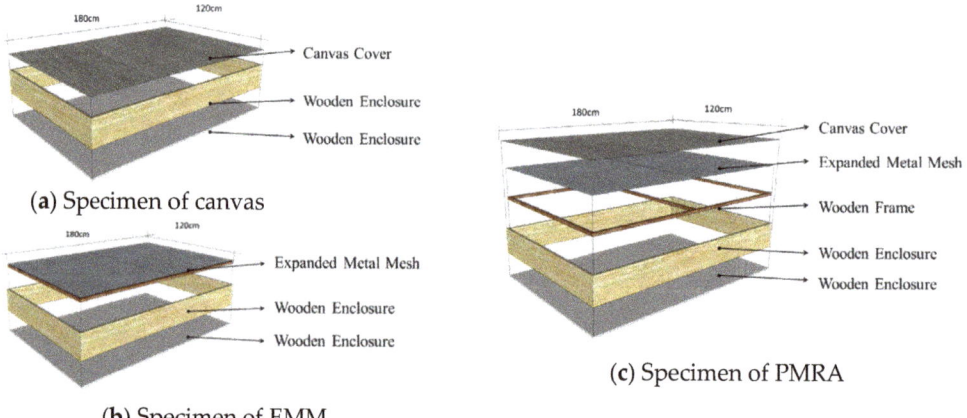

Figure 2. Composition of specimens.

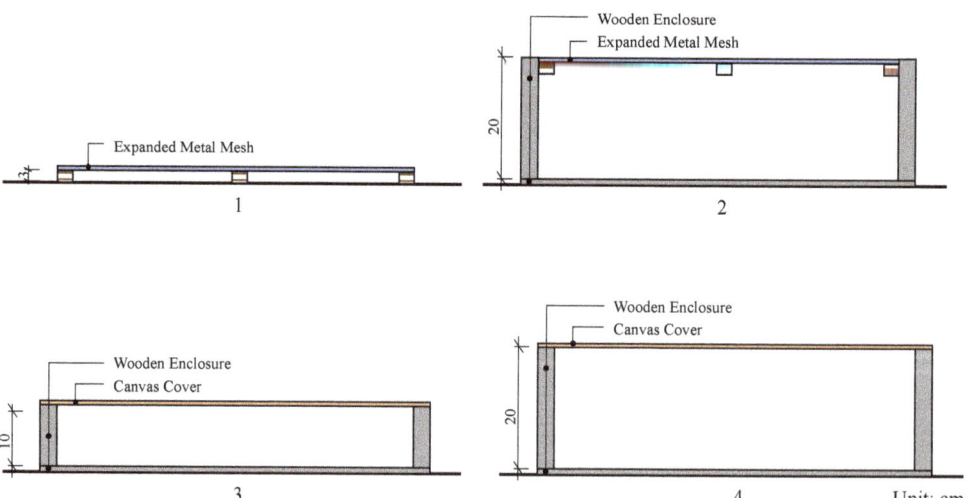

Figure 3. Specimen section in stage 1, as Table 1.

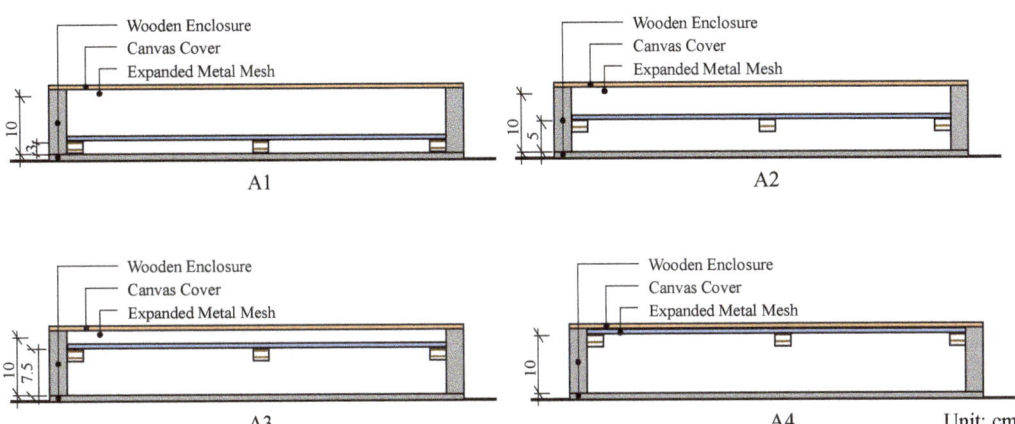

Figure 4. Group A section in stage 2, as Table 2.

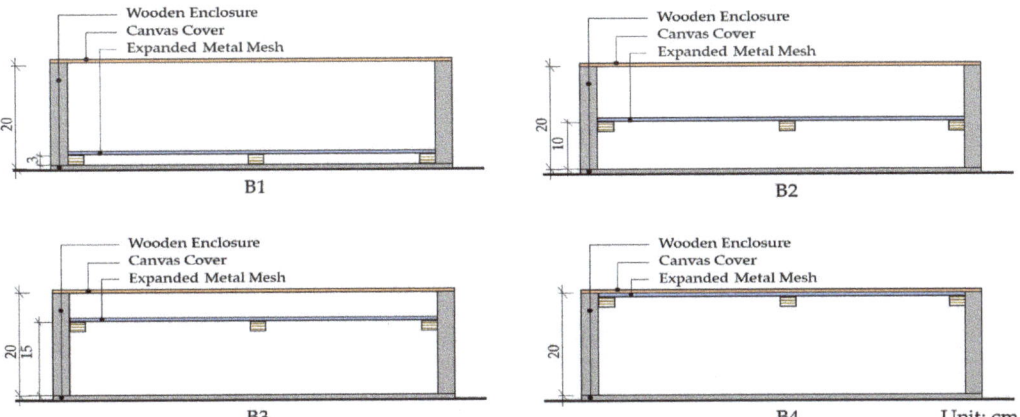

Figure 5. Group B section in stage 2, as Table 2.

2.2. Experiments

In this study, the sound absorption efficiency was measured using the reverberation room, which conforms with the ISO/IEC 17025 [21] testing and calibration laboratory operation regulations, and the methodology of measurement suite is in accordance with ISO 354:2003 [22]. The reverberation room is an unshaped hexahedron. The volume of the reverberation room is 171.3 m^3, its surface area is 184.3 m^2, and its floor area is 32.8 m^2. The laboratory adopts a floating structure to reduce the outside interference on the experiment. As described above, the single PMRA was 2.16 m^2 (1.8 m × 1.2 m), and the total area of the test specimen was 4.32 m^2 (1.8 m × 2.4 m), which was placed on the center of the floor. Figure 6 shows the reverberation room environment, and the receive point and calculation of the sound absorption coefficient are shown in Equation (1).

$$\alpha_s = 55.3 \times V \left(\frac{1}{c_2 T_2} - \frac{1}{c_1 T_1} \right) - 4V(m_2 - m_1) \tag{1}$$

where V is the volume of the empty reverberation room (m^3); c is the propagation speed of sound in air (m/s); T_1 is the reverberation time of the empty reverberation room (s);

T_2 is the reverberation time of the reverberation room after the test specimen has been introduced (s); and m_1, m_2 is the power attenuation coefficient (m^{-1}).

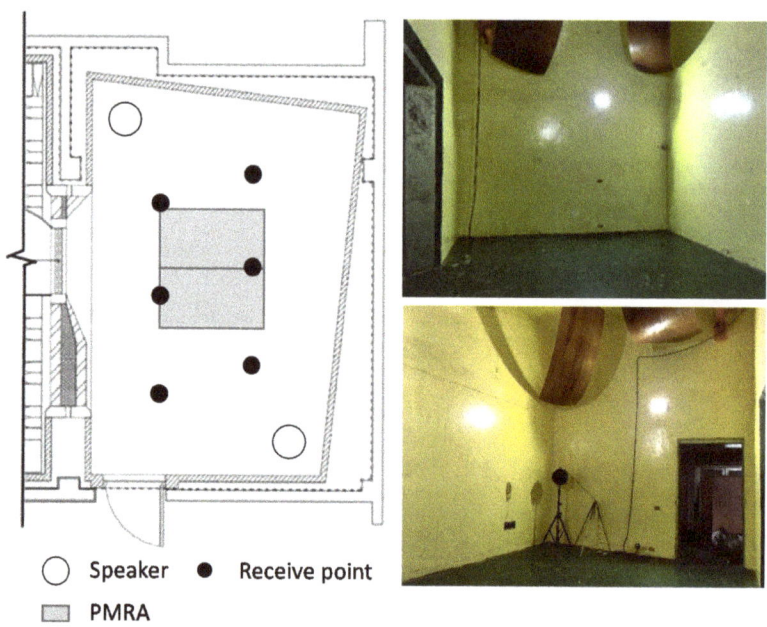

Figure 6. Reverberation room of National Cheng Kung University Architectural Acoustics Lab.

3. Measurement Results of PMRA

Figures 7 and 8 demonstrate the results of the first stage. By increasing the air layer behind the expanded metal mesh, we found that the absorption frequency band became wider, and the resonance frequency moved to low frequency. The surface density of the canvas was small. Although the low frequency was slightly improved by increasing the air layer behind it, the sound absorption efficiency was relatively weak throughout the entire frequency band. Due to the limitation of the materials' surface density, changing the air layer had a greater impact on the low frequency of absorption efficiency with the expanded metal mesh than with the canvas.

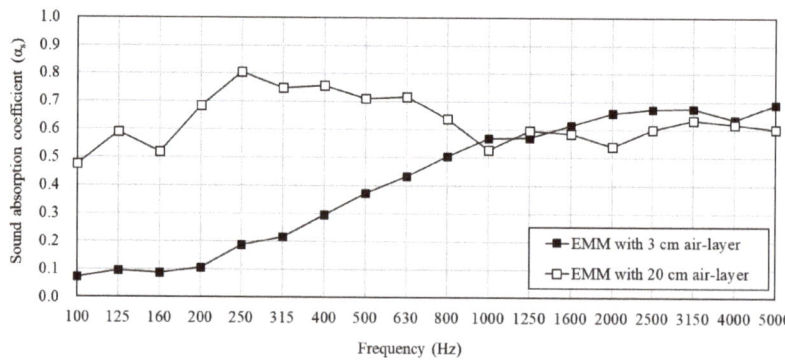

Figure 7. The sound absorption coefficient of expanded metal mesh (EMM) with single-layer structure in stage 1.

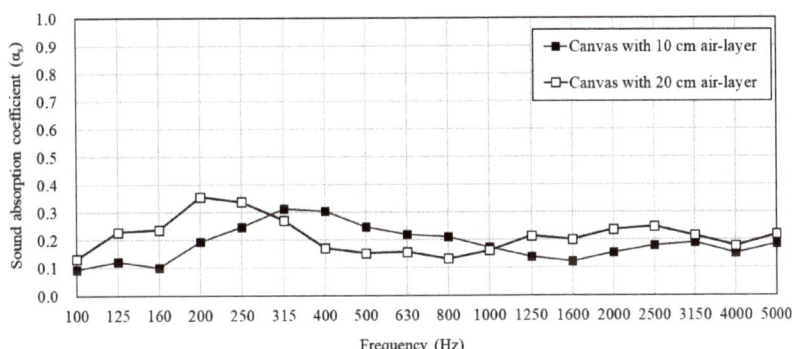

Figure 8. The sound absorption coefficient of canvas with single-layer structure in stage 1.

The results of the second stage are shown in Figures 9 and 10. In Group A, the sound-absorbing performance significantly increased at a frequency range from 125 to 250 Hz via increased air space behind EMM, that is, at 125 Hz, it increased from 0.14 to 0.33, and at 250 Hz from 0.53 to 0.75. Although the sound absorption coefficient at low frequency increased, it was still lower than 0.6 when under 250 Hz.

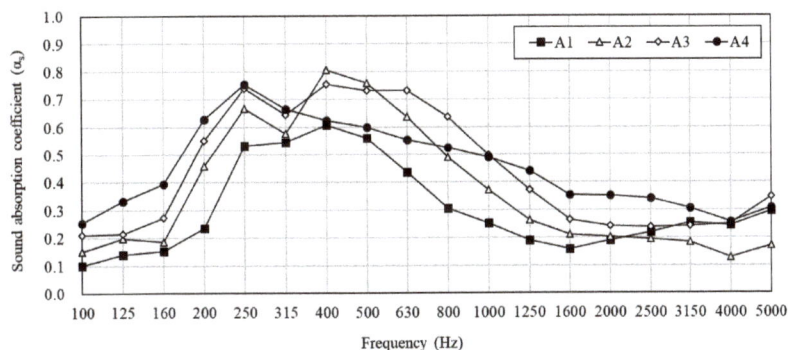

Figure 9. The sound absorption coefficient of Group A in stage 2 (specimen height 10 cm). A1: canvas with 5.8 cm air-layer + EMM with 3 cm air-layer; A2: canvas with 3.8 cm air-layer + EMM with 5 cm air-layer; A3: canvas with 1.3 cm air-layer + EMM with 7.5 cm air-layer; A4: canvas with 0 cm air-layer + EMM with 10 cm air-layer.

In Group B, the air space was increased to 20 cm, and the overall sound absorption performance was significantly improved at low frequencies compared to Group A. Therefore, the sound absorption coefficient rose above 0.4; at 250 Hz, it increased from 0.48 to 0.91, at 125 Hz, from 0.35 to 0.80. B4 sound absorption performance not only performed better than the other specimens in Group B at 100 Hz and 125 Hz, but also at medium and high frequencies.

As shown above, in Group A, as the air layer increased, the sound absorption coefficient of each frequency band improved. The sound absorption coefficients of A2 to A4 at 250–500 Hz were all above 0.6. However, the objects of this study were 125 and 250 Hz. Therefore, in Group B, we increased the air layer to 20 cm and found that the sound absorption coefficient moved to low frequency. B4 performed well at 125 Hz, and the 250 Hz sound absorption coefficient was 0.76. Therefore, this study chose B4 as the specimen for subsequent development.

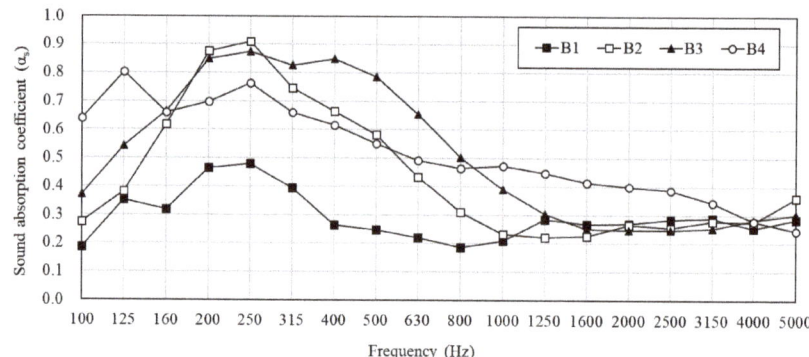

Figure 10. The sound absorption coefficient of Group B in stage 2 (specimen height 20 cm). B1: canvas with 15.8 cm air-layer + EMM with 3 cm air-layer. B2: canvas with 8.8 cm air-layer + EMM with 10 cm air-layer. B3: canvas with 3.8 cm air-layer + EMM with 15 cm air-layer. B4: canvas with 0 cm air-layer + EMM with 20 cm air-layer.

4. Field Validation of PMRA

4.1. The Historic Building

In this study, we adopted Ge-Chi Hall of National Cheng Kung University as the object of field verification. Ge-Chi Hall has a historical and cultural background and is a typical small auditorium, as shown in Figure 11. The building is approximately 220 m², with a volume of 1600 m³, and a total interior surface area of 1060 m². The overall wall was made of cement, the first floor was made of wood and cement, and the second floor was made of wood without fixed seats. The first floor was for the auditorium, while the second floor was for the media. As described, these materials were all smooth surface materials, which causes a long RT. However, Ge-Chi Hall is primarily used for ceremonial activities, including musical performances, speeches, dinner parties, and evening parties. As a result, we targeted the RT and C_{50} in this study, especially at low frequency.

Figure 11. Ge-Chi Hall environment and section diagram.

4.2. Acoustic Index

This study refers to the bass ratio by Beranek [3], which is identified as the ratio of RT between 125 Hz, 250 Hz, and middle frequency (500 Hz and 1000 Hz), as shown in Equation (2). Beranek classified the ratio of RT into four levels, as shown in Table 3.

$$\text{Ratio of RT} = \begin{cases} T_{125}/T_{mid} \\ T_{250}/T_{mid} \end{cases} \quad (2)$$

$$T_{mid} = (T_{500} + T_{1000})/2$$

where T_{125} is the reverberation time of 125 Hz (s), T_{250} is the reverberation time of 250 Hz (s), and T_{mid} is the reverberation time of 500 and 1000 Hz (s).

Table 3. Ratio of reverberation time (RT) at low frequency (Beranek, 1962).

Category	T_{250}/T_{mid}	T_{125}/T_{mid}
Excellent bass	1.14	1.27
Good bass	1.06	1.03
Fair bass	0.97	0.95
Poor bass	0.90	0.86

According to ISO 3382-1 [22], the C_{50} is the ratio of early-to-late arriving sound energy ratio, and it can be calculated through Equation (3). When $C_{50} > 0$, the early sound energy dominates the sound field and satisfies basic speech intelligibility. In general, the C_{50} have a high relation with RT—the lower the RT, the better the C_{50}.

However, the target in this paper is to compare the RT and C_{50} at a low frequency in Ge-Chi Hall with and without PMRA. RT is valued by BR, and we observed how much C_{50} increased.

$$C_{50} = 10 \lg \frac{\int_0^{50} p^2(t) dt}{\int_{50}^{\infty} p^2(t) dt} \, dB \quad (3)$$

where C_{50} is the early-to-late index, and $p(t)$ is the instantaneous sound pressure of the impulse response measured at the measurement point.

4.3. Field Measurement

The measurement environment had air conditioning, NC was 35, temperature was 26 °C, and relative humidity was 55%. In this study, the sound source was an omnidirectional loudspeaker via B&K Dirac software that output MLS digital signals and analysis after a 1/2 free-field microphone received the sound power, as shown in Figure 12. In Figure 13, the sound source is shown set on the stage, and all receive points are evenly distributed on the first floor (P1–P5) and second floor (P6–P7); the measured data were the total average.

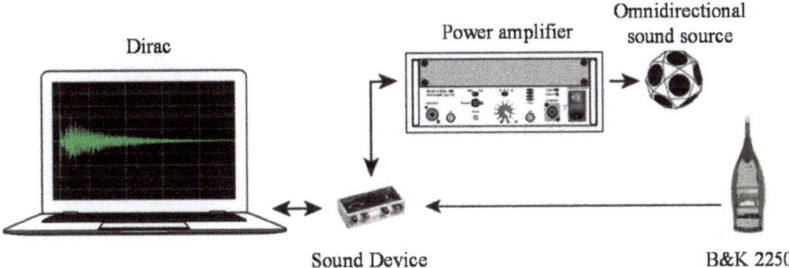

Figure 12. System of the field measurement.

Figure 14 shows the RT results of Ge-Chi Hall without PMRA. At 125, 250, 500, and 1000 Hz, the RT values were 1.74, 1.53, 1.31, and 1.21 s, respectively. According to the RT ratio proposed by Beranek [3], 500 and 1000 Hz of RT were substituted into Equation (2) for the field measured, and the calculation revealed that the 125 and 250 Hz RT of the space should be between 1.19 and 1.60 s, and 1.22 and 1.43 s, respectively. The comparison result shows that 125 and 500 Hz need to be reduced by at least 0.14 s and 0.1 s, respectively, to fall within an appropriate RT.

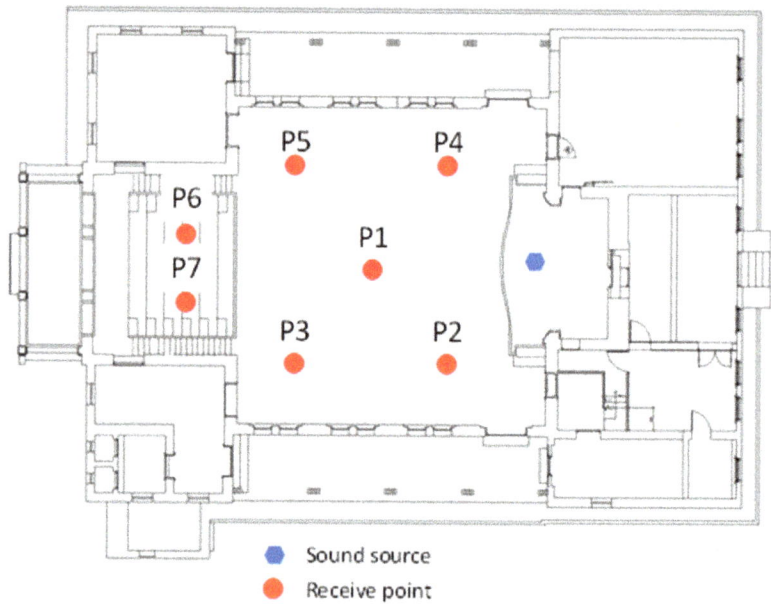

Figure 13. Sound source and measurement points.

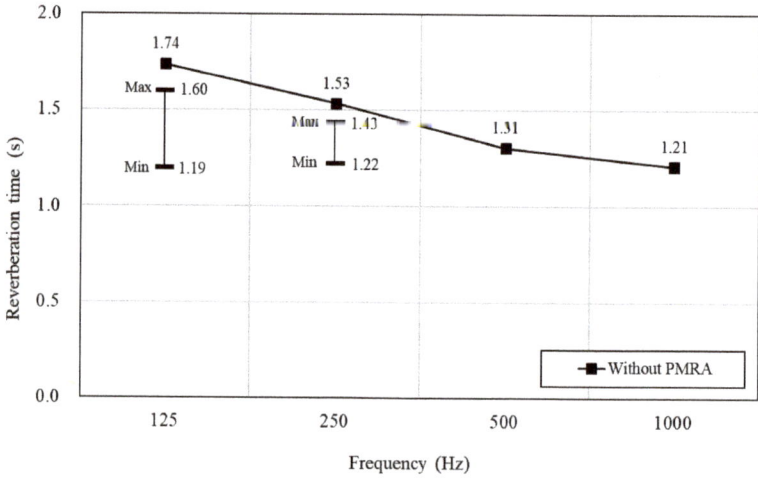

Figure 14. RT of Ge-Chi Hall without panel membrane resonant absorber (PMRA).

4.4. Installation of PMRA

As described herein, for the field verification, we conducted a two-phase measurement of current situation investigation and improvement investigation, followed by the position measurement of RT and C_{50}. After improvement, the survey installed PMRA on both sides of the front and back walls of the auditorium on the first floor, as well as on both sides of the back and the walls on both sides of the media booth on the second floor. The PMRA was based on type B4 for field verification implementation. The following two sizes were used: 180 (L) × 125 (W) × 20 cm (H) with seven pieces and 120 (L) × 90 (W) × 20 cm (H) with two pieces. The installation position is shown in Figure 15.

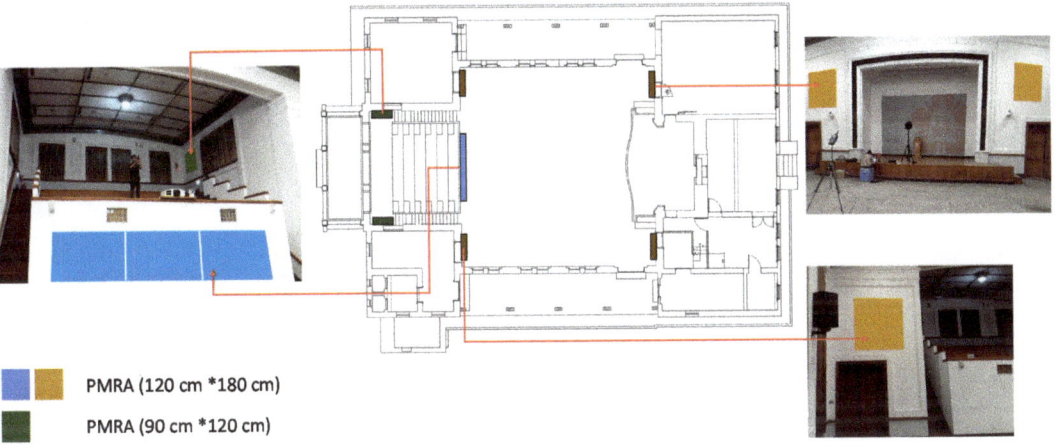

Figure 15. PMRA setting position.

4.5. Field Performance of PMRA

Figure 16 shows the RT of Ge-Chi Hall with PMRA. The RT results were 1.55, 1.40, 1.28, and 1.16 s at 125, 250, 500, and 1000 Hz, respectively. The 500 Hz and 1000 Hz of RT in the measured field were substituted into Equation (2), which indicated that 125 Hz and 250 Hz should be between 1.16 and 1.47 s, and 1.19 and 1.37 s, respectively. Therefore, the PMRA effectively reduced the RT at low frequency, which was within a suitable RT range at both 125 and 250 Hz. Overall, by minimizing the high-frequency sound absorption as much as possible in this study, we found that PMRA can effectively reduce the RT at 125 and 500 Hz; thus, the result was consistent with the purpose of this research.

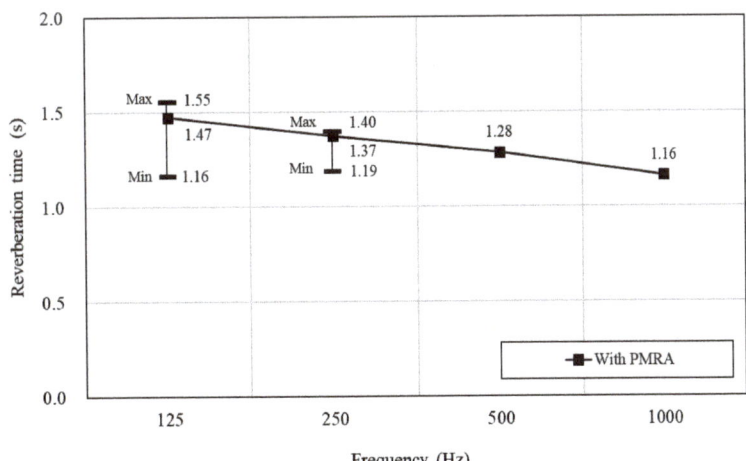

Figure 16. RT of Ge-Chi Hall with PMRA.

As shown in Figure 17, the C_{50} of Ge-Chi Hall without PMRA were −4.26, −2.41, and −2.23 dB at 125, 250, and 500 Hz, respectively. After PMRA was installed, the C_{50} was −2.19, −0.73, and −1.35 dB, reflecting increases of 2.07, 1.68, and 0.98 dB, respectively. Therefore, PMRA can effectively increase C_{50} performance at 125, 250, and 500 Hz. However, whether PMRA was installed or not, we observed no significant effect at 1000 Hz to 8000 Hz.

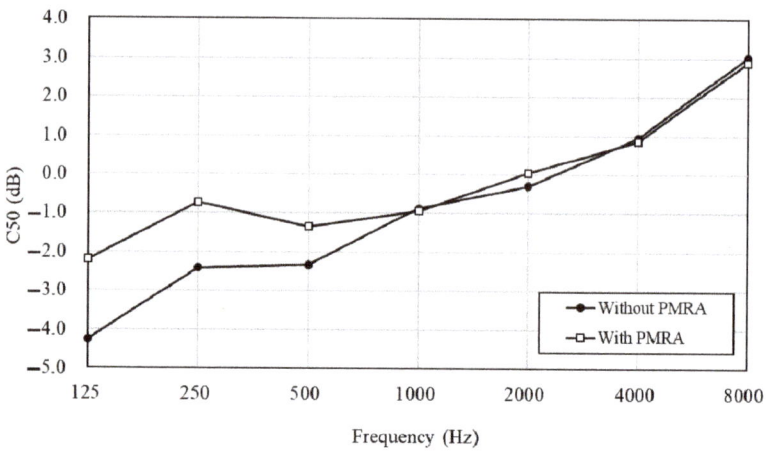

Figure 17. A comparison of C_{50} with or without PMRA at each band.

Figure 18 shows the comparison of the C_{50} with and without the PMRA at 500 Hz. Due to the PMRA installed point, speculated P1 had a long distance with PMRA, and P2 was close to outside noise. Therefore, C_{50} had an increased limitation, while the others were significantly increased.

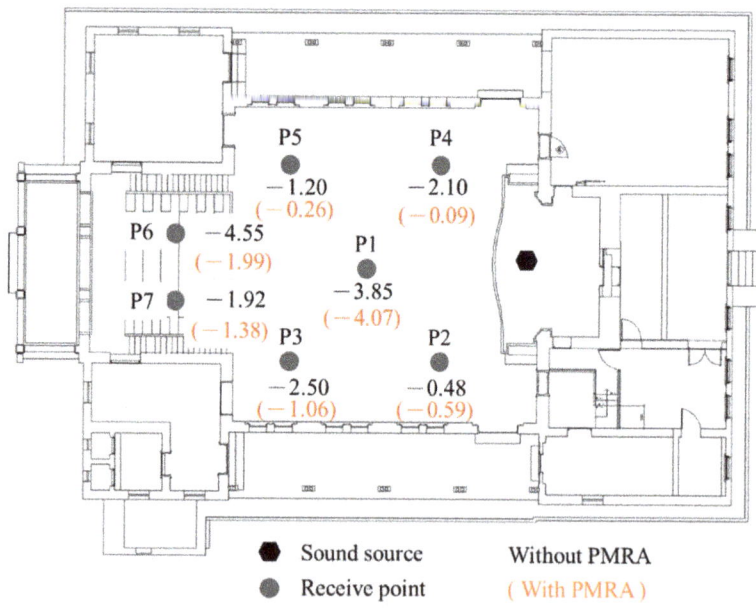

Figure 18. A comparison of C_{50} with or without PMRA at 500 Hz.

5. Conclusions

In this paper, we developed a PMRA prototype set with different structure combinations and used laboratory measurements to confirm the basic sound-absorbing characteristics of PMRA, choose a better sample on the basis of the research results, apply it to the actual field, and then study the low-frequency improvement of building acoustics.

The laboratory measurement was separated into two stages. In the first stage, we studied the sound absorption performance of the surface materials. The second stage was to study the membrane structure with single-layer EMM and to design a composite plate mold resonance sound absorber, which we used to explore each group's sound absorption characteristics of different materials and air space. We ultimately found that B4 had a better sound absorption performance than others at low frequency (125 Hz), and thus we chose and installed B4 in field validation.

For the difference between PMRA being installed in Ge-Chi Hall or not, the RT was reduced by 0.19 s at 125 Hz and 0.13 at 250 Hz, while C_{50} increased by 2.07 and 1.68 at 125 and 250 Hz, respectively. The overall results show that PMRA not only effectively reduced low frequency and increased C_{50}, but also was both practical and aesthetic as a sound absorber.

Author Contributions: Conceptualization, Y.-S.T.; Formal analysis, Y.-S.T.; Investigation, J.-Y.L.; Project administration, Y.-S.T.; Resources, Y.-S.T.; Supervision, Y.-S.T.; Writing—original draft, F.M.; Writing—review & editing, J.-Y.L. All authors have read and agreed to the published version of the manuscript.

Funding: Ministry of Science and Technology, Taiwan: MOST 109-2622-E-006-032.

Institutional Review Board Statement: Not applicable.

Informed Consent Statement: Not applicable.

Data Availability Statement: Not applicable.

Conflicts of Interest: The authors declare no conflict of interest.

References

1. Knudsen, V.O.; Harris, C.M. *Acoustical Design in Architecture*, 6th ed.; John Wiley & Sons, Inc.: New York, NY, USA, 1962; pp. 194–195.
2. Ehmer, R.H. Masking Patterns of Tones. *J. Acoust. Soc. Am.* **1959**, *31*, 1115–1120. [CrossRef]
3. Beranek, L.L. *Music, Acoustics & Architecture*, 1st ed.; Wiley: New York, NY, USA, 1962; pp. 433–443.
4. Fuchs, H.V.; Zha, X. Requirement for Low-Frequency Reverberation in Spaces for Music: Part 1: Smaller Rooms for Different Uses. *Psychomusicol. Music Mind Brain* **2015**, *25*, 272–281. [CrossRef]
5. Vasudevan, R.; Gordon, C.G. Experimental Study of Annoyance Due to Low Frequency Environmental Noise. *Appl. Acoust.* **1977**, *10*, 57–69. [CrossRef]
6. Leventhall, H.G. Low Frequency Noise and Annoyance. *Noise Heal* **2004**, *6*, 59–72.
7. Alimohammadi, I.; Sandrock, S.; Gohari, M.R. The Effects of Low Frequency Noise on Mental Performance and Annoyance. *Environ. Monit. Assess.* **2013**, *185*, 7043–7051. [CrossRef] [PubMed]
8. Waye, K.P.; Rylander, R. The Prevalence of Annoyance and Effects after Long-Term Exposure to Low-Frequency Noise. *J. Sound Vib.* **2001**, *240*, 483–497. [CrossRef]
9. Caniato, M.; Bettarello, F.; Schmid, C.; Fausti, P. Assessment Criterion for Indoor Noise Disturbance in the Presence of Low Fre-Quency Sources. *Appl. Acoust.* **2016**, *113*, 22–33. [CrossRef]
10. Falourd, X.; Lissek, H.; René, P.J. Active Low-Frequency Modal Noise Cancellation for Room Acoustics: An Experimental Study. In Proceedings of the 16th International Congress on Sound and Vibration (ICSV), Kraków, Poland, 7 July 2009.
11. Abbasi, A.M.; Motamedzade, M.; Aliabadi, M.; Golmohammadi, R.; Tapak, L. Study of the Physiological and Mental Health Effects Caused by Exposure to Low-Frequency Noise in a Simulated Control Room. *Build. Acoust.* **2018**, *25*, 233–248. [CrossRef]
12. Čudina, M.; Prezelj, J.; Pušlar-Čudina, M. The Impact of Paintings Hung on Lecture Room Walls on the Speech Intelligibility and Perception of Background Noise. *Indoor Built Environ.* **2015**, *25*, 659–673. [CrossRef]
13. Zainulabidin, M.H.; Wan, L.M.; Ismail, A.E.; Kasron, M.Z.; Kassim, A.S.M. Effect of membrane surface tension and backed-air gap distance on sound absorption characteristics. *J. Eng. Appl. Sci.* **2006**, *11*, 5494–5498.
14. Yang, M.; Sheng, P. Sound Absorption Structures: From Porous Media to Acoustic Metamaterials. *Annu. Rev. Mater. Res.* **2017**, *47*, 83–114. [CrossRef]

15. Zhao, H.; Wang, Y.; Yu, D.; Yang, H.; Zhong, J.; Wu, F.; Wen, J. A Double Porosity Material for Low Frequency Sound Absorption. *Compos. Struct.* **2020**, *239*, 111978. [CrossRef]
16. Dupont, T.; LeClaire, P.; Panneton, R.; Umnova, O. A Microstructure Material Design for Low Frequency Sound Absorption. *Appl. Acoust.* **2018**, *136*, 86–93. [CrossRef]
17. Liu, C.R.; Wu, J.H.; Chen, X.; Ma, F. A Thin Low-Frequency Broadband Metasurface with Multi-Order Sound Absorption. *J. Phys. D: Appl. Phys.* **2019**, *52*, 105302. [CrossRef]
18. Zhu, X.-F.; Lau, S.-K.; Lu, Z.; Jeon, W. Broadband Low-Frequency Sound Absorption by Periodic Metamaterial Resonators Embedded in a Porous Layer. *J. Sound Vib.* **2019**, *461*, 114922. [CrossRef]
19. Tang, Y.; Ren, S.; Meng, H.; Xin, F.; Huang, L.; Chen, T.; Zhang, C.; Lu, T.J. Hybrid Acoustic Metamaterial as Super Absorber for Broadband Low-Frequency Sound. *Sci. Rep.* **2017**, *7*, 1–11. [CrossRef]
20. ISO. *354 Acoustics — Measurement of Sound Absorption in a Reverberation Room*; ISO: Geneva, Switzerland, 2003.
21. ISO/IEC. *17025 — General Requirements for the Competence of Testing and Calibration Laboratories*; ISO: Geneva, Switzerland, 2003.
22. ISO/IEC. *3382-1 — Acoustics — Measurement of Room Acoustic Parameters — Part 1: Performance Spaces*; ISO: Geneva, Switzerland, 2009.

Article

Acoustical Properties of Fiberglass Blankets Impregnated with Silica Aerogel

Hasina Begum * and Kirill V. Horoshenkov

Department of Mechanical Engineering, The University of Sheffield, Sheffield S1 3JD, UK; k.horoshenkov@sheffield.ac.uk
* Correspondence: hbegum3@sheffield.ac.uk; Tel.: +44-75-2157-0011

Abstract: It is known that aerogel impregnated fibrous blankets offer high acoustic absorption and thermal insulation performance. These materials are becoming very popular in various industrial and building applications. Although the reasons for the high thermal insulation performance of these materials are well understood, it is still largely unclear what controls their acoustic performance. Additionally, only a small number of publications to date report on the acoustical properties of fibrous blankets impregnated with powder aerogels. There is a lack of studies that attempt to explain the measured absorption properties with a valid mathematical model. This paper contributes to this knowledge gap through a simulation that predicts the measured complex acoustic reflection coefficient of aerogel blankets with different filling ratios. It is shown that the acoustic performance of a fibrous blanket impregnated with aerogel is generally controlled by the effective pore size and porosity of the composite structure. It is shown that there is a need for refinement of a classical Biot-type model to take into account the sorption and pressure diffusion effects, which become important with the increased filling ratio.

Keywords: acoustics; aerogels; modeling; fiber; porous materials

Citation: Begum, H.; Horoshenkov, K.V. Acoustical Properties of Fiberglass Blankets Impregnated with Silica Aerogel. *Appl. Sci.* **2021**, *11*, 4593. https://doi.org/10.3390/app11104593

Academic Editor: Edoardo Piana

Received: 23 April 2021
Accepted: 14 May 2021
Published: 18 May 2021
Corrected: 10 March 2022

Publisher's Note: MDPI stays neutral with regard to jurisdictional claims in published maps and institutional affiliations.

Copyright: © 2021 by the authors. Licensee MDPI, Basel, Switzerland. This article is an open access article distributed under the terms and conditions of the Creative Commons Attribution (CC BY) license (https://creativecommons.org/licenses/by/4.0/).

1. Introduction

There is a global need to reduce the use of fossil fuels and the release of greenhouse gases. Currently, 40% of energy consumption in Europe comes solely from the building sector [1], which is a major source of greenhouse gases. Due to this high level of energy consumption, the European council has introduced a 27% energy efficiency target for 2030 [2]. This has led to industries sourcing better energy-saving products for the market, with thermal insulation being the most effective way to reduce the energy consumption and loss. Achieving such a significant energy efficacy requires the development and upscaling of new commercial products based on aerogels.

One popular emerging thermal insulation product is aerogel blankets. Aerogel blankets consist of a silica aerogel embedded in a reinforcing fibrous matrix, which allows the brittle aerogel to become a flexible, durable solid used for buildings [3] and pipelines. The silica aerogel can undergo a surface modification process (typically hydrophobization) to enhance surface life stability [4], thus reducing the aerogel's susceptibility to moisture and rapid spoilage [5]. Silica aerogels themselves have porosity values as high as 98%, densities as low as 0.05–0.5 g/cm^3, surface areas in the range of 300–1000 m^2/g [6] and thermal conductivity values as low as 0.02 W/mK [7]. Application of aerogels on their own are limited due to their fragility and low mechanical modulus. Using them as composites in the form of aerogel blankets removes their fragility, as the aerogel grains are now incorporated within a fibrous matrix such as fiberglass or rockwool, giving them impeccable mechanical strength and a breadth of flexibility in terms of product development [8].

Conventional porous materials, such as nonwovens and polymer foams [9], can also prevent the reflection of sound incident waves to provide a high sound absorption performance [6,10] that is a highly desired property. Nonwovens in particular are ideal for sound absorption due to their large surface area and high porosity, which offers increased frictional losses between sound waves and the fibrous matrix, leading to their good sound absorption performance [11].

Monolithic silica aerogels alone have unusual viscoelastic properties and have been used in the form of clamped plates to become the main source of intrinsic losses allowing them to exhibit subwavelength resonances for high sound absorption [12,13]. However, these materials are highly fragile. Utilizing them as aerogel powder into a fibrous, flexible matrix results in a multi-functional system that can fulfill a range of practical needs in many industry and domestic applications. Their fused nanoparticles in particular result in extremely low elastic stiffness, which provides a relatively low acoustic impedance and exceptionally low flexural wave speed, making it ideal for use as a subwavelength flexural element for controlling airborne sound [14]. Super-insulative acoustic absorbing materials such as aerogel blankets can be tailored and combined with other products to widen their applications and to provide lighter, thinner and more economical products.

It is known that the acoustic properties of aerogels alone are greatly influenced by the interstitial gas type, pore structure and aerogel density [15,16], and more recently the pioneering efforts to embed granular aerogels into a reinforced fibrous network [3] have shown promising acoustical behavior. The combination of the density and granular size of aerogel [17] and fiber reinforcement and decreased pore size greatly influences the sound absorption [18]. Motahari et al. [19] investigated the aging time of silica aerogels in cotton nonwoven mats on the sound absorption performance. They found that the presence of low density (0.088 g/cm^3) silica aerogel at different molar ratios of the precursors MeOH/TEOS used and the low aging time enhanced the sound absorption coefficient in the low frequency range of 250 to 2500 Hz. Furthermore, Eskandari et al. [20] investigated the acoustical behavior of synthesized silica aerogels mixed into UPVC blankets of different weight ratios. They found that neat UPVC only had a maximum sound absorption of 17% at a frequency of 1800 Hz; however, when silica aerogel was applied at 0.5, 1.5 and 3 weight %, the maximum sound absorption of UPVC increased to 24, 28 and 43%, respectively, therefore highlighting that acoustical properties were greatly increased upon the addition of silica aerogel. A more extensive review of acoustical properties of aerogels can be found in reference [4].

However, there is a general lack of understanding regarding what leads to the observed acoustical properties of granular aerogels embedded into fibrous mats. A majority of previous works have not attempted to apply any valid theoretical models to predict key acoustical properties of these systems to explain the measured data. There are limited data on the effect of the filling ratio on the acoustical properties of aerogel impregnated fibrous blankets. Additionally, despite some previous efforts (e.g., [6,9]), there is a limited understanding on the ability of some prediction models to explain the general acoustical behavior of these materials. There was no discussion on the values of the non-acoustical parameters that the authors of references [6,9] had to use in the prediction models they chose in their works to simulate the measured absorption coefficient data.

Our work aims to address this gap via a careful characterization of the acoustical behavior of granular silica aerogels impregnated into fiberglass mats. The acoustical properties of five samples of aerogel blankets with varying concentrations of aerogel powder (at micrometric particle sizes) at filling ratios of 0, 25, 50, 75 and 100% were measured and predicted using a mathematical model. This work helps to better understand the relation between their micro-structure and measured acoustical performance.

The structure of this paper is as follows. Section 2 highlights the various techniques used to characterize the chemical and physical material properties of aerogel blankets. Section 3 looks at the experimental acoustical data derived from the analysis of these materials. Section 4 attempts to explain these data with a mathematical model to understand what intrinsic properties of aerogel blankets make them acoustically absorbing.

2. Materials and Methods

2.1. Materials Preparation

As specified in the patent [21], sodium silicate diluent was prepared using distilled water to achieve 3 to 10 weight % of SiO_2 and stirred with hexamethydisilazane (HDMS) whilst slowly adding nitric acid (HNO_3) to allow gelation to occur. The silylated hydrogel and co-precursor were gradually immersed in n-hexane for a one-step solvent exchange and sodium ion removal. Water present in the hydrogels is detached due to surface modification of the organic groups (–CH_3)$_3$ in HDMS. The hydrogel from which water was removed was then dried at ambient pressure and pulverized to form a superhydrophobic synthetic silica aerogel powder [22] with the particle diameter in the range of 1–20 µm impregnated into a fiberglass blanket at different weight % of 25, 50, 75 and 100 powder to blanket at a later manufacturing process. This is a standard process [23]. The fiber diameter in the blanket was 10 microns and its density was approximately 73 kg/m^3. It is a standard commercial E-glass fiber needle mat produced by Lih Feng Jiing Enterprise Co Ltd (Tainan City, Taiwan) [23]. The impregnated fiberglass blankets were then cut to a 10 mm diameter size using a hand-held hole saw that had smooth blade edges to ensure a perfect fit into the impedance tube when tested for acoustical properties.

2.2. Materials Characterization

Microstructural observations such as particle distribution of the silica aerogels within fiberglass mats were performed using scanning electron microscopy (SEM). Images were obtained with a FEI Nova NanoSEM 230 instrument (FEI, Hillsboro, OR, USA) at an accelerating voltage of 10 kV and a minimum working distance of 5 mm. The silica aerogels were fixed on the sample holder using a carbon pad and subsequently coated with 15–20 nm of platinum for SEM analysis.

The acoustical properties of aerogel blankets were measured in a 10 mm impedance tube that was custom made by Materiacustica [24]. This 2-microphone tube setup was developed to test small material specimens in accordance with the standard ISO 10534-2:2001 [25]. This setup enabled us to measure the normalized surface acoustic impedance, complex reflection coefficient and sound absorption coefficient of a hard-backed porous layer in the frequency range of 300–3000 Hz. The spacing between the two microphones was 30 mm, which is usual for this frequency range as recommended in the standard [25]. The thickness of the samples used in the acoustic experiments was between 7 and 11 mm, which is a typical thickness of a commercial product [23,26]. Figure 1 illustrates a typical specimen of fiberglass blanket impregnated with aerogel that was used in the acoustic experiments. Figure 2 shows a photograph and jigsaw drawing of the vertically standing impedance tube.

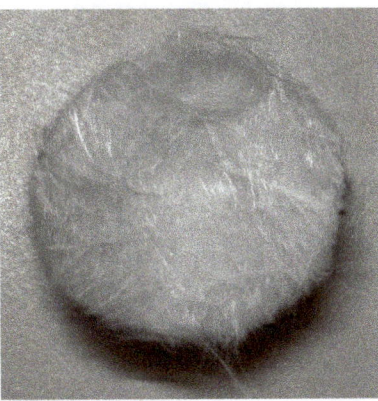

Figure 1. 10 mm diameter of fiberglass blanket samples cut for fitting into the impedance tube.

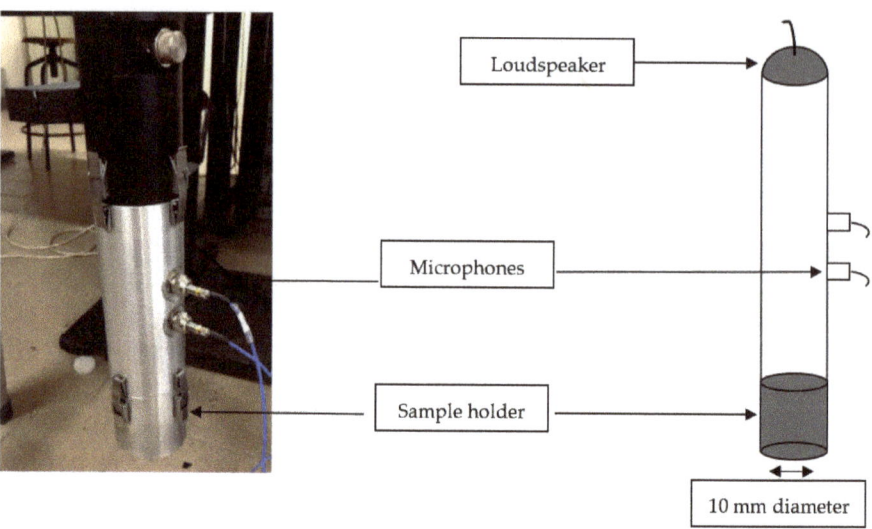

Figure 2. 2-Microphone impedance tube setup to measure the surface impedance of a porous layer [25].

3. Modeling of the Acoustical Properties of Fibrous and Granular Media

Basic modeling of the acoustical properties of this kind of material requires a mathematical model that takes into account the classical visco-thermal effects in the voids' between the fibers and loose granules of powder. However, a fibrous blanket impregnated with aerogel is a more complicated void structure that has at least three scales of porosity. The fiberglass blanket itself consist of 10 μm interlaced fibers that form a porous structure with sub-millimeter size pores of approximately 0.1 mm. The aerogel particles are around 20 μm in size and contain nano-pores of 20 nm in size.

There are several models that exist that can predict the acoustical properties of classical fibrous media [27]. In this work we attempt to use the model proposed by Horoshenkov et al. [28], which is based on the following three parameters: (i) the median pore size, $\bar{s}$; (ii) porosity, ϕ; and (iii) the standard deviation in pore size, σ_s. This reduced number of parameters allows easier inversion of key morphological characteristics of porous media from acoustical data. This model predicts the dynamic density, $\tilde{\rho}$, and complex compressibility, $\tilde{C}$, of air in the material pores. These quantities are given by the analytical equations, which are presented in reference [28]. The MATLAB code to predict these quantities can be found in reference [29].

The normalized surface impedance of a hard-backed layer of porous material that is typically measured in the impedance tube is:

$$Z_s = -jZ_c \cot(k_c d)/\rho_0 c_0 \tag{1}$$

where $j = \sqrt{-1}$, d is the sample thickness, ρ_0 is the ambient density of air, c_0 is the sound speed in air,

$$Z_c = \sqrt{\frac{\tilde{\rho}}{\tilde{C}}} \tag{2}$$

is the characteristic impedance and

$$k_c = \omega\sqrt{\tilde{\rho}\tilde{C}} \tag{3}$$

is the wavenumber in the porous material. Here, ω is the angular frequency of sound. In this work, we use the complex reflection coefficient data

$$R = \frac{Z_s - 1}{Z_s + 1} \tag{4}$$

to fit the model. The work presented in reference [30] shows that the complex reflection coefficient is a reliable quantity to determine the effective values of the three non-acoustical parameters in the model [28] through the parameter inversion. This is the complex acoustical quantity that is measured directly using the standard impedance tube method [25]. The real and imaginary parts of this quantity are bounded between −1 and +1, which makes them attractive to use in the parameter inversion process. The complex reflection coefficient can also be used to predict the acoustic absorption coefficient

$$\alpha = 1 - |R|^2 \tag{5}$$

which is a usual measure of the ability of the porous layer to absorb sound.

4. Results and Discussion

4.1. Microstructural Analysis

Figures 3–7 present SEM images of the fiberglass blankets with a progressive increase in the aerogel powder filing ratio from 0 to 100%. These images can be used to identify the aerogel particle distribution in fiberglass blankets and the structure of the fiber network. The SEM magnification scale in each of these images changes between 40, 100 and 500 microns to provide a better view inside into the microstructure. We note that SEM image analysis is sensitive to the loading of samples on to the carbon stub; a large amount deposited will affect the coating and this may fracture the image surfaces. Furthermore, there may be sampling bias causing the contrast/brightness settings to be adjusted and this may also affect the results.

Figure 3 clearly shows that there is little to no aerogel powder present in virgin fiberglass. It also shows that the spacing between individual fibers is in the order of 100 s of microns and that these randomly oriented fibers form a complicated network. The addition of a relatively small (25%) amount of aerogel powder does not significantly affect the inter-fiber space (see Figure 4). For this case, aerogel particles mainly attach themselves to the fibers (see Figure 4a) causing an apparent increase in the fiber diameter (see Figure 4). In the case of the samples with 50 and 75% concentrations (Figures 5 and 6, respectively), a similar effect can be visually observed, but the apparent increase in the fiber diameter is more significant whereas the size of the inter-fibrous space is clearly reduced. In the ultimate case, when the aerogel filling ratio in the fibrous sample is 100% (see Figure 7), a considerable proportion of the inter-fibrous space is occupied with aerogel powder so that the effective pore size appears to be significantly reduced visually.

(a)

(b)

(c)

Figure 3. SEM images taken at different magnifications (3000× (a), 800× (b) and 200× (c)) showing the fiberglass blanket without any aerogel.

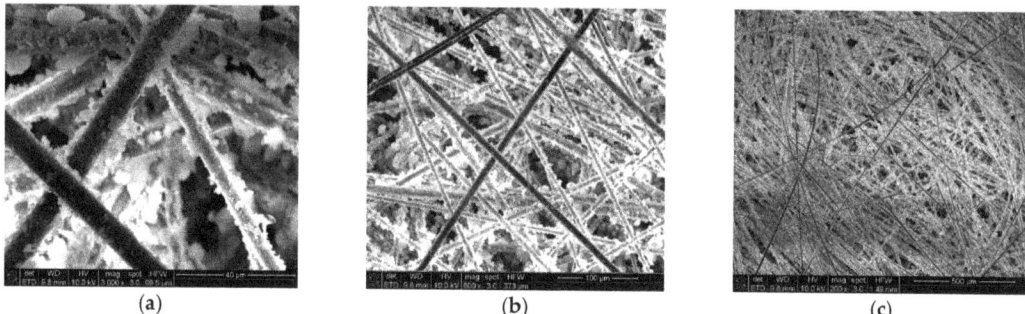

Figure 4. SEM images taken at different magnifications (3000× (**a**), 800× (**b**) and 200× (**c**)) showing the fiberglass blanket structure with an aerogel filling ratio of 25%.

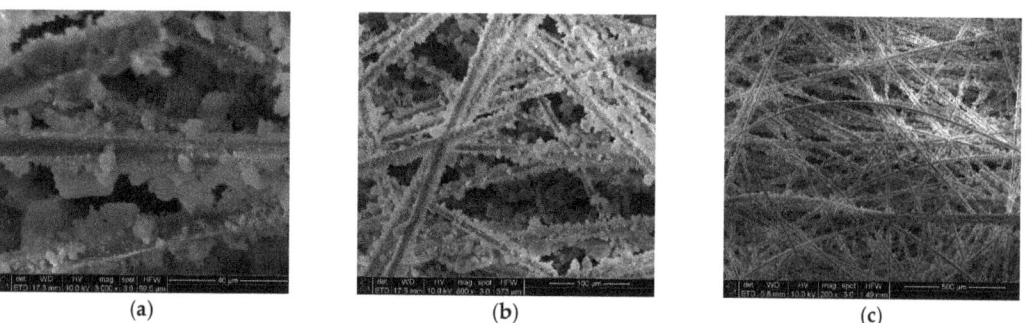

Figure 5. SEM images taken at different magnifications (3000× (**a**), 800× (**b**) and 200× (**c**)) showing the fiberglass blanket structure with an aerogel filling ratio of 50%.

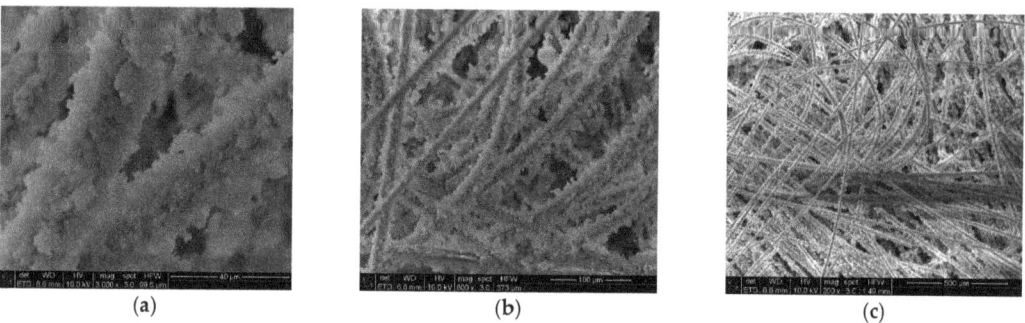

Figure 6. SEM images taken at different magnifications (3000× (**a**), 800× (**b**) and 200× (**c**)) showing the fiberglass blanket structure with an aerogel filling ratio of 75%.

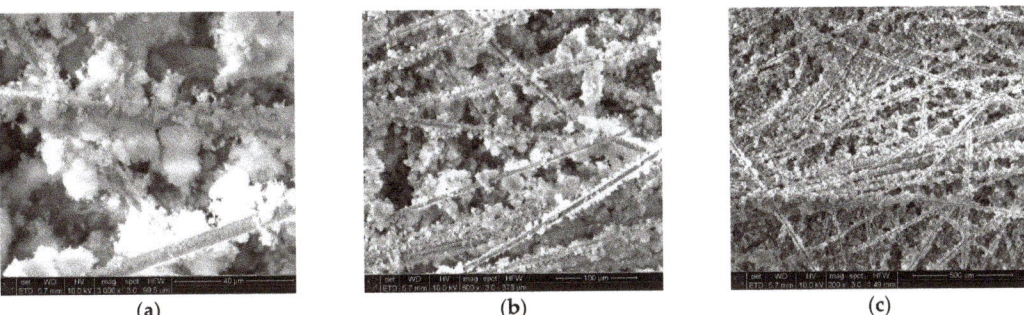

Figure 7. SEM images taken at different magnifications (3000× (**a**), 800× (**b**) and 200× (**c**)) showing the fiberglass blanket structure with an aerogel filling ratio of 100%.

4.2. Acoustical Properties

The acoustical properties were measured at the University of Sheffield in a 10 mm impedance tube [25]. Five specimens were cut from different areas on a sample of each type of fibrous blanket and their properties were measured. The repeatability of each measurement was found within ±2.9% for the absorption coefficient and ±5.8% for the reflection coefficient. Figure 8 shows a comparison between the measured absorption coefficients for the five samples. Figure 9 presents a comparison between the measured and predicted real and imaginary parts of the complex reflection coefficients for these five materials.

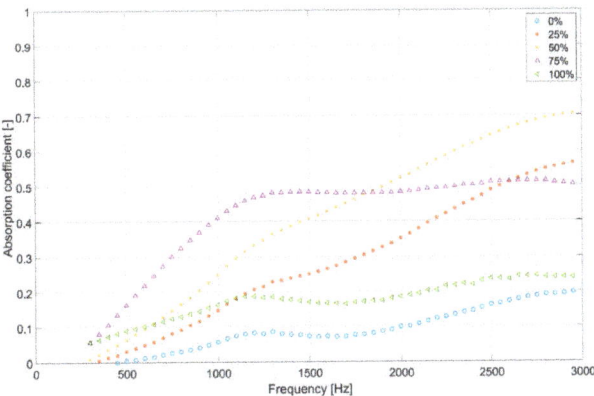

Figure 8. An example of the measured sound absorption coefficient of a 8–9 mm thick hard-backed layer of the five fibrous blankets with a progressive increase in the aerogel filling ratio.

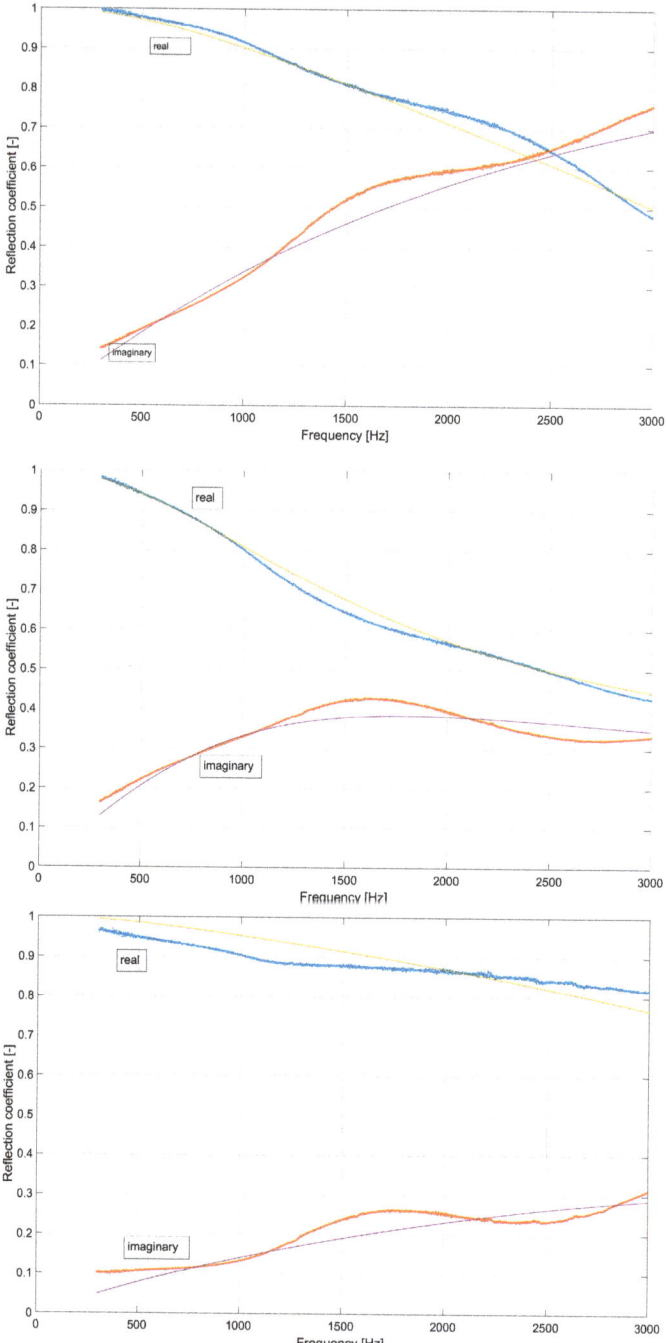

Figure 9. Examples of the measured (marker) and predicted (solid lines) complex reflection coefficient data for fiberglass blanket without any aerogel (**top**), 50% aerogel impregnated blanket (**middle**) and 100% aerogel impregnated blanket (**bottom**).

The results presented in Figure 8 suggest that there is a progressive increase in the absorption coefficient as the aerogel impregnation increases from 0 to 50%. When the aerogel filling ratio reaches 75% this increase becomes less pronounced. Increasing the filling ratio beyond 75% reduces the absorption coefficient significantly. This reduction makes sense because it is likely associated with a densely packed inter-fibrous space, which becomes almost full with aerogel (see Figures 6 and 7), causing a considerable reduction in the pore size (see Table 1) in a relatively thin material layer. For the filling ratios of 75% and above the characteristic impedance (see Figure 9) and attenuation of sound in a layer with such small pores becomes very high, limiting the value of the absorption coefficient [27]. The absorption coefficient of this relatively thin fibrous blanket with 50–75% filling ratios is still relatively high (30–70%) particularly above 1000 Hz (see references [4,13]). This level of absorption has a practical value in applications related to engineering noise control.

Table 1. Values of the non-acoustical parameters inverted from fitting the model [28] to the measured complex reflection coefficient data for the five types of fiberglass blankets.

Filling Ratio, %	Layer Thickness, d, mm	Pore Size, $\bar{s}^{(i)}$, μm	Porosity, $\phi^{(i)}$	Standard Deviation in Pore Size, $\sigma_s^{(i)}$	Calculated Porosity, ϕ	RMS Error, %
0	8.12 ± 0.77	99.4 ± 4.15	0.994 ± 0.0098	0	0.965 ± 0.0041	1.4
25	9.33 ± 1.60	48.0 ± 20.2	0.938 ± 0.018	0.160 ± 0.213	0.960 ± 0.0044	1.7
50	9.26 ± 0.47	32.8 ± 2.00	0.929 ± 0.011	0	0.952 ± 0.0026	1.8
75	10.35 ± 0.85	20.5 ± 1.35	0.959 ± 0.032	0	0.951 ± 0.0036	3.6
100	9.34 ± 0.84	83.0 ± 2.04	0.505 ± 0.091	0.55 ± 0.015	0.94 ± 0.0067	2.5

An obvious question here is: *What happens to the fiberglass pore properties when the percentage of aerogel powder impregnating the blanket increases?* In order to answer this question we attempted to fit the mathematical model [28] to the complex acoustic reflection coefficient data measured in the impedance tube. We used the optimization procedure described in reference [30] to invert the three parameters of the best fit. This procedure has been used extensively by many researchers (see [27] for a review of parameter inversion methods). Figure 9 shows three examples of this fit for fiberglass blankets with aerogel filling ratios of 0, 50 and 100%.

Table 1 presents a summary of the mean values of the three non-acoustical parameters in the adopted theoretical model [28], which were inverted from its fit to the measured data for the five filling ratios. This table also provides the porosity values calculated from the material density data, mean layer thickness measured directly and root mean square error (RMS) calculated between the predicted and measured reflection coefficient spectra. The superscript $^{(i)}$, which appears with a non-acoustic parameter in this table, means that the values of this parameter were inverted rather than measured directly.

The results shown in Figure 9 and the parameter values listed in Table 1 suggest that the model generally provides a very close fit to the data (an RMS error better than 2.5%), particularly when the filling ratio is equal to or below 50%. The agreement between the predicted and measured reflection coefficient spectra reduces slightly with the increased filling ratio. The inverted value of the median pore size (Table 1) decreases progressively from 99.4 to 20.5 μm as the filling ratio increases from 0 to 75%. This makes physical sense, as the SEM images in Figures 3–7 illustrate this. This range of pore sizes is also consistent with that measured non-acoustically for similar materials [6]. When the filling ratio increases, the inter-fiber pores are progressively replaced with much smaller inter-grain pores. The transport (inner) pores in the grains of aerogel do not seem to contribute significantly to the measured acoustical properties. This is reflected in a consistently underpredicted porosity value, $\phi^{(i)}$. The progressive change in the inverted porosity value make sense for the filling ratios between 0 and 50%, dropping from 99.4 to 92.9%, respectively. These values match the measured porosity values within 3%. When the filling ratio increases to 100%, the inverted porosity of $\phi^{(i)} = 50.5\%$ is significantly below the measured porosity of $\phi = 93.6\%$. Additionally, the median pore size inverted for this type of blanket is not realistic. This suggests that the physical behavior of the blanket layer with 100% filling ratio is no longer captured accurately by the model. As the proportion of aerogel powder in the material approaches 100%, the sorption and thermal diffusion effects are likely to become much more important [31]. These effects are not captured by the adopted model [28], which only accounts for the classical visco-thermal and inertia effects.

5. Conclusions

This work is a systematic study of the acoustical properties of fibrous blankets that are impregnated with an aerogel powder. The level of impregnation (filling ratio) has been progressively changed from 0 to 100% with respect to the material weight. The complex acoustic reflection coefficient of these materials was measured in the frequency range of 300–3000 Hz using a standard impedance tube setup [25]. These data were used to invert the three parameters of the theoretical model [28] via the best fit method [30]. It was found that the adopted model can predict the reflection coefficient spectrum relatively accurately with the RMS error being below 4%. The absorption coefficient of these relatively thin (8–9 mm thick) fibrous blankets with 50–75% filling ratios is relatively high (30–50%), particularly above 1000 Hz. This level of absorption has a practical value in applications related to engineering noise control.

The results of the parameter inversion obtained with the adopted model suggest that the impregnation of fibrous blanket with an aerogel powder results in a progressive reduction in the effective pore size. For the filling ratios in the range of 0–50% there is also a small but progressive reduction in the inverted porosity, which is within 3% of that measured directly. The absorption coefficient increases progressively with the increased filling ratio, reaching its maximum when the filling ratio is between 50% and 75%. This decrease in the effective pore size results in an increased acoustic attenuation and better coupling, which are important to maximize the acoustic absorption for such a thin porous layer. Increasing the filling ratio beyond 75% results in a significant drop in the absorption. This drop is associated with a considerable drop in the porosity value ($\phi = 0.505$) and substantial increase in the pore size ($\bar{s} = 83$ µm) inverted for the filling ratio of 100%. The discrepancy between the model and data for this filling ratio increases. As the proportion of aerogel powder in the material approaches 100%, the open porosity does not drop significantly, i.e., the proportion of the open interconnected pores remains relatively constant. However, the sorption and thermal diffusion effects in the inner pores in the aerogel grains become much more important [31]. These pores have nanometer scales [6], which is much smaller than the values of $\bar{s}$ inverted with the model [28] (see Table 1). The effects that occur in nanometer pores cannot be captured by the adopted model [28], which only accounts for the classical visco-thermal and inertia effects in pores that are much larger than the mean free path (68 nm in air at ambient pressure and temperature).

This work suggests that in order to predict the acoustic behavior of fibrous blankets with high aerogel filling ratios there is a clear need to refine the model [28] to include the sorption and pressure diffusion effects. The adopted model does require unrealistic values of the median pore size and porosity to achieve a good fit. This model can be refined by including in it the work by Venegas and Umnova [31]. In this way the dynamic compressibilities of the air filling the inter-fiber pores and in the nanoscale pores in the aerogel grains can be combined to account for all of the physical effects that contribute to the observed acoustical behavior.

Author Contributions: Conceptualization, H.B. and K.V.H.; methodology, H.B.; software, K.V.H.; validation, formal analysis, H.B.; investigation, H.B.; resources, H.B.; data curation, H.B.; writing—original draft preparation, H.B.; writing—review and editing, K.V.H.; visualization, H.B.; supervision, K.V.H.; project administration, K.V.H.; funding acquisition, K.V.H. All authors have read and agreed to the published version of the manuscript.

Funding: This research was partly funded by the EPSRC-sponsored Centre for Doctoral Training in Polymers, Soft Matter and Colloids, grant number EP/L016281/1, and industry sponsors—Armacell.

Institutional Review Board Statement: Not applicable.

Informed Consent Statement: Not applicable.

Data Availability Statement: The data are available online (see ref. [29]).

Acknowledgments: The authors would like to thank the EPSRC-sponsored Centre for Doctoral Training in Polymers, Soft Matter and Colloids at The University of Sheffield for their financial support of this work. We would also like to thank our industry partner Armacell and Mark Swift and Pavel Holub for their continued support throughout this research study. We extend our thanks to Shanyu Zhao at the Swiss Federal Laboratories for Materials Science and Technology for allowing us to use their electron microscopy center for high magnification SEM image analysis.

Conflicts of Interest: The authors declare no conflict of interest. The funders had no role in the design of the study; in the collection, analyses, or interpretation of data; in the writing of the manuscript, or in the decision to publish the results.

References

1. Directive 2012/27/EU of the european parliament and of the council of 25 October 2012 on energy efficiency, amending directives 2009/125/EC and 2010/30/EU and repealing Directives 2004/8/EC and 2006/32/EC. *OJEU* **2012**, *55*, 315/97.
2. Directive (EU) 2018/2002 of the European parliament and of the council of 11 December 2018 amending Directive 2012/27/EU on energy efficiency. *OJEU* **2018**, *328*/20. Available online: https://eur-lex.europa.eu/legal-content/EN/TXT/?uri=uriserv%3AOJ.L_.2018.328.01.0210.01.ENG (accessed on 17 May 2021).
3. Riffat, S.B.; Qiu, G. A review of state-of-the-art aerogel applications in buildings. *Int. J. Low-Carbon Technol.* **2013**, *8*, 1–6. [CrossRef]
4. Mazrouei-Sebdani, Z.; Begum, H.; Schoenwald, S.; Horoshenkov, K.V.; Malfait, W.J. A review on silica aerogel-based materials for acoustic applications. *J. Non Cryst. Solids* **2021**, *562*, 120770. [CrossRef]
5. Duer, K.; Svendsen, S. Monolithic silica aerogel in superinsulating glazings. *Sol. Energy* **1998**, *63*, 259–267. [CrossRef]
6. Talebi, Z.; Soltani, P.; Habibi, N.; Latif, F. Silica aerogel/polyester blankets for efficient sound absorption in buildings. *Constr. Build. Mater.* **2019**, *220*, 76–89. [CrossRef]
7. Koebel, M.M.; Rigacci, A.; Achard, P. Aerogel-based thermal superinsulation: An overview. *J. Sol. Gel. Sci. Technol.* **2012**, *63*, 315–339. [CrossRef]
8. Nocentini, K.; Achard, P.; Biwole, P.; Stipetic, M. Hygro-thermal properties of silica aerogel blankets dried using microwave heating for building thermal insulation. *Energy Build.* **2018**, *158*, 14–22. [CrossRef]
9. Rwawiire, S.; Tomkova, B.; Militky, J.; Hes, L.; Kale, B.M. Acoustic and thermal properties of a cellulose nonwoven natural fabric (barkcloth). *Appl. Acoust.* **2017**, *116*, 177–183. [CrossRef]
10. Ramamoorthy, M.; Pisal, A.A.; Rengasamy, R.S.; Rao, A.V. In-situ synthesis of silica aerogel in polyethylene terephthalate fibre nonwovens and their composite properties on acoustical absorption behavior. *J. Porous Mater.* **2018**, *25*, 179–187. [CrossRef]
11. Tascan, M.; Vaughn, E.A.; Stevens, K.A.; Brown, P.J. Effects of total surface area and fabric density on the acoustical behavior of traditional thermal-bonded highloft nonwoven fabrics. *J. Text. Inst.* **2011**, *102*, 746. [CrossRef]
12. Fernandez-Marin, A.A.; Jimenez, N.; Groby, J.-P.; Sanchez-Dehesa, J.; Romero-Garcia, V. Aerogel-based metasurfaces for perfect acoustic energy absorption. *Appl. Phys. Lett.* **2019**, *115*, 061901. [CrossRef]
13. Geslain, A.; Groby, J.-P.; Romero-Garcia, V.; Cervera, F.; Sanchez-Dehesa, J. Acoustic characterization of silica aerogel clamped plates for perfect absorption, *J. Non Cryst. Solids* **2018**, *499*, 283–288. [CrossRef]
14. Guild, M.D.; Garcia-Chocano, V.M.; Sanchez-Dehesa, J. Aerogel as a soft acoustic metamaterial for for airborne sound. *Phys. Rev. Appl.* **2016**, *5*, 034012. [CrossRef]
15. Gross, J.; Fricke, J. Sound propagation in SiO_2 aerogels. *J. Acoust. Soc. Am.* **1992**, *91*, 2004–2006. [CrossRef]
16. Forest, L.; Gibiat, V.; Woignier, T. Biot's theory of acoustic propagation in porous media applied to aerogels and alcogels. *J. Non Cryst. Solids* **1998**, *225*, 287–292. [CrossRef]
17. Gibiat, V.; Lefeuvre, O.; Woignier, T. Acoustic properties and potential applications of silica aerogels. *J. Non Cryst. Solids* **1995**, *186*, 244–255. [CrossRef]
18. Forest, L.; Gibiat, V.; Hooley, A. Impedance matching and acoustic absorption in granular layers of silica aerogels. *J. Non Cryst. Solids* **2001**, *285*, 230–235. [CrossRef]
19. Motahari, S.; Javadi, H.; Motahari, A. Silica-aerogel cotton composites as sound absorber. *J. Mater. Civ. Eng.* **2014**, *27*, 1–6. [CrossRef]
20. Eskandari, N.; Motahari, S.; Atoufi, Z.; Motlagh, G.H.; Najafi, M. Thermal, mechanical, and acoustic properties of silica aerogel/UPVC composites. *J. Appl. Polym. Sci.* **2017**, *134*, 1–8. [CrossRef]
21. Joung, Y.C.; Roe, M.J.; Yoo, Y.J.; Park, J.C.; Choi, H.J.; Kim, M.W. Method of Preparing Silica Aerogel Powder. U.S. Patent No. US 2012/0225003 A1, 6 September 2012.

22. Sobha Rani, T.; Subha, M.C.S.; Venkata Reddy, G.; Kim, Y.-H.; Ahn, Y.-S. Synthesis of Water-Glass-Based Silica Aerogel Powder via with and Without Squeezing of Hydrogels. *J. Appl. Polym. Sci.* **2009**, *115*, 1675–1679. [CrossRef]
23. Available online: https://www.lih-fe.com/en/product/Fiberglass-Needle-Mat-E-650C/fiberglass_needled_mat-001.html (accessed on 14 April 2021).
24. Materiacustica Srl. Measurement Kit for Acoustical Complex Properties Testing. Available online: http://www.materiacustica.it/mat_UKProdotti_MAA.html (accessed on 27 January 2021).
25. International Organisation for Standardization. *Acoustics—"Determination of Sound Absorption Coefficient and Impedance in Impedance Tubes—Part 2: Transfer-Function Method"*; ISO10534-2; International Organisation for Standardization: Geneva, Switzerland, 1998.
26. Available online: https://local.armacell.com/fileadmin/cms/downloads/others/armagel/marketing-brochure/ArmaGelHT_Marketing_Brochure_English.pdf (accessed on 14 April 2021).
27. Horoshenkov, K.V. A review of acoustical methods for porous material characterization. *Int. J. Acoust. Vib.* **2017**, *22*, 92–103.
28. Horoshenkov, K.V.; Hurrell, A.; Groby, J.-P. A three-parameter analytical model for the acoustical properties of porous media. *J. Acoust. Soc. Am.* **2019**, *145*, 2512–2517. [CrossRef] [PubMed]
29. Available online: https://drive.google.com/drive/folders/1rA10utMecuzzuiiX5O-nHDrA8mzgCuEn (accessed on 16 April 2021).
30. Hurrell, A.; Horoshenkov, K.V. On the relationship of the observed acoustical and related non-acoustical behaviours of nanofibers membranes using Biot and Darcy-type models. *Appl. Acoust.* **2021**, *179*, 108075. [CrossRef]
31. Venegas, R.; Umnova, O. Influence of sorption on sound propagation in granular activated carbon. *J. Acoust. Soc. Am.* **2016**, *140*, 755–766. [CrossRef] [PubMed]

Article

More Than Just Concrete: Acoustically Efficient Porous Concrete with Different Aggregate Shape and Gradation

Louena Shtrepi [1,*], Arianna Astolfi [1], Elena Badino [1], Giovanni Volpatti [2] and Davide Zampini [3]

1. Department of Energy (DENERG), Corso Duca degli Abruzzi 24, Politecnico di Torino, 10129 Torino, Italy; arianna.astolfi@polito.it (A.A.); elena.badino@polito.it (E.B.)
2. CEMEX Innovation Holding AG—Brügg Branch, Römerstrasse 13, 2555 Brügg, Switzerland; giovanni.volpatti@cemex.com
3. CEMEX Innovation Holding AG, General-Guisan-Strasse 6, 6300 Zug, Switzerland; davide.zampini@cemex.com
* Correspondence: louena.shtrepi@polito.it

Featured Application: The use of acoustically efficient porous concrete with weighted absorption coefficients (α_w) in the range of 0.30 to 0.75 for noise control in outdoor and indoor applications.

Abstract: The interest in the use of resistant acoustic materials has put further attention on the use of porous concrete in the building industry. This work investigates the acoustic properties of four different mix designs of porous concrete obtained with two types of aggregates, that is, normal weight and lightweight aggregates. The assessment of the sound-absorbing performances has been conducted in the small-scale reverberation room (SSRR) at Politecnico di Torino (Italy), in agreement with the procedure indicated in the ISO 354 Standard. For each concrete type, three panel thicknesses, i.e., 20 mm, 40 mm, and 60 mm, were tested. Moreover, different mounting conditions were investigated, considering the combination of single panels in multiple layers, adding an air gap between the panel and the backing, and inserting a layer of rock wool in the air gap itself. The results show weighted absorption coefficients (α_w) in the range of 0.30 to 0.75 depending on the thickness and mounting conditions. These encouraging values make these materials useful for efficient practical applications in indoor and outdoor environments.

Keywords: acoustics; acoustic measurements; sound absorption coefficient; cement-based materials; building materials; pervious concrete; acoustic concrete

1. Introduction

The implementation of noise control strategies in outdoor environments is a challenging task for several professionals, and an increasing number of studies highlight the importance of the architectural design on urban noise mitigation in canyon streets [1,2] squares [3] and inner yards [4]. A detailed overview of the acoustic strategies used for the building envelope design in order to improve the urban acoustic environment is given in [5]. These studies have pointed out the need for sound-absorbing and -scattering materials suitable for outdoor environments. Moreover, several indoor spaces such as airports, train stations, schools, etc. are characterized by requirements similar to those of outdoor spaces regarding highly durable and resistant acoustic materials. Therefore, this work aims to investigate the sound absorbing properties of porous concrete of different mix designs, thicknesses and mounting conditions, as this material results suitable for outdoor and indoor applications. Compared to other porous sound absorbers, porous concrete has the capability to withstand the atmospheric elements, and therefore it is suitable for applications in outdoor and indoor environments when resistance, low deformability, and high durability are required.

Porous absorbers are the most widespread type of sound absorbers. According to their microstructure, porous absorbers can be further classified into granular, cellular, and fibrous [6,7]. The most fundamental properties of porous materials influencing their sound absorbing properties are flow resistivity and porosity and second, pore shape factor and tortuosity [7].

Conventional concrete is generally characterized by poor sound-absorbing properties, as the prevailing phenomena occurring are sound reflections. In general, normal concrete has an absorption coefficient value of 0.05–0.10 [8]. However, porous concrete has the capability to work as a porous sound-absorbing material as it is characterized by high porosity, i.e., open pore structure on its surface and an interconnected network of pores. It is also known as pervious, gap-graded, permeable, or enhanced porosity concrete [9] and is currently widely used in urban environments as paving material to support environmentally sustainable rainwater management [10]. It has been also exploited for its acoustic absorbing properties in traffic noise barriers and railway noise reduction [11–13]. Pervious concrete mainly consists of normal Portland cement, coarse aggregates (aggregate dimension greater than 5 mm), and water, which generate a void content that generally ranges from 15% to 35% [10,14–16]. Pervious concrete acoustic panels belong to the class of granular sound absorbers with pores created by the presence solid aggregates which are bonded together by a cementitious binder. The key factor to allow sound absorption to occur is the accurate definition of the quantity of binder to ensure that there is enough binder to keep the aggregate together without clogging the pore network and still allow for an appropriate resistance for its use and handling. Overall, the sound-absorbing properties of granular materials tend to be uneven in frequency and to be characterized by peaks [17].

Different strategies have been proposed with the intent to improve the sound absorbing properties, i.e., with the aim to enhance the rate and the evenness of the sound absorption provided by altering the microstructural properties of the pervious concrete. Note that these strategies applied to the mix design aim to vary the fundamental properties, i.e., flow resistivity, porosity, pore shape factor, and tortuosity, which control the absorbing performance. Indeed, the sound absorption properties of porous concrete are strictly related to the void ratio of the concrete. Therefore, it is important to adequately control the void ratio and aggregate type, which influence tortuosity and flow resistivity [18], pore size, and pore aperture size, which are used to control porosity [8]. A higher void ratio leads to higher and wider peak values in acoustic absorption coefficients, resulting in a shift of the peak of the coefficient towards the higher frequencies [12,19,20].

The effect on sound absorption of the aggregate size and different aggregate types by blending or combining them in multiple layers has been studied in [11,13,21,22]. Aggregate size can be used to control the pore dimensions, as the median pore size increases for increasing aggregate size [19,21]. With respect to aggregate size, it has been observed that most previous studies endorse the use of aggregate with dimensions in the range 1 to 10 mm [11,21,22], as smaller aggregates would clog the pores, thus reducing porosity, and bigger ones, despite increasing the pore volume, would reduce the tortuosity of the pore network. When considering the use of different aggregate types such as lightweight and normal-weight aggregates, the study in [22] suggests that lightweight aggregates can absorb cement paste from micropores on the surface of the aggregates. As a result, for an equal absolute volume ratio of aggregates, smaller size lightweight aggregates result in slightly higher sound absorbing performance, as they have a larger total surface area compared to bigger ones, and therefore the cement paste covering the aggregates can be better absorbed when smaller aggregates are used and result in higher void ratio values with respect to normal weight aggregates [22]. Other studies have investigated the use of different materials as aggregates, such as crumb rubber, cenospheres, and recycled aggregates [12,13,23–25]. The possibility of blending aggregates with different size in the concrete matrix has been studied in [19,21], highlighting that, as a general rule, aggregate size should be selected in order to ensure that smaller aggregates do not enter the pores created by the bigger ones. Porous concretes with blends of aggregates of different materials have been tested in [11], where expanded perlite aggregates were replaced by different percentages of slag, evidencing a nonlinear impact on the sound absorption performance of the panels. Concrete samples featuring aggregates of different dimensions or material have been combined into layers in [11,13,22], evidencing the coupling two layers of concrete with the external one featuring aggregates with lower bulk densities or bigger pores sizes compared to the back layer lead to increased sound absorbing performances.

Slight differences in sound absorption have been reported regarding the shape of the aggregates; for instance, this was shown in [22], i.e., which has compared round shape (lightweight) and irregular shape (normal weight) aggregates with similar gradation.

Moreover, as for all the acoustic porous materials, the thickness of the porous layer also results as important for the acoustic absorption coefficient spectra. The principal maximum peak of the absorption coefficient is displaced to lower frequencies when the thickness increases [13,18,21]. However, there is a threshold regarding the thickness of granular materials above which the absorption does not increase further [7]. Table A1 (Appendix A) briefly summarizes the details and the main findings of previous research investigating the effects of design factors on the sound absorption coefficient of porous concrete. The studies which analyzed different aggregate size, material and shape, and on panel thickness have been clustered evidencing if and the extent to which such variable was found to have an influence on the sound absorbing properties of the panels.

Recent reviews on the strategies that have been proposed to enhance the sound absorbing performances of concrete have been presented in [17,26]. However, these reviews highlight the fact that further research is required to provide larger datasets to refine and produce better estimation of the sound absorption of concrete materials.

Therefore, the following study aims to provide further experimental data on the investigation of some design guidelines for sound absorbing concrete emerging from the past research regarding the aggregate shape and size. The present study investigates, through a systematic research approach, the effects of concrete mix design (four different conditions), sample thickness (three different conditions), and mounting conditions (three different conditions) on the absorption properties of porous concrete tested in a small-scale reverberation room (SSRR). Therefore, the main aim of this study is to define the sample configuration that could lead to an increase of the sound absorption properties of concrete panels. More than 30 different combinations of the aforementioned variables have been considered. Note that besides providing a useful database of measured data in addition to previous research, this work presents novel configurations, that is, mounting conditions with an air gap and combination in multiple layers with other porous materials. To the authors' knowledge, this has not been studied in previous literature.

This work aims to increase awareness on the porous concrete properties among several professionals such as architect, designers, acousticians, policy-makers, etc. that deal with noise control strategies in outdoor and indoor environments.

2. Materials and Methods

The research has been organized through the following steps:

(1) Selection of different concrete mix design and preparation of samples for the measurements.
(2) Selection of different mounting methods.
(3) Measurement of the frequency-dependent sound absorption αs in the SSRR.
(4) Computation of the weighted sound absorption coefficients as single index α_w and comparisons.

2.1. Tested Concretes

Information regarding the porous concrete types, identified with the letters A, B, C, and D, are summarized in Table 1. The following parameters are reported: aggregate size (according to EN 933-2:2020 [27]), aggregate particle density (according to EN 1097-6:2013 [28]), void ratio (according to ASTM C1754/C1754M [29]), flexural strength (according to EN 12390-5:2019 [30]), previous concrete density (according to ASTM C1754/C1754M [29]), and water permeability (according to ASTM D2434-19 [31]). Two different types of aggregates have been used in the mix design: normal weight and lightweight. The normal weight aggregates have been used in concrete type A and have an irregular shape with an average dimension of 4–8 mm, while the lightweight aggregates have an almost perfect round shape, i.e., spherical, with different dimensions ranging between 4 and 8 mm, 2 and 4 mm, and 0.5 and 1 mm for concretes B, C, and D, respectively.

Table 1. Four mix design of porous concrete characteristics with respect to: aggregate size, aggregate particle density, void ratio, flexural strength, previous concrete density, and water permeability.

Concretes	Aggregate Typology	Aggregate Size [mm]	Aggregate Particle Density [kg/m³]	Void Ratio [%]	Flexural Strength [MPa]	Pervious Concrete Density [kg/m³]	Water Permeability [mm/s]
A	crushed normal weight aggregates	4–8	2650 ± 30	25 ± 2	3.5 ± 0.5	1955 ± 20	9.5 ± 1.1
B	round lightweight aggregates	4–8	905 ± 85	25 ± 3	1.5 ± 0.3	932 ± 35	10.9 ± 1.7
C	round lightweight aggregates	2–4	325 ± 35	25 ± 2	1 ± 0.2	514 ± 20	7.4 ± 0.9
D	round lightweight aggregates	0.5–1	510 ± 70	20 ± 2	0.5 ± 0.1	682 ± 15	3.6 ± 0.5

Details of the aggregate shape can be visualized in Figure 1.

Figure 1. Sample (**A**): crushed normal weight aggregates 4–8 mm; Sample (**B**): round lightweight aggregates 4–8 mm; Sample (**C**): round lightweight aggregates 2–4 mm; Sample (**D**): round lightweight aggregates 0.5–1 mm.

Concrete A differs significantly from the other three regarding the concrete density value, which is strongly affected by the higher values of the aggregate particle density. The four concretes present a similar void ratio. However, while this parameter is constant for concretes A, B, and C, it decreases for concrete type D, which features smaller aggregates. It can also be noticed that there is a decrease in the flexural strength for lower densities and smaller aggregate dimensions.

For each concrete, three different sample types have been manufactured with three different thicknesses, i.e., 20 mm, 40 mm, and 60 mm (Figure 1); for each of them, three samples have been produced. The panels are square-shaped in plan with a side dimension of 60 cm. Three different mounting conditions were tested for the samples with a thicknesses of 20 and 40 mm, that is, coupling different samples in multiple layers (Figure 2), adding a 50 mm air gap between the sample and the room floor (Figure 3), and adding a layer of fibrous material (rock wool) in the air gap itself (Figure 4). The identification codes of the samples and mounting conditions have been summarized in Table 2. The coupling of different samples in multiple layers has been performed only within the same concrete in order to compare their performance with single layers of the same thickness and investigate any anisotropy at the back surface of each layer. The multiple layer configuration is obtained by superimposing one panel to the other, with no joint or glue connecting them. This mounting solution could be practically useful when modular solutions are explored and would limit the need for different formwork thicknesses. The introduction of a rock wool layer in the air gap has been tested with sample D of 20 mm thickness only as it resulted in the highest sound absorption performances compared to the 20 mm samples of A, B, and C concretes. In this case, two thicknesses of the rock wool layer—30 and 50 mm—have been introduced in the air gap.

Figure 2. Multiple layers of 20 + 20 mm and 20 + 40 mm. Sample (**A**): crushed normal weight aggregates 4–8 mm; Sample (**B**): round lightweight aggregates 4–8 mm; Sample (**C**): round lightweight aggregates 2–4 mm; Sample (**D**): round lightweight aggregates 0.5–1 mm.

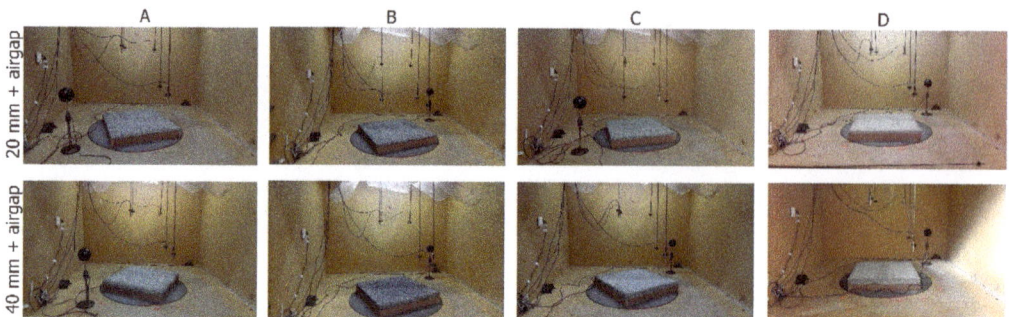

Figure 3. Mounting on 50 mm air gap. Sample (**A**): crushed normal weight aggregates 4–8 mm; Sample (**B**): round lightweight aggregates 4–8 mm; Sample (**C**): round lightweight aggregates 2–4 mm; Sample (**D**): round lightweight aggregates 0.5–1 mm.

Figure 4. (**a**) 30 mm and (**b**) 50 mm rock wool filling 50 mm air gap. (**c**) Sample D of 20 mm over one of the two conditions.

Table 2. Summary of the tested samples and configurations of the porous concrete. Single layers have been tested in configurations of multiple layers, with air gap and with rock wool in the airgap (+tested and −untested configurations of single layers).

Concrete Type	Overall Thickness [mm]	Layer Thickness [mm]		Air Gap 50 mm	Rock Wool Thickness [mm]
		Single Layer	Multiple Layers		
A	20	20		+	-
	40	40	20 + 20	+	-
	60	60	20 + 40	-	-
B	20	20		+	-
	40	40	20 + 20	+	-
	60	60	20 + 40	-	-
C	20	20		+	-
	40	40	20 + 20	+	-
	60	60	20 + 40	-	-
D	20	20		+	-
					30
					50
	40	40	20 + 20	+	-
	60	60	20 + 40	-	-

The assessment of the sound absorbing performances has been conducted in the small-scale reverberation room (SSRR) of Politecnico di Torino (Italy), following the procedure indicated in the ISO 354 Standard [32]. The reliability of the measurement was tested with respect to reproducibility and repeatability, by repeating the measures three times on three different samples of the same typology and considering their arithmetic mean to describe the performances of each type. The sound absorbing properties are expressed as 1/3 octave band sound absorption coefficients (α) and also as weighted sound absorption coefficients (α_w) for an easier comparison.

2.2. Sound Absorption Coefficient Measurements

The small-scale reverberation room (Figures 1–4) is installed in the Applied Acoustics laboratory at DENERG (Department of Energy, Politecnico di Torino, Torino, Italy). The room has been primarily built for random-incidence scattering coefficient measurements according to ISO 17497-1 [33], but it is also suitable for measurement of sound absorption coefficient according to ISO 354 [32,34]. It is an oblique angled room with pairs of non-parallel walls with a volume of 2.86 m^3 and a total area of 12.12 m^2. A more detailed description of the room construction has been provided in Shtrepi and Prato [35].

The measurement procedure consists in using the integrated impulse response method [32] for simultaneous measurements on six different microphone positions in two conditions, i.e., with and without the sample inside the room. The measurement chain consists of six 1/4" BSWA Tech MPA451 microphones and ICP104 (BSWA Technology Co., Ltd., Beijing, China), two ITA High-Frequency Dodecahedron Loudspeakers with their specific ITA power amplifiers (ITA-RWTH, Aachen, Germany), and a sound card Roland Octa-Capture UA-1010 (Roland Corporation, Shizuoka, Japan). This setup allows to perform 12 measurements, which refer to the minimum number required by ISO 354:2003 [32]. The software used for the measurements, i.e., sound generation, recording, and signal processing, is MATLAB combined with the functions of the ITA-Toolbox (an opensource toolbox by RWTH-Aachen, Aachen, Germany) [36].

For each of the 12 measurements the reverberation time relative to a 20 dB decay, i.e., T_{20}, is evaluated and used to estimate the T_{60}, i.e., the reverberation time occurring for a 60 dB decay, as done in the full-scale reverberation room (FSRR) data processing. The data are spatially averaged with the ensemble averaging method in order to obtain the reverberation times T_1 and T_2, which are obtained without and with the sample inside the room, respectively. Equations (1) and (2) are applied to estimate the random-incidence absorption coefficient α_s.

The difference between T_1 and T_2 measurements is used to calculate the variation of the equivalent sound absorption area A_T [m^2] based on Sabine's theory:

$$A_T = 55.3V \left(\frac{1}{c_2 T_2} - \frac{1}{c_1 T_1} \right) - 4V(m_2 - m_1) \quad (1)$$

where T_1 and T_2 [s] are the reverberation times of the empty reverberation room and of the reverberation room with the test specimen, respectively; V [m^3] is the volume of the empty reverberation room; c_1 and c_2 [m/s] are the propagation speed of sound in air in the room without and with the sample: $c_1 = 331 + 0.6\, t_1$, t_1 [°C] is the air temperature; and m_1 and m_2 [m^{-1}] is the power attenuation coefficient of the climatic conditions in the reverberation room without and with the sample (calculated according to ISO 9613-1 [37]).

The random-incidence absorption coefficient α_s is defined as

$$\alpha_S = \frac{A_T}{S} \quad (2)$$

where S [m^2] is the area covered by the test sample. Note that the edge area is included in the calculations of S considering the four concretes as isotropic materials [38].

3. Results

The results of the measured sound absorption coefficients are reported in the graphs in Figures 5, 7 and 8 and discussed in separate sections, based on the tested conditions, i.e., thickness and mounting method for each concrete type (A–D). Figures 5, 7 and 8 present an immediate reading of the design factors considered within the sample typology to evidence improvements/deterioration given the mix design. Furthermore, the figures in Appendix B compare the results of considered panel samples (A–D) for a given design factor, in order to help the reader with a more immediate understanding of the differences between samples (A–D). In the end, more general conclusions are drawn to compare the performances of the different sample types. Moreover, the single index for weighted sound absorption (α_w) in SSRR measurements has been estimated and used for comparisons.

3.1. Effect of Sample Thickness and Concrete Type

Figure 5 shows the graphs of the four samples (A–D) for three different thicknesses of the single layers. Overall, the absorption spectra of panels A are uneven, and tend to provide poor absorption (<0.25) at frequencies lower than 630 Hz, while at higher frequencies, the sound absorption coefficients ranges between 0.40 and 0.70 for panels with either 40 mm or 60 mm thicknesses. The 20 mm thick panel features an absorption peak at 3150 Hz, which reaches the value of 0.90 and provides a poor absorption (<0.25) at frequencies lower than 2000 Hz. The 40 and 60 mm panels present a higher absorption coefficient with respect to the 20 mm panels in the 500–2000 Hz frequency range.

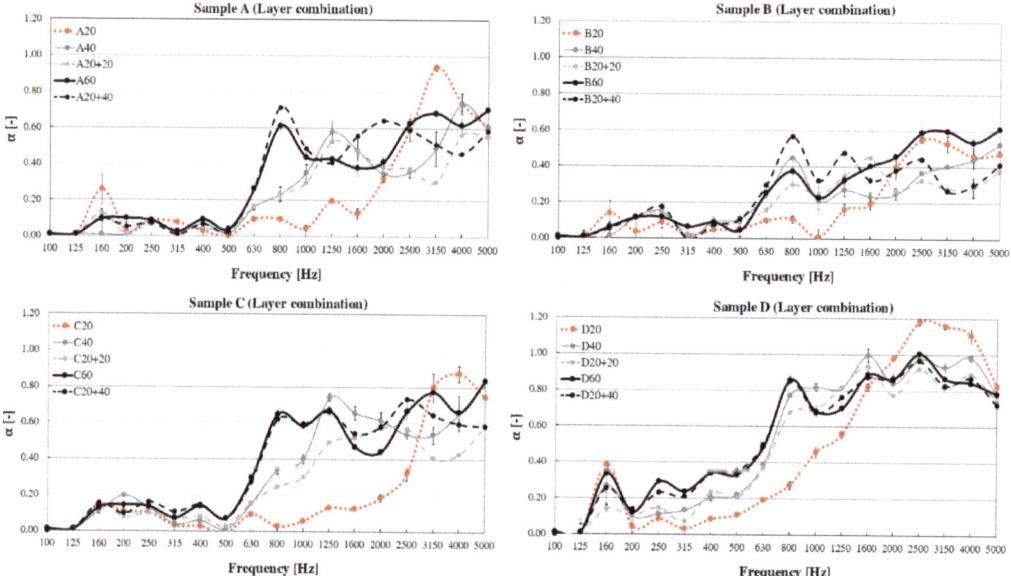

Figure 5. Comparison of the absorption coefficients for samples (A–D) with different thicknesses obtained from multiple layer combinations (20, 40, 20 + 20, 60, and 20 + 40 mm). Sample (**A**): crushed normal weight aggregates 4–8 mm; Sample (**B**): round lightweight aggregates 4–8 mm; Sample (**C**): round lightweight aggregates 2–4 mm; Sample (**D**): round lightweight aggregates 0.5–1 mm.

The absorption spectra of samples B are uneven and tend to provide poor absorption (<0.25) at frequencies lower than 630 Hz for panels with either 40 mm or 60 mm thicknesses, while at higher frequencies the absorption coefficient ranges between 0.20 and 0.60. The 20 mm thick panel features an absorption peak at 2500 Hz of about 0.60 and provides poor absorption (<0.25) at frequencies lower than 1600 Hz. This might be due to the curing process of the 40 mm sample, which might have led to lower porosity of these samples.

The absorption spectra of panels C are also slightly uneven and tend to provide poor absorption (<0.25) at frequencies lower than 630 Hz for panels with either 40 mm or 60 mm thicknesses, while at higher frequencies, the absorption ranges between 0.40 and 0.80. The 20 mm thick panel features an absorption peak around 4000 Hz, achieving a value of 0.90 and provides poor absorption (<0.25) at frequencies lower than 1600 Hz.

The absorption coefficient for this thickness becomes lower than 0.25 at frequencies below 2000 Hz. The 60 mm sample reaches significant high values of absorption coefficient (>0.40) at 800 Hz, while the 40 mm panel at 1250 Hz.

The absorption spectra of panel D are more even than the other three typologies, and tend to provide significant absorption (>0.40) at frequencies higher than 630 Hz for panels with either 40 mm or 60 mm thicknesses, where the sound absorption ranges between 0.40 and 1. The 20 mm thick panel feature an absorption peak between 2500 Hz and 4000 Hz, achieving a value of 1.20; the peak is broader than those featured by 20 mm thick panels of types A–C. Values higher than 1 may occur in the measurements with finite sample size for materials with high absorption properties [39,40]. The 20 mm sample of panel D achieves significant absorption (>0.40) above 1000 Hz, while for panels A–C, this occurred above 2500 Hz, 2000 Hz, and 3150 Hz, respectively. The sound absorbing performances of thicker panels are extended towards the lower frequencies, in the range below 1600 Hz. Indeed, for the thicker panels (40 mm and 60 mm), the significant absorption range is extended in a similar way down to 630 Hz.

3.2. Effect of Sample Mounting in Multiple Layers

The graphs in Figure 5 show the absorption coefficients of the four sample types both in the single layer and multiple layer configurations with panel thicknesses of 20, 40, and 60 mm, for an easier comparison. Sample A graph shows that the sound-absorbing performances achieved when coupling two panels of 20 mm thick are comparable to those achieved by a single panel with a thickness of 40 mm. A similar trend is observed comparing the 60 mm thick panel with the combination of 20 + 40 mm thick panels. However, there are some differences occurring above 1250 Hz. It can be observed that above 2500 Hz both the 20 + 20 mm and the 20 + 40 mm combination show lower values of sound absorption compared to the 40 and the 60 mm single layers samples, respectively. It can be noticed that the multiple layer 20 + 40 mm of sample A outperforms the 60 mm sample only at the 800 Hz peak and in the frequency range 1250 to 2500 Hz.

Sample B graph shows that the sound absorbing performances achieved when coupling two panels 20 mm thick are comparable to those achieved by a single panel with a thickness of 40 mm. However, the combination 20 + 20 outperforms the 40 mm single layer panel in the range of 1000 to 2000 Hz. By contrast, the performances of the 60 mm thick panel are higher than those of 20 + 40 mm thick panels combined for frequencies higher than 1600 Hz. The multiple layer 20 + 40 outperforms the 60 mm sample in the range 630–1250 Hz.

The results of Sample C show that the sound absorbing performances achieved when coupling two panels that are 20 mm thick are slightly lower than those achieved by a single panel with a thickness of 40 mm, particularly for frequencies range 800–2000 Hz and above 3150 Hz. The performances of the 60 mm thick panel are comparable with those achieved by the combination of 20 + 40 mm thick panels. However, the multiple layer 20 + 40 outperforms the 60 mm sample in the range 1250–2500 Hz.

Sample D results show that the sound absorbing performances achieved when coupling two panels 20 mm thick are comparable to those achieved by a single panel with a thickness of 40 mm. A similar trend is observed comparing the performances achieved by a 60 mm thick panel with that of the combination of 20 + 40 mm thick panels. This might be due to the high and uniform porosity obtained for all the samples of type D compared to the other panel types, as seen in Figure 6. In these cases, further care should be put in the treatment of the mix design and its curing in samples A, B, and C, as heavier aggregates might sediment and result in nonuniform distribution of the pores within the panel and its front/back surfaces.

Figure 6. Back surface for Sample (**A**): crushed normal weight aggregates 4–8 mm; Sample (**B**): round lightweight aggregates 4–8 mm; Sample (**C**): round lightweight aggregates 2–4 mm; Sample (**D**): round lightweight aggregates 0.5–1 mm.

3.3. Effect of Sample Mounting with an Air Gap

The graphs in Figure 7 show the four sample types (A–D) mounted with an air gap of 50 mm between the panel and the rigid backing, i.e., the SSRR floor. The graph of Sample A shows that the performance is enhanced at the lower frequencies when an air gap is left between the panel of 20 mm and the backing, while the sound absorption at high frequencies decreases. The maximum peak is shifted at lower frequencies, i.e., at ~630 Hz, with an absorption coefficient of ~0.60. The 40 mm layer seems to be less affected by the presence of the air gap and the maximum peaks remain unvaried in frequency for this thickness. However, a slight decrease is reported at high frequencies and an increase of about 0.10 is observed at the peak value corresponding to 1250 Hz.

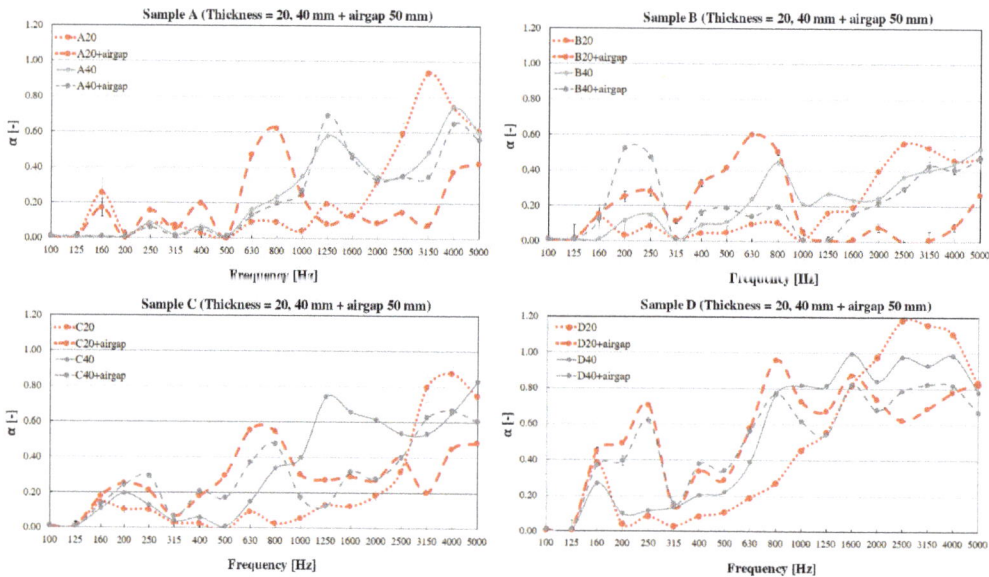

Figure 7. Comparison of the absorption coefficients for samples (**A–D**) of different thicknesses (20 and 40 mm) mounted with an air gap of 50 mm. Sample (**A**): crushed aggregates 4–8 mm; Sample (**B**): round lightweight aggregates 4–8 mm; Sample (**C**): round lightweight aggregates 2–4 mm; Sample (**D**): round lightweight aggregates 0.5–1 mm.

Sample B shows different trends for the 20 mm and 40 mm layers. However, when an air gap is left between the panels and the backing, the performance is enhanced at the lower frequencies for the 20 mm and 40 mm layers. The high frequency sound absorption decreases for the 20 mm layer when the air gap is added, while the maximum peak is shifted at lower frequencies, i.e., at ~630 Hz, with an absorption coefficient of ~0.60. The 40 mm layer seems to be less affected by the presence of the air gap at high frequencies above 2000 Hz. Conversely, the air gap seems to decrease the absorption over the 630 to 2000 Hz range for the 40 mm layer. A peak value appears at the frequency of 200 Hz with a value of about 0.55 of the absorption coefficients.

Sample C shows a decrease of the absorption coefficient at high frequencies for both 20 mm and 40 mm layers when an air gap is left between the panels and the backing. For the 20 mm panel, this is significant above 2500 Hz, while for the 40 mm panel, it is more evident in the 1000 to 2500 Hz range. The performances are slightly enhanced at the lower frequencies in the range 315 to 800 Hz for the 20 mm sample and in the range 315 to 2500 Hz for the 40 mm sample, with the maximum peaks that are shifted at 630 Hz and 800 Hz, respectively.

The sound-absorbing performances of sample D show a decrease at high frequencies when an air gap is left between the panels and the backing above 1600 Hz and above 800 Hz for the 20 mm and 40 mm panels, respectively. Nevertheless, the sound absorption coefficients in those ranges result above 0.55. The performances are enhanced at the lower frequencies, where several peaks appear around 250 Hz, 400 Hz, and 800 Hz. The absorption coefficient increases for both thicknesses in the 160 to 630 Hz range when the air gap is added, showing a very similar trend for both 20 mm and 40 mm panels.

Effect of Sample Mounting with an Air Gap Filled with Porous Material

The previous sections showed that sample D presents the highest sound absorption coefficients extended over the broader range of frequencies. In order to further improve the performance of the combination of panel D with an air gap, another strategy has been used considering the air gap filled with porous material. The introduction of a rock wool layer in the air gap has been tested with the sample of 20 mm thickness only. Two thicknesses of the rock wool layer, that is, 30 and 50 mm, have been introduced in the air gap. Recall that the air gap considered here is of 50 mm. Therefore, the first layer of rock wool (30 mm) allowed to have a 20 mm air gap left between the concrete sample and the rock wool layer, while the 50 mm rock wool allowed to test a fully filled air gap.

Figure 8 shows that the with the insertion of 30 mm and 50 mm rock wool in the air gap the sound absorption coefficients have very similar trends above 630 Hz. Generally, the combination of an air gap with a porous material (e.g., rock wool) is shown to improve the acoustic performance down to 250 Hz. A peak value at 800 Hz is further increased when the air gap is filled with rock wool compared to the empty condition. Furthermore, a significant improvement is obtained in the 250 to 800 Hz frequency range reaching values of sound absorption coefficients of 0.60–0.90.

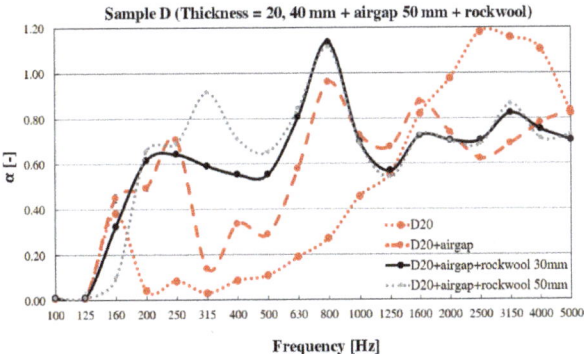

Figure 8. Sample D single layer of 20 mm combined with an air gap of 50 mm filled with a rock wool layer of 30 and 50 mm.

3.4. Single Number Acoustic Index α_w

Based on the above results, the weighted sound absorption coefficients α_w derived from the SSRR measurements were calculated. These single indices are useful for an immediate and practical comparison of the performance of different conditions. The higher the α_w values, the better the material capability in sound absorption. Their values normally range from 0 to 1, with 1 meaning 100% sound absorption.

The weighted sound absorption coefficient α_w is derived from practical sound absorption coefficients, α_p which is calculated as an average of the one-third octave sound absorption coefficients within the octave in accordance with ISO 11,654 [41]. Weighted sound absorption coefficient α_w can be obtained with the reference curve ($\alpha_{250} = 0.8$; $\alpha_{500} = 1$; $\alpha_{1000} = 1$; $\alpha_{2000} = 1$; $\alpha_{4000} = 0.9$), which is shifted in steps of 0.05 towards the α_p values until the sum of unfavorable deviations is less or equal to 0.10. The unfavorable deviations occur when the measured value is lower than the value of the reference curve. Finally, the weighted sound absorption coefficient is the value of the adjusted reference curve at 500 Hz.

Table 3 shows that there are a few differences among the single indices within each concrete data. It is evident from these values that the highest performance is obtained for panel type D. The α_w values for the single layer of type D samples become significant (>0.40) for a thickness of 60 mm. The single layers of 20 mm and 40 mm present an improvement of the α_w values when they are mounted with an air gap behind ($\alpha_w = 0.50$). This mounting condition performance is further improved when the air gap is filled with a porous material. It can be noticed that when the entire gap is filled with rock wool (50 mm), the highest α_w is obtained. A significant improvement due to the air gap is also obtained for sample C, while a slight improvement is reported for sample A. Conversely, depending on the sample thicknesses, sample B values of α_w are either not affected or reduced when the air gap is added at the back of the 20 mm and 40 mm thick layers, respectively.

Table 3. Comparison of single acoustic indices related to the weighted absorption coefficient (α_w) for the four concrete types (A–D).

Sample Characteristics	A	B	C	D
20 mm	0.10	0.10	0.10	0.20
40 mm	0.15	0.25	0.15	0.30
60 mm	0.25	0.25	0.25	0.45
20 + 20 mm	0.15	0.25	0.15	0.30
20 + 40 mm	0.20	0.25	0.25	0.40
20 mm + 50 mm air gap	0.20	0.10	0.35	0.50
40 mm + 50 mm air gap	0.20	0.10	0.30	0.50
20 mm + 50 mm air gap (rock wool 30 mm)				0.70
20 mm + 50 mm air gap (rock wool 50 mm)				0.75

4. Discussion

Given the results herein, a few aspects can be highlighted with respect to previous findings presented in Section 1 and Appendix A. The sound-absorbing properties of the panels under examination (i.e., A–D) were generally found to be extended towards the lower frequencies with increasing thicknesses of the panels (i.e., 20 mm, 40 mm, or 60 mm). The result is coherent with the findings of previous studies, such as in [13,18,21]. However, panel B exhibits an unexpected behavior, as while the sound absorbing properties of the thicker panels are higher at lower frequencies compared to the 20 mm sample, as it can be seen in the 500 to 1600 Hz frequency range, the 20 mm thick sample outperforms the 40 mm thick one in the range of 1600 to 4000 Hz. Moreover, no peak shift towards the lower frequencies is reported for the 60 mm thick panel compared to the 40 mm thick one, as both present an absorption peak at 800 Hz. These two aspects may suggest that the superficial and inner porosity of panels B are not uniform among the different thicknesses. Moreover, it can be argued that for this typology that the thickness threshold is ~40 mm, i.e., no further increase of the absorption coefficient below 800 Hz is obtained with the thickness increase from 40 to 60 mm [7]. Sample D outperforms the other typologies and confirms that its superficial and inner structures are made of many small and uniformly distributed pores and apertures connected with each other and with the outer surface [11].

When comparing samples with round lightweight aggregates, i.e., B–D, it can be observed that there is a decrease in the sound absorption when the aggregate size increases from 0.5–1 mm (sample D) to 4–8 mm (sample B). This is due to an increase in the median pore size when increasing aggregate size as shown in [21], which would reduce the tortuosity of the pore network, thus resulting in lower absorption values. Indeed, sample D has a lower water permeability (Table 1), which is inversely correlated to tortuosity [42]. Moreover, note that sample A with crushed normal weight aggregates results in higher values of the absorption coefficient when compared to sample B, which has similar void ratio (25%) and aggregate dimensions (4–8 mm) to sample A, but features different aggregate shapes and densities, i.e., round lightweight aggregates. This might be due to a higher tortuosity enabled by internal pores with varied size connected to the surface, which is coherent with the aspects highlighted in [11]. This kind of difference was not observed in previous studies, that is, the work in [22], where only slight differences between round-shape (lightweight) and irregular shape (normal weight) aggregates with the same gradation were found.

When considering panels composed of two layers, the presented results have highlighted some discrepancies between the sound absorbing performances of multilayered panels and those of a single layer panel of the same thickness in case of panel samples A–C. Conversely, samples D in the multilayered and single layer solution of equal thickness exhibit similar performances. This behavior may be linked to the different degrees of uniformity in the pore distribution of the different panel samples. In samples D, both sides of the panel present a uniform distribution of the pores apertures and the measurement results also suggest a higher connection of the internal pores to the surface as highlighted in [11]. Differently, for samples A–C, the closed pores presented in the back side of the panels (Figure 6) may not allow full activation of the absorption of the second layer. This highlights that the sound absorption performances of such sample may be improved if greater attention is paid during the treatment of the mix design and its curing in samples.

By comparing the sound absorbing performances of the different panel types measured mounted with an air gap of 50 mm, it emerges that the panel type D outperforms the other typologies. It presents a more uniform frequency-dependent sound absorption, a broader frequency range of high values of absorption coefficient, and absorption coefficients higher than those of other panel typologies. The performances of panels type C are slightly better than those of panels A and B. The worst performance is presented by panel type B, which is generally associated with the lower sound absorbing coefficient throughout the spectrum. This might be due to the effect of regular and bigger aggregates, which lead to reduced tortuosity of the pore network [21]. However, the behavior of samples A, B and C does not change much with the air gap, suggesting that the sound is at least partly blocked by the sample. Indeed, as it was highlighted also for the multilayer investigation, for the other three typologies the back sides of the panels (Figure 6) present a higher number of closed pores, which do not allow to fully activate the absorption due to the combination with the air gap.

Generally, when considering the additional layer of air gap, note that the performance of the 20 mm sample behaves as a layer of microperforated panel mounted with an air gap, i.e., presenting a clear sound absorption coefficient peak at low frequencies with poor values at higher frequencies [7]. This similarity is more evident for samples A and B, which are expected to have pore networks with lower tortuosity due to the greater dimension of the aggregates (4–8 mm) as presented in [21]. The 40 mm sample shows a similar behavior, which can resemble that of a multilayer microperforated panel (MPP) [43]. In this case, the thickness of the panel allows for a higher tortuosity of the pore network, which still allows for some absorption at higher frequencies. Indeed, the microperforated panel sound absorption model presented by Maa [44,45] has been used in several studies to describe the acoustic behavior of concrete.

By partially or completely filling the air gap at the back of the 20 mm thick sample D with rock wool as porous material within the air gap, the sound absorbing performances were reported to improve down to 250 Hz. This is because the air resonance in the air gap and porous material layer is further damped by the porous material layer. This is coherent with the findings related to MPPs [43] and highlights the improvements on absorption with broader bandwidth and lower frequencies efficiency. These solutions' results are appropriate for several outdoor applications dealing with railway noise and traffic noise reductions and feature a spectrum of interest in the range of 125 to 4000 Hz [46]. Moreover, the investigated mounting systems could be integrated with structural multilayer building facades [47,48].

Note that it was observed that although sample D results with the highest performance in terms of evenness and rate, it presents poor performances related to wear resistance compared to the other types, which may hamper their application in actual scenarios if no facings or other protective solutions are used. Another option is to use panels of type B and C, which, when coupled in layers of 20 + 40 mm, reach sound-absorbing performances close to those of the same configuration of panels type D for frequencies higher than 800 Hz. Alternatively, a systematic investigation may be useful to detect the thresholds values of the concrete parameters (e.g., paste volume) in order to obtain acceptable mechanical properties and still preserve highly efficient acoustical properties.

The study highlights the necessity to develop a higher number of experimental investigations by controlling the variables of the mix design in more systematic way. This approach has been possible to follow only through model applications as in [45].

5. Conclusions

The present study has been carried out in order to characterize the sound absorbing performances of a set of porous concrete panels varying in concrete mix design (A–D), thickness and mounting method. The measurements have been conducted in the 1:5 scale reverberation room of the Politecnico di Torino, in accordance with the ISO 354-1:2003 standard. The sound absorbing performances of the different panels have been described as 1/3 octave band and as weighted sound absorption coefficient α_w. The following conclusions have been drawn.

(i) The mix design with the smallest round lightweight aggregate dimensions (0.5–1 mm), referred to as panel D, gave the most effective sound absorption coefficient for all the three sample thicknesses as well as for the mounting condition with an air gap at their back. It was shown that the worst performing mix design feature round lightweight aggregate with the greater dimensions (4–8 mm) referred to as panel B.

(ii) Samples with crushed normal weight aggregates of 4–8 mm, referred to as panel A, showed higher values of absorption coefficients compared to samples with round lightweight aggregates of the same dimensions. The performance is comparable to that of the sample with round lightweight aggregates of smaller gradation (2–4 mm) referred to as panel C. This was attributed to the pores dimensions and inner distribution which affects the pores tortuosity.

(iii) The sound-absorbing performances of the porous concrete panels tend to increase at low frequencies for greater panel thicknesses. In most cases, solutions with single panels or double-layered panels of an equivalent thickness provide similar performances. This mounting solution could be useful in practice for modular solutions and to limit the need for different formwork thicknesses.

(iv) The mounting method is shown to greatly influence the sound-absorbing performances. For all porous concrete types considered, the sound absorption performances are enhanced for lower frequencies by leaving a 50 mm air gap behind the panel. However, the air gap significantly lowers the high frequencies performance of the thinnest samples (20 mm).

(v) The frequency dependent absorption coefficient and the weighted absorption coefficient α_w comparisons showed that, depending on the mounting method, the performance of the concrete samples with aggregate dimensions of 0.5–1 mm, i.e., panel D, can be further improved. The α_w reaches values 0.50 and 0.75 for the condition with an empty air gap of 50 mm and air gap completely filled with a rock wool layer, respectively. These values are comparable to those of most used conventional porous materials.

Note that the mix design mechanical properties remain a crucial aspect that need to be considered when the applicability of such materials is discussed. It was observed that the material with higher acoustic performance (round lightweight aggregate of 0.5–1 mm) presents poor performances related to wear resistance, which makes the application of such panels in actual scenario impractical. Therefore, we endorse further testing in the attempt to find the most performing solution balancing sound absorption with wear resistance performances. Alternatively, when wear resistance is required, it is possible to use panels of type B and C, which, when coupled in layers of 20 + 40 mm, reach sound-absorbing performances close to those of the same configuration of panels type D for frequencies higher than 800 Hz.

Further research could be conducted along this line of research to explore other mix design and mounting method strategies to hopefully increase awareness about the potential benefits of the application of sound absorbing porous concrete in the frame of the architectural and urban design strategies. Such research may include (1) acoustic absorption of materials with blended aggregates of different dimensions, weights and shapes, (2) acoustic absorption for alternative mounting methods, (3) acoustic absorption modeling of porous concrete of single layers and multilayer structure, and (4) possible applications in case studies for outdoor and indoor environments.

Author Contributions: Conceptualization, L.S., A.A., G.V., and D.Z.; methodology, L.S. and A.A.; formal analysis, L.S. and E.B.; investigation, L.S. and E.B.; resources, G.V. and D.Z.; data curation, L.S. and E.B.; writing—original draft preparation, L.S. and E.B.; writing—review and editing, L.S., A.A., E.B., and G.V.; visualization, L.S. and E.B.; supervision, L.S. and A.A.; project administration, L.S., A.A., and G.V.; funding acquisition, A.A. and L.S. All authors have read and agreed to the published version of the manuscript.

Funding: The work has been funded by CEMEX Innovation Holding AG.

Institutional Review Board Statement: Not applicable.

Informed Consent Statement: Not applicable.

Data Availability Statement: Not applicable.

Acknowledgments: The authors are grateful to Marta Bivanti and Giuseppe Vannelli for their contribution to the small-scale reverberation room measurements. They would like to thank the colleagues of CEMEX Innovation Holding AG who helped in manufacturing the samples.

Conflicts of Interest: The authors declare no conflict of interest.

Appendix A

Summary of the main findings of past studies on the effect on sound absorption of aggregate size.

Table A1. Summary of the main findings of past studies on the effect on sound absorption of aggregate size, dimensions and type, and panel thickness. Abbreviations used in the table body: lightweight (LW); normal weight (NW); limestone (LS); aggregate (aggr.); sound absorption (α).

Mix Design Variable	Effect [Refs]	Details	Method	Main Findings
Aggregate size	Influence [11]	0–2 mm/ 1–5 mm/1–3 mm	Single sized	1–3 mm and 1–5 mm aggr. result in higher α
	Influence [19,21]	2.36–4.75 mm/ 4.75–9.5 mm/ 9.5–12 mm	Single sized	Concrete with 2.36–4.75 mm and 4.75–9.5 mm aggr. provide higher α than that with 9.5–12 mm aggr.
			Blended	The effect of blending aggr. on α varies depending on the aggr. size. Best performance with blends of 2.36–4.75 mm and 4.75–9.5 mm aggr.
	Limited influence [22]	4–8 mm/8–12 mm/ 12–19 mm	Single sized	Slight increase in α for smaller aggr. (4–8 mm) compared to bigger ones
	Influence [12,13]	>5 mm/ 1.25–5 mm/ <1.25 mm	Single sized	Concrete with aggr. dimensions >5 mm feature higher α than alternatives with smaller aggr.
			Layered	Three-layered solutions with the aggr. dimensions (from exterior layer) of >5 mm/1.25–5 mm/ <1.25 mm result in the higher α
	No influence [22]	8–13 mm/ 13–19 mm	Layered	The variation of aggr. dimensions in the back layer does not affect the α
Aggregate material	Influence [11]	Expanded perlite/slag/ clay ceramsite	Single type	Expanded perlite aggr. provides the highest α with respect to slag and clay ceramsite
		Expanded perlite/slag	% replacement	The α decrease with the relative increase in content of slag over expanded perlite aggr.
			Layered	The combination of 8 cm slag (lower layer) and 12 cm expanded perlite (upper layer) is the most performing one among those considered
	Influence [22]	LW + NW aggr./only LW aggr.	Layered	Layered solution with LW aggr. in the exterior layer and NW aggr. in the back layer outperform single layer with LW aggr.
	Limited influence [22]	NW/LW aggr.	Single type	A slight increase in α is reported for crushed NW aggr. in comparison to rounded LW ones with similar sizes. The results do not seem consistent when varying the thickness of the concrete panel
	Influence [13]	Bottom ash vs. normal aggr.	Single type	Bottom ash concrete results in higher or comparable α than a typical porous concrete sample
	Influence [23]	Crumb rubber/fine normal aggr.	% replacement	Replacing fine aggr. with crumb rubber ones increase α, for increasing percentages of replacement (up to 20%)
	Influence [24]	Bottom ash/recycled/ LS aggr.	% replacement	The replacement of LS aggr. with bottom ash and recycled aggr. result in higher α; the 2 nd peak shifts towards the higher frequencies for higher percentages of replacement
	No influence [20]	Recycled aggr./ LS aggr.	% replacement	With equal target void ratio, the effect of replacing LS aggr. with recycled ones had very slight influence
	Influence [25]	Cenosphere addition	Single type	The increase of volume fraction of cenospheres result in increased α from 0 to 20 to 40%; further increases result in lower performance

Table A1. Cont.

Mix Design Variable	Effect [Refs]	Details	Method	Main Findings
Aggregate shape	Limited influence [22]	Crushed/rounded aggr.	Single type	A slight increase of α is reported for crushed NW aggregates in comparison to rounded LW ones with similar sizes. The results do not seem consistent when varying the thickness of the concrete panel
Thickness	Influence [13,18,21]	Panel thickness variation	Single layer	The peak of the α is displaced to lower frequencies for increasing panel thicknesses

Appendix B

Graphs supplemental to the results provided as a direct comparison between different concrete typologies regarding thickness variation, multilayer combination, and mounting condition over an airgap.

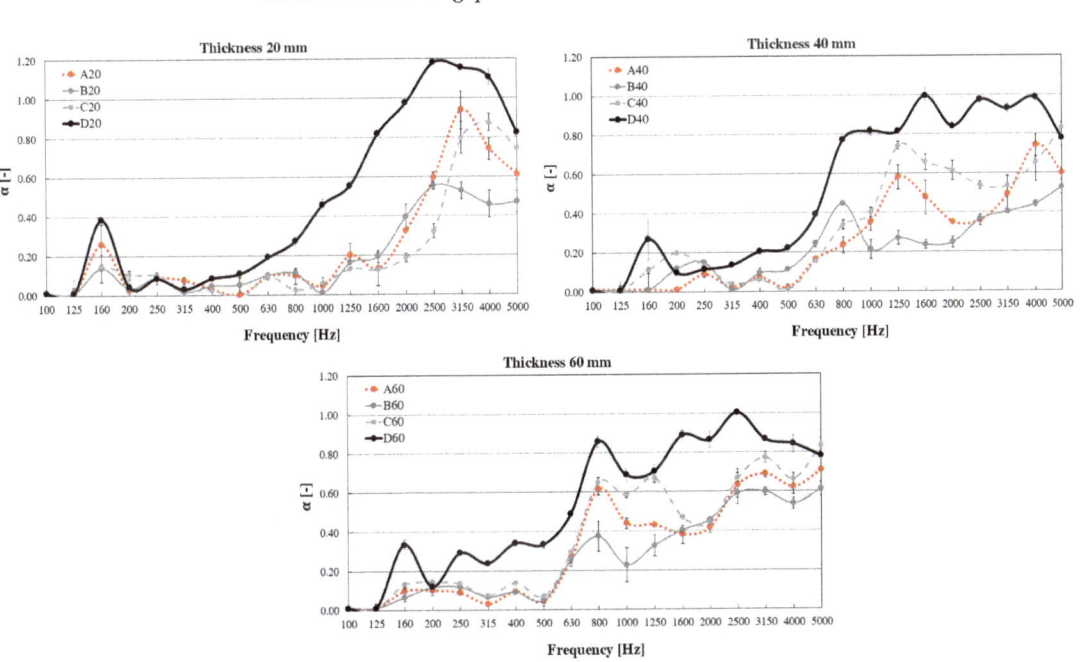

Figure A1. Comparison of the absorption coefficients for samples A–D with different thicknesses. Sample A: crushed normal weight aggregates 4–8 mm; Sample B: round lightweight aggregates 4–8 mm; Sample C: round lightweight aggregates 2–4 mm; Sample D: round lightweight aggregates 0.5–1 mm.

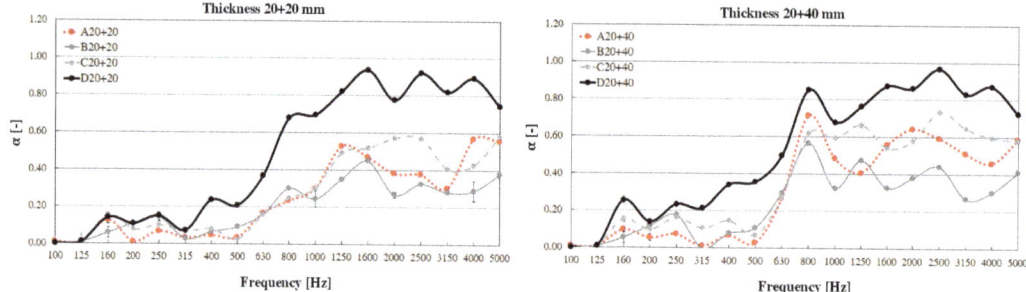

Figure A2. Comparison of the absorption coefficients for samples A–D with different thicknesses obtained from multiple layer combinations (20 + 20 and 20 + 40 mm). Sample A: crushed normal weight aggregates 4–8 mm; Sample B: round lightweight aggregates 4–8 mm; Sample C: round lightweight aggregates 2–4 mm; Sample D: round lightweight aggregates 0.5–1 mm.

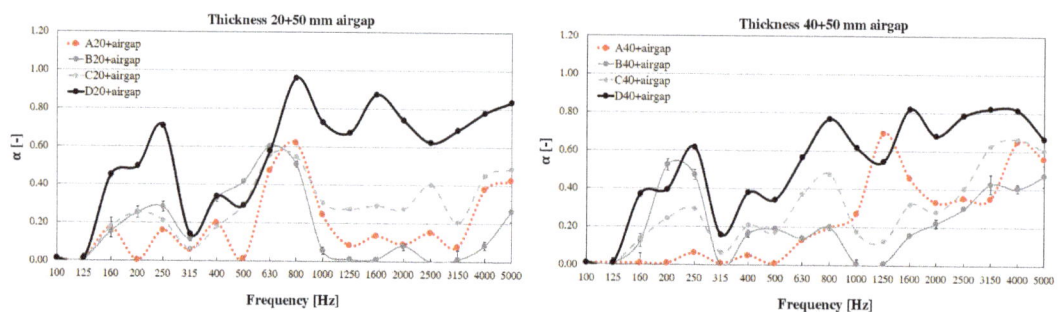

Figure A3. Comparison of the absorption coefficients for samples A–D with different thicknesses (20 and 40 mm) mounted over an airgap of 50 mm. Sample A: crushed normal weight aggregates 4–8 mm; Sample B: round lightweight aggregates 4–8 mm; Sample C: round lightweight aggregates 2–4 mm; Sample D: round lightweight aggregates 0.5–1 mm.

References

1. Sanchez, G.M.E.; Van Renterghem, T.; Thomas, P.; Botteldooren, D. The Effect of Street Canyon Design on Traffic Noise Exposure along Roads. *Build. Environ.* **2016**, *97*, 96–110. [CrossRef]
2. Badino, E.; Manca, R.; Shtrepi, L.; Calleri, C.; Astolfi, A. Effect of Façade Shape and Acoustic Cladding on Reduction of Leisure Noise Levels in a Street Canyon. *Build. Environ.* **2019**, *157*, 242–256. [CrossRef]
3. Calleri, C.; Shtrepi, L.; Armando, A.; Astolfi, A. Evaluation of the Influence of Building Façade Design on the Acoustic Characteristics and Auditory Perception of Urban Spaces. *Build. Acoust.* **2018**, *25*, 77–95. [CrossRef]
4. Taghipour, A.; Sievers, T.; Eggenschwiler, K. Acoustic Comfort in Virtual Inner Yards with Various Building Facades. *Int. J. Environ. Res. Public Health* **2019**, *16*, 249. [CrossRef] [PubMed]
5. Yang, W.; Jeon, J.Y. Design Strategies and Elements of Building Envelope for Urban Acoustic Environment. *Build. Environ.* **2020**, *182*. [CrossRef]
6. Adams, T. *Sound Materials*; Frame Publisher: Amsterdam, The Netherlands, 2016; ISBN 94-92311-01-1.
7. Cox, T.J.; D'Antonio, P. *Acoustic Absorbers and Diffusers: Theory, Design and Application*, 3rd ed.; Taylor & Francis: Abingdon-on-Thames, UK, 2017; ISBN 978-0-367-65841-0.
8. Neithalath, N.; Weiss, J.; Olek, J. Characterizing Enhanced Porosity Concrete Using Electrical Impedance to Predict Acoustic and Hydraulic Performance. *Cem. Concr. Res.* **2006**, *36*, 2074–2085. [CrossRef]
9. Ibrahim, A.; Mahmoud, E.; Yamin, M.; Patibandla, V.C. Experimental Study on Portland Cement Pervious Concrete Mechanical and Hydrological Properties. *Constr. Build. Mater.* **2014**, *50*, 524–529. [CrossRef]
10. Scholz, M.; Grabowiecki, P. Review of Permeable Pavement Systems. *Build. Environ.* **2007**, *42*, 3830–3836. [CrossRef]
11. Zhao, C.; Wang, P.; Wang, L.; Liu, D. Reducing Railway Noise with Porous Sound-Absorbing Concrete Slabs. *Adv. Mater. Sci. Eng.* **2014**, *2014*, 1–11. [CrossRef]
12. Arenas, C.; Vilches, L.F.; Cifuentes, H.; Leiva, C.; Vale, J.; Fernández-Pereira, C. Development of Acoustic Barriers Mainly Composed of Co-Combustion Bottom Ash. In Proceedings of the World of Coal Ash (WOCA) Conference, Denver, CO, USA, 9–12 May 2011.

13. Arenas, C.; Leiva, C.; Vilches, L.F.; Cifuentes, H. Use of Co-Combustion Bottom Ash to Design an Acoustic Absorbing Material for Highway Noise Barriers. *Waste Manag.* **2013**, *33*, 2316–2321. [CrossRef] [PubMed]
14. ACI Committee 522-10. *Report on Pervious Concrete*; American Concrete Institute: Farmington Hills, MI, USA, 2010; ISBN 978-0-87031-364-6.
15. Kovác, M.; Sicáková, A. Pervious Concrete as a Sustainable Solution for Pavementsin Urban Areas. In Proceedings of the 10th International Conference "Environmental Engineering"; VGTU Technika, Vilnius, Lithuania, 27–28 April 2017.
16. Kosmatka, S.H.; Wilson, M.L. *Design and Control. of Concrete Mixtures*, 15th ed.; Portland Cement Association: Skokie, IL, USA, 2011; Volume EB001, ISBN 0-89312-272-6.
17. Tie, T.S.; Mo, K.H.; Putra, A.; Loo, S.C.; Alengaram, U.J.; Ling, T.-C. Sound Absorption Performance of Modified Concrete: A Review. *J. Build. Eng.* **2020**, *30*, 101219. [CrossRef]
18. Neithalath, N. Development and Characterization of Acoustically Efficient Cementitious Materials. Ph.D. Thesis, Purdue University, West Lafayette, IN, USA, 2004.
19. Neithalath, N.; Weiss, J.; Olek, J. Improving the Acoustic Absorption of Enhanced Porosity Concrete with Fiber Reinforcement. In Proceedings of the International RILEM Symposium on Concrete Science and Engineering: A Tribute to Arnon Bentur, Evanston, IL, USA, 21–24 March 2004; Kovler, K., Marchand, J., Mindess, S., Weiss, J., Eds.; RILEM Publications SARL: Paris, France, 2004.
20. Park, S.B.; Seo, D.S.; Lee, J. Studies on the Sound Absorption Characteristics of Porous Concrete Based on the Content of Recycled Aggregate and Target Void Ratio. *Cem. Concr. Res.* **2005**, *35*, 1846–1854. [CrossRef]
21. Marolf, A.; Neithalath, N.; Sell, E.; Wegner, K.; Weiss, J.; Olek, J. Influence of Aggregate Size and Gradation on Acoustic Absorption of Enhanced Porosity Concrete. *ACI Mater. J.* **2004**, *101*, 82–91.
22. Kim, H.K.; Lee, H.K. Influence of Cement Flow and Aggregate Type on the Mechanical and Acoustic Characteristics of Porous Concrete. *Appl. Acoust.* **2010**, *71*, 607–615. [CrossRef]
23. Sukontasukkul, P. Use of Crumb Rubber to Improve Thermal and Sound Properties of Pre-Cast Concrete Panel. *Constr. Build. Mater.* **2009**, *23*, 1084–1092. [CrossRef]
24. Ngohpok, C.; Sata, V.; Satiennam, T.; Klungboonkrong, P.; Chindaprasirt, P. Mechanical Properties, Thermal Conductivity, and Sound Absorption of Pervious Concrete Containing Recycled Concrete and Bottom Ash Aggregates. *KSCE J. Civ. Eng.* **2018**, *22*, 1369–1376. [CrossRef]
25. Tiwari, V.; Shukla, A.; Bose, A. Acoustic Properties of Cenosphere Reinforced Cement and Asphalt Concrete. *Appl. Acoust.* **2004**, *65*, 263–275. [CrossRef]
26. Fediuk, R.; Amran, M.; Vatin, N.; Vasilev, Y.; Lesovik, V.; Ozbakkaloglu, T. Acoustic Properties of Innovative Concretes: A Review. *Materials* **2021**, *14*, 398. [CrossRef]
27. EN 933-2:2020. *Tests for Geometrical Properties of Aggregates. Part. 2: Determination of Particle Size Distribution-Test. Sieves, Nominal Size of Apertures*; The British Standards Institution: London, UK, 2020.
28. EN 1097-6:2013. *Tests for Mechanical and Physical Properties of Aggregates. Part. 6: Determination of Particle Density and Water Absorption*; The British Standards Institution: London, UK, 2013.
29. ASTM C1754/C1754M. *Standard Test. Method for Density and Void Content of Hardened Pervious Concrete*; ASTM International: West Conshohocken, PA, USA, 2012.
30. EN 12390-5:2019. *Testing Hardened Concrete. Part 5: Flexural Strength of Test. Specimens*; The British Standards Institution: London, UK, 2019.
31. ASTM D2434−19. *Test. Method for Permeability of Granular Soils (Constant Head)*; ASTM International: West Conshohocken, PA, USA, 2019.
32. ISO 354:2003. *Acoustics-Measurement of Sound Absorption in a Reverberation Room*; International Organization for Standardization: Geneva, Switzerland, 2003.
33. ISO 17497-1:2004. *Acoustics-Sound-Scattering Properties of Surfaces. Part 1: Measurement of the Random-Incidence Scattering Coefficient in a Reverberation Room*; International Organization for Standardization: Geneva, Switzerland, 2004.
34. Shtrepi, L.; Astolfi, A.; D'Antonio, G.; Vannelli, G.; Barbato, G.; Mauro, S.; Prato, A. Accuracy of the Random-Incidence Scattering Coefficient Measurement. *Appl. Acoust.* **2016**, *106*, 23–35. [CrossRef]
35. Shtrepi, L.; Prato, A. Towards a Sustainable Approach for Sound Absorption Assessment of Building Materials: Validation of Small-Scale Reverberation Room Measurements. *Appl. Acoust.* **2020**, *165*, 107304. [CrossRef]
36. *ITA-Toolbox for MATLAB® v.R2018b*; Developed at the Institute of Technical Acoustics at RWTH Aachen University; RWTH Aachen University: Aachen, Genmary, 2018.
37. ISO 9613-1:1993. *Acoustics-Attenuation of Sound during Propagation Outdoors. Part 1: Calculation of the Absorption of Sound by the Atmosphere*; International Organization for Standardization: Geneva, Switzerland, 1993.
38. Bartel, T.W. Effect of Absorber Geometry on Apparent Absorption Coefficients as Measured in a Reverberation Chamber. *J. Acoust. Soc. Am.* **1981**, *69*, 1065–1074. [CrossRef]
39. Embleton, T.F.W. Absorption Coefficients of Surfaces Calculated from Decaying Sound Fields. *J. Acoust. Soc. Jpn.* **1971**, *50*. [CrossRef]
40. Scrosati, C. Towards More Reliable Measurements of Sound Absorption Coefficient in Reverberation Rooms: An Inter-Laboratory Test. *Appl. Acoust.* **2020**, *165*, 107298. [CrossRef]

41. ISO 11654:1997. *Acoustics-Sound Absorbers for Use in Buildings–Rating of Sound Absorption*; International Organization for Standardization: Geneva, Switzerland, 1997.
42. Ahmad, S.; Azad, A.K.; Loughlin, K.F. A Study of Permeability and Tortuosity of Concrete. In Proceedings of the 30th Conference on Our World in Concrete and Structures (OWICS), Singapore, 23–24 August 2005.
43. Liu, Z.; Zhan, J.; Fard, M.; Davy, J.L. Acoustic Properties of Multilayer Sound Absorbers with a 3D Printed Micro-Perforated Panel. *Appl. Acoust.* **2017**, *121*, 25–32. [CrossRef]
44. Maa, D.-Y. Microperforated-Panel Wideband Absorbers. *Noise Control Eng. J.* **1987**, *29*, 77–84. [CrossRef]
45. Kim, H.K.; Lee, H.K. Acoustic Absorption Modeling of Porous Concrete Considering the Gradation and Shape of Aggregates and Void Ratio. *J. Sound Vib.* **2010**, *329*, 866–879. [CrossRef]
46. Kephalopoulos, S.; Paviotti, M.; Anfosso-Lédée, F. *Common Noise Assessment Methods in Europe (CNOSSOS-EU)*; Publications Office of the European Union: Luxembourg, 2012.
47. Calleri, C.; Astolfi, A.; Shtrepi, L.; Prato, A.; Schiavi, A.; Zampini, D.; Volpatti, G. Characterization of the Sound Insulation Properties of a Two-Layers Lightweight Concrete Innovative Façade. *Appl. Acoust.* **2019**, *145*, 267–277. [CrossRef]
48. Kousis, I.; Pisello, A.L. For the Mitigation of Urban Heat Island and Urban Noise Island: Two Simultaneous Sides of Urban Discomfort. *Environ. Res. Lett.* **2020**, *15*, 103004. [CrossRef]

 *applied sciences*

Article

Sound Absorbing and Insulating Low-Cost Panels from End-of-Life Household Materials for the Development of Vulnerable Contexts in Circular Economy Perspective

Manuela Neri [1,*], Elisa Levi [1], Eva Cuerva [2], Francesc Pardo-Bosch [3], Alfredo Guardo Zabaleta [4] and Pablo Pujadas [2]

[1] Department of Mechanical and Industrial Engineering, University of Brescia, via Branze 38, 25121 Brescia, Italy; elisa.levi@unibs.it
[2] Department of Project and Construction Engineering, Escola Tècnica Superior d'Enginyers Industrials de Barcelona (ETSEIB), Universitat Politècnica de Catalunya (UPC), Av. Diagonal 647, 08028 Barcelona, Spain; eva.cuerva@upc.edu (E.C.); pablo.pujadas@upc.edu (P.P.)
[3] Department of Project and Construction Engineering, Escola Superior d'Enginyeries Industrial, Aeroespacial yi Audiovisual de Terrassa, Universitat Politècnica de Catalunya (UPC), Carrer de Colom 15, 08222 Terrassa, Spain; francesc.pardo@upc.edu
[4] Centre de Diagnòstic Industrial i Fluidodinàmica (UPC CDIF), Escola Tècnica Superior d'Enginyers Industrials de Barcelona (ETSEIB), Universitat Politècnica de Catalunya (UPC), Av. Diagonal 647, 08028 Barcelona, Spain; alfredo.guardo-zabaleta@upc.edu
* Correspondence: manuela.neri@unibs.it

Citation: Neri, M.; Levi, E.; Cuerva, E.; Pardo-Bosch, F.; Zabaleta, A.G.; Pujadas, P. Sound Absorbing and Insulating Low-Cost Panels from End-of-Life Household Materials for the Development of Vulnerable Contexts in Circular Economy Perspective. *Appl. Sci.* **2021**, *11*, 5372. https://doi.org/10.3390/app11125372

Academic Editor: Luís Picado Santos

Received: 3 May 2021
Accepted: 2 June 2021
Published: 9 June 2021

Publisher's Note: MDPI stays neutral with regard to jurisdictional claims in published maps and institutional affiliations.

Copyright: © 2021 by the authors. Licensee MDPI, Basel, Switzerland. This article is an open access article distributed under the terms and conditions of the Creative Commons Attribution (CC BY) license (https://creativecommons.org/licenses/by/4.0/).

Abstract: From a construction point of view, neighborhoods with residents living at or below the poverty threshold are characterized by low energy efficiency buildings, in which people live in acoustic discomfort with no viable options for home improvements, as they usually can not afford the materials and labor costs associated. An alternative to this is to use low-cost insulating elements made of non-conventional materials with acceptable acoustic properties. Given that household materials at their end-of-life (EoLHM) are free of costs and available also to the more disadvantaged population, they can be used to build acoustic panels for such contexts. This approach embraces several benefits since it reduces the amount of waste produced, the footprint deriving from the extraction of new raw materials and, by highlighting the potential of the EoLHM, discourages the abandonment of waste. In this paper, the acoustic properties of EoLHM, such as cardboard, egg-cartons, clothes, metal elements and combinations of them, are investigated by means of the impedance tube technique. The measured sound absorption coefficient and transmission loss have shown that EoLHM can be used for the realization of acoustic panels. However, since none of the analyzed materials shows absorbing and insulating properties at the same time, EoLHM must be wisely selected. This innovative approach supports the circular economy and the improvement for the living condition of low-income households.

Keywords: household end-of-life materials; building retrofitting; sound insulation; sound absorption; vulnerable houses; circular economy; egg-box; cardboard; textile waste; reuse

1. Introduction

The Sustainable Development Goals are a universal call embraced by all Member States of the United Nation in 2015 for eradicating poverty and protecting the environment. According to the call, for improving the living condition on a global scale, economy and social aspects must go hand-in-hand. For this reason, issues such as education, health, social protection, job opportunities, climate change and environmental protection must be taken into account through global, local and people actions [1]. Among the 17 Goals, number 11 deals with sustainable cities and communities, and it requires to ensure access for everyone to adequate, safe and affordable housing and basic services. Indeed, it is estimated that by 2030 the 60% of the world's population will live in cities that account for about the 70% of global carbon emission and 60% of resource use. The rapid urbanization that the world has been facing since 2007 is resulting in air pollution, unplanned urbanization, inadequate services and infrastructures. The growth and development of cities must be controlled, so to guarantee cities inclusive, safe, resilient and sustainable.

Since people with similar socioeconomic status tend to cluster in the same urban areas disadvantaged contexts can be easily identified in the urban fabric: in these places, the vulnerable population lives and it consists of refugees, migrants, elderly persons, people with disabilities and children [1]. In these specific contexts, people live below the threshold of poverty, and sometimes in conditions of great discomfort. This phenomenon is responsible of inequalities and it has been identified in several European cities, as in the case of Barcelona [2,3]. Between 2001 and 2011, in the city of Barcelona the migrant population increased from about 5% to 17%, and the new-low income immigrants reside mostly either in the historical center, usually on degraded 19th century buildings, or in peripheral districts characterized by poor quality houses built in the 1960s and in the 1970s [2]. In the case of the historical center, dwellings are in some cases small, overcrowded and lacking of openings with consequent insufficient natural light and poor air quality. When present, windows are crumbling and do not guarantee adequate acoustic insulation. Since many of these neighborhoods are also touristic destinations with noisy anthropic activities also during the night-time, the aspect related to the sound quality of dwellings should not be underestimated.

The urban environment is characterized by multiple simultaneous sounds due to transportation, industry and neighbors. When the sound pressure level exceeds a certain value it is perceived as noise and even if sound perception is subjective, noise control is very important. The exposure to excessive and prolonged levels of noise affects people's well-being, behavior, productivity, mental and physical health, with negative consequences such as sleep disturbances, stress, irritability and other health issues [2,4–6]. However, noise pollution and acoustic discomfort in buildings are not limited to disadvantaged neighborhoods. To depict the acoustic situation, the European Union, through the Environmental Noise directive [7], has requested to map the noise pollution sources and to define an action plan to reduce the effects on the population. It is estimated that 40% of the population does not experience acoustic well-being because of noise from neighbors and traffic [5], and the 65% of Europeans living in major urban areas are exposed to high-noise levels [8]. If in virtuous contexts the improvement of the indoor acoustic comfort is possible, in disadvantaged contexts this task is much more difficult to achieve. In fact, these interventions require specialized personnel and expensive insulating/absorbing acoustic solutions. Acoustic panels must be aesthetics, safe, acoustically efficient, easy to install and maintain, resistant to wear and environmental factors. Although inexpensive acoustic materials can be found on the market, in disadvantaged contexts they can not be easily purchased because people have little or no financial resources. An alternative can be the realization of no-cost panels featuring acoustic properties.

While on the one hand there is growing attention to the well-being of people, on the other it is necessary to define actions aimed at protecting the environment, optimizing the system that provides us with the raw materials necessary to make the products, and which houses the waste. To lighten the load on the environment, it is necessary to use raw materials in a conscious way, for example, by extending the life of the products as much as possible. Additionally, since many materials still possess exploitable properties when they are discarded, they can be reused for other purposes. This model is called Circular Economy (CE) which is in contrast to the linear economy model. In the linear economy model, the raw material is extracted, processed to make the product that, at the end of its life, is discarded. The circular economy model, on the other hand, is based on the 7R principle: reduce, reuse, recycle, repair, replace, recovery, remanufacture as shown in Figure 1.

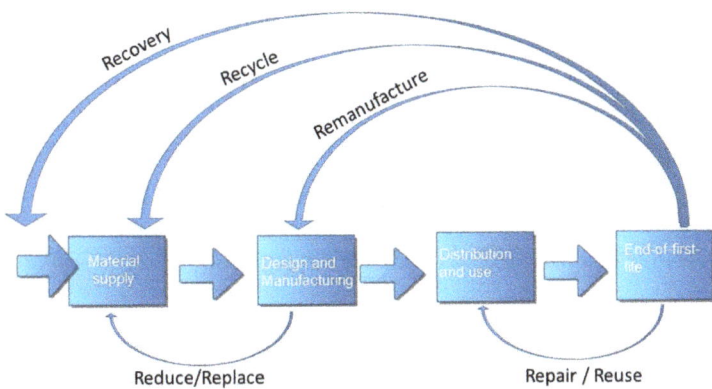

Figure 1. Comparison between circular and linear economy models [9].

With a view to the circular economy and sustainable cities, household end-of-life materials (EoLHM), such as clothes or packaging, could be reused to realize acoustic panels. EoLHM can be defined as household waste materials which still possess exploitable properties, thus making them suitable for reuse. Many EoLHM still have properties when discharged and are largely available: for example, the estimated yearly global production is about 241 million tons for cardboard and paper packaging [10,11], 380,000 million tons for plastic packaging [12], and 92 million tons for textile waste [13] of which only the 12% is recycled [14]. The large availability of EoLHM and the problems related to recycling can support the approach of converting them into acoustic panels: as suggested in [15], this avoids the generation of waste, reduces the footprint due to raw materials extraction, and makes them accessible also to vulnerable population that can not afford commercial acoustic materials. Moreover, since EoLHM are largely available, this approach could incentive buildings renovation and facilitate the achievement of the energy and environmental international goals set by the European Parliament [16,17].

The study presented in this paper explores the possibility of converting EoLHM into panels featuring interesting acoustic properties, and it is focused mainly on those EoLHM that can be reused without any type of processing so that they are directly available to low-income households. Indeed, any treatment would entail costs that would affect end-users and, consequently, the vulnerable population may not be able to afford them. Specifically, the aim of the experimental analysis presented in this paper is to understand which EoHLM can be used to make acoustic panels of limited thickness, and how these materials can be assembled to meet both sound insulation and sound absorption requirements. Since the panels are intended for the most disadvantaged population, they must be easy to be assembled and installed, so that these people, once trained, can collect the necessary EoLHM and assemble the panels independently. The first part of the study addresses the state of the art regarding the reuse of EoLHM to realize acoustic panels. There are several studies in the literature that address the recycling of these materials, but only a limited number analyzes their possible reuse. This highlights that the approach proposed in this paper is quite innovative. In the second part of the paper, EoHLM suitable for low-cost acoustic insulation panels for indoor comfort improvement are investigated by means of experimental tests performed with a 4-microphone impedance tube technique. Five sets of samples have been tested. In the first set of samples, the acoustic performance of egg-cartons has been evaluated. The second set of samples consists in egg-cartons coupled with fibrous materials and metal elements. In the third set of samples, cardboard has been featured. Finally, in the fourth and fifth sets of samples, the acoustic properties of different fabrics coupled with egg-cartons and metal elements have been evaluated.

2. Theoretical Background

When a sound wave with a certain acoustic power W_i impinges a wall-partition, its energy is divided into three components. One portion of the power is reflected back (W_r), while another portion (W_a) is able to pass through the surface of the material. The energy that passes through the surface can be divided into two components W_d and W_t. The component W_d represents the part of the absorbed energy actually converted into heat due to the internal friction and viscoelastic effects. The component W_t represents the portion of the energy that passes through the partition and it is related to the power transmitted through the wall. The relation among incident, reflected and absorbed power is

$$W_i = W_r + W_a = W_r + W_d + W_t \qquad (1)$$

as depicted in Figure 2. By dividing the single components for the incident power W_i, the sound reflection coefficient, the sound dissipation coefficient δ, and the sound transmission coefficient τ are defined:

$$r = W_r/W_i \qquad (2)$$

$$\delta = W_d/W_i \qquad (3)$$

$$\tau = W_t/W_i \qquad (4)$$

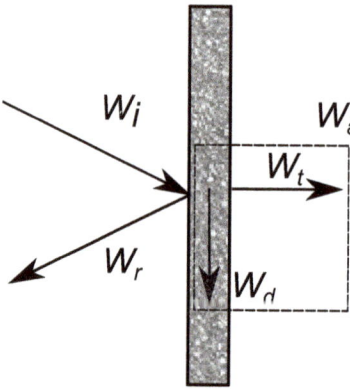

Figure 2. Decomposition of a sound wave W_i impinging a wall into its reflected W_r, dissipated W_d and transmitted W_t components. The sum of the dissipated and transmitted components represents the absorbed W_a component.

Building acoustics usually investigates the frequency range going from 100 Hz to 3150 Hz [18]. The reason of the 100 Hz lower frequency limit is that, in general, the first speech tones range between 100 Hz and 125 Hz for men, and they are an octave higher for women. As concerns the emission due to traffic noise, the encompassed frequency range is 125–2500 Hz and depends on the vehicles' speed. The two main properties to be considered for indoor acoustic comfort are the apparent sound absorption coefficient α and the sound transmission loss TL. The apparent absorption coefficient is defined as:

$$\alpha = 1 - r \qquad (5)$$

and it represents the portion of incident energy absorbed (or not reflected) by the partition. In practice, sound absorbing materials and structures reduce the possibility of multiple reflections and are able to 'clean' the indoor acoustic environment from the annoying effects of reverberation. Sound absorbing materials and structures can be classified as porous materials, acoustic resonators (Helmholtz resonators that include perforated and microperforated panels respectively), vibrating panels and mixed systems (Figure 3).

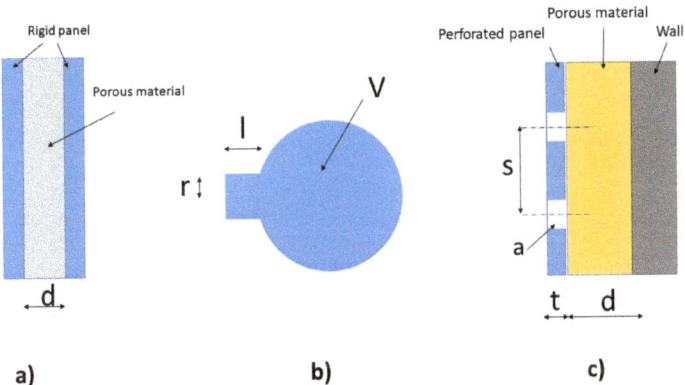

Figure 3. Representation of (**a**) a double partition made of two rigid leafs with an internal porous layer, (**b**) Helmholtz resonator and (**c**) mixed system—multiple resonator.

2.1. Sound Absorption

The absorbing performance of a given material depends on the angle of incidence of the sound wave, on the frequency, on the material properties and thickness, and on the surface finishing. The absorption coefficient is usually measured in single reverberation rooms, that allows an evaluation of the absorption properties in diffuse field, or by two or four microphones impedance tubes that evaluate only the properties for a sound wave impinging normally on the sample surface. In spite of this, the impedance tube requires small samples and, for this reason, it is particularly suitable during the research and development phase. To easily compare the properties of different materials, the weighted Noise Reduction Coefficient (NRC) is one of the most used indicators [19].

$$NRC = \frac{\alpha_{125} + \alpha_{250} + \alpha_{500} + \alpha_{1000} + \alpha_{2000}}{5} \tag{6}$$

The NRC summarizes the absorption characteristic of a material through a single value ranging between 0 (perfectly reflective material) and 1 (perfectly absorbent material).

2.1.1. Porous Materials

This kind of materials is characterized by high porosity, low density and, if possible, a high surface area. Porous materials include fibrous, cellular (foams) and granular materials. The absorption properties depend on a number of parameters including flow resistivity and tortuosity. The dissipation of sound energy is due to three phenomena that are the friction between air and material fibers, the compression and decompression of air, and viscous effects [20,21].

In the literature, several empirical and theoretical models have been proposed for the prediction of porous materials sound absorption. One of the first available models was proposed by Delany-Bazley [22] and requires only the flow resistivity σ as an input parameter, but since it neglects the thermal conductive effects, it is accurate in the $0.01 < (\rho_0 f / \sigma) < 1$ range only, where ρ_0 is the air density and f is the sound frequency [23]. More accurate but, at the same time, more complex models were defined by several authors [24–27]. One of the most popular models was proposed by Johnson-Champoux-Allard (JCA) and takes into account the flow resistivity σ, open porosity ϕ, tortuosity α_∞, the viscous characteristic length Λ and the thermal characteristic length Λ' [20].

2.1.2. Acoustic Resonators

A Helmholtz resonator consists of a cavity with one or more holes and necks, as represented in Figure 3b. The air inside the neck behaves like an oscillating piston (mass) while the air in the cavity behaves like an elastic element (spring). When the resonance frequency of the mass-spring system is equal to the frequency of the incident wave, the resonator express its maximum absorption. For these systems, the resonance frequency f_0 is defined as:

$$f_0 = \frac{c_0}{2\pi}\sqrt{\frac{r^2}{V(l+\frac{\pi}{2r})}} \tag{7}$$

where c_0 is the speed of sound in air, r is the radius of the hole, V is the volume of the cavity and l is the length of the neck. However, Helmholtz resonators do not express any sound absorption outside the resonance frequency region. The transmission loss TL and the absorption coefficient of a Helmholtz resonator are defined as:

$$TL = -10\log\left|\frac{p_t}{p_i}\right|^2 = 20\log\left|1 + \frac{1}{2}\frac{S_0\rho c_0}{SZ}\right| \tag{8}$$

$$\alpha = 1 - \left|\frac{p_t}{p_i}\right|^2 = \frac{4c_0\rho_0 \frac{S}{S_0} Z_{Re}}{(\frac{S}{S_0}Z_{Re} + \rho_0 c_0)^2 + \frac{S^2}{S_0^2}Z_{Im}} \tag{9}$$

where S is the cross-sectional area of the neck, S_0 is the total areas of all necks, Z is the acoustic impedance of the resonator and represent the ratio between pressure amplitude and the particle velocity at the interface of the resonator [28].

2.1.3. Vibrating Panels

Another type of sound absorbing mechanism is the one involving vibrating panels placed at a distance from a rigid wall. Vibrating panels are thin, rigid and flat leafs and the absorption mechanism is again of the mass-spring type. The resonance frequency, at which the maximum absorption occurs, is determined as:

$$f_0 = 60/\sqrt{\mu'' d} \tag{10}$$

where μ'' is the mass per unit area of the panel and d is the thickness of the panel as depicted in Figure 3c.

2.2. Sound Transmission Loss

The Transmission Loss represents the ability of a structure to block the sound propagation in neighboring ambient and is defined as

$$TL = 10 \cdot \log\frac{1}{\tau} \tag{11}$$

Materials characterized by a low transmission coefficient have a high TL. The sound insulation properties depend mainly on the mass per unit area of the structure, the angle of incidence and the frequency of the impinging wave. Other factors influencing the transmission of the sound are the nature of the partition (single, double), the internal losses and the boundary conditions [29]. The acoustic insulation performance of a homogeneous wall can be divided into four regions as shown in Figure 4.

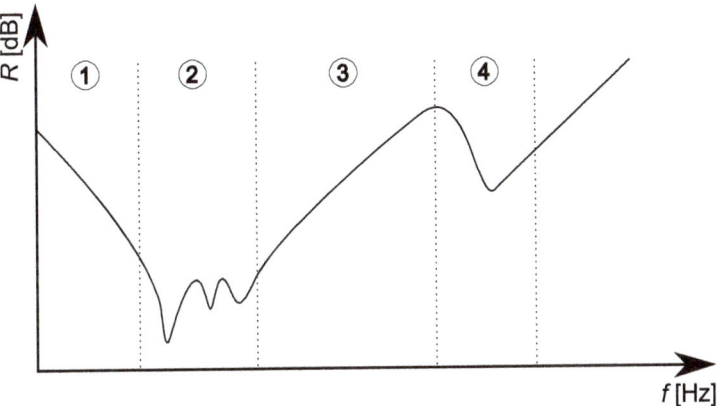

Figure 4. Sound transmission loss of a single panel: (1) stiffness controlled region, (2) resonances region, (3) mass law region, (4) coincidence region.

In the low frequency region, the TL is governed by the material stiffness and it decreases 6 dB/oct. The behavior of the panel is then dominated by the modes of the specimen, which depend on the elastic and geometric properties of the wall. When the modal density is sufficiently high, the wall behaves according to the mass law [30]. In this region, the transmission loss has a linear trend and increases 6 dB/oct. The mass-law region is limited by the coincidence effect that occurs when the wavelength of the sound in the air is the same as the wavelength of the bending waves in the partition. In this region the partition does offer a weak opposition to sound propagation. The coincidence frequency f_c of a homogeneous board is related to its size, thickness, Young's modulus, and surface density:

$$f_c = \frac{c^2}{2\pi}\sqrt{\frac{\mu''}{D}} \qquad (12)$$

where D is the bending stiffness calculated as

$$D = E \cdot I_b \qquad (13)$$

E is the Young modulus, and I_b is the moment of inertia. The bending stiffness can be computed also for complex structures, once the Young's modulus and the moment of inertia of the elements are known [31].

The sound insulation of a wall can be significantly increased if it is built as a multiple structure. One common way to increase the sound insulation of a partition, without increasing the mass per unit area, is to build it with two or more layers separated by an air gap, possibly filled by sound absorbing material. In this case the wall behaves like a multiple mass-spring-mass system. When an acoustic wave passes through such a construction, the total transmission factor τ_{tot} is:

$$\tau_{tot_{n=1}}^{n=N} = \tau_1 \cdot \tau_2 \cdot \ldots \cdot \tau_n \qquad (14)$$

in which the assumption is that the N layers have a transmission factor τ_n. The equation holds at sufficiently high frequency (above the mass-spring-mass frequency f_0), for large enough distances between the layers and when the damping of the gap, in the form of sound absorbing material, is sufficiently high. Below the mass-spring-mass resonance standing waves between the layers modify the transmission factor. The most common case is the one featuring a double wall. If the mass law holds, then the following equation can be applied:

$$R_\perp = 20 log(\mu'' \cdot f) - 42 \text{ for } f < f_c \qquad (15)$$

In case of a finite double wall, the sound transmission loss can be computed as:

$$R_\perp^{double} = 20\log\left[\frac{2\cdot\pi\cdot f\cdot \mu_1''}{(2\rho_0\cdot c_0)}\right] + 20\cdot\log\left[\frac{(2\cdot\pi\cdot f\cdot \mu_2'')}{(2\rho_0\cdot c_0)}\right] \text{ for } f < f_c \quad (16)$$

The mass law has a lower bound given by the lower mechanical resonance of the system. This resonance corresponds to the mass-spring-mass resonance of the wall, where the air enclosed in the gap acts as a spring, while the walls act like two masses. A two degrees of freedom system has a resonance frequency equal to:

$$f_0 = \frac{\pi}{2}\left(\frac{\rho_0\cdot c^2\cdot(\mu_1''+\mu_2'')}{(\mu_1''\cdot\mu_2''\cdot h)}\right)^{1/2} \quad (17)$$

Below the mass-air-mass frequency the wall behaves like a single wall with a total mass per unit area equal to the sum of the mass per unit areas of the two walls composing the entire wall. As concerns the coincidence effects, the discussion made for single walls also applies to double walls. For double walls, the coincidence frequency is determined by the mass per unit area and thickness of each element, while the TL is higher than that predicted by the mass-law for a single panel of the same mass. As suggested in [32], it can be an advantage to realize the double panel with two panels having different thicknesses to avoid that the coincidence effect takes place at the same frequency.

2.3. Acoustic Performance of EoLHM in the Literature

In this section, the acoustic performances reported in the literature of some EoLHM are collected. It is worth noting that the performances of acoustic materials deriving from agriculture have not been analyzed, because they are not directly available to disadvantaged people. Neither organic waste has been analyzed, even if in the literature several studies, such as the one presented in [33], can be found.

2.3.1. Textile Waste

Textile waste includes clothes, carpets, tablecloths and pieces from the textile sector. In literature, a very recurring classification is between woven (WF) and non-woven (NWF) fabrics: WF are obtained by threading fibers together perpendicularly, whereas NWF are bounded together by using heat, chemical, or mechanical treatment. Textile waste have been widely investigated from the acoustic point of view because they are largely available and their porous structure makes them suitable for acoustic absorption. The sound absorption of NWF waste was investigated in relation to the fiber content and the fiber diameter [34], and NWF shows higher sound reduction than WF [35]. A panel made of waste wool and polyamide fibers was designed in [36], and it presented a sound absorption coefficient equal to 0.91 and NRC equal to 0.56. The study pointed out that the sound absorption coefficient in the low-frequency range is affected by the thickness, while the volume density affects the absorption properties in the middle-frequency range. Blankets for building roofing and internal walls insulation were realized with polyester fabrics of different sizes and they showed an NRC ranging between 0.54 and 0.74 [37]. The study in [38] investigated the correlation between the humidity content and the transmitted wave through cotton fabric: for moisture content between 0 and 100%, the transmitted wave ranges between 31% and 7%.

2.3.2. Cardboard

According to [39], cardboard panels from the packaging industry present promising acoustic insulation performance but slightly lower than common insulation panels. Cardboard performance intended as the combination of acoustic properties, transportability, lightweight, cost and recyclability was evaluated for several cardboard design options in [40], and honeycomb panels filled with cellulose fiber presented the best performance. To evaluate the conservation status of the beer during transport by trucks, the acoustic properties of beer packaging was investigated in [41]. The sound absorption of a cover made of porous sponge and cardboard was 0.58 [42]. In [43], sound absorber obtained by mixing recycled paper and a blowing agent showed a NRC of 0.75.

2.3.3. Plastic Bottles and Metal Cans

Plastic bottles of different sizes (500 mL, 750 mL, 1 L, 1.25 L and 2 L) can be easily found on the market [18]. In the literature, bottles have been analyzed mainly from the structural point of view when incorporated in the construction of walls since, if compared to ceramic and concrete blocks, they are faster to build, require less water and cement and do not produce waste [44]. For these reasons, plastic bottles are continuously investigated. According to [45], polyethylene terephthalate-based material shows good sound-absorbing characteristics, especially at high frequencies. Panels made of recycled PET and sheep wool showed an absorption coefficient α higher than 0.7 in the range of 50–5700 Hz regardless of the humidity content [46]. The sound absorption of light-soft-plastic bottles with net capacity from 7 to 2000 mL is affected by the capacity in the range of 100 and 1000 Hz [47]. Plastic bottles are often used to hold materials that lack structural strength. For example, a slightly lower TL than those of traditional construction materials was measured for PET bottles filled with plastic bags [18]. End-of-life PET bottles were incorporated in a wall 12 cm thick and tests showed a reduction between 29.8 dB and 55.8 dB than the wall without bottles [48]. Additionally, the acoustic properties of aluminum cans were investigated [49]: a sandwich panel made of polystyrene, pressed aluminum cans, rockwool and corrugated cardboard showed a better acoustic performance than gypsum panels, but lower than panels made of rock-wool and egg-boxes.

2.3.4. Egg-Boxes and Trays

Egg-boxes and trays can be made of different materials such as plastic, recycled paper, cardboard, but what distinguishes them is their shape. For a long time, egg-cartons have been considered good sound absorbing materials, and they have been widely used for this purpose since they are inexpensive, easy-to-install and easily available [50]. However, their acoustic performances have been recently questioned. It was pointed out that egg-boxes provide good sound absorption only at high frequencies, their NRC equal to 0.4 is too low for considering them sound absorbing elements, and the sound absorption coefficient profile is irregular [51]. The experimental tests presented in [52] showed that the sound absorption coefficient of egg-boxes and fruit trays is affected by the material, orientation of the boxes, and by if they are closed or open. Experimental tests showed that egg-cartons can reduce the reverberation time at mid-frequency [53]. In spite of this, researches have been looking for a way to improve their sound performance by coupling them with other materials. A sound absorbent made of egg-boxes pulp showed an optimized NRC equal to 0.5 [54]. A non-standardized test method showed that filling egg-boxes with mineral wool blocks a percentage of sound ranging between 14.42% and 17.71% depending on the frequency. Egg-boxes were filled with shredded rice straw paper and textile waste [50], and with polyurethane foam [52]. The panels proposed in [50] showed higher sound absorption coefficients than common egg-boxes cartons at all frequencies, and those presented in [52] featured a NRC equal to 0.87.

3. Methods

The review presented in the previous section shows that, even if a limited number of papers investigated the EoLHM acoustic performances, these materials have exploitable properties for the improvement of the indoor acoustic quality. An ideal panel suitable to be used as a façade element posses both good sound absorption and high transmission loss. As concerns the transmission loss, it must be remembered that the final acoustic performance will also depend on the basic wall on which they will be installed. In this study, the acoustic properties of different panels, realized by coupling different EoLHM, are experimentally investigated to understand whether further studies are required. Tests have been performed on samples made of easily obtainable EoLHM such as cardboard, textile waste, egg-boxes, metallic elements and their combination. Since the acoustic conditions of the environment in which these panels will be installed are unknown, configurations with high sound absorption coefficient and good TL are considered interesting and worth to be further investigated. Since this analysis is exploratory, the experimental tests have been performed by means of the impedance tube method that requires small samples and gives reproducible results. However, this technique allows the determination of the properties for sound waves impinging normally on the sample surface.

The experimental investigation of the acoustic properties was performed following the standard procedure given by the ASTM E2611 [55] that required the use of a four-microphone impedance tube (Figures 5 and 6). This device consists of two tubes of equal internal cross section connected to a test sample holder. Four microphones were placed along the tube (two on either side of the specimen). A source emitting a pink noise was placed at one end of the tube. A multi-channel Fast Fourier Transform (FFT) analyzer acquired the signals captured by the microphones. The second endpoint of the tube could be equipped with an anechoic or a reflecting termination, allowing us to perform the tests with two different boundary conditions. The pressure and particle velocity of the traveling waves and of reflected waves could be determined by means of a MATLAB script implemented on the basis of the E2611 ASTM standard [55]. The frequency range investigated went from 100 Hz to 3150 Hz.

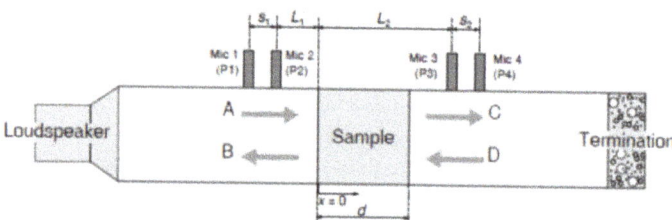

Figure 5. Schematic drawings of a four-microphones impedance tube. A represents the energy emitted by the loudspeaker, C is the component that crosses the sample, D is the component reflected by the termination, and B is the component reflected by the sample and/or that crosses the sample after being reflected by the termination.

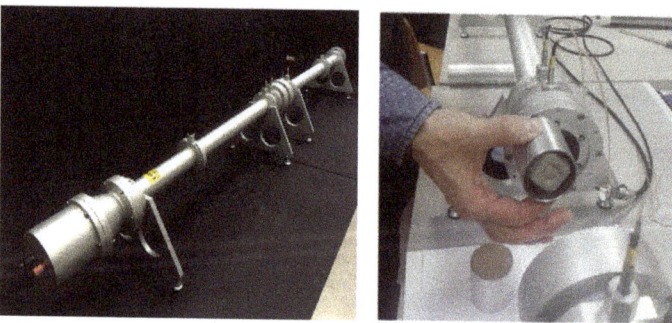

Figure 6. Impedance tube used for the determination of the acoustic properties of EoLHM.

Defining the wave number in air, $k = 2\pi \cdot f/c_0$, the traveling and reflected components of the plane wave propagation in the tube (A, B, C and D) can be calculated using the following correlations, once the complex acoustic transfer functions $H_{i,ref}$ between the ith microphone and the reference microphone are measured:

$$A = 0.5 \times j(H_{1,ref}e^{-jkL_1} - H_{2,ref}e^{-jk(L_1+s_1)})/\sin(ks_1) \qquad (18)$$

$$B = 0.5 \times j(H_{2,ref}e^{+jk(L_1+s_1)} - H_{1,ref}e^{+jk(L_1)})/sin(ks_1) \qquad (19)$$

$$C = 0.5 \times j(H_{3,ref}e^{+jk(L_2+s_2)} - H_{4,ref}e^{-jk(L_2)})/sin(ks_2) \qquad (20)$$

$$D = 0.5 \times j(H_{4,ref}e^{-jkL_2} - H_{3,ref}e^{-jk(L_2+s_2)})/sin(ks_2) \qquad (21)$$

where, in the case at hand, microphone 1 was selected as the reference microphone. For a given boundary condition, it is possible to determine the acoustic pressure p and the particle velocity u on each face of the specimen using the following equations:

$$p_0 = A + B \qquad p_d = Ce^{-jkd} + De^{+jkd} \qquad (22)$$

$$u_0 = \frac{A - B}{\rho_0 c_0} \qquad u_d = (Ce^{-jkd} - De^{+jkd})/\rho_0 c_0 \qquad (23)$$

where ρ_0 is the density of air. In general, the elements of a transfer matrix T, putting into relation pressures and particle velocities at either side of the specimen under test, can be calculated from the acoustic pressures and particle velocities measured during two different experimental sessions performed using an anechoic (a) and a reflecting (b) termination:

$$[T] = \begin{bmatrix} T_{11} & T_{12} \\ T_{21} & T_{22} \end{bmatrix} = \begin{bmatrix} \dfrac{p_{0a}u_{db} - p_{0b}u_{da}}{p_{da}u_{db} - p_{db}u_{da}} & \dfrac{p_{0b}p_{da} - p_{0a}p_{db}}{p_{da}u_{db} - p_{db}u_{da}} \\ \dfrac{u_{0a}u_{db} - u_{0b}u_{da}}{p_{da}u_{db} - p_{db}u_{da}} & \dfrac{p_{da}u_{0b} - p_{db}u_{0a}}{p_{da}u_{db} - p_{db}u_{da}} \end{bmatrix} \qquad (24)$$

The absorption coefficient can be computed as:

$$\alpha = 1 - \left| \frac{T_{11} - \rho c T_{21}}{T_{11} + \rho c T_{21}} \right|^2 \qquad (25)$$

The sound transmission loss TL is expressed as:

$$TL = 20 \times \log_{10} \left| \frac{T_{11} + (T_{12}/\rho c) + T_{21}\rho c + T_{22}}{2e^{jkd}} \right| \qquad (26)$$

Samples

The analyzed samples were made putting together different types of EoLHM and are shown in Figures 7 and 8, where the sequence described in the caption starts with the material nearest to the sound source. The layers of the samples were only placed close to and not connected to each other. The samples were 50 mm long, except for samples 13 and 14 that had a length of 24.2 mm, and sample 26 that was 100 mm long. The weight of the samples is reported in Table 1. For each sample, three repetitions were performed and the results of the experimental tests were averaged. This has made it possible to evaluate how manual skills influenced the panel acoustic performances.

Table 1. Weight in grams of the samples.

Sample	3	22	4	5	7	8	13	14	17	26
Weight	3.6	4.19	12.63	12.63	13.33	13.33	6.47	15.4	4.36	19.31
Sample	27	28	29	30	32	33	34	35	36	
Weight	12.53	13.81	8.45	17.41	8.91	20.07	29.03	21.83	21.83	

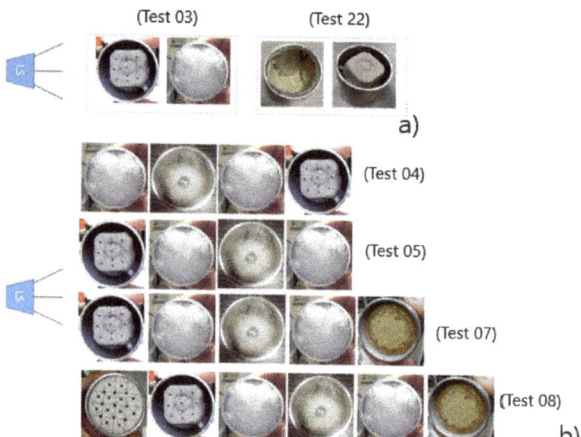

Figure 7. Configurations analyzed with the impedance tube: (**a**) samples made of egg-boxes and polyester, and (**b**) samples made of egg-box, polyester and a metallic element. Samples 04 and 05 are made of the same elements but in sample 04 the polyester faces the loudspeaker. Sample 08 has an additional perforated cardboard layer.

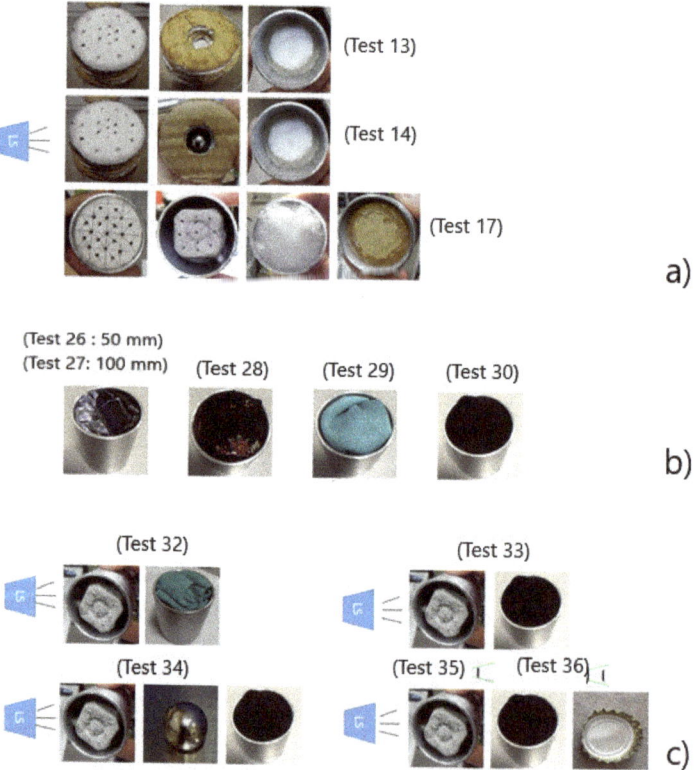

Figure 8. Configurations analyzed with the impedance tube: (**a**) samples made of several layers of cardboard, (**b**) samples made of clothes (one fabric at a time), (**c**) samples made of egg-boxes and clothes.

Since the acoustic properties of egg-boxes have been questioned in a number of papers [51,52,56], to analyze this aspect, the first set of samples (03, 22) was made at least by one egg-carton 2.79 g in weight made of recycled paper with a density of 355 kg/m^3. In sample 03, the egg-carton facing the sound source was coupled with loose polyester. The egg-carton was perforated and the holes were less than 1 mm in diameter. This element was used for realizing the other samples that included egg-boxes, which exception of sample 22 that was made of two not-perforated spaced egg-cartons whose cavity faced the sound source.

To improve the acoustic performance, in the following set of samples (04, 05, 07, 08) the perforated egg-carton was coupled to other EoLHM such as loose polyester, a metallic element and cardboard 197 kg/m^3 in density. The cardboard was made of two external linear boards 0.11 mm thick and an internal board with 130 flutes/m. The metal element was a steel sphere with an external diameter of 13 mm, and a weight of 8.95 g.

In particular, samples 04 was made of a box-carton, polyester and a metallic sphere. Sample 05 was similar but had mounted reverse. Samples 07 and 08 were realized to exploit the double panel characteristics. Indeed, a plane wave impinging a double-panel system saw the impedance of the panel closest to the sound source, the impedance of the airspace, the impedance of the second panel, and finally the impedance of the air beyond. The cavity acted as a spring element reducing significantly the TL, especially at higher frequencies. In the cavity the absence of absorptive material contributed to the transmission of sound, while the addition of damping elements such as fibrous materials attenuated the modes of the cavity. For this reason, in samples 07 and 08 cardboard layers were added to create a sort of cavity. In sample 07, to reduce the permeability, only a cardboard was added on the back of the sample. In sample 08 a perforated layer was added in the front of the sample: the first panel being perforated allowed the passage of a certain quantity of sound and behaved like a Helmholtz resonator.

To characterize cardboard panels, a third set of samples (13, 14, 17) was prepared. In the last few years, cardboard is largely available at domestic level as a result of the e-commerce. For this reason, highlighting its acoustic properties would encourage its conversion into a building element. Since very sound reflective materials could have a negative impact on acoustic indoor comfort, especially in very crowded ambient such as homes in disadvantaged contexts, the first cardboard layer of the samples was perforated to increase the sound absorption capability. Sample 13 and 14 were made of nine cardboard elements: the first two were perforated, the internal five disks presented a central hole 17 mm in diameter, while the last two disks were not perforated. In sample 14 a metal sphere was housed in the central layers. The weight of the whole cardboard disk was 0.77 g. Sample 17 was similar to samples 08 except for the presence of the metal sphere and, consequently, the weight of the sample was (13.33 g for sample 08, and 4.36 g for sample 17).

In the fourth set of samples (26–32) different fabrics were tested. Samples 26 and 27 were made of cotton, while samples 28, 29 and 30 were respectively made of polyester, plush cotton, and viscose. Since the fabrics had no structural strength, it was necessary to fold them inside the impedance tube. This revealed that the installation of the fabrics was strongly influenced by the operator's skills.

In the fifth and last set of samples (32–36), textile waste was coupled with other EoLHMs to improve their insulation performance. To reach a certain degree of stiffness, these samples were realized with a perforated egg-carton facing the sound source. Sample 32 was made of cotton, while the others are made of viscose. By means of tests performed on samples 34–36, the influence of metallic elements was investigated. In particular, a metallic sphere was inserted in sample 34, while a metal cap 1.75 g in weight and 26 mm in diameter was included in samples 35 and 36 but only in sample 35 there was contact with the egg-carton.

4. Results and Discussion

The results of the tests described in the previous section are reported in Figures 9–13 showing the sound absorption coefficient α and the transmission loss TL obtained by means of the impedance tube measurements. For each sample, the NRC has been calculated and reported in Table 2.

Table 2. NRC of the samples tested in this paper.

Sample	3	22	4	5	7	8	13	14	17	26
NRC	0.49	0.45	0.56	0.48	0.54	0.60	0.45	0.44	0.58	0.84
Sample	27	28	29	30	32	33	34	35	36	
NRC	0.69	0.64	0.71	0.69	0.52	0.46	0.45	0.38	0.37	

Figure 9 shows that, for samples 03 and 22, the most interesting sound insulation performance was given by sample 22, with a TL following the mass law up to 800 Hz and then a behavior typical of double walls, with a coincidence frequency around 1800 Hz. Sample 03 was not able to reach the same performances. As regards the absorption coefficient, it was characterized by wide peaks at given frequencies due to holes in the egg-cardboard behaving like Helmholtz resonators. In the case of sample 03, the peak around 700 Hz was very wide due to the presence of sound absorbing polyester fibers inside the main volume. This result suggests that to reach a good TL it was important to arrange the egg boxes upside down, but they still had to be coupled with other materials to improve their performances. The presence of the holes improved the absorption characteristics.

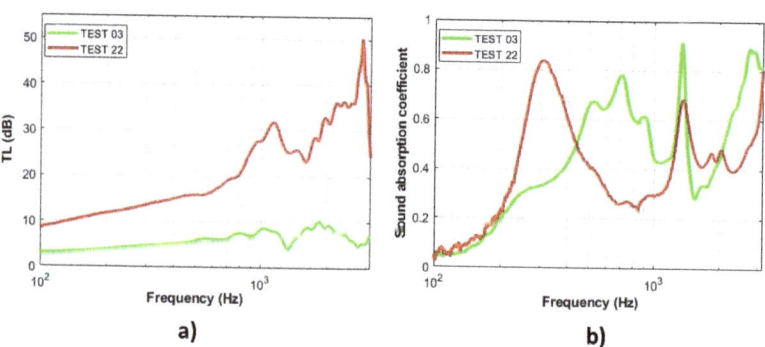

Figure 9. Transmission loss (a) and absorption coefficient (b) of samples made of at least on egg-box and polyester.

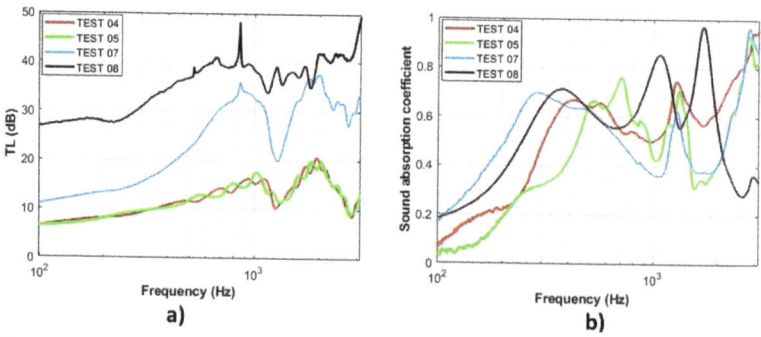

Figure 10. Transmission loss (a) and absorption coefficient (b) of samples made of egg-box, cardboard, polyester and a metallic element.

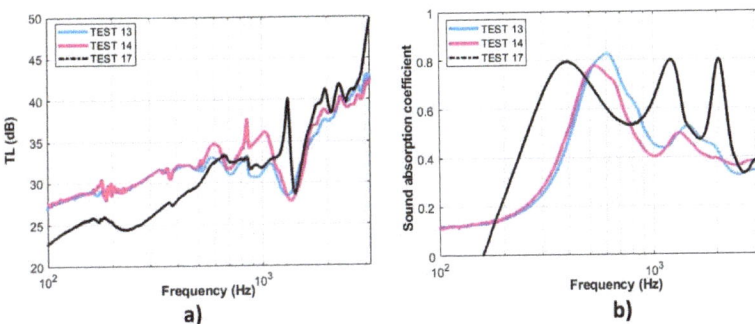

Figure 11. Transmission loss (**a**) and absorption coefficient (**b**) of samples made of several layers of cardboard.

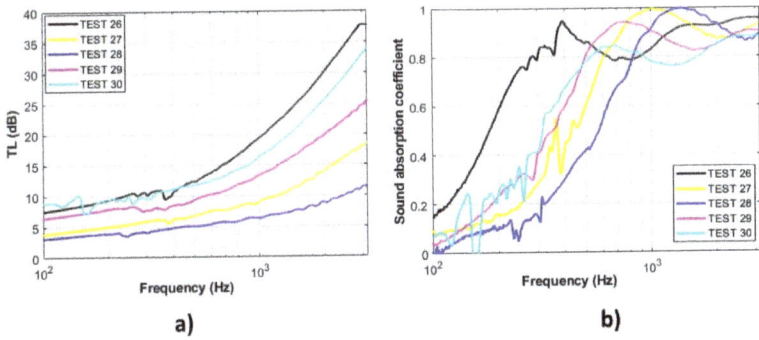

Figure 12. Transmission loss (**a**) and absorption coefficient (**b**) of samples made of clothes (one fabric at a time).

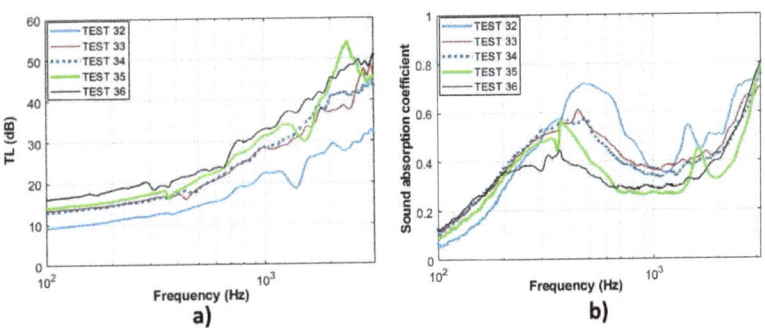

Figure 13. Transmission loss (**a**) and absorption coefficient (**b**) of samples made of egg-boxes and clothes.

The TL curves just analyzed were very similar to the curves obtained for the second set of samples and reported in Figure 10. This behavior can be explained by the nature of the samples which were built with the same elements: the egg-box, the polyester foam and steel spheres. The only variables were the orientation of the samples and the presence of a cardboard disk. The TLs of samples 04 and 05 were characterized by the typical mass law behavior due to the single egg cardboard, except a dip around 1200 Hz. Samples 04 and 05 showed an interesting absorption coefficient, and sample 04 featured better performances since it did not present valleys at high frequency. However, since these samples were permeable to air, the TL was very weak. Reducing the permeability, in samples 07 and 08 the additional cardboard layer caused an increase of the curve slope due to the mass-spring-mass behavior of the layers. Sample 08 exhibited very interesting performances at low frequencies and the highest TL of the group also at high frequencies. In sample 08 the additional perforated cardboard layer facing the sound source captured sound energy at some specific frequency bands. Part of the energy that passed through the egg-box was absorbed by the fibrous material. Finally, the final last cardboard reduced the transmitted energy. For these samples, the absorption coefficient was characterized by multiple peaks typical of the resonators featured in the cardboard portions. The width of the peaks depended again on the presence of polyester fibers. The best performance belonged to sample 08, characterized by a rather good sound absorption coefficient also at high frequency, with a maximum of 0.95 at 2 kHz.

As regards the third set of samples, Figure 11 shows very similar TL curves for all the samples. This group of TL was the highest among the entire group of tested materials. Such behavior is due to the high density of the samples that made the samples similar to sandwich materials featuring non compressible cores. For this reason the trend was characterized by a mass-law behavior followed by the typical coincidence dip. For samples 13 and 14, the sound absorption coefficient was marked out by a maximum around 600 Hz due to the resonance of the Helmholtz resonators featured in the cardboard. For sample 17, the graph of the sound absorption was very similar to the one of sample 08 (having a very similar structure), with three peaks reaching a value of 0.8.

The results of the fourth set of test samples, which were made of fabrics, are shown in Figure 12. The absorption curves were similar for all the samples and typical of porous materials. The best performance was given by sample 30 having the highest density of the group. Additionally, sample 26 showed a good performance but since it was 100 mm thick it could not be directly compared with the other samples. However, this result shows that better performances could be achieved by increasing the thickness of the panels. Additionally, in this case, the sound absorption coefficient had a shape typical for porous materials, featuring an S shape, with low values at low frequencies and values approaching 1 at high frequencies. By comparing the NRC measured for samples 26 and 27 and reported in Table 2, it emerged that the operator skills affected the acoustic performances of the panels. Indeed, even if the samples were made of the same material and the same NRC should be obtained, a higher value of NRC was measured for the thinner sample (26) and this is probably due to the assembling mode.

The fifth and last set of samples was a combination of fabrics, egg-boxes and metal parts. As can be observed in Figure 13, all the TL curves had very similar trends. If compared to the TL in Figure 12, for samples 32–36, values were generally higher at low frequency due to the higher mass per unit area of the samples. Sample 36 had the best performances for this group and this is probably due to the fact that the metal element could vibrate because it was not in contact with the rigid egg-carton. As concerns the sound absorption coefficient, the behavior was dominated by the Helmholtz resonator featuring a peak around 400 Hz followed by an increase of the coefficient due to the presence of the tissues.

5. Conclusions

The study presented in this paper has shown that EoLHM, such as cardboard, egg-boxes, clothes and metal elements, can be reused to realize low-cost acoustic panels for the improvement of the indoor comfort. Since these panels are easy realizable and cheap, they can be used in disadvantaged contexts where low-income people live and can not afford commercial acoustic panels. By wisely coupling EoLHM, good acoustic performances can be obtained for panels of limited thickness. Measurements performed with the impedance tube technique have shown that samples made of fabrics present a sound absorption coefficient greater than 0.8 in the range 300–3500 Hz. The higher insulation performance has been measured for samples made of perforated cardboard that present a TL of

25–30 dB in the range 100–300 Hz, and 30–40 dB in the range 300–2000 Hz. To reach interesting performances from both the insulation and the absorption point of view, it is necessary to couple egg-cartons, cardboard, polyester and metal elements. For this configuration, NRC is higher than 0.54 and the TL varies between 25 and 40 dB in the range 250–2000 Hz. Since in this study only the performance related to normal waves has been analyzed, in future investigation the most performing configurations will be tested in a reverberation room. Since the acoustic panels will be realized by not-skilled personnel and the manual skills affect the panels acoustic performance, it will be necessary to provide courses and guidelines for illustrating how the panels must be realized and installed.

Author Contributions: All authors conceived the presented idea. M.N. and E.L. designed the experimental campaign and wrote the paper with input from all authors. All authors have read and agreed to the published version of the manuscript.

Funding: The authors would like thank the Department of Mechanical and Industrial Engineering of University of Brescia for funding the research through the MetATer PRD project.

Acknowledgments: All the authors would like to thank the Applied Acoustics Laboratory of University of Brescia and Edoardo Alessio Piana for the opportunity to carry out the experimental tests and for the support in designing the experimental campaign.

Conflicts of Interest: The authors declare no conflict of interest.

References

1. United Nations. Transforming Our World: The 2030 Agenda for Sustainable Development. Available online: https://sustainabledevelopment.un.org/post2015/transformingourworld/publication (accessed on 2 March 2021).
2. Lagonigro, R.; Martori, J.C.; Apparicio, P. Environmental noise inequity in the city of Barcelona. *Transp. Res. Part D Transp. Environ.* **2018**, *63*, 309–319. [CrossRef]
3. Moreno-Jiménez, A.; Cañada-Torrecilla, R.; Vidal-Domínguez, M.J.; Palacios-García, A.; Martínez-Suárez, P. Assessing environmental justice through potential exposure to air pollution: A socio-spatial analysis in Madrid and Barcelona, Spain. *Geoforum* **2016**, *69*, 117–131. [CrossRef]
4. Chiesura, A. The role of urban parks for the sustainable city. *Landsc. Urban Plan.* **2004**, *68*, 129–138. [CrossRef]
5. Rasmussen, B. Acoustic classification of buildings in Europe—Main characteristics of national schemes for housing, schools, hospitals and office buildings. In Proceedings of the Euronoise, Crete, Greece, 27–31 May 2018.
6. Kryter, K.D. *The Effects of Noise on Man*; Academic Press: New York, NY, USA, 1985.
7. European Parliament and the Council of the European Union. Directive 2002/49/EC of the European Parliament and of the Council of 25 June 2002 Relating to the Assessment and Management of Environmental Noise. Available online: http://eur-lex.europa.eu/legalcontent/EN/TXT/PDF/?uri=CELEX:32002L0049&from=EN (accessed on 8 April 2021).
8. European Parliament and the Council of the European Union. Decision No 1386/2013/EU of the European Parliament and of the Council of 20 November 2013 on a General Union Environment Action Programme to 2020 Living Well, within the Limits of Our Planet. Available online: https://eur-lex.europa.eu/eli/dec/2013/1386/oj (accessed on 26 April 2021).
9. UNIDO—United Nations Industrial Development Organization. Circular Economy. Available online: https://www.unido.org/our-focus-cross-cutting-services/circular-economy (accessed on 15 May 2020).
10. Common Objective. Sustainability Issues—How Sustainable Is Paper and Cardboard Packaging? Available online: www.commonobjective.co/article/how-sustainable-is-paper-and-cardboard-packaging (accessed on 26 February 2021).
11. Chua, J.C. Asos, H&M Seek to Keep Ancient, Endangered Forests Out of Packaging. Available online: https://sourcingjournal.com/topics/sustainability/canopy-pack4good-ecommerce-packaging-sustainable-recycled-asos-hm-kontoor-vf-172028/ (accessed on 31 March 2021).
12. Ritchie, H.; Roser, M. Plastic Pollution. Available online: https://ourworldindata.org/plastic-pollution (accessed on 31 March 2021).
13. Beall, A. Why Clothes Are so Hard to Recycle. Available online: https://www.bbc.com/future/article/20200710-why-clothes-are-so-hard-to-recycle (accessed on 13 July 2020).
14. Ellen MacArthur Foundation. A New Textile Economy: Redesigning Fashion's Future. Available online: www.ellenmacarthurfoundation.org (accessed on 31 March 2021).
15. Neri, M.; Pilotelli, M.; Traversi, M.; Levi, E.; Piana, E.A.; Bannò, M.; Cuerva, E.; Pujadas, P.; Guardo, A. Conversion of End-of-Life Household Materials into Building Insulating Low-Cost Solutions for the Development of Vulnerable Contexts: Review and Outlook towards a Circular and Sustainable Economy. *Sustainability* **2021**, *13*. [CrossRef]
16. European Parliament and Council of the European Union. Directive 2010/31/EU of the European Parliament and of the Council of 19 May 2010 on the Energy Performance of Buildings. Available online: https://eur-lex.europa.eu/LexUriServ/LexUriServ.do?uri=OJ:L:2010:153:0013:0035:en:PDF (accessed on 26 April 2021).

17. European Parliament and Council of the European Union. Directive 2012/27/EU of the European Parliament and of the Council of 25 October 2012 on Energy Efficiency, Amending Directives 2009/125/EC and 2010/30/EU and Repealing Directives 2004/8/EC and 2006/32/EC. Official Journal of the European Union, L 315, 14 November 2012. Available online: https://eur-lex.europa.eu/LexUriServ/LexUriServ.do?uri=OJ:L:2012:315:0001:0056:en:PDF (accessed on 29 April 2021).
18. Taaffe, J.; O'Sullivan, S.; Rahman, M.E.; Pakrashi, V. Experimental characterisation of Polyethylene Terephthalate (PET) bottle Eco-bricks. *Mater. Des.* **2014**, *60*, 50–56. [CrossRef]
19. *ASTM C423—Complete Document Standard Test Method for Sound Absorption and Sound Absorption Coefficients by the Reverberation Room Method*; ASTM International: West Conshohocken, PA, USA, 2017.
20. Cao, L.; Fu, Q.; Si, Y.; Ding, B.; Yu, J. Porous materials for sound absorption. *Compos. Commun.* **2018**, *10*, 25–35. [CrossRef]
21. Arenas, J.; Crocker, M. Recent trends in porous sound-absorbing materials. *Sound Vib.* **2010**, *44*, 12–17.
22. Delany, M.E.; Bazley, E.N. Acoustical properties of fibrous absorbent materials. *Appl. Acoust.* **1970**, *3*, 105–116. doi:10.1016/0003-682X(70)90031-9 [CrossRef]
23. Oldham, D.J.; Egan, C.C.R. Sustainable acoustic absorbers from the biomass. *Appl. Acoust.* **2011**, *72*, 350–363. doi:10.1016/j.apacoust.2010.12.009 [CrossRef]
24. Wang, Y.H.; Zhang, C.C.; Ren, L.Q.; Ichchou, M.; Galland, M.A.; Bareille, O. Sound absorption of a new bionic multi-layer absorber. *Compos. Struct.* **2014**, *108*, 400–408. [CrossRef]
25. Pelegrinis, M.T.; Horoshenkov, K.V.; Burnett, A. An application of kozeny-carman flow resistivity model to predict the acoustical properties of polyester fibre. *Appl. Acoust.* **2016**, *101*, 1–4. [CrossRef]
26. Othmani, C.; Taktak, M.; Zein, A.; Hentati, T.; Elnady, T.; Fakhfakh, T.; Haddar, M. Experimental and theoretical investigation of the acoustic performance of sugarcane wastes based material. *Appl. Acoust.* **2016**, *109*, 90–96. [CrossRef]
27. Meric, C.; Erol, H.; Ozkan, A. On the sound absorption performance of a felt sound absorber. *Appl. Acoust.* **2016**, *114*, 275–280. [CrossRef]
28. Langfeldt, F.; Hoppen, H.; Gleine, W. Resonance frequencies and sound absorption of Helmholtz resonators with multiple necks. *Appl. Acoust.* **2019**, *145*, 314–319. [CrossRef]
29. Nilsson, A.; Baro, S.; Piana, E.A. Vibro-acoustic properties of sandwich structures. *Appl. Acoust.* **2018**, *139*, 259–266. [CrossRef]
30. Piana, E.; Nilsson, A. Prediction of the sound transmission loss of sandwich structures based on a simple test procedure. In Proceedings of the 17th International Congress on Sound and Vibration 2010, ICSV 2010, Cairo, Egypt, 18–22 July 2010; International Institute of Acoustics and Vibrations, IIAV: Cairo, Egypt, 2010; Volume 1, pp. 109–116.
31. Piana, E.; Petrogalli, C.; Solazzi, L. Dynamic and acoustic properties of a joisted floor. In Proceedings of the SIMULTECH 2016—International Conference on Simulation and Modeling Methodologies, Technologies and Applications, Lisbon, Portugal, 29–31 July 2016; Obaidat, M., Merkuryev, Y., Oren, T., Eds.; SciTePress: Lisbon, Portugal, 2016; pp. 277–282.
32. Bruel & Kjaer. *Measurements in Building Acoustics*; Bruel & Kjaer: Nærum, Denmark, 1998.
33. Iannace, G.; Umberto, B.; Bravo-Moncayo, L.; Ciaburro, G.; Puyana-Romero, V. Organic waste as absorbent materials. In Proceedings of the 2020 International Congress on Noise Control Engineering, INTER-NOISE 2020, Seoul, Korea, 23–26 August 2020.
34. Lee, Y.; Joo, C. Sound absorption properties of recycled polyester fibrous assembly absorbers. *Autex Res. J.* **2003**, *3*, 139–146.
35. Saravana Kumar, T.; Ramesh Kumar, M. Development of needle punched non woven fabrics for acoustic application. *Int. J. ChemTech Res.* **2015**, *8*, 21–26.
36. Lyu, L.; Li, C.; Wang, Y.; Lu, J.; Guo, J. Sound absorption, thermal, and flame retardant properties of nonwoven wall cloth with waste fibers. *J. Eng. Fibers Fabr.* **2020**, *15*. [CrossRef]
37. Trajković, D.; Jordeva, S.; Tomovska, E.; Zafirova, K. Polyester apparel cutting waste as insulation material. *J. Text. Inst.* **2017**, *108*, 1238–1245. [CrossRef]
38. Asami, T.; Miura, H. Basic study of the acoustic characteristics of cotton fabric with differing moisture content using 28 kHz ultrasound. *Jpn. Appl. Phys.* **2019**, *58*, SGGD08. [CrossRef]
39. Asdrubali, F.; Pisello, A.L.; D'Alessandro, F.; Bianchi, F.; Cornicchia, M.; Fabiani, C. Innovative cardboard based panels with recycled materials from the packaging industry: Thermal and acoustic performance analysis. *Energy Procedia* **2015**, *78*, 321–326. [CrossRef]
40. Secchi, S.; Asdrubali, F.; Cellai, G.; Nannipieri, E.; Rotili, A.; Vannucchi, I. Experimental and environmental analysis of new sound-absorbing and insulating elements in recycled cardboard. *J. Build. Eng.* **2015**, *5*, 1–12. [CrossRef]
41. Paternoster, A.; Van Camp, J.; Vanlanduit, S.; Weeren, A.; Springael, J.; Braet, J. The performance of beer packaging: Vibration damping and thermal insulation. *Food Packag. Shelf Life* **2017**, *11*, 91–97. [CrossRef]
42. Kang, C.W.; Kim, M.; Jang, E.S.; Lee, Y.H.; Jang, S.S. Sound absorption coefficient and sound transmission loss of porous sponge attached corrugated cardboard of noise insulation cover. *Palpu Chongi Gisul/J. Korea Tech. Assoc. Pulp Pap. Ind.* **2020**, *52*, 38–44. [CrossRef]
43. Jun-Oh, Y.; Kyoung-Woo K.; Kwan-Seop, Y.; Jea-Min, K.; Myung-Jun, K. Physical properties of cellulose sound absorbers produced using recycled paper. *Constr. Build. Mater.* **2014**, *70*, 494–500. [CrossRef]
44. Shoubi, M.V.; Shoubi, M.V.; Barough, A.S. Investigating the Application of Plastic Bottle as a Sustainable Material in the Building Construction. *Int. J. Sci. Eng. Technol. Res. (IJSETR)* **2013**, *2*, 28–34.
45. Iannace, G.; Ciaburro, G. Modelling sound absorption properties for recycled polyethylene terephthalate-based material using Gaussian regression. *Build. Acoust.* **2020**. [CrossRef]

46. Patnaik, A.; Mvubu, M.; Muniyasamy, S.; Botha, A.; Anandjiwala, R.D. Thermal and sound insulation materials from waste wool and recycled polyester fibers and their biodegradation studies. *Energy Build.* **2015**, *92*, 161–169. [CrossRef]
47. Iwase, T.; Sugie, S.; Kurono, H.; Abe, M.; Okada, Y.; Yoshihisa, K. Sound absorption characteristic of glass and plastic bottles: Considerations of their dependences on material properties. In Proceedings of the ASME 2018 Noise Control and Acoustics Division Session Presented at INTERNOISE 2018, Chicago, IL, USA, 26–29 August 2018; [CrossRef]
48. Viegas, L.; Bezerra, U.; Barbosa, N. Blocks for Performance of Masonry Using PET Bottle Seal: Thermal, acoustic, and Mechanical and evaluation. *Key Eng. Mater.* **2014**, *600*, 753–767. [CrossRef]
49. Kassim, U.; Goh, J.K.S. Recycle materials as industrialised building system (IBS) internal partition. *J. Built Environ. Technol. Eng.* **2016**, *1*, 330–334. ISSN 0128-1003.
50. Satwiko, P.; Gharata, V.D.; Setyabudi, H.; Suhedi, F. Enhancing egg cartons' sound absorption coefficient with recycled materials. *Build. Acoust.* **2017**, *24*, 115–131. [CrossRef]
51. Quintero-Rincon, A. Measurement of the sound-absorption coefficient on egg cartons using the Tone Burst Method. In Proceedings of the 11th WSEAS International Conference on Acoustics and Music: Theory and Applications, AMTA 10, Iasi, Romania, 13–15 June 2010.
52. Carvalho, A.P.O.; Vieira, S.C.P. Sound absorption of egg boxes and trays. In Proceedings of 44th International Congress and Exposition on Noise Control Engineering, San Francisco, CA, USA, 9–12 August 2015.
53. Iannace, G.; Berardi, U.; Ciaburro, G.; Trematerra, A. Egg cartons used as sound absorbing systems. In Proceedings of the INTER-NOISE and NOISE-CON Congress and Conference Proceedings, Seoul, Korea, 23–26 August 2020.
54. Sim J.; Zulkifli, R.; Tahir, M.; Khidir, E.. Recycled paper fibres as sound absorbing material. *Appl. Mech. Mater.* **2014**, *663*, 459–463. [CrossRef]
55. *ASTM E2611 Standard Test Method for Normal Incidence Determination of Porous Material Acoustical Properties Based on the Transfer Matrix Method*; ASTM International: West Conshohocken, PA, USA, 2019.
56. Kassim, U.; Goh, J. Acoustic Myths and Realities: Can Egg Carton Be Used as an Acoustical Treatment? Available online: http://www.acousticsfirst.com/eggc.htm (accessed on 29 April 2021).

Article

Optimization of Shunted Loudspeaker for Sound Absorption by Fully Exhaustive and Backtracking Algorithm

Zihao Li, Xin Li and Bilong Liu *

School of Mechanical & Automobile Engineering, Qingdao University of Technology, No. 777 Jialingjiang Road, Qingdao 266520, China; zihao_li0401@163.com (Z.L.); jz03-4lx@163.com (X.L.)
* Correspondence: liubilong@qut.edu.cn

Abstract: The shunted loudspeaker with a negative impedance converter is a physical system with multiple influencing parameters. In this paper, a fully exhaustive backtracking algorithm was used to optimize these parameters, such as moving mass, total stiffness, damping, coil inductance, force factor, circuit resistance, inductance and capacitance, in order to obtain the best sound absorption in a specific frequency range. Taking the maximum average sound absorption coefficient in the range of 100–450 Hz as the objective function, the optimized parameters of the shunted loudspeaker were analyzed. Simulation results indicated that the force factor and moving mass can be sufficiently reduced in comparison with that of a typical four-inch loudspeaker available on the market. For a given loudspeaker from the market as an example, the four optimized parameters of the shunted loudspeaker were given, and the sound absorption coefficient was measured for verification. The measured results were in good agreement with the predicted results, demonstrating the applicability of the algorithm.

Keywords: shunted loudspeaker; optimal sound absorption; fully exhaustive method

Citation: Li, Z.; Li, X.; Liu, B. Optimization of Shunted Loudspeaker for Sound Absorption by Fully Exhaustive and Backtracking Algorithm. *Appl. Sci.* **2021**, *11*, 5574. https://doi.org/10.3390/app11125574

Academic Editor: Yoshinobu Kajikawa

Received: 9 May 2021
Accepted: 13 June 2021
Published: 16 June 2021

Publisher's Note: MDPI stays neutral with regard to jurisdictional claims in published maps and institutional affiliations.

Copyright: © 2021 by the authors. Licensee MDPI, Basel, Switzerland. This article is an open access article distributed under the terms and conditions of the Creative Commons Attribution (CC BY) license (https://creativecommons.org/licenses/by/4.0/).

1. Introduction

Low-frequency sound absorption within a limited space is always a challenge in noise control engineering. Traditional passive acoustic structures usually have the disadvantage of being large in size, but active noise control technology also has drawbacks, such as instability and high cost. In recent years, the semi-active structure of a shunted loudspeaker (SL) for sound absorption has attracted much attention. For an SL with a negative impedance converter (NIC), the circuit parameters, such as resistance, capacitance and inductance, are transformed due to the negative impedance converter. This can effectively adjust the acoustic impedance of the coupled system to match that of the air in a wide frequency range [1]. Initially, Forward [2] proposed a preliminary experiment on the feasibility of using shunted damping in optical systems. Lissek et al. [3–6] introduced shunt circuits to loudspeakers and used the SL to control the acoustic impedance of walls for indoor sound absorption. Good sound absorption for low frequencies can be achieved in a relatively narrow frequency band. In their later research, analogous analysis, experimental optimization of the SL and active control theory were also carried out. Due to the low-frequency sound absorption properties of the SL, many structures relevant to the SL that have better sound absorption performance have been reported [7–10].

Some references can be found for the optimal design of an SL. Lissek et al. [5] established a low-order polynomial function and the effect of four parameters on sound absorption was investigated by using the response surface method (RSM). These four parameters were the moving mass of the loudspeaker, the enclosure volume, the filling density of mineral fiber within the enclosure and the electrical load value to which the loudspeaker was connected. Rivet et al. [11] introduced the SL for interior damping optimization and they determined the interior eigenfrequency by using a finite element model established in COMSOL Multiphysics. They also calculated the optimal location and orientation of the loudspeaker by establishing the linear equations of the system. Liu et al. [12] applied the SL to the pipe by means of a polar configuration of the system's characteristic equations. The optimal resistance, inductance and location of the SL were derived. This method effectively improved the insertion loss of the pipe. Zhang et al. [13] analyzed the effect of the circuit resistance, inductance and capacitance (RLC) on the acoustic impedance and absorption coefficient of the SL in detail. They provided an experimental procedure for achieving effective broadband sound absorption from the low to the middle frequency range. An array of 64 SLs was experimentally investigated by Qiu et al. [14], and the optimal array alignment spacing, to control 100 Hz and 200 Hz tone noise, was also discussed.

The loudspeaker in a reported SL is oriented for sound generation. This means that this type of loudspeaker would not be suitable for optimal sound absorption due to its large force factor and moving mass. Designing a loudspeaker from the perspective of sound absorption has not been reported in the literature. To achieve this task, the loudspeaker and shunt circuit parameters must be taken into account. Since the SL is a coupled field consisting of electrical, mechanical and acoustic components, the system contains a large number of parameters and potential interactions among these parameters. The problem of multi-parameter optimization is rather complex.

The fully exhaustive backtracking algorithm (EBA) is a programming method frequently used in programming design. EBA is often applied to solve the problems that cannot be solved by conventional mathematical methods [15]. The fully exhaustive algorithm allows multivariate functions, with potential interactions, to be solved numerically according to a combined enumeration [16]. After the multi-dimensional database is created by the fully exhaustive method, the backtracking algorithm is then used to search for the target value by using loop traversal according to the optimal conditions [17]. Genetic algorithms (GA) and simulated annealing algorithms (SAA) are stochastic optimization algorithms that are based on probabilistic convergence [18]. In the optimization process of multi-peaked objective functions, GA and SAA may converge to a local optimal solution prematurely, and there is no effective quantitative analysis method for the convergence and reliability of the solution [19,20]. The global search feature of the EBA can effectively avoid these disadvantages. Although the EBA has the advantage of a simple computational process, it usually has the disadvantage of requiring a large amount of computing resources. In SL optimization problems, the amount of computation required is very limited; therefore, the EBA is well suited for SL multi-parameter optimization.

In this paper, six main parameters of the SL, namely moving mass ΔM_m, system stiffness ΔK_m, force factor Bl, total resistance ΔR, total inductance ΔL and capacitance C_e, are considered in an optimization algorithm. In the following section, the principle of the SL is introduced briefly; then, an optimized sound absorption algorithm based on a six-dimensional EBA is described, and the simulation and analysis of the loudspeaker parameters suitable for sound absorption are demonstrated. For a given loudspeaker from the market, the experimental method to determine the key parameters of the loudspeaker by an impedance tube is provided, and, finally, the optimization results of the four parameters are verified by an experiment.

2. Theoretical Model of an SL

The layout of a typical SL is shown in Figure 1 and the technical date of the loudspeaker used in the experiment are listed in Table 1. The SL with an NIC is assembled at the end of the impedance tube, and the effective absorption can be achieved after reasonable adjustment of the electrical parameters. From an energy perspective, it can be understood that the sound energy is dissipated in the form of mechanical and electrical energy, reducing the reflected sound energy and achieving the purpose of sound absorption.

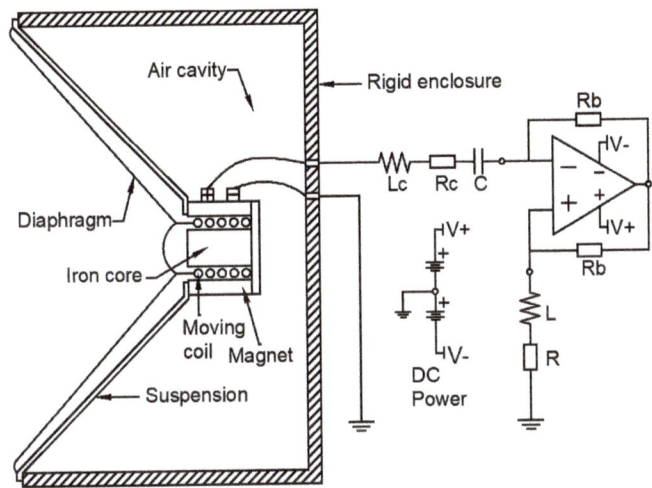

Figure 1. Schematic of the shunted loudspeaker with an NIC.

Table 1. Technical data for the loudspeaker Hivi–M4N.

Bl	R_c	L_c	M_m	K_m	δ_m
3.1 Tm	6.5 Ω	0.5 mH	4.8 g	926 N/m	1.74 sN/m

When the SL is in an open-circuit state, it can be considered a single-degree-of-freedom, second-order system, which consists of stiffness, mass and damping [21]. The mechanical impedance under the case of an air cavity of depth D can be expressed as:

$$Z_m = \delta_m + j\omega M_m + \frac{1}{j\omega K_m} + \frac{\rho_0 c_0 A}{i \tan(kD)} \qquad (1)$$

where ω is the angular frequency, c_0 is the speed of sound in air, M_m, K_m, δ_m are the moving mass, suspension diaphragm stiffness and damping of the moving-coil loudspeaker, respectively. $Z_{air} = \rho_0 c_0 A$ is the acoustic impedance of air, and A is the cross-section area of the impedance tube. k is the wavenumber and D is the cavity depth, where a more specific impedance expression can be obtained after making a second-order approximation to $\tan(kD)^{-1}$ [22]:

$$Z_m(\omega) = \delta_m + j\omega(M_m + \frac{\rho_0 A D}{3}) + (K_m + \frac{\rho_0 c_0^2 A}{D})/j\omega \qquad (2)$$

From Equation (2), it can be seen in the acoustic model of the SL with an air cavity that the total stiffness is the sum of the suspension diaphragm stiffness and the air spring of the air cavity, where the second item dominates. For example, a cylindrical cavity with a depth of 10 cm and radius of 5 cm can produce a stiffness of 11 KN/m, while a four-inch loudspeaker's diaphragm stiffness is generally 1 KN/m. The total vibrating mass is the sum of the mechanical vibrating mass and one-third of the cavity air mass; the latter is usually negligible.

An NIC can generate the equivalent value of a negative electrical parameter between the in-phase input and ground [23]. It can flexibly adjust the impedance caused by a larger resistance and inductance of the loudspeaker itself, enabling impedance of the SL to match with air over a wider frequency band. When connecting the SL with an NIC, the impedance of the circuit is:

$$Z_e(\omega) = (R_c - R) + j\omega(L_c - L) + \frac{1}{j\omega C} \tag{3}$$

The following is a derivation of the electrical force and impedance analogy. When the sound waves are transmitted to the loudspeaker's diaphragm, it will produce a vibration with speed of v. The loudspeaker's coil will cut the magnetic field of the permanent magnet, producing an induced electrical potential Blv. As the induced current is Blv/Z_e, the electromagnetic force applied to the coil is $F_e = B^2l^2v/Z_e$. The equivalent mechanical impedance induced by the circuit can be obtained by $Z_{\Delta m}(\omega) = F_e/v = (Bl)^2/Z_e(\omega)$. Here, the total impedance of the SL can be expressed as:

$$Z_{sys}(\omega) = Z_m(\omega) + (Bl)^2/Z_e(\omega) \tag{4}$$

The normal incident absorption coefficient of the SL is:

$$\alpha(\omega) = 1 - \left|\frac{Z_{sys} - Z_{air}}{Z_{sys} + Z_{air}}\right|^2 = \frac{4Z_{air}\text{Re}(Z_{sys})}{[Z_{air} + \text{Re}(Z_{sys})]^2 + \text{Im}(Z_{sys})^2} \tag{5}$$

Equation (5) shows that the sound absorption of the SL depends on the acoustic impedance of the system. The impedance matching condition should be satisfied when the sound is completely absorbed:

$$\text{Re}(Z_{sys}) = \delta_m + \frac{(Bl)^2 \Delta R}{\Delta R^2 + (\omega \Delta L - 1/\omega C)^2} = \rho_0 c_0 A \tag{6}$$

$$\text{Im}(Z_{sys}) = \omega M_m - \frac{\Delta K_m}{\omega} - \frac{(Bl)^2(\omega \Delta L - 1/\omega C)}{\Delta R^2 + (\omega \Delta L - 1/\omega C)^2} = 0 \tag{7}$$

where $\Delta R = R_e - R$, $\Delta L = L_e - L$ and $\Delta K_m = K_m + \rho_0 c_0^2 A/D$. The connection of the shunt circuit introduces new mechanical resistance and reactance. These parameters are mostly constant for the actual device, but the total impedance of the system changes with frequency. It is impractical to achieve an exact theoretical match, so a comprehensive optimization of sound absorption, based on experimental and theoretical calculation, is needed.

3. Algorithm Model and Simulation of the EBA
3.1. Procedure of the Algorithm Model

Loudspeakers used in the SL are for sound absorption, not sound generation. In contrast, loudspeakers available on the market are always used for sound generation. From the perspective of sound absorption, the loudspeaker in the SL must be redesigned. Through the simple analysis of the loudspeaker parameters, a certain trend of sound absorption can be obtained. However, the parameters influencing the sound absorption are coupled with each other and are difficult to analyze from a numerical point of view. The EBA is a method to obtain the ideal solution by calculating and analyzing all possible scenarios within the constraint. It can be expressed as enumerating all possible combinations of parameters within the boundaries, according to the step size of each variable, and then performing numerical analysis. Therefore, Matlab's powerful matrix solving capability can be used to perform the EBA. The optimal parameters for $\Delta R, \Delta L, C_e, \Delta K_m, M_m, Bl$ can be calculated by the EBA and then used as design values for the SL. The following describes the EBA optimization algorithm for six parameters.

3.1.1. Parameter Boundary

Since the algorithm corresponds to the actual physical system, a realistic boundary condition should be set for $\Delta R, \Delta L, C_e, \Delta K_m, M_m, Bl$. The characteristic equations of this system can be obtained by stability analysis. According to the Rouse criterion, $\Delta R, \Delta L$

and C_e must be positive, which determines the lower boundary of the $\Delta R, \Delta L$ and C_e [24]. Usually, the resistance of a typical four-inch loudspeaker does not exceed 25 Ω. Considering the actual component size, $\Delta L, C_e$ should be limited to the magnitude of mF and mH, respectively.

The upper boundary of the mechanical parameters can be set reasonably, according to the actual size of the speaker and the assembly model. Here, M_m is limited to 10 g, ΔK_m is limited to 1.95×10^4 N/m, and Bl is limited to 6 Tm. It is necessary to set a reasonable step size for these six parameters in this calculation. If the step size is small, it will lead to long computation time or even be impossible to compute. By using multiple iterations of the EBA to improve the computational efficiency of the program, sufficiently accurate solutions can be obtained in a relatively short time.

Under excitation of sound pressure, the SL generates an output voltage. The transfer function of the circuit section is shown in Equation (8). The maximum amplification can be obtained at the resonant frequency of the circuit. The actual output voltage at resonance can be calculated by multiplying the output signal obtained from the experimental test with Equation (9). When the actual transmission voltage can maximize the op-amp saturation value, the balancing resistance R_b can be determined [22].

$$G(S) = \frac{R_b + R + sL}{R - R_c + s(L - L_c) - \frac{1}{sC_e}}, \quad \omega_0 = \frac{1}{\sqrt{(L_c - L) \cdot C_e}} \tag{8}$$

$$|G(\omega_0)| = \frac{\sqrt{(R_b + R)^2 + \frac{L^2}{(L_c - L) \cdot C}}}{R_c - R} \tag{9}$$

3.1.2. Database Creation

The nonlinearity of the damping δ_m is usually difficult to predict accurately after assembly. To obtain an accurate theoretical calculation, the damping corresponding to the open circuit should be sampled for replacing the damping in Equation (2). The absorption coefficient at each frequency in any group within the boundary can be calculated in a nested cycle using Equations (2)–(5). Then, the absorption coefficients of each group are stored after taking the average values, and thus the database of the average absorption coefficients of the six-dimensional parameters of the SL is established.

3.1.3. Optimal Results of $\Delta R, \Delta L, C_e, \Delta K_m, M_m, Bl$

Once the database is created, the optimal average absorption coefficient values, and structural parameters such as $\Delta R, \Delta L, C_e, \Delta K_m, M_m, Bl$, can be searched in the database by the backtracking method. Thus, the circuit parameters R, L, C_e, and the equivalent depth D of the air cavity required for the design, can be calculated. Then, the sound absorption performance of the multi-parameter SL can be analyzed.

3.2. Optimal Sound Absorption for a Six-Parameter SL

In this simulation, the frequency range was 100–450 Hz and the inner diameter of the impedance tube was 10 cm. The mechanical damping as a constant was used in calculations and had a value of 1.74 sN/m. The optimized absorption coefficient and acoustic impedance of a six-parameter SL are shown in Figure 2. As observed in Figure 2a, the optimized six-parameter SL had an excellent sound absorption coefficient close to 1 in a wide frequency range of 100–450 Hz. By the EBA optimization search, a matched acoustic resistance close to 1 and a flat acoustic reactance trending toward 0 can be obtained in the specified frequency range, as shown in Figure 2b,c, respectively. In addition, it can be found that the first resonance occurs at 120 Hz, which is due to the resistance being close to 1 and the reactance being close to 0 at this frequency. Similarly, the second resonance is located at approximately 320 Hz.

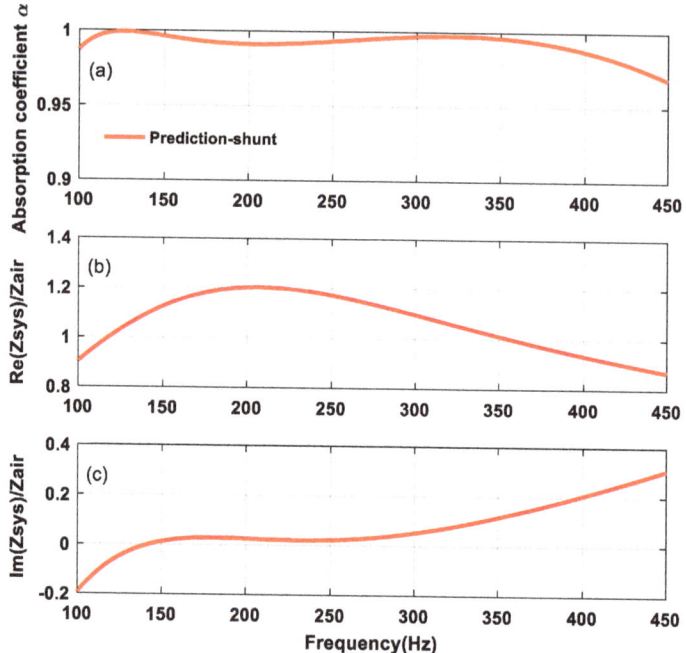

Figure 2. Optimized sound absorption of the SL by a six–dimensional EBA, (**a**) the sound absorption coefficient, (**b**) the specific acoustic resistance, (**c**) the specific acoustic reactance.

The optimized mechanical and electrical parameters of the SL by the six-dimensional EBA are listed in Table 2. The optimized results indicated that the moving mass and force factor were smaller than that of a typical loudspeaker available on the market. The decrease in force factor can effectively reduce the cost and the weight of the loudspeaker magnet. This would be an obvious potential benefit for practical applications. The results also revealed that the total stiffness was smaller than that of a typical SL reported in the literature. Lower stiffness suggests that the backing air cavity needs to be larger; for example, when the loudspeaker suspension diaphragm stiffness is 900 N/m, a cubic cavity with a side length of 23.5 cm is needed to provide the remaining stiffness.

Table 2. Parameter upper bounds and step size settings.

Parameter	Upper Bound	Step Size	Optimal
ΔR	20 Ω	0.2 Ω	2 Ω
ΔL	5 mH	50 μH	0.85 mH
C_e	5 mF	50 μF	0.7 μF
ΔK_m	1.95×10^4 N/m	390 N/m	1560 N/m
M_m	10 g	0.2 g	1 g
Bl	6 Tm	0.2 Tm	2.2 Tm

3.3. Optimal Sound Absorption for a Five-Parameter SL

The optimization results of the six parameters showed that the loudspeaker suitable for optimal sound absorption has the advantage of smaller Bl. In practical applications, the thickness of the loudspeaker should be as small as possible, which means that the Bl should be as small as possible. As an example, for the value of Bl set to 0.5 Tm, is taken into account in the algorithm; thus, the optimization procedure becomes an EBA of the remaining five variables. The optimized mechanical and electrical parameters of the SL by the five-dimensional EBA are listed in Table 3. The theoretical absorption coefficients under this condition are shown in Figure 3, and the average absorption coefficient is up to 0.96.

Table 3. Parameter upper bounds and step size settings.

Parameter	Upper Bound	Step Size	Optimal
ΔR	20 Ω	0.2 Ω	0.2 Ω
ΔL	5 mH	50 μH	0.15 mH
C_e	5 mF	50 μF	2 mF
ΔK_m	1.95×10^4 N/m	390 N/m	1170 N/m
M_m	10 g	0.1 g	0.5 g

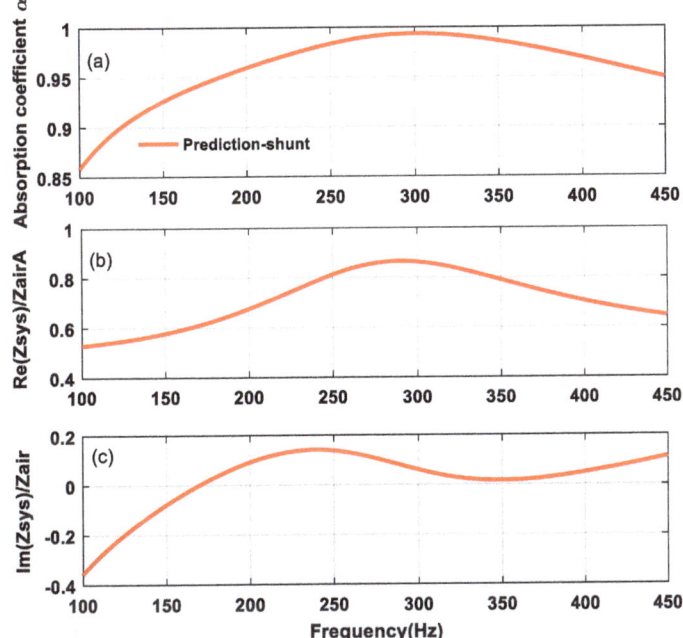

Figure 3. Optimized sound absorption of the SL by a five–dimensional EBA, (a) the sound absorption coefficient, (b) the specific acoustic resistance, (c) the specific acoustic reactance.

Below 150 Hz, the system resistance is less than half of that of the air, and the absolute value of sound reactance deviates from the zero point, which together leads to a lower value of the sound absorption coefficient in this frequency band. The peak of sound absorption occurs around 300 Hz, where the system resistance is close to 1 and the system reactance trends towards 0, as shown in Figure 3b,c.

The optimized total stiffness shown in Table 3 is relatively small. In this case, when the loudspeaker's suspension diaphragm stiffness is 900 N/m, a cubic cavity with a side length of 31.8 cm is required to provide the remaining stiffness. If the volume of the air cavity needs to be sufficiently reduced, the loudspeaker's suspension diaphragm stiffness must be set relatively low. Compared with Table 2, when the Bl becomes smaller, the total resistance and inductance are relatively reduced, and the required capacitance is increased.

4. Experiment of Optimal Sound Absorption for a Four-Parameter SL

Since there were no loudspeakers available that were specifically suitable for optimal sound absorption, a commercial loudspeaker was used for the experimental verification.

Thus, only four parameters of the SL, namely $\Delta R, \Delta L, C_e, \Delta K_m$, needed to be optimized. The experimental setup is shown in Figure 4 and a photograph of the setup is shown in Figure 5. The inside diameter of the impedance tube (SW422 (BSWA, Beijing, China)) was 100mm, and the noise signal generated by the computer was amplified by a power amplifier (PA50 (BSWA, Beijing, China)). When the loudspeaker is excited to emit a sound source, the end of the impedance tube uses a dual microphone (BSW416 (BSWA, Beijing, China)) to pick up the sound signal. The four-channel digital collector (MC3242 (BSWA, Beijing, China)) samples the signal and sends it to the computer for data processing. The loudspeaker (M4N (HiVi, Zhuhai, China)) was fixed at the end of the pipe by an air cavity equipped with a piston.

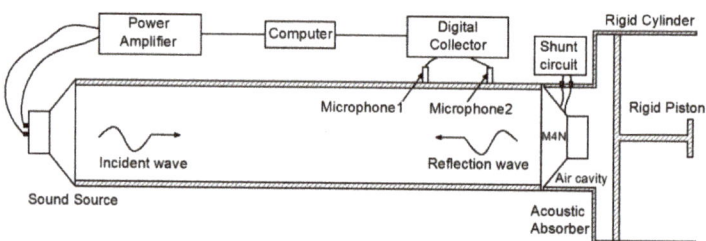

Figure 4. Experimental setup of the SL.

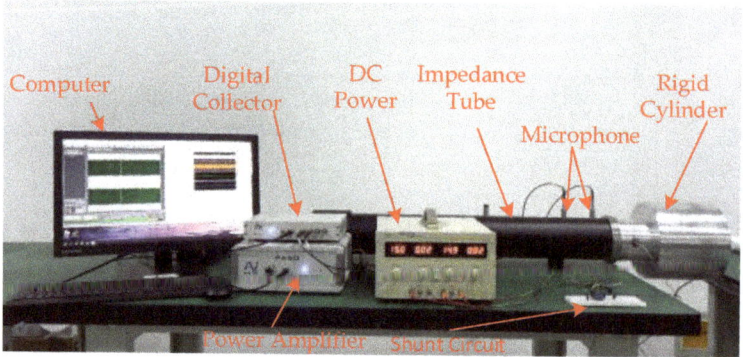

Figure 5. Photograph of the experimental setup.

For the accurate establishment of an SL absorption model, the exact mechanical and electrical parameters of the loudspeaker need to be known. Generally, the factory-calibrated parameters of the loudspeaker are accurate, but the actual parameters will change after it is assembled due to the coupling influence in the impedance. After assembly, the damping of the loudspeaker is nonlinear and difficult to predict accurately [22]. This will lead to a mismatch between the results of the theoretical predictions and the actual experiments, so, in our experiment, the actual damping was used in the calculation. The following describes how to experimentally determine the values of $\Delta\delta, \Delta K_m, M_m, R_c, L_c, BL$.

4.1. The Experiment of Parameter Determination

4.1.1. Determination of Mechanical Parameters

The loudspeaker was assembled at the end of the standing wave tube, in accordance with the open-circuit state. The cylinder piston was placed on the leftmost side. The resistance and reactance diagram is shown in Figure 6a,b. The theoretical equation of acoustic impedance is:

$$\begin{cases} \text{Im}[Z_m(\omega)] = j\omega M_m + \Delta K_m/j\omega & (10a) \\ \text{Re}[Z_m(\omega)] = \delta_m & (10b) \end{cases}$$

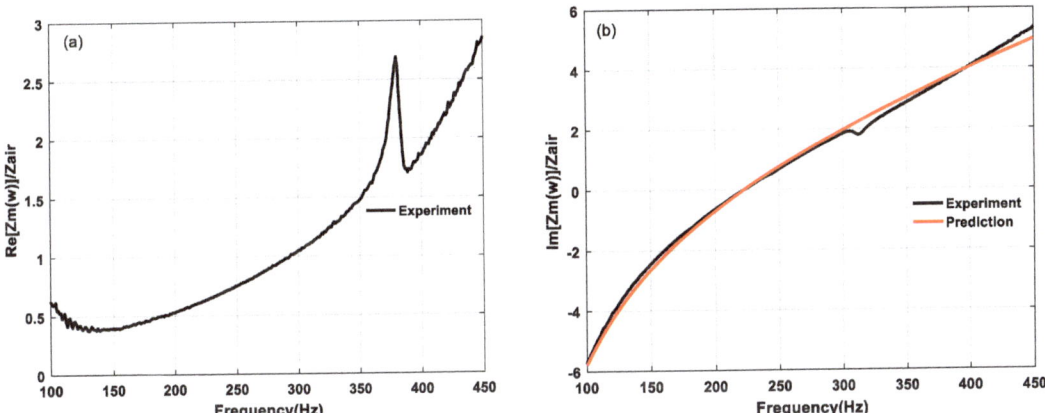

Figure 6. Experimental impedance of the open circuit: (a) the specific acoustic resistance; (b) the specific acoustic reactance.

As shown in Figure 6a, the actual resistance of the system was not a constant value, but a nonlinear function that is dependent on the frequency. There was a damping peak at 380 Hz, which was caused by the resonance of the mechanical system. According to Equation (10a), the reactance of the system was only related to the moving mass and stiffness. Therefore, the equivalent moving mass and stiffness can be calculated by fitting the measured acoustic reactance using the least squares method. The equivalent moving mass of the loudspeaker in this experiment was 7.5 g and the system stiffness was 14,724 N/m; therefore, the three mechanical parameters of the loudspeaker could be accurately determined.

4.1.2. Determination of Electrical Parameters

The coil resistance R_c can be measured directly using a Digital Multi-Meter. In contrast, the coil inductance L_c has a frequency-dependent nonlinearity, so its value as determined by multi-meter measurement would be inaccurate. L_c can be fitted under short-circuit states, and when the R_c, L_c, Bl are introduced, the system acoustic impedance can be expressed as:

$$Z_{short} = j\omega[M_m - \frac{(Bl)^2 L_c}{R_c^2 + \omega^2 L_c^2}] + [\delta_m + \frac{(Bl)^2 R_c}{R_c^2 + \omega^2 L_c^2}] + \frac{\Delta K_m}{j\omega} \quad (11)$$

First, according to the frequency at the resonance peak and the absorption coefficient, the Bl and the coil L_c can be counted out at the resonance frequency f_0, as shown in Equations (12) and (13).

$$f_0 = \sqrt{\frac{K_{sys}}{M_{sys}}}/2\pi = \sqrt{\frac{\Delta K_m}{M_m - \frac{(Bl)^2 \cdot L_c}{R_c^2 + \omega_0^2 L_c^2}}}/2\pi \quad (12)$$

$$\alpha_0 = 1 - \left|\frac{Z_{sys} - Z_0}{Z_{sys} + Z_0}\right|^2 = 1 - \left|\frac{j\omega_0(M_m - \frac{(Bl)^2 \cdot L_c}{R_c^2 + \omega_0^2 L_c^2}) + (\delta_m + \frac{(Bl)^2 \cdot R_c}{R_c^2 + \omega_0^2 L_c^2}) + \frac{\Delta K_m}{j\omega_0} - \rho_0 c_0 S}{j\omega_0(M_m - \frac{(Bl)^2 \cdot L_c}{R_c^2 + \omega_0^2 L_c^2}) + (\delta_m + \frac{(Bl)^2 \cdot R_c}{R_c^2 + \omega_0^2 L_c^2}) + \frac{\Delta K_m}{j\omega_0} + \rho_0 c_0 S}\right|^2 \quad (13)$$

The resistance measured from the three sets of experiments for the short circuit and the open circuit are shown in Figure 7. According to Equations (10b) and (11), the resistance difference between the short circuit and the open circuit is expressed as $(Bl)^2 R_e/(R_e^2 + \omega^2 L_e^2)$. For a small signal input, Bl can be regarded as a constant value. By using least squares method at each frequency, the theoretical value of L_c can be calculated. The calculated Bl was 4 Tm, and L_c was 0.68 mH. The actual parameters of the loudspeaker were all obtained. In Figure 8, the theoretical calculation results and the actual sound absorption results are shown to match better in the short-circuit state, which verifies the parameters obtained.

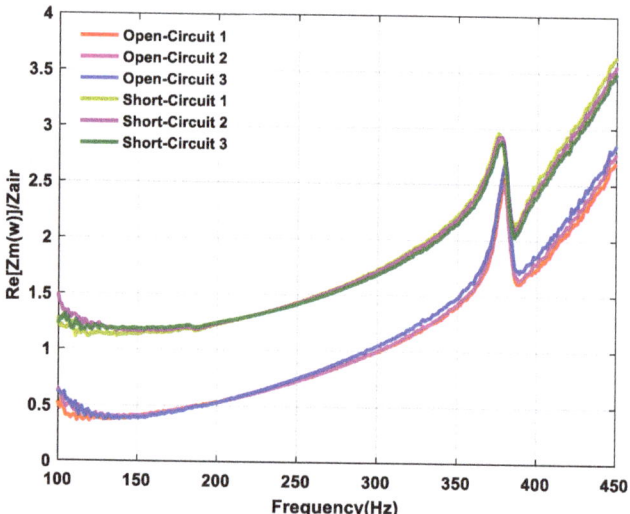

Figure 7. Short-circuit and open-circuit resistance comparison.

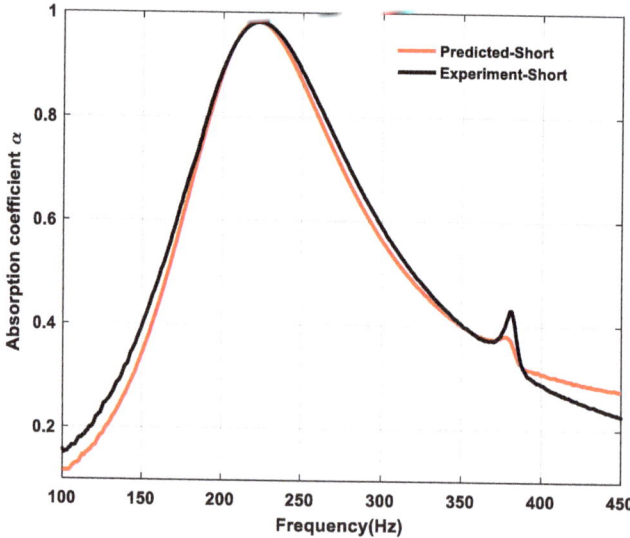

Figure 8. Short-circuit absorption coefficient comparison.

4.2. Experimental Results

The resistance obtained from the experiments in the open-circuit state was sampled and used in the optimization program as the actual damping. M_m and Bl obtained in the previous section were taken as fixed parameters. The optimization procedure thus becomes EBA about $\Delta R, \Delta L, C_e, \Delta K_m$. The upper bound settings, step size settings and optimal parameters are shown in Table 4.

Table 4. Parameter upper bounds and step size settings.

Parameter	Upper Bound	Step Size	Optimal
ΔR	25 Ω	0.1 Ω	1.6 Ω
ΔL	5 mH	50 μH	1.6 mH
C_e	5 mF	50 μF	0.4 mF
ΔK_m	1.8×10^4 N/m	360 N/m	11,880 N/m

The experimental balance resistance R_b is 1 Ω, and the selected operational amplifier is OPA552 – PA with a ±15 V power supply. The experimental and theoretical predictions were in good agreement in the overall frequency band. As shown in Figure 9a, in the target frequency band, the average absorption coefficient was 0.65, and the overall absorption coefficient was improved compared with the short-circuit condition. However, due to the larger M_m and Bl of the loudspeaker, the SL was less adjustable. Compared with the open-circuit case in Figure 6b, the total reactance of the SL shown in Figure 9c was significantly lower over a wide frequency band, especially in the 150–300 Hz band, where it trended toward zero, which allowed the reactance to better meet the matching conditions. As shown in Figure 9b, the resistance below 450 Hz was much larger than the air acoustic resistance, so the SL over-damping limited further improvement of the sound absorption level.

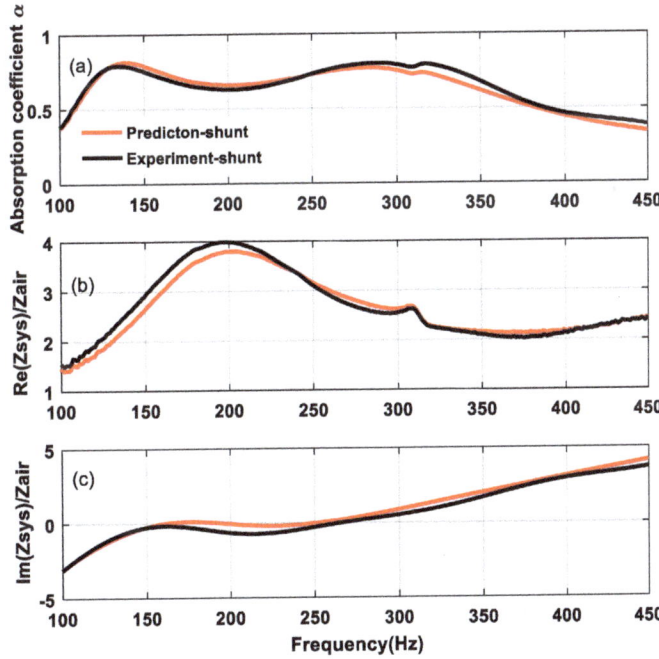

Figure 9. Comparison of the four–dimensional EBA simulation and measurement: (**a**) the sound absorption coefficient, (**b**) the specific acoustic resistance, (**c**) the specific acoustic reactance.

4.3. Discussion

The experimental results of the four–parameter optimization showed that loudspeakers on the market have large values of moving mass and force factor, which limit the sound absorption performance improvement of the SL. The EBA optimization simulation indicated that a loudspeaker suitable for sound absorption should be characterized by small moving mass and force parameters. This would facilitate the miniaturization and design of a lightweight SL, as well as allowing for innovation in the loudspeaker structure. As shown in Equations (6) and (7), the introduction of the shunt circuit inevitably increases the acoustic resistance, while reducing the system acoustic reactance. Since excessive damping is a disadvantage for sound absorption, designing a loudspeaker with small amounts of linear damping should be the focus of future research. In addition, designing a large-area SL for diffuse field sound absorption would also be worth studying.

5. Conclusions

In order to obtain excellent sound absorption in the frequency range of 100–450 Hz, a fully exhaustive backtracking algorithm was proposed for optimizing the loudspeaker and shunt circuit parameters. For a given loudspeaker, the experimental method to determine its parameters was provided, and the optimal sound absorption algorithm under four parameters was verified by measurement. Through multiple-parameter optimization, it was found that the force factor and moving mass can be sufficiently reduced in comparison with that of a typical four-inch loudspeaker available on the market. The results imply that if an air cavity is properly sized, the SL can be redesigned to achieve good sound absorption, while also significantly reducing the weight and volume of the loudspeaker.

Author Contributions: Conceptualization, Z.L. and B.L.; Methodology, Data curation and Investigation, Z.L.; Validation and Software, Z.L. and X.L.; Resources and Supervision, B.L.; Writing—Original Draft Preparation, Z.L.; Writing—Review and Editing, Z.L. and X.L. All authors have read and agreed to the published version of the manuscript.

Funding: Financial support was given by NSFC through Grant No. 11874034, as well as the Taishan Scholar Program of Shandong (No.ts201712054). Both are highly appreciated.

Institutional Review Board Statement: Not applicable.

Informed Consent Statement: Not applicable.

Data Availability Statement: The data presented in this study are available on request from the corresponding author.

Conflicts of Interest: The authors declare no conflict of interest.

References

1. Černík, M.; Mokry, P. Sound reflection in an acoustic impedance tube terminated with a loudspeaker shunted by a negative impedance converter. *Smart Mater. Struct.* **2012**, *21*, 115016. [CrossRef]
2. Forward, R.L. Electronic damping of vibrations in optical structures. *Appl. Opt.* **1979**, *18*, 690–697. [CrossRef] [PubMed]
3. Lissek, H.; Meynial, X. A preliminary study of an isodynamic transducer for use in active acoustic materials. *Appl. Acoust.* **2003**, *64*, 917–930. [CrossRef]
4. Lissek, H.; Boulandet, R. Pierre-Jean René. Shunt loudspeakers for modal control in rooms. In Proceedings of the 16th International Congress on Sound and Vibration (ICSV), Krakow, Poland, 5–9 July 2009.
5. Boulandet, R.; Lissek, H. Optimization of electroacoustic absorbers by means of designed experiments. *Appl. Acoust.* **2010**, *71*, 830–842. [CrossRef]
6. Lissek, H.; Boulandet, R.; Fleury, R. Electroacoustic absorbers: Bridging the gap between shunt loudspeakers and active sound absorption. *J. Acoust. Soc. Am.* **2011**, *129*, 2968. [CrossRef] [PubMed]
7. Tao, J.; Jiao, Q.; Qiu, X. A composite sound absorber with micro-perforated panel and shunted loudspeaker. *Proc. Meet. Acoust.* **2013**, *19*, 015068.
8. Jing, R.; Tao, J.; Qiu, X. Sound absorption of a finite micro-perforated panel backed by a shunted loudspeaker. *J. Acoust. Soc. Am.* **2014**, *135*, 231.
9. Zhang, Y.; Chan, Y.J.; Huang, L. Thin broadband noise absorption through acoustic reactance control by electro-mechanical coupling without sensor. *J. Acoust. Soc. Am.* **2014**, *135*, 2738–2745. [CrossRef] [PubMed]

10. Cong, C.; Tao, J.; Qiu, X. A Multi-Tone Sound Absorber Based on an Array of Shunted Loudspeakers. *Appl. Sci.* **2018**, *8*, 2484. [CrossRef]
11. Rivet, E.; Boulandet, R.; Lissek, H. Optimization of electroacoustic resonators for semi-active room equalization in the low-frequency range. *J. Acoust. Soc. Am.* **2013**, *133*, 3348. [CrossRef]
12. Liu, W.; Mao, Q. Design of shunt loudspeaker by pole configuration method. *Vib. Shock* **2018**, *37*, 97–101.
13. Zhang, Y.; Wang, C.; Huang, L. Tuning of the acoustic impedance of a shunted electro-mechanical diaphragm for a broadband sound absorber. *Mech. Syst. Signal Process.* **2019**, *126*, 536–552. [CrossRef]
14. Zhang, P.; Cong, C.; Tao, J.; Qiu, X. Dual frequency sound absorption with an array of shunt loudspeakers. *Sci. Rep.* **2020**, *10*, 10806. [CrossRef] [PubMed]
15. Sun, Y.; Feng, N. The application of exhaustive method in programming. *Comput. Age* **2012**, *8*, 50–52.
16. Zhang, T.; Zhang, F.; Sheng, J. Study of Exhaustive Algorithm for the Unit Commitment Optimization. *J. Qingdao Univ. Technol.* **2011**, *32*, 87–92.
17. Pei, N.; Bi, C. Application of Backtracking Method in Computer Programming. *Comput. Knowl. Technol.* **2017**, *13*, 262–264.
18. Yang, H.; Lin, H. Summarization of Optimizations of Genetic Algorithm and Simulated Annealing Algorithm. *Mach. Build. Autom.* **2010**, 73–75.
19. Li, Y.; Yuan, H.; Yu, J.; Zhang, G.; Liu, K. A review on the application of genetic algorithm in optimization problems. *Shandong Ind. Technol.* **2019**, *290*, 242–245.
20. Zhu, Y.; Zhong, Y. A Kind of Renewed Simulated Annealing Algorithm. *Comput. Technol. Dev.* **2009**, *19*, 32–35.
21. Eargle, J. *Loudspeaker Handbook*, 2nd ed.; Kluwer Academic: Boston, MA, USA, 2003; Chapters 1–4; pp. 1–63.
22. Zhang, Y. Dynamic Mass Modification by Electric Circuits. Master's Thesis, University of Hong Kong, Pokfulam, Hong Kong, 2012.
23. Yu, C. Negative impedance converter and its application in circuit experiments. *Teach. Electr. Courses High. Educ.* **1982**, 54–57.
24. Zhang, Y.; Chan, Y.; Huang, L. Low-frequency noise absorption by a shunted loudspeaker. In Proceedings of the 20th International Congress on Sound and Vibration (ICSV), Bangkok, Thailand, 7–11 July 2013.

Article

Acoustic Characterization of Some Steel Industry Waste Materials

Elisa Levi *, Simona Sgarbi and Edoardo Alessio Piana

Department of Industrial and Mechanical Engineering, University of Brescia, via Branze 38, 25123 Brescia, Italy; s.sgarbi001@studenti.unibs.it (S.S.); edoardo.piana@unibs.it (E.A.P.)
* Correspondence: elisa.levi@unibs.it; Tel.: +39-0303715571

Abstract: From a circular economy perspective, the acoustic characterization of steelwork by-products is a topic worth investigating, especially because little or no literature can be found on this subject. The possibility to reuse and add value to a large amount of this kind of waste material can lead to significant economic and environmental benefits. Once properly analyzed and optimized, these by-products can become a valuable alternative to conventional materials for noise control applications. The main acoustic properties of these materials can be investigated by means of a four-microphone impedance tube. Through an inverse technique, it is then possible to derive some non-acoustic properties of interest, useful to physically characterize the structure of the materials. The inverse method adopted in this paper is founded on the Johnson–Champoux–Allard model and uses a standard minimization procedure based on the difference between the sound absorption coefficients obtained experimentally and predicted by the Johnson–Champoux–Allard model. The results obtained are consistent with other literature data for similar materials. The knowledge of the physical parameters retrieved applying this technique (porosity, airflow resistivity, tortuosity, viscous and thermal characteristic length) is fundamental for the acoustic optimization of the porous materials in the case of future applications.

Keywords: steel industry by-products; circular economy; sound absorption; sound reduction index; granular materials; inverse method

1. Introduction

The steel industry is one of the main global economic sectors providing raw materials for a wide variety of manufacturing processes. During the various activities, a steel plant produces large amounts of waste under different forms. In recent decades, this type of industry is also trying to gradually leave the linear economy model and aim for the global and ambitious "zero waste" target [1], focusing its efforts on the development of innovative and sustainable production schemes. The emerging principle of the circular economy supports the reuse and recycling of industrial by-products, creating a symbiosis [2] which encourages collaboration and synergy with different sectors. The final goal is to develop new business opportunities through the conversion of waste into valuable raw materials or secondary materials exploitable in other sectors [3]. These activities allow the steel industry to reduce its environmental impacts: indeed, the reduction in waste materials can be ensured by providing an alternative solution to safe and environmentally friendly disposal of polluting industrial wastes and by avoiding the extraction of new natural resources. In this way, it is possible to achieve both environmental and economic benefits for all the industries involved in the symbiosis.

The main waste product of the steel industry is represented by slags. There are different types of slag, depending on the type of furnaces, raw materials and process adopted during production. The slag deriving from melting the scrap iron by an electric arc furnace (EAF—Figure 1a) is generically defined as "black slag". Such a type of waste material results from the oxidation of the scrap and includes impurities and compounds generated by the additives used to control the chemical processes. These elements form a layer that floats on top of the molten steel in the furnace, insulating the liquid part from the external environment and helping maintain the temperature inside the furnace at the right set-point. At the end of the process, the floating layer is collected and cooled down, resulting in "black slag". The melted steel is then processed and refined in a ladle furnace (LF—Figure 1b). The slag deriving from this process is defined as "white dross", or "white slag", and has completely different chemical and physical properties if compared to the black slag.

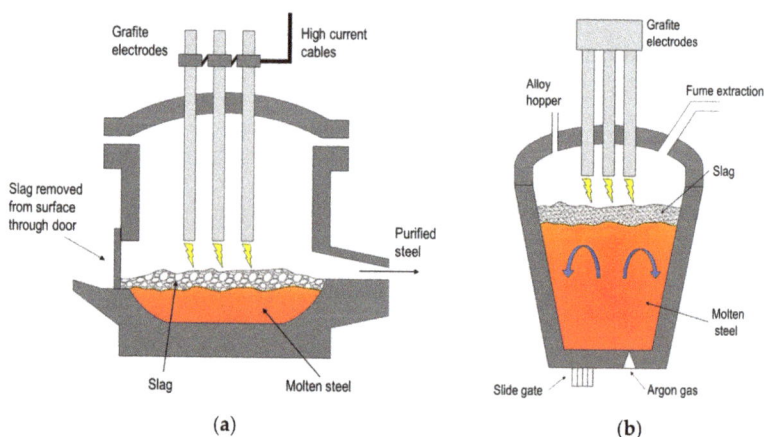

Figure 1. Schematic drawings of EAF and LF furnaces: (**a**) EAF furnace; and (**b**) ladle furnace.

The two slag types are kept separate as they have a different chemical composition and must be treated differently. Black slag can be assimilated to natural effusive rocks of volcanic origin, takes on granular characteristics and mainly consists of a ternary mixture of calcium oxide (CaO), silicon dioxide (SiO_2) and iron oxides (FeO), to which heavy metals and other components, in percentages, are mixed. The white dross chemically differs from the black slag, particularly for the content in iron oxides and calcium; therefore, this dross, after cooling, undergoes a transformation of the crystalline lattice which leads to the formation of a fine and lightweight material.

Some studies are actually investigating the physical properties and the environmental compatibility of these materials, to establish the environmental impact of the slags and how to treat them. Depending on the application field, several studies have been carried out to characterize steel slags. One of the first practical applications of steel slags outside the steel production cycle is as sustainable (alternative) aggregates in pavement layers for road construction. They have been used not only for unbound layers, like road bases and sub-bases, but also for bituminous mixtures in surface layers [4]. In [5], the EAF steel slag was preliminarily investigated from chemical, leaching, physical and mechanical points of view. The bituminous conglomerates have also been characterized to verify their potential application in high performance asphalt concretes for road and airport pavements. The comparison with the corresponding traditional natural aggregates shows that using slags as coarse under-pavement material brings both technical and environmental advantages [5,6]: the mixtures with EAF slag improve the mechanical properties and prevent the depletion of raw materials.

Several studies also investigated the suitability of steel slags for civil engineering applications in cement-based materials. In particular, they were used for replacing natural sand [7] in the production of concrete [8–13], as armor stones for hydraulic engineering constructions [14,15] (during the restoration of marine environments and stabilization of shores), and finally, as an agricultural fertilizer. In [2], steel slags were investigated as to help in the removal of harmful elements and wastewater treatment. More recently, slags have been used as green resource in ceramic tile production and for biomedical applications.

The development of innovative sustainable solutions, by means of already existing or new technologies, is a goal that the steel industry is willing to pursue in order to further reduce its environmental impacts. Recently, some critical environmental aspects emerged regarding the use of steel slags [2,14]. The concerns are about volume instability and leaching behavior, the latter being a crucial aspect for environmental considerations, especially in terms of possible water and soil pollution caused by the release of heavy metals. Such aspects must be deeply investigated and solved, depending on the characteristics of the specific chemical composition of the recycled slag and the exposure to atmospheric elements.

The study reported in [16] aimed to find an inertization process for the recovery of steelwork slags and granite cutting waste as raw materials for the production of rockwool, which is a good thermal insulator and acoustic absorber for the construction and automotive sectors. It was found that the partial replacement of traditional raw materials does not influence the thermal insulation and fireproof properties of rockwool.

In [17,18], a recent improvement consisting of a new production method was introduced: high-pressure cold air is passed through the molten slag and the result is a material consisting of slag granules characterized by an almost spherical shape. The studies provide a comprehensive experimental characterization, in terms of fundamental and durability properties. The outcomes of both studies confirmed that a fine aggregate of spheric slags is a promising and advantageous alternative to natural sand in concrete pavement, also in terms of workability, water content and cement mechanical requirements.

Granular materials are emerging as an interesting alternative to the more popular and conventional sound absorbers. This trend is also encouraged by the large amount of industrial waste or by-products available in granular shape. If properly treated, these materials could become a valuable "second raw" resource, instead of using them as waste material for landfill, with all the related costs in terms of money and environmental impact. In this way, these materials can re-enter the production cycle and can be addressed in different application fields. Of course, this depends on how much their properties and potentialities are investigated and optimized. In this perspective, the steel industry is continuing its path towards the "zero waste" and circular economy goals by funding studies on the waste reuse and sustainable recycling and developing new technological solutions in an effort to find new fields of application. For instance, the traditional mineral wool production process can be applied to steelwork slag: by means of spin dryers and a high-speed air flow, the white dross molten slag forms long fibers and a sort of wool that could represent a partial or complete substitute to the traditional rockwool.

This paper aims to analyze the acoustic behavior of some steelwork waste materials. In particular, slags shaped as wool, granules and spheres. As previously mentioned, the literature describes many studies focused on the investigation of the chemical, mechanical and thermal properties of steelwork slags, focusing on their reuse for various outcomes, especially when combined with other materials and mixtures, such as cement, concrete and soils. The novelty of the present study lies in the fact that, to the knowledge of the authors, steelwork slags have never been acoustically characterized before, especially in the form of wool, granules or spheres. It can be highlighted that the process adopted to obtain the spheres is relatively recent. Once the acoustic properties of these waste slags are obtained, the aim is to evaluate and optimize them as a function of the specific noise control application at hand modifying their non-acoustical parameters. Their acoustic characterization will be performed by means of a four-microphone impedance tube. This technique allows one to obtain the complex acoustical properties of the tested samples. This study will mainly be focused on the sound absorption properties of the slags. However, the sound transmission loss (TL) will also be reported for the sake of completeness and because it is included in the acoustic properties retrieved from the four-microphone impedance tube method. Finally, the Johnson–Champoux–Allard (JCA) model will be employed to better understand the relations between the acoustic behavior and the microstructure of the investigated materials. In particular, this theoretical model was based on the knowledge of five intrinsic properties of the material. Such properties are usually determined using specific laboratory equipment. In order to have a rough estimation of these parameters, a well-established inverse characterization method was applied to find the main non-acoustic characteristics of the materials.

The paper is organized as follows: Section 2 describes the samples analyzed and the experimental set up, including the laboratory equipment, providing the methodology for the experimental and analytical investigation; in Section 3, the experimentally obtained results are reported and discussed, including the comparison with the predicted results; finally, Section 4 draws the conclusions and highlights future research directions/perspectives.

2. Materials and Methods

2.1. Porous Materials

Porous materials are the most used sound-absorbing materials in many engineering and industrial applications. The Biot theory [19] describes how acoustic and elastic waves propagate and dissipate energy inside a porous medium characterized by air-saturated open-cell structures. When excited by a sound wave, the solid skeleton of the material can be considered as acoustically rigid (i.e., motionless) over a wide frequency range. Consequently, the compression and shear waves in the solid phase can be neglected. Thus, only a compression wave is able to propagate in the fluid phase and the porous material can be assumed to behave like an equivalent fluid. The absorption mechanism is possible thanks to the structure of the porous medium: it is made by a large number of small pores that are interconnected with each other and with the external air, thus allowing the sound wave to enter and propagate within the cavities. During the propagation process, the viscosity of air in the pores causes viscous losses. The conversion of sound energy in internal energy and the subsequent dissipation caused by the viscosity of air enables obtaining a certain sound absorption [20].

Recently, increasing interest has emerged in granular porous materials [20–24], considered to be a promising alternative to the more traditional fibrous or foam sound absorbers, thanks to their advantage of merging a good sound absorption with interesting mechanical properties and low production costs [25,26].

Granular materials are made of assemblies of particles that can have the same or different shape and diameter. The grains, that can be hollow, porous or solid, represent the rigid frame of the medium while the fluid (i.e., air), saturating the interconnected cavities, can be assumed as an equivalent homogeneous fluid, characterized by two effective (or equivalent) properties: the equivalent dynamic density ρ_{eq} and equivalent dynamic bulk modulus K_{eq}. At the macroscopic level, the viscous and thermal losses that occur in porous media and are responsible of the energy sound dissipation, can be related to the so-called transport (or non-acoustic or macroscopic) parameters: depending on the model chosen to characterize the acoustic performance of the investigated materials, these parameters differ in number and type. The appropriate knowledge of the relationships relating the acoustic behavior to the microstructure is of importance to customize the material for specific target frequencies. As effectively summarized and described in [27,28], these models can be mainly sorted into empirical, phenomenological, and semi-phenomenological/microstructural models. The Delany-Bazley model [29], designed for fibrous and cellular materials and based on airflow resistivity as relevant parameter, and the Miki model [30], which improved the previous one with the inclusion of two additional non-acoustic parameters, porosity and tortuosity, belong to the first group. The Voronina–Horoshenkov model [31], suitable for loose granular materials, is of empirical type as well, and considers the characteristic particle dimension and specific density of the grain base in addition to porosity and tortuosity. In [32], the authors assumed that pore geometry and pore size distribution obey an approximately statistical distribution. The Hamet–Berengier [33] and Attenborough [34] models are located in the phenomenological group: the first results useful for porous pavements, the latter for fibrous and granular materials and is based on five parameters (airflow resistivity, porosity, tortuosity, steady flow shape factor and dynamic shape factor). The Johnson–Champoux–Allard [35,36] and the Champoux–Stinson [37] models fall into the semi-phenomenological/microstructural group and involve five non-acoustic parameters: porosity, airflow resistivity and tortuosity are common to both, whereas the JCA model uses thermal and viscous characteristic lengths, and the Champoux–Stinson model considers viscous and thermal shape factors.

Subsequent implementations of the JCA model, such as the six-parameter Johnson–Champoux–Allard–Lafarge (JCAL) model or the eight-parameter model of Johnson–Champoux –Allard–Pride–Lafarge (JCAPL), involve more parameter, such as viscous and thermal tortuosities and permeabilities. Compared to the JCA model, they provide more precision at low frequencies [38]. In general, the more sophisticated models require more parameters and have better performances. Nevertheless, as a counterpart, they are more complex and demanding. All the aforementioned models require physical techniques to measure the non-acoustic parameters. Some of them involve expensive set-ups and even complex or destructive tests. Recently, multiscale analyses have been developed to compute non-acoustic parameters by means of numerical simulations at the microstructural level [21,22]. The multiscale approach, which establishes micro–macro relationships, bypasses the difficulty of direct measurements by developing specific finite-element analyses.

Each model has its application field, related to the type of material its development is based on, and respective limitations and advantages. More details about these aspects and model comparisons can be found in [21,22,25,27,28,39–41].

In this work, the five-parameter JCA model, better described in Section 2.2, was selected to perform the investigation: it is one of the most known generalized models, suitable for the accurate description of the wide-band sound propagation in porous materials. It is a robust model as it is applicable to the random geometry of porous materials, it allows rapid calculation and the five parameters, having a physical meaning, and can be directly measured by experiments. The JCA model, coupled with the four-microphone impedance tube and inversion methods, results to be a well-established and fast technique to investigate the intrinsic properties of a material, thus being a valuable alternative whenever direct measurements are not available.

2.2. JCA Model and Inverse Method

The JCA model assumes that rigid-frame open-cell porous media can be seen as an equivalent fluid of effective, or equivalent, dynamic density ρ_{eq} and equivalent dynamic bulk modulus K_{eq}. These equivalent properties depend on five transport (or macroscopic–non-acoustic) parameters: open porosity Φ; static airflow resistivity σ; tortuosity α_∞; viscous characteristic length Λ; and thermal characteristic length Λ'. These parameters are referred to the geometry of the porous material and describe the complexity of the porous network.

By definition, open porosity Φ is a measure of the volume fraction of air (V_{fluid}) in the total volume (V_{tot}) or the complement to unit of the ratio between the solid volume of the frame (V_{solid}) on the total volume [42]:

$$\Phi = \frac{V_{fluid}}{V_{tot}} = 1 - \frac{V_{solid}}{V_{tot}} \tag{1}$$

Airflow resistivity expresses the resistance opposed to the airflow while passing through the material. It can be calculated as [42]

$$\sigma = \frac{\Delta p}{v_{airflow} d} \quad \left[\text{Ns/m}^4\right] \tag{2}$$

with Δp as the pressure drop across the medium, $v_{airflow}$ the amount of airflow passing through the material and d its thickness.

Tortuosity α_∞ is an intrinsic property of the porous frame, related to the microgeometry of the interlinked cavities. It is a dimensionless quantity that expresses the tortuous fluid paths through the porous material. It can be calculated as [42]

$$\alpha_\infty = \frac{1}{V}\int_V v^2\, dV \bigg/ \left|\frac{1}{V}\int_V v\, dV\right|^2 \qquad (3)$$

where v is the microscopic velocity of an ideal inviscid fluid within the pores and V a homogenization volume that expresses the volume of free fluid contained in the cavities. Tortuosity cannot be lower than 1.

Viscous characteristic length Λ is used to describe the viscous forces generating within the cavities at high frequencies and is related to the characteristic dimension of the connection between pores—particularly to the mean diameter of the hole connecting two adjacent cells, expressed in micrometers. It is given by [42]

$$\Lambda = 2\int_V |v|^2 dV \bigg/ \int_S |v|^2 dS \quad [\mu m] \qquad (4)$$

where S is the specific surface that denotes the total contact surface between the frame and the pores.

Thermal characteristic length Λ' describes the thermal exchanges between the solid frame and its saturating fluid at high frequencies and it is related to the pores dimension, especially to the mean diameter of the cell in micrometers; it can be expressed as [42,43]:

$$\Lambda' = 2\int_V dV \bigg/ \int_S dS = 2V/S \quad [\mu m] \qquad (5)$$

Alternatively, Λ and Λ' can be calculated in function of the above-described parameters, as follows [38]:

$$\Lambda = \frac{1}{c_1}\left[\frac{8\alpha_\infty \eta}{\sigma \Phi}\right]^{1/2} \qquad (6)$$

$$\Lambda' = \frac{1}{c_2}\left[\frac{8\alpha_\infty \eta}{\sigma \Phi}\right]^{1/2} \qquad (7)$$

where η is the viscosity of air, c_1 and c_2 are pore shape parameters, related, respectively, to the viscous and thermal dissipation, and they can assume values in the following ranges:

$$0.3 \leq c_1 \leq 3.3 \qquad (8)$$

$$0.3 \leq c_2 \leq c_1 \qquad (9)$$

In the case of the granular material shaped in spheres, the calculation of the macroscopic parameters can be simplified in function of the porosity Φ and particle radius r as follows [21,23]:

$$\sigma = \frac{45(1-\Phi)(1-\theta)\eta}{2\Phi^2 r^2 \left(5 - 9\theta^{1/3} + 5\theta - \theta^2\right)} \qquad (10)$$

$$\alpha_\infty = 1 + \frac{1-\Phi}{2\Phi} \qquad (11)$$

$$\Lambda = \frac{4(1-\theta)\Phi \alpha_\infty}{9(1-\Phi)} r \qquad (12)$$

$$\Lambda' = \frac{d}{3}\left(\frac{\Phi}{1-\Phi}\right) \qquad (13)$$

where θ is expressed as

$$\theta = \frac{3(1-\Phi)}{\pi 2^{1/2}} \qquad (14)$$

The purpose of the model is to finally obtain the acoustic behavior of the analyzed material, so the procedure to compute the sound absorption coefficient is made with the following steps:

- Once the five non-acoustic parameters (Φ, σ, α_∞, Λ, Λ') are obtained with one of the methods described below, it is possible to calculate the effective quantities ρ_{eq} and K_{eq};
- From the equivalent properties, one can predict the acoustic parameters: characteristic impedance Z_c and complex wave number k_c;
- From Z_c and k_c, the surface impedance Z_s can be deduced;
- Finally, from Z_s the normal incident sound absorption coefficient α can be calculated.

Starting from the five non-acoustic parameters, the equivalent properties ρ_{eq} and K_{eq} can be computed as follows:

$$\rho_{eq} = \frac{\alpha_\infty \rho_0}{\Phi} + \frac{\sigma}{i\omega}\left(1 + \frac{4i\alpha_\infty^2 \eta \rho_0 \omega}{\sigma^2 \Lambda^2 \Phi^2}\right)^{1/2} \quad [\text{kg/m}^3] \tag{15}$$

$$K_{eq} = \frac{\kappa P_0/\Phi}{\kappa - (\kappa - 1)\left[1 + \frac{8\eta}{i\rho_0 \omega N_p \Lambda'^2}\left(1 + \frac{i\rho_0 \omega N_p \Lambda'^2}{16\eta}\right)^{1/2}\right]^{-1}} \quad [\text{kg/ms}^2] \tag{16}$$

where ρ_0 is the density of air, $\omega = 2\pi f$ is the angular frequency, η is the air viscosity, κ is the specific heat ratio and N_p is Prandtl number of the saturating air.

Once the effective properties are obtained, it is possible to determine the complex acoustical parameters [44]; the characteristic impedance Z_c:

$$Z_c = (\rho_{eq} Z_{eq})^{1/2} \quad [\text{Ns/m}^3] \tag{17}$$

and the complex wave number k_c:

$$k_c = \omega (\rho_{eq}/Z_{eq})^{1/2} \quad [\text{m}^{-1}] \tag{18}$$

From these acoustic properties, the surface impedance Z_s can be derived as follows:

$$Z_s = Z_c \cdot \cot(k_c d) \quad [\text{m}^{-1}] \tag{19}$$

Finally, the normal incidence sound absorption coefficient α is calculated as

$$\alpha = \frac{4Re\{Z_s\}\rho_0 c_0}{|Z_s|^2 + 2\rho_0 c_0 Re\{Z_s\} + (\rho_0 c_0)^2} \quad \text{or} \quad \alpha = 1 - \left|\frac{Z_s - \rho_0 c_0}{Z_s + \rho_0 c_0}\right|^2 \tag{20}$$

where c_0 is the speed of sound in air.

Classical methods to estimate the non-acoustic properties can be mainly classified in three groups [45]:

1. Direct methods, which allow obtaining the macroscopic parameters through direct measurements, thus requiring specific laboratory equipment or a dedicated setup for the determination of each single property;
2. Indirect methods, based on an acoustic model providing the relations and formulas that link the non-acoustic parameters to the acoustic measurements;
3. Inverse methods, consisting of an optimization problem where, once the difference between the experimentally measured and analytically estimated acoustic performances is minimized, the non-acoustic properties are progressively refined to an optimum value.

Indirect and inverse methods are based on impedance tube measurements or ultrasound measurements. The indirect method uses the equivalent properties, ρ_{eq} and K_{eq}, obtained from measured Z_c and k_c values by using an impedance tube, and combine (17) with (18) as follows [45]:

$$\rho_{eq} = \frac{Z_c k_c}{\omega} \quad \text{and} \quad K_{eq} = \frac{Z_c \omega}{k_c} \tag{21}$$

At this point, it is possible to extract non-acoustic parameters from the limit behavior of the effective properties [44]:

$$\Phi = \frac{\rho_0 \alpha_\infty}{\left(\lim_{\omega \to \infty} Re\{\rho_{eq}\}\right)} \tag{22}$$

$$\sigma = -\lim_{\omega \to 0} \left[Im\{\rho_{eq}\}\omega\right] \tag{23}$$

$$\alpha_\infty = \left\{ \lim_{\omega^{-1/2} \to 0} (c/c_0) \right\}^{-2} \tag{24}$$

$$\Lambda = \lim_{\omega \to \infty} \left(\alpha_\infty \left(\frac{2\rho_0 \eta}{\omega \Phi Im\{\rho_{eq}\}(\rho_0 \alpha_\infty - \Phi Re\{\rho_{eq}\})} \right)^{1/2} \right) \tag{25}$$

$$\Lambda' = \left[\frac{(N_P)^{1/2}}{\kappa - 1} \left(\lim_{\omega \to \infty} \left\{ \frac{Re\{k_c c\}}{Im\{k_c c\}} \left(\frac{2\eta}{\omega \rho_0} \right)^{1/2} \right\} - \frac{1}{\Lambda} \right) \right]^{-1} \tag{26}$$

where c is the speed of sound within the material.

Alternatively, in [45], a straightforward procedure is proposed where, in addition to the effective properties ρ_{eq} and K_{eq}, the direct measurement of the open porosity Φ is necessary. In this case, the analytical solutions suitable to obtain the macroscopic parameters starting from the effective properties are reported below [45,46]:

$$\sigma = -\frac{1}{\Phi} \lim_{\omega \to 0} \left[Im\{\rho_{eq}\omega\}\right] \tag{27}$$

$$\alpha_\infty = \frac{1}{\rho_0} \left[Re\{\rho_{eq}\} - \left(Im\{\rho_{eq}\}^2 - \left(\frac{\sigma \Phi}{\omega}\right)^2 \right)^{1/2} \right] \tag{28}$$

$$\Lambda = \alpha_\infty \left[\frac{2\rho_0 \eta}{\omega Im\{\rho_{eq}\}(\rho_0 \alpha_\infty - Re\{\rho_{eq}\})} \right]^{1/2} \tag{29}$$

$$\Lambda' = \left(\frac{2\eta}{\rho_0 \omega} \right)^{1/2} \left[2 \left(-Im\left\{ \left(\frac{1 - K_{eq}/K_a}{1 - \kappa K_{eq}/K_a} \right)^2 \right\} \right)^{-1} \right]^{-1/2} \tag{30}$$

where $K_a = \kappa P_0/\Phi$, with P_0 static pressure, is the equivalent adiabatic bulk modulus of the equivalent fluid.

Inverse methods generally need a surface acoustic property to start with, such as the sound absorption coefficient or surface impedance, both obtained from impedance tube measurements. The optimization process is based on the fact that the unknown parameters (in this paper, the five non-acoustic parameters) are adjusted so that the estimated surface acoustic property is as close as possible to the one experimentally obtained. The objective function is designed as a cost function where small values mean close agreement.

There are different optimizing methods: for instance, the group of global optimization techniques includes the simulated annealing [20], based on Monte Carlo iteration, and the class of evolutionary algorithms, such as genetic algorithms [42,44] and differential evolution algorithms [38]; moreover, there are standard minimization procedures, such as nonlinear best-fit [42,47], which is a direct search method that requires an initial trial guess of the parameters and operates within a research domain set on the lower and upper bound constraints for all the variables.

2.3. Experimental Characterization—Four-Microphone Impedance Tube

In this paragraph, the experimental set-up used for the characterization of the samples is described. The measurements of the acoustic properties have been performed by means of the four-microphone impedance tube method, following the process given by the ASTM E2611 standard [48]. On one end of the apparatus features, a loudspeaker generates a plane wave field inside the tube. The other end can be configured with two different types of termination (anechoic and/or reflecting), to perform the investigation with two different boundary conditions. Two microphones are mounted in front of the sample, at the "emitting side" of the tube, and the other two microphones are placed close to the sample at the "receiving side" of the tube.

A transfer matrix approach can be used, allowing to relate the particle velocities (u_i) and the sound pressures (p_i) at both surfaces of the tested sample. Denoting the front surface of the sample with the coordinate $x = 0$ and the back surface with $x = d$, the resulting transfer matrix can be written as

$$\begin{bmatrix} p_0 \\ u_0 \end{bmatrix} = \begin{bmatrix} T_{11} & T_{12} \\ T_{21} & T_{22} \end{bmatrix} \begin{bmatrix} p_d \\ u_d \end{bmatrix} \tag{31}$$

Thanks to the comparison between the signals measured by the four microphones, it is possible to apply the decomposition technique: referring to Figure 2, the upstream and downstream sound field can be distinguished in two forward travelling waves (A and C) and two backward travelling waves (B and D).

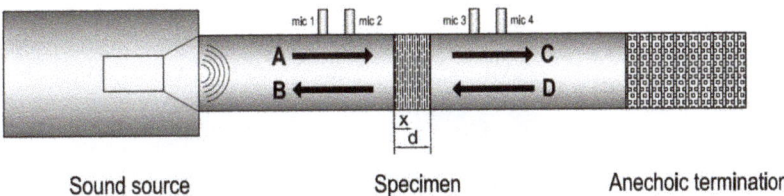

Figure 2. Schematic drawing of a four-microphone impedance tube.

The wave components A–D represent the complex amplitudes of the incident and reflected waves on both sides of the sample and can be derived from the complex transfer functions $H_{i,ref}$ measured between the -ith microphone ($i = 1, \ldots, 4$) and the reference (ref) microphone. In this study, the first microphone was selected as the reference microphone, but generally any of the four microphones can be chosen for this role. At this point, an interchanging procedure must be applied between the transducers to correct the measured transfer functions for amplitude and phase mismatches. Once the corrected transfer functions are obtained by dividing the measured transfer functions by relative correction transfer functions, the four components A, B, C and D can be obtained. These coefficients are used for the derivation of the transfer matrix terms. Pressures and particle velocities at both sides of the sample can be determined in terms of incident and reflected plane wave components. In the case of geometrically symmetric specimens, since the physical properties are the same on either side, reciprocity and symmetry can be applied and a single set of measurements is sufficient to characterize the material. The acoustical properties of the sample can thus be calculated as a function of the transfer matrix elements, the acoustic impedance of air, the sample thickness and the wavenumber in air. In particular, the following properties are obtained:

- Normal incidence sound absorption coefficient, α;
- Normal incidence sound transmission loss, TL;
- Propagation wavenumber inside the material, k_c;
- Characteristic impedance inside the material, Z_c.

The Applied Acoustic Laboratory impedance tube at the University of Brescia is composed of two 1200 mm long-segments, with an internal diameter of 46 mm, determining a cross-section that ensures that the plane-wave assumption is verified up to approximately 3700 Hz. The loudspeaker is installed in an isolated and sealed volume at the source endpoint of the tube. Through the connection to the generator of a multichannel analyzer, a wide-band white noise test signal (50 Hz–5 kHz) is created inside the tube. As the samples tested in this article are symmetric, it was not necessary to use a double boundary condition, and the second endpoint of the tube was equipped with an anechoic termination.

The sample holder is a detachable unit, made of separate segments of tube of appropriate length, which can be usually chosen to be 50, 100 or 200 mm long. Once carefully filled with the material to be tested, the holder is placed in the central section of the tube, between two microphone pairs, and it is additionally sealed to the main parts of the tube by means of O-rings and petroleum jelly for assuring air tightness. Four PCB microphones Type 130F22 are inserted in openings sealed with O-rings and flush mounted with the inner surface of the tube. The microphone pairs are spaced 500 mm for low-frequency measurements and 45 mm for high-frequency measurements. It is worth noting that this study focuses on high-frequency characterization (200–3150 Hz). This choice was made because the JCA model used for the inverse characterization is less accurate in the low frequency range, as discussed in [38]. The transducers are connected to an OROS OR 36 multichannel analyzer which measures the complex transfer functions between the microphones. All the microphones were calibrated before the test by using a Bruel and Kjaer pistonphone Type 4228. In Figure 3, some details of the four-microphone impedance tube used for the experiments are shown.

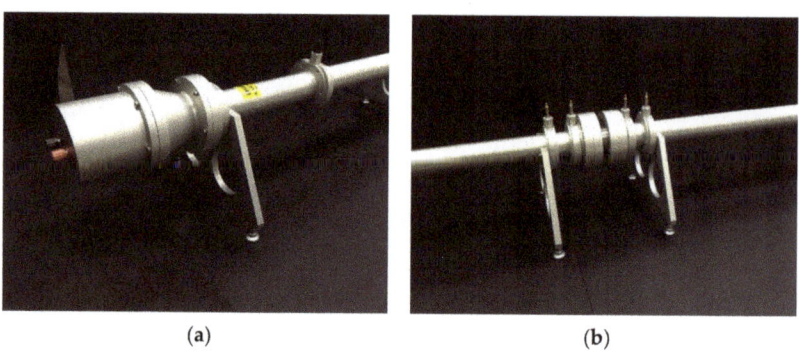

(a) (b)

Figure 3. Details of the four-microphone impedance tube: (**a**) the sound source; and (**b**) central part with the inserted sample holder and the two microphone pairs.

To determine the transfer matrix elements, it is necessary to measure the complex sound pressure, including amplitude and phase, at four positions. Once microphone 1 is chosen as a reference, the standard procedure requires a first measurement with all the microphones placed in the port corresponding to their respective number, and then three other measurements are made by physically switching the location of each microphone with the reference microphone 1. This enables obtaining the correction of the transfer functions for phase and amplitude mismatches. In this way, for each tested sample, four measurements have to be executed. A self-built MATLAB® code allows one to post-process the measured transfer functions and to describe the acoustic behavior of the tested material, giving as an output the normal incidence sound absorption coefficient α, the normal incidence sound transmission loss TL, the characteristic acoustic impedance Z_c, the speed of sound c and the propagation wavenumber k_c in the tested material. To correct the speed of sound in the air and the air density values, the temperature and atmospheric pressure were measured before each test and then considered during the post-processing phase.

3. Tested Samples

Among the different types of waste resulting from the steel production, slags probably represent the main (90% by mass) and most hazardous one, due to the possible content of heavy metals such as chromium, manganese and iron. In order to make slag suitable for recycling and reuse, a deep knowledge of its composition and physical properties is needed, to apply appropriate stabilization and inertization methods that allow environmentally sustainable applications of slags.

In this work, three types of steelwork waste materials were analyzed: wool derived from white dross, spheres derived from black slag, and spheres encapsulated in an inert material. The first material is a white wool, made of long fibers, similar to mineral wool or glasswool. This material is derived from a centrifuge process of the white dross and it features inclusions of transparent spheres and thin dark flakes, as shown in Figure 4.

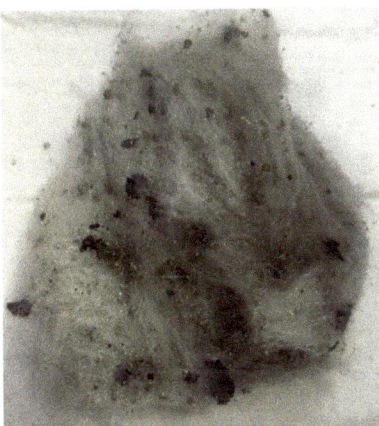

Figure 4. Sample of wool derived from white dross.

The second material is a conglomerate of spheres derived from black slag, as shown in Figure 5. Three diameters (⌀) ranges were obtained by using progressive sieves on a sample of unselected byproduct. The samples are categorized as "BIG" (⌀ ∈ [1.4; 2.0) mm), "MEDIUM" (⌀ ∈ [0.71; 1.4) mm) and "SMALL" (⌀ ∈ (0; 0.71) mm) depending on the dimension of the spheres. The composition of the sample is approximately: 15% BIG, 35% MEDIUM and the remaining 50% SMALL spheres.

The third material is made of spherical black slag embedded in inert material, resulting in an irregular granular assembly, as shown in Figure 6. After the spherification process, a fluid cement consisting of mixtures of hydraulic binders (lime, silica and alumina) is mixed with the slag spheres. This mixture completely covers the granules and makes them inert. Table 1 reports the samples thickness, the net weight and the density of the different materials considered in this work, together with the diameter ranges of slag spheres specimens.

Figure 5. Conglomerate of spheres derived from black slag: (**a**) sample "BIG", with $\varnothing \in [1.4; 2.0)$ mm; (**b**) sample "MEDIUM" with $\varnothing \in [0.71; 1.4)$ mm; and (**c**) sample "SMALL" with $\varnothing \in (0; 0.71)$ mm.

Figure 6. Sample of slag spheres encapsulated in inert material.

Table 1. Characteristics of the analyzed specimen: sample thickness, net weight and density.

Material	Sample Thickness (mm)	Net Weight (kg ∗ 10⁻³)	Density (kg/m³)
White dross wool	50	29.23	368
Slag spheres "BIG" $\varnothing \in [1.4; 2.0)$ mm	100	312.96	1968
	50	164.72	2071
Slag spheres "MEDIUM" $\varnothing \in [0.71; 1.4)$ mm	50	175.38	2204
Slag spheres "SMALL" $\varnothing \in (0; 0.71)$ mm	50	185.64	2334
Incapsulated spheres	50	136.46	1716

The second and third material specimens were prepared in the following way:

1. The front surface of the sample holder cylinder was terminated with a protective layer, sealed by glue along the perimeter to contain loose granules and guarantee flat surface;

2. A quantity of granules freely fell and randomly into the sample holder while kept in vertical position;
3. A slight manual vibration was applied to pack the granules;
4. Occasionally, the loose samples were compacted with a soft pressure on the top end to ensure the correct filling and to level the surface;
5. A non-woven fabric layer, glued along the perimeter, was applied to close the other side of the sample holder.

Previous separate measurements had confirmed that the protective layer, Figure 7, has no influence on the acoustic properties of the tested samples.

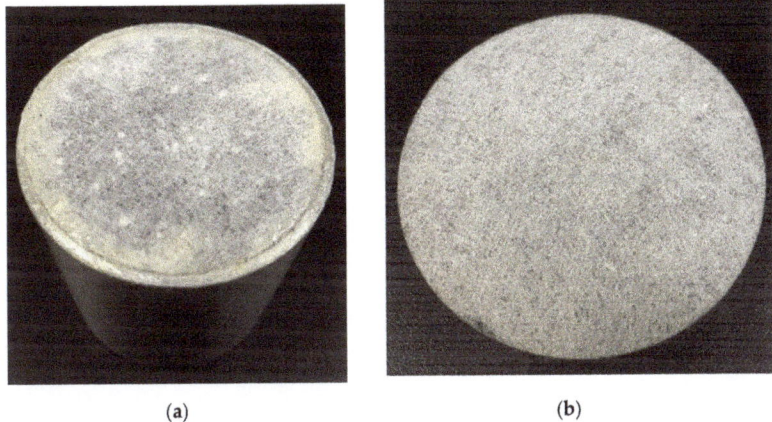

Figure 7. Examples of protective layers: (a) top surface of the sample closed by the protective layer sealed by glue; and (b) protective layer.

4. Results and Discussion

In Figure 8, the measured sound absorption coefficient and transmission loss of the white dross wool are presented. This material features an "S-shaped" absorption curve with the characteristic behavior typical of porous–fibrous materials, that is low values at low frequencies and values approaching a unit value at high frequencies: in particular, α starts with a value of 0.13 at 200 Hz, it linearly increases and around 1700 Hz, it reaches the unit value. The *TL* curve is also typical for fibrous materials, it does not reach high values but at about 1250 Hz, it shows a change in slope with an increasing trend.

In Figure 9, the acoustic performances of all the samples made of slag spheres of the three diameter ranges are shown in the same graph. The absorption coefficient curves of BIG and MEDIUM samples can be referred to the typical quarter wavelength resonance behavior of granular materials: the oscillations of the sound absorption for granular materials are caused by the air gap around the granules. If the gap between granules is too small or too large, not enough friction and subsequent heat transfer can develop between the air and the solid skeleton of the pore wall during the propagation of sound waves [20]. The first peaks are, respectively, at about 580 Hz for sample BIG of 100 mm length, 1330 Hz for sample BIG with 50 mm of thickness and about 1190 Hz for sample MEDIUM, which is 50 mm long. As the dimension of the sample increases, a more complex gap distribution occurs together with longer channels. While the acoustic wave propagates, the air particle collisions and the flow volume raise within the pores, resulting in a higher dissipation of energy. When the natural frequency of the spheres mix decreases, the sound absorption peak shifts to a lower frequency.

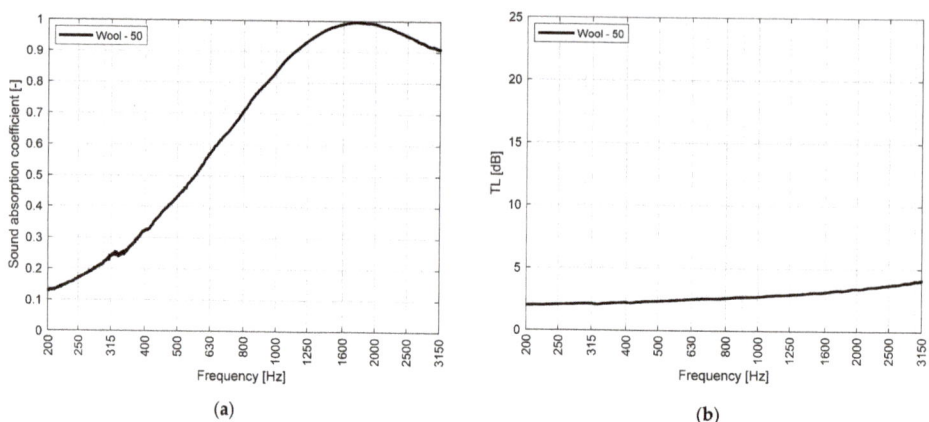

Figure 8. Acoustic properties of white dross wool sample: (**a**) sound absorption coefficient; and (**b**) transmission loss.

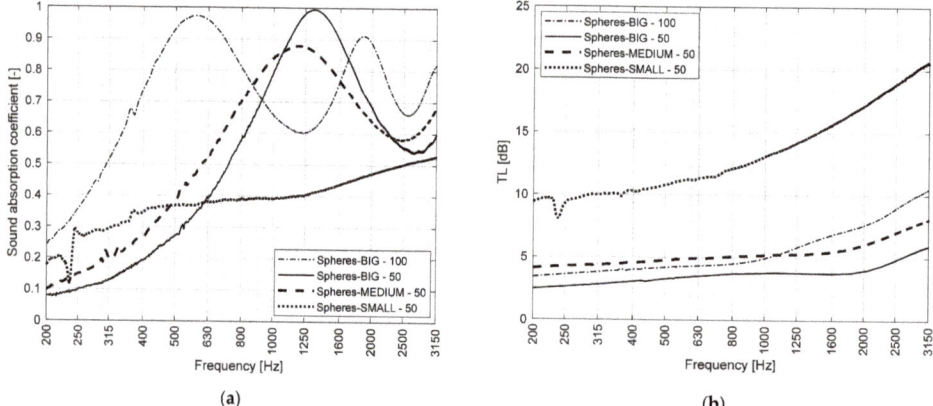

Figure 9. Acoustic properties of slag spheres samples BIG, MEDIUM and SMALL: (**a**) sound absorption coefficient; and (**b**) transmission loss.

It can be observed that for the SMALL sample, a smooth absorptive behavior is present where the resonance peaks and throughs are suppressed. As stated in [31], for large grain mixes, the absorption coefficient spectrum shows an oscillating trend, corresponding to resonance maxima and minima. On the contrary, small grain mixes lose the resonant behavior, featuring a less pronounced trend. For this reason, the transmission loss of SMALL sample is higher than the one measured for the BIG and MEDIUM samples throughout the whole frequency range of interest. This may be caused by the nature of the SMALL sample, featuring spheres with $\varnothing \in (0; 0.71)$ mm. Such structure can be considered since compact sand and its higher density results in a very high airflow resistance. This gives rise to a reflective behavior. In the frequency range between 200 and 300 Hz, a drop in both α and TL values of the SMALL sample were observed, probably because of the rigid frame resonance of the system.

Figure 10 shows the absorption curve of the slag spheres sample embedded inside an inert material. Additionally, in this case, the graph shows the typical quarter wavelength resonance behavior of granular materials. The first peak almost reaches a unit value around 1390 Hz. The transmission loss remains quite low throughout the whole frequency range of interest.

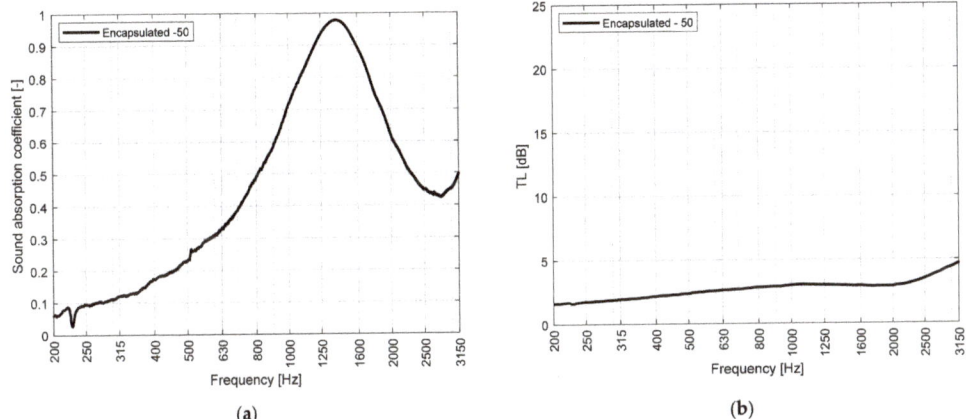

Figure 10. Acoustic properties of slag spheres encapsulated in inert material: (**a**) sound absorption coefficient; and (**b**) transmission loss.

In order to easily compare the performances of different materials, the weighted noise reduction coefficient (NRC) and the sound absorption average (SAA) [49] are used to summarize the absorption characteristics of the tested samples by single rating numbers: they range between 0 and 1, in the case of perfectly reflective or perfectly absorptive materials, respectively. As stated by the standard, NRC is rounded off to the nearest multiple of 0.05, while SAA is rounded off to the nearest multiple of 0.01. Table 2 reports the sound absorption coefficients for the twelve one-third octave bands from 200 to 2500 Hz of the investigated waste materials and their respective NRC and SAA values.

Table 2. Sound absorption coefficients for the twelve one-third octave bands from 200 to 2500 Hz of the tested materials and the respective noise reduction coefficient (NRC) and sound absorption average (SAA).

Material	Frequency (Hz)												SAA	NRC
	200	250	315	400	500	630	800	1000	1250	1600	2000	2500		
Wool-50	0.127	0.172	0.235	0.319	0.435	0.571	0.707	0.838	0.937	0.988	0.988	0.950	0.61	0.60
BIG-100	0.245	0.360	0.522	0.736	0.925	0.950	0.812	0.661	0.614	0.767	0.861	0.685	0.68	0.70
BIG 50	0.074	0.099	0.132	0.194	0.278	0.399	0.576	0.796	0.972	0.893	0.682	0.559	0.47	0.45
MEDIUM-50	0.101	0.146	0.203	0.273	0.391	0.530	0.698	0.836	0.867	0.769	0.639	0.589	0.50	0.50
SMALL-50	0.180	0.243	0.297	0.347	0.368	0.379	0.389	0.394	0.407	0.437	0.473	0.504	0.37	0.35
Encapsulated-50	0.065	0.087	0.118	0.168	0.241	0.335	0.487	0.712	0.930	0.888	0.622	0.452	0.43	0.45

In this paragraph, the inverse method based on the standard minimization approach is applied in order to derive the main non-acoustic parameters of the different materials considered in this article. For this analysis, the selected optimization objective function is the difference between the sound absorption coefficient measured by means of the four-microphone impedance tube and the absorption coefficient predicted by using the JCA model. Thus, the investigated cost function is defined as

$$CF\{|\alpha|\} = \sum |\alpha_{measured} - \alpha_{JCA_{model}}| \qquad (32)$$

The purpose is to determine the best solution of the unknown parameters to minimize the cost function. According to the literature [20,26,38], the intervals of the five non-acoustic parameters are set as

$$\begin{cases} \Phi \in [0.1\,;\,0.9] \\ \sigma \in [1000\,;\,150000] \\ \alpha_\infty \in [1\,;\,4] \\ c_1 \in [0.3\,;\,3.3] \\ c_2 \in [0.3\,;\,c_1] \end{cases} \tag{33}$$

To better understand the degree of agreement between measurements and predictions, using the method described in [44], the relative error $E\%$ was estimated for all the predictions as

$$E\% = \left| \frac{Measured - Predicted}{Measured} \right| \tag{34}$$

As shown in Table 3, the error was evaluated for each computed third octave band and then the average value of the relative error for the single material is given in the last column.

Table 3. Relative errors for third octave bands and average values of the relative errors.

Material	\multicolumn{11}{c	}{Relative Error E%}	Average Relative Error E%
	200 Hz	250 Hz	315 Hz	400 Hz	500 Hz	630 Hz	800 Hz	1000 Hz	1250 Hz	1600 Hz	2000 Hz	2500 Hz	3150 Hz	
Wool-50	5.55	12.95	14.98	13.30	7.33	2.13	0.01	1.03	0.63	0.35	1.79	4.48	4.85	5.34
BIG-100	13.26	6.33	0.24	4.53	4.98	0.90	2.53	0.75	1.77	1.03	0.12	1.93	7.59	3.54
BIG 50	14.22	16.27	16.13	5.75	0.26	1.59	1.19	1.40	0.83	1.05	0.14	2.49	4.86	5.09
MEDIUM-50	17.09	14.75	10.97	5.82	8.18	7.30	6.13	2.93	0.36	1.33	1.34	3.61	3.03	6.37
SMALL-50	13.91	18.75	17.70	15.65	8.41	2.27	0.94	2.07	5.19	4.96	0.42	6.47	10.48	8.25
Encapsulated-50	1.08	7.93	13.04	18.00	18.78	12.01	3.91	3.06	2.81	1.34	1.26	6.30	9.73	7.64

Figure 11 refers to the wool sample and shows the comparison between the absorption experimentally obtained coefficient and the one estimated by using the JCA model—achieved by means of the iterative minimization method. It can be noted that there is a good agreement between the two curves with respect to the frequency range considered, except for a slight overestimation upstream of 630 Hz in the predicted curve, and a little drop downstream of 1600 Hz which is not present in the measured curve.

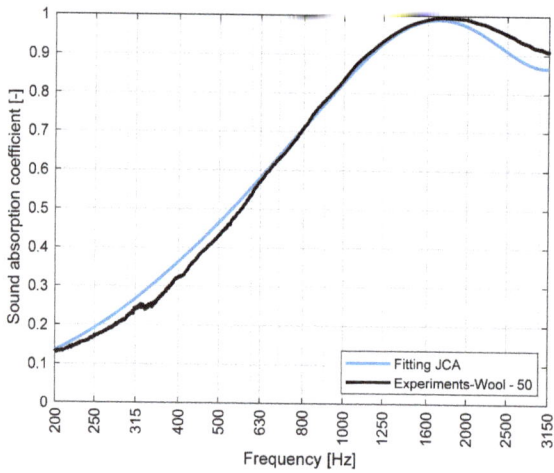

Figure 11. Comparison between experimental and predicted sound absorption coefficient for the wool sample derived from white dross.

In Figure 12, the experimental and predicted curves are depicted for the three slag spheres samples: BIG, MEDIUM and SMALL. The predictions referring to BIG and MEDIUM samples are in good agreement with the experimental curves, showing the classic resonant behavior. In particular, sample BIG—50 features a high degree of agreement between the two curves above 500 Hz. In the high frequency range, a slight discrepancy can be observed for sample BIG—100. For the sample SMALL, the estimated curve fairly approximates the measured curve, but it does not follow the trend in an optimal way along the entire frequency range. This is probably caused by the nature of the SMALL sample, which is neither an absorbing nor an insulating material.

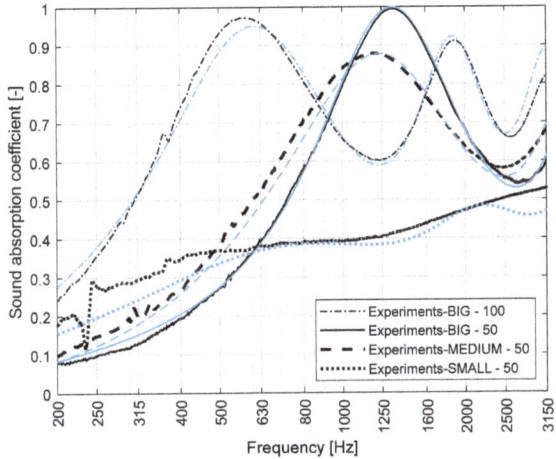

Figure 12. Comparison between experimental and predicted sound absorption coefficients for slag spheres samples BIG, MEDIUM and SMALL. Blue lines are referred to the respective JCA fittings.

Figure 13 shows, overall, a good correspondence between the estimated and the measured absorption curves relative to the sample made of encapsulated slag spheres.

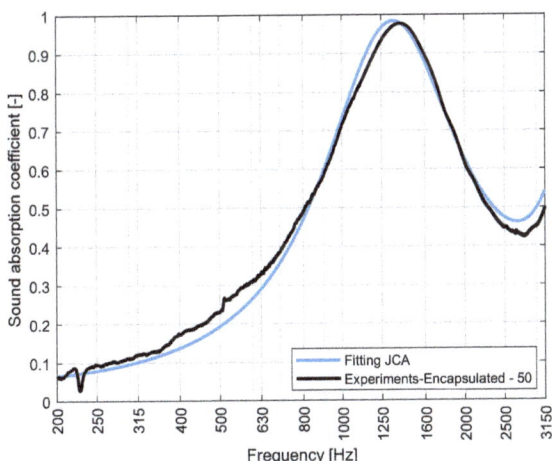

Figure 13. Comparison between experimental and predicted sound absorption coefficient for the sample made of encapsulated spheres.

Table 4 summarizes the values of the five non-acoustic parameters obtained by applying the optimization procedure. The achieved parameters seem to be consistent with what can be found in the literature for similar materials. Nevertheless, in [21], the authors stated that the porosity of the random close packing of spherical beads should remain constant to a value of approximately 0.36, when the ratio between the sample holder diameter and the tested spheres diameter exceeds the value of 10. This corresponds to the characteristics of the case at hand, since the internal diameter of the sample holder is 46 mm and the diameter of the largest spheres is 2 mm. However, the discrepancies may be due to the fact that, in this study, the spherical particles have not a single diameter value, but they are indeed assembled in diameter ranges, thus, the internal arrangement may be different from the one described in [21]. In order to completely validate the optimal parameters identified by the inverse technique, the next step of the research will be the direct experimental measurement of the five non-acoustic parameters.

Table 4. Inversely determined non-acoustic parameters.

Material	d (mm)	Φ (-)	σ (Pa * s/m^2)	α_∞ (-)	Λ (μm)	Λ' (μm)
White dross wool	50	0.87	10550	1	114	209
Slag spheres "BIG"	100	0.50	10600	1.46	182	333
$\varnothing \in [1.4; 2.0)$ mm	50	0.52	11350	1.33	164	301
Slag spheres "MEDIUM" $\varnothing \in [0.71; 1.4)$ mm	50	0.44	30250	1.47	115	211
Slag spheres "SMALL" $\varnothing \in (0; 0.71)$ mm	50	0.39	144550	4	92	169
Encapsulated spheres	50	0.52	9100	1.37	186	512

5. Conclusions

In this paper, the acoustic characterization of some steel industry waste materials derived from black and white slags is provided. The measurements performed by using a four-microphone impedance tube allowed us to obtain the acoustic properties of the tested samples. As a result, the analyzed materials can be mainly considered as porous media featuring interesting sound absorption and insulation characteristics. The wool derived from white dross exhibits a trend of the sound absorption which is typical of fibrous material, while slag spheres and encapsulated spheres behave as granular materials, with an oscillating tendency whose peaks are due to the resonance of the particle frame at a frequency corresponding to the one of a quarter wavelength resonator having the same thickness. Only the SMALL sample showed a more insulating than absorptive behavior, due to its higher density and airflow resistance values. It can be said that the SMALL sample acoustically behaves like compact sand. In order to determine the non-acoustic parameters of the samples, without the possibility of performing direct measurements, an inverse characterization technique was applied. Based on the JCA model, the inverse technique used relies on a standard iterative optimization procedure: the minimization is performed between the sound absorption coefficient measured in a four-microphone impedance tube and the one estimated by optimizing the inversion values into the JCA model. The optimization intervals were set according to the literature data. The five resulting non-acoustic parameters are compatible and comparable with the ones which can be found in other studies dealing with porous and granular media. The fact that some samples are made by spheres assembled by ranges of diameters and not by single diameter values explains possible discrepancies with literature data. The next step of the research will be focused on the validation of the inversion procedure and of the optimized non-acoustic parameters, by means of specific experimental measurements. Further investigations on the microstructure and the particle arrangements will allow the optimization and customization of the material for specific noise control applications.

Author Contributions: Investigation, data curation, writing—original draft preparation, visualization, E.L. Methodology, resources, supervision, E.A.P. Software, S.S. Conceptualization, writing—review and editing, E.A.P. and E.L. All authors have read and agreed to the published version of the manuscript.

Funding: This research received no external funding.

Institutional Review Board Statement: Not applicable.

Informed Consent Statement: Not applicable.

Data Availability Statement: Not applicable.

Acknowledgments: The authors would like to thank ORI Martin (Brescia), particularly Maurizio Zanforlin, for providing the material and technical insight on the manufacturing and inertization processes.

Conflicts of Interest: The authors declare no conflict of interest.

References

1. Smol, M. Towards Zero Waste in Steel Industry: Polish Case Study. *J. Steel Struct. Constr.* **2015**, *1*, 102. [CrossRef]
2. Branca, T.A.; Colla, V.; Algermissen, D.; Granbom, H.; Martini, U.; Morillon, A.; Pietruck, R.; Rosendahl, S. Reuse and Recycling of By-Products in the Steel Sector: Recent Achievements Paving the Way to Circular Economy and Industrial Symbiosis in Europe. *Metals* **2020**, *10*, 345. [CrossRef]
3. Neri, M.; Pilotelli, M.; Traversi, M.; Levi, E.; Piana, E.A.; Bannò, M.; Cuerva, E.; Pujadas, P.; Guardo, A. Conversion of End-of-Life Household Materials into Building Insulating Low-Cost Solutions for the Development of Vulnerable Contexts: Review and Outlook towards a Circular and Sustainable Economy. *Sustainability* **2021**, *13*, 4397. [CrossRef]
4. Motz, H.; Geiseler, J. Products of steel slags an opportunity to save natural resources. *Waste Manag.* **2001**, *21*, 285–293. [CrossRef]
5. Pasetto, M.; Baldo, N. Mix design and performance analysis of asphalt concretes with electric arc furnace slag. *Constr. Build. Mater.* **2011**, *25*, 3458–3468. [CrossRef]
6. Gökalp, İ.; Uz, V.E.; Saltan, M.; Tutumluer, E. Technical and environmental evaluation of metallurgical slags as aggregate for sustainable pavement layer applications. *Transp. Geotech.* **2018**, *14*, 61–69. [CrossRef]
7. Brand, A.S.; Fanijo, E.O. A Review of the Influence of Steel Furnace Slag Type on the Properties of Cementitious Composites. *Appl. Sci.* **2020**, *10*, 8210. [CrossRef]
8. Abu-Eishah, S.I.; El-Dieb, A.S.; Bedir, M.S. Performance of concrete mixtures made with electric arc furnace (EAF) steel slag aggregate produced in the Arabian Gulf region. *Constr. Build. Mater.* **2012**, *34*, 249–256. [CrossRef]
9. Pellegrino, C.; Cavagnis, P.; Faleschini, F.; Brunelli, K. Properties of concretes with Black/Oxidizing Electric Arc Furnace slag aggregate. *Cem. Concr. Comp.* **2013**, *37*, 232–240. [CrossRef]
10. Coppola, L.; Buoso, A.; Coffetti, D.; Kara, P.; Lorenzi, S. Electric arc furnace granulated slag for sustainable concrete. *Constr. Build. Mater.* **2016**, *123*, 115–119. [CrossRef]
11. Faleschini, F.; Brunelli, K.; Zanini, M.A.; Dabalà, M.; Pellegrino, C. Electric Arc Furnace Slag as Coarse Recycled Aggregate for Concrete Production. *J. Sustain. Metall.* **2016**, *2*, 44–50. [CrossRef]
12. Rondi, L.; Bregoli, G.; Sorlini, S.; Cominoli, L.; Collivignarelli, C.; Plizzari, G. Concrete with EAF steel slag as aggregate: A comprehensive technical and environmental characterization. *Compos. Part B Eng.* **2016**, *90*, 195–202. [CrossRef]
13. Saxena, S.; Tembhurkar, A.R. Impact of use of steel slag as coarse aggregate and wastewater on fresh and hardened properties of concrete. *Constr. Build. Mater.* **2018**, *165*, 126–137. [CrossRef]
14. Fisher, L.V.; Barron, A.R. The recycling and reuse of steelmaking slags—A review. *Resour. Conserv. Recy.* **2019**, *146*, 244–255. [CrossRef]
15. Guadagnino, P.; Cantone, L.; Conte, P.; Pocina, G.; Matarazzo, A.; Bertino, A. Techniques of reuse for slags and flakes from the steel industry: A circular economy perspective. In Proceedings of the Procedia Environmental Science, Engineering and Management, Rimini, Italy, 6–9 November 2018; Volume 5, pp. 93–99.
16. Alves, J.; Espinosa, D.; Tenório, J. Recovery of Steelmaking Slag and Granite Waste in the Production of Rock Wool. *Mater. Res.* **2015**, *18*, 204–211. [CrossRef]
17. Roy, S.; Miura, T.; Nakamura, H.; Yamamoto, Y. Investigation on applicability of spherical shaped EAF slag fine aggregate in pavement concrete—Fundamental and durability properties. *Constr. Build. Mater.* **2018**, *192*, 555–568. [CrossRef]
18. Roy, S.; Miura, T.; Nakamura, H.; Yamamoto, Y. Investigation on material stability of spherical shaped EAF slag fine aggregate concrete for pavement during thermal change. *Constr. Build. Mater.* **2019**, *215*, 862–874. [CrossRef]
19. Biot, M.A. Theory of Propagation of Elastic Waves in a Fluid-Saturated Porous Solid. I. Low-Frequency Range. *JASA* **1956**, *28*, 168–178. [CrossRef]
20. Zhou, B.; Zhang, J.; Li, X.; Liu, B. An Investigation on the Sound Absorption Performance of Granular Molecular Sieves under Room Temperature and Pressure. *Materials* **2020**, *13*, 1936. [CrossRef] [PubMed]

21. Viet Dung, V.; Panneton, R.; Gagné, R. Prediction of effective properties and sound absorption of random close packings of monodisperse spherical particles: Multiscale approach. *JASA* **2019**, *145*, 3606–3624. [CrossRef]
22. Zieliński, T.G. Microstructure-based calculations and experimental results for sound absorbing porous layers of randomly packed rigid spherical beads. *JASA* **2014**, *116*, 034905. [CrossRef]
23. Tsuruha, T.; Yamada, Y.; Otani, M.; Takano, Y. Effect of casing on sound absorption characteristics of fine spherical granular material. *JASA* **2020**, *147*, 3418–3428. [CrossRef] [PubMed]
24. Boubel, A.; Bousshine, S.; Garoum, M.; Ammar, A. Experimental Sound Absorption of Several Loose Uncooked Granular Materials. *IJITEE* **2019**, *9*, 4578–4583. [CrossRef]
25. Zalewski, R.; Rutkowski, M. The use of Vacuum Packed Particles with adaptable properties in acoustic applications. *J. Ther. Appl. Mech.* **2018**, *56*, 403–416. [CrossRef]
26. Asdrubali, F.; Schiavoni, S.; Horoshenkov, K. A Review of Sustainable Materials for Acoustic Applications. *Build. Acoust.* **2012**, *19*, 283–312. [CrossRef]
27. Cobo, P.; Simón, F. A comparison of impedance models for the inverse estimation of the non-acoustical parameters of granular absorbers. *Appl. Acoust.* **2016**, *104*, 119–126. [CrossRef]
28. Cobo, P.; Simón, F. Using simulating annealing for the inverse estimation of the non-acoustical parameters of sound absorbers. *Build. Acoust.* **2017**, *24*, 295–306. [CrossRef]
29. Delany, M.E.; Bazley, E.N. Acoustical properties of fibrous absorbent materials. *Appl. Acoust.* **1970**, *3*, 105–116. [CrossRef]
30. Miki, Y. Acoustical properties of porous materials-Generalizations of empirical models. *J. Acoust. Soc. Jpn.* **1990**, *11*, 25–28. [CrossRef]
31. Voronina, V.V.; Horoshenkov, K.V. Acoustic properties of unconsolidated granular mixes. *Appl. Acoust.* **2004**, *65*, 673–691. [CrossRef]
32. Horoshenkov, K.; Swift, M. The acoustic properties of granular materials with pore size distribution close to log-normal. *JASA* **2001**, *110*, 2371–2378. [CrossRef] [PubMed]
33. Bérengier, M.; Stinson, M.; Daigle, G.; Hamet, J. Porous road pavements: Acoustical characterization and propagation effects. *JASA* **1997**, *101*, 155–162. [CrossRef]
34. Attenborough, K. Acoustical characteristics of rigid fibrous absorbents and granular materials. *JASA* **1983**, *73*, 785–799. [CrossRef]
35. Johnson, D.; Koplik, J.; Dashen, R. Theory of dynamic permeability and tortuosity in fluid-saturated porous media. *J. Fluid Mech.* **1987**, *176*, 379–402. [CrossRef]
36. Allard, J.-F.; Atalla, N. *Propagation of Sound in Porous Media: Modelling Sound Absorbing Materials*, 2nd ed.; Wiley: Hoboken, NJ, USA, 2009; pp. 77–110.
37. Champoux, Y.; Stinson, M.R. On acoustical models for sound propagation in rigid frame porous materials and the influence of shape factors. *JASA* **1992**, *92*, 1120–1131. [CrossRef]
38. Atalla, Y.; Panneton, R. Inverse acoustical characterization of open cell porous media using impedance tube measurements. *Can. Acous.* **2005**, *33*, 11–24.
39. Kidner, M.R.F.; Hansen, C.H. A comparison and review of theories of the acoustics of porous materials. *IJAV* **2008**, *13*, 112–119.
40. Horoshenkov, K.V. A Review of Acoustical Methods for Porous Material Characterisation. *IJAV* **2017**, *22*, 99–103. [CrossRef]
41. Alba, J.; del Rey, R.; Ramis, J.; Arenas, J. An Inverse Method to Obtain Porosity, Fibre Diameter and Density of Fibrous Sound Absorbing Materials. *Arch. Acoust.* **2011**, *36*, 561–574. [CrossRef]
42. Bonfiglio, P.; Pompoli, F. Inversion problems for determining physical parameters of porous materials: Overview and comparison between different methods. *Acta Acust. United Ac.* **2013**, *99*, 341–351. [CrossRef]
43. Allard, J.F.; Henry, M.; Tizianel, J.; Kelders, L.; Lauriks, W. Sound propagation in air-saturated random packings of beads. *JASA* **1998**, *104*, 2004–2007. [CrossRef]
44. Bonfiglio, P.; Pompoli, F. Comparison of different inversion techniques for determining physical parameters of porous media. In Proceedings of the 19th International Congress on Acoustics, Madrid, Spain, 2–7 September 2007.
45. Doutres, O.; Salissou, Y.; Atalla, N.; Panneton, R. Evaluation of the acoustic and non-acoustic properties of sound absorbing materials using a three-microphone impedance tube. *Appl. Acoust.* **2010**, *71*, 506–509. [CrossRef]
46. Olny, X.; Panneton, R. Acoustical determination of the parameters governing thermal dissipation in porous media. *JASA* **2008**, *123*, 814–824. [CrossRef] [PubMed]
47. Caniato, M.; D'Amore, G.K.O.; Kaspar, J.; Gasparella, A. Sound absorption performance of sustainable foam materials: Application of analytical and numerical tools for the optimization of forecasting models. *Appl. Acoust.* **2020**, *161*, 107166. [CrossRef]
48. *ASTM Standard E2611-19, Test Method for Normal Incidence Determination of Porous Material Acoustical Properties Based on the Transfer Matrix Method*; ASTM International: West Conshohocken, PA, USA, 2019. [CrossRef]
49. *ASTM C423, Complete Document Standard Test Method for Sound Absorption and Sound Absorption Coefficients by the Reverberation Room Method*; ASTM International: West Conshohocken, PA, USA, 2017.

Article

The Influence of Floor Layering on Airborne Sound Insulation and Impact Noise Reduction: A Study on Cross Laminated Timber (CLT) Structures

Federica Bettarello [1], Andrea Gasparella [2] and Marco Caniato [2,*]

[1] Department of Engineering and Architecture, University of Trieste, 34127 Trieste, Italy; fbettarello@units.it
[2] Faculty of Science and Technology, Free University of Bozen, 39100 Bolzano, Italy; andrea.gasparella@unibz.it
* Correspondence: mcaniato@unibz.it

Abstract: The use of timber constructions recently increased. In particular, Cross Laminated Timber floors are often used in multi-story buildings. The development of standardization processes, product testing, design of details and joints, the speed of construction, and the advantages of eco-sustainability are the main reasons why these structures play a paramount role on the international building scene. However, for further developments, it is essential to investigate sound insulation properties, in order to meet the requirements of indoor comfort and comply with current building regulations. This work presents the results obtained by in field measurements developed using different sound sources (tapping machine, impact rubber ball, and airborne dodecahedral speaker) on Cross Laminated Timber floors, changing different sound insulation layering (suspended ceiling and floating floors). Results clearly show that the influence on noise reduction caused by different layering stimulated by diverse noise source is not constant and furthermore that no available analytical model is able to correctly predict Cross Laminated Timber floors acoustic performances.

Keywords: cross laminated timber; impact noise; rubber ball; sustainable; sound insulation; timber

1. Introduction

At present, the need of sustainable buildings is rising all over Europe and thus their construction is growing quickly [1]. Therefore, high-rise wooden edifices are more and more requested in the market [2–4]. These edifices are composed using different elements. Often, timber frame is used for the construction of walls [5,6] and Cross Laminated Timber (CLT) for floors [7,8]. In this light, CLT horizontal partitions have to fulfil many requisites like structural integrity etc., but recently sound insulation and impact noise reduction as well as indoor acoustic comfort are becoming important issues to manage. Anyway, bare horizontal partitions do not easily fulfill acoustic law requirements [9] and thus many other layers have to be added.

In order to solve these problems, many works were developed in years to study the acoustic behavior of this type of timber element. In a recent review, Di Bella and Mitrovic [10] focused on bare structures elucidating their properties and construction phases. Such structures have several advantages:
(1) eco-sustainability;
(2) anti-seismicity;
(3) thermally insulating;
(4) possibility of dry construction;
(5) possibility of raising existing structures thanks to the reduced weight.

When focusing on layered CLT elements, Pérez and Fuente [11] presented a dedicated study using laboratory and field measurements of sound insulation and impact noise reduction of some CLT components. Anyway, no parametric study related to the influence of the single layer is included. The same consideration could be applied to many other works [12–15].

Due to the reduced weight of CLT elements, their poor acoustic performances could lead to problems in the lower frequency range when in presence of impact noises such as children or adults walking or running. In order to reduce impact noise or to increase sound insulation, some other technologies have to be coupled to the bare timber floor. Two of the most used are (i) floating floor and (ii) suspended ceiling.

Kim et al. [16] found that a floating floor addition using resilient materials ensures good performance against lightweight impact noise, but has rather negative effects due to the resonance on the heavy weight impact noise caused by the falling of heavy objects or children walking/running.

It is thus evident how there is a lack of parametric studies, discussing the influence of single noise reduction action on CLT floors and, in addition, their overall contribution when laid together on the same horizontal partition. Furthermore, there is a lack of studies comprising different acoustic excitation techniques on such floors [17], providing single configuration influence on final sound reduction.

Timber constructions are relatively new in the European market. People usually live in traditional heavyweight ones made of masonry and/or concrete. When moving on new sustainable edifices, people feel new indoor environment and new noises, which were not present in traditional houses. Thus, subjective evaluations are now part of the research order to understand if timber buildings could provide a suitable environment from the point of view of acoustic comfort [18]. In this view, the rubber impact ball was demonstrated to be the noise source most associated with subjective reactions [19,20]. However, to the authors' knowledge, no parametric research comparing the influence of noise reduction technologies on CLT floors is available in literature, using such a source.

For these reasons, this research presents the results of acoustic measurements using rubber ball and tapping machine for impact noise and dodecahedral source for airborne noise. Tests were carried out in situ in a timber building featuring CLT floors. The measurements were made step-by-step during the construction phase, firstly considering the bare CLT floor and after all the various layers. The aim of this research is to parametrically determine the influence of different layers on impact and airborne noise reduction as well as to understand if available analytical models could predict the measured values.

2. Materials and Methods

The test-building where the in situ measurements (airborne and impact noise tests) were performed consists of five CLT floors (Figure 1), featuring timber frame walls, as depicted in Figure 2.

Figure 1. Realization of the test-building.

Figure 2. Pictures of the internal partition.

In these conditions, thanks to (i) the rock wool included within the timber studs of the vertical partitions, (ii) the coupling of massive (CLT) and lightweight (timber frame) partitions and (iii) the point connections, flanking transmissions are very limited (up to 1 dB overall) [21–24].

2.1. Investigated Structures

Different configurations of floor structures were built and tested, in order to understand their influence on sound insulation and impact noise reduction, as follows:

1. Bare floor;
2. Bare floor coupled with suspended ceiling;
3. Bare floor coupled with a floating floor;
4. Bare floor coupled both with suspended ceiling (rigid connections) and floating floor.

The first configuration deals with the characterization of the bare floor. This structure features a thickness of 180 mm of Cross Laminated Timber as reported in Figure 3.

Figure 3. Configuration 1: Bare floor.

The second studied configuration presents a common solution used in timber buildings: suspended ceiling (configuration 2). A suspended ceiling is used for the following most frequent reasons: (i) including HVAC systems and thermos-hygrometric indoor conditions [25], (ii) including air or fluids pipes or ducts [26,27], (iii) protecting timber structures from fire [28]. Less frequently, it is intended to be used as a sound insulation layer or impact noise reduction technology. In Figure 4, the configuration 2 is depicted.

This solution does not interfere in vibration transmission but does on the airborne noise one. Accordingly, the suspended ceiling acts as an added layering, namely another and different impedance from the bare floor. Thus, it constitutes a sound insulating element laid between the source (vibrating floor) and the receiver (room). Subsequently, its influence is related to the airborne noise more than the structure borne one.

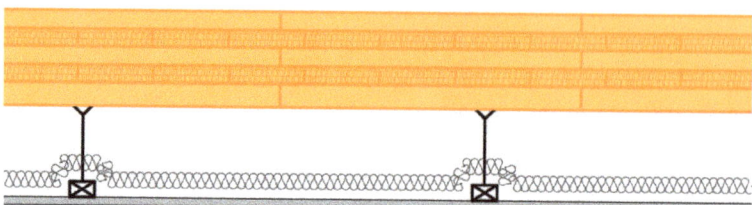

Figure 4. Configuration 2: Bare floor coupled with suspended ceiling.

The third configuration features a well-established technology for impact noise reduction: a floating floor. Using this decoupling approach, vibration transmission is decreased by means of the mass-spring effect [29,30]. It is known that this technology diminishes the transmitted noise by decoupling the covering heavyweight screed from the bare floor. In this way, vibrations are reduced and thus the transmission to the other room will be significantly reduced. Configuration 3 is represented in Figure 5.

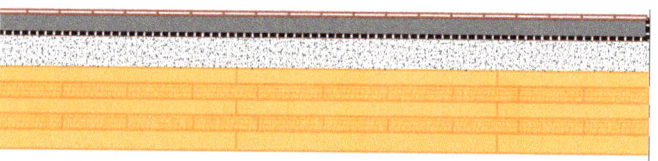

Figure 5. Configuration 3: Bare floor coupled with floating floor.

In order to investigate also the coupled effect of both suspended ceiling and floating floor on cross laminated timber, a further configuration (configuration 4, -Figure 6) was considered.

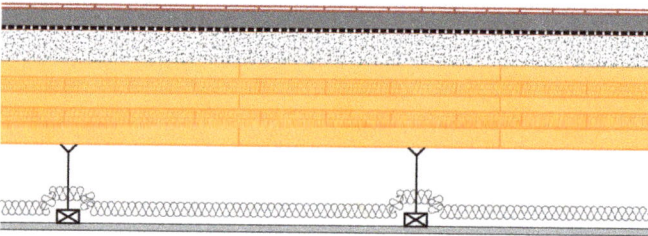

Figure 6. Configuration 4: Bare floor coupled with floating floor and suspended ceiling.

In Table 1, different layers used and tested are reported, describing their thickness, density, and elasticity.

Table 1. Floor elements description.

Element	Thickness d [mm]	Density ρ [kg/m^3]	Dynamic Stiffness s' [Mn/m^3]
Screed	40	1150	-
Resilient layer	9	700	11
Screed	100	400	-
Waterproof membrane	0.2	33	-
CLT floor panel	180	470	-
Air layer	62	1	-
Rock wool panel	60	70	-
Gypsum board	1.25	730	-

2.2. Experimental Structures Characterization

In order to investigate the influence of different layers on bare CLT, three different noise excitation sources were used: dodecahedral speaker for airborne noise generation, ISO tapping machine for heavyweight impact noise generation, and rubber ball for lightweight noise generation (Figure 7). Four different floors were tested for each configuration. For the sake of brevity, only average results are presented and discussed.

Figure 7. Tapping machine and rubber ball used to test the impact noise of CLT floors.

The measurement methods of airborne and impact sound insulation were conducted in accordance with international standards ISO 16283 part 1 (airborne noise) [31] and part 2 (impact noise) [32]. In particular, part 2 of the standard has recently introduced the use of the rubber ball also at an international level, associating it to subjective perception evaluation. The indices are calculated in accordance with the procedures indicated in the ISO 717 standards part 1 (airborne noise) and part 2 (impact noise).

The used tapping machine features the following characteristics:

a. five hammers placed in a line. The distance between centerlines of hammers is (100 ± 3) mm;
b. the distance between the center of the supports of the tapping machine and the centerlines of neighboring hammers is at least 100 mm;
c. height of fall of the hammers is 40 ± 2 mm;
d. the mass of each hammer is 500 ± 12 g from which it follows that the velocity at impact should be 0.886 ± 0.022 m/s. The tolerance limits of the velocity may be increased to a maximum of ± 0.033 m/s if it is ensured that the hammer mass lies within accordingly reduced limits of 500 ± 6 g;
e. the falling direction of the hammers is perpendicular to the test surface to within $\pm 0.5°$.
f. the part of the hammer carrying the impact surface is cylindrical with a diameter of 30 ± 0.2 mm;
g. the impact surface shall be of hardened steel and is spherical with a curvature radius of 500 ± 100 mm;
h. the mean time between impacts is 100 ± 5 ms. The time between successive impacts is 100 ± 20 ms;
i. the time between impact and lift of the hammer is less than 80 ms;
j. the weight of the tapping machine is less than 25 kg.

The rubber ball generates the impact force exposure level L_{FE} in each octave band shown in Table 2, when it is dropped vertically in a free fall from the height of 100 cm $\pm$ 1 cm, measured from the bottom of the rubber ball to the surface of the floor under test. The used rubber ball features the following characteristics:

(a) hollow ball of 180 mm in diameter with 30 mm thickness;
(b) effective mass of (2.5 ± 0.1) kg;
(c) coefficient of restitution of 0.8 ± 0.1.

The impact force exposure level, L_{FE}, is expressed by Equation (1):

$$L_{FE} = 10 \lg \left[\frac{1}{T_{ref}} \int_{t_1}^{t_2} \frac{F^2(t)}{F_0^2} dt \right] \text{ (dB)} \quad (1)$$

where F(t) is the instantaneous force acted on the floor under test when the rubber ball is dropped on the floor [N], $F_0 = 1$ N is the reference force, $t_2 - t_1$ is the time range of the impact force [s], and $T_{ref} = 1$ s is the reference time interval. In Table 2, the standard rubber ball force is depicted.

Table 2. Impact force exposure level octave band of the rubber ball [32].

Octave Band Centre Frequency [Hz]	Impact Force Exposure Level, L_{FE} (dB re 1 N)
31.5	39.0 ± 1.0
63	31.0 ± 1.5
125	23.0 ± 1.5
250	17.0 ± 2.0
500	12.5 ± 2.0

The dodecahedral source features 12 speaker units. All speaker units in the same cabinet radiate in phase. The directivity of loudspeakers is approximately uniform and omnidirectional.

2.3. Acoustic Parameters

The apparent sound reduction index R' is calculated in accordance with Equation (2):

$$R' = L_1 - L_2 + 10 \log \frac{S}{A} \text{ (dB)} \quad (2)$$

L_1 is the energy-average sound pressure level in the source room (dB);
L_2 is the energy-average sound pressure level in the receiving room (dB);
S is area of the common partition [m²];
A is the equivalent absorption area in the receiving room [m²];
The normalized impact sound pressure level generated by standard tapping machine is calculated using Equation (3):

$$L'_n = L_i + 10 \lg \frac{A}{A_0} \text{ (dB)} \quad (3)$$

where $A_0 = 10$ m² is the reference equivalent absorption area.

The maximum impact sound pressure level measured with rubber ball $L'_{i,Fmax}$ is the maximum sound pressure level, tested using the "fast" time constant.

From the values measured in 1/3 octave bands it is possible to derive the evaluation indices R'_w, $L'_{n,w}$, and $L'_{iA,Fmax}$ according to ISO 717 part 1 and 2 standard. R'_w and $L'_{n,w}$ are evaluated in the frequency range 100–3150 Hz, while $L'_{iA,Fmax}$ is the A-weighted sound pressure level evaluated both in the frequency range 50–630 Hz and 20–2500 Hz. This last extended range was performed in order to consider low frequency comfort according to Späh et al. [20].

2.4. Acoustic Models

In order to verify if available traditional models are suitable for acoustic performance predictions of Cross Laminated Timber floors, in the following, for the four presented configurations, analytical equations retrieved from literature and standard are presented. It has to be highlighted here that, at present, for the impact rubber ball, no analytical model is available for the noise prediction in the receiving room.

For the bare floor, the traditional model is the ISO 12354-2 [32]. In this view, analytic expression is reported in Equation (4):

$$L_n = 155 - \left[(30 \log m'_{floor}) + (10 \log T_s) + (10 \log \sigma) + \left(10 \log \frac{f}{f_{ref}}\right)\right] \text{ (dB)} \quad (4)$$

where m'_{floor} is the mass per square meter [kg/m^2] of the bare floor, T_s is the structural reverberation time, σ is the radiation efficiency, f is the excitation frequency, and f_{ref} is the reference frequency at 1000 Hz.

The structural reverberation time is calculated according to Equation (5):

$$T_s = \frac{2.2}{f \eta} \text{ [s]} \quad (5)$$

where η is the overall damping.

The radiation efficiency is calculated according to Equation (6), using the Waterhouse correction [33]:

$$\sigma = \frac{\frac{p^2}{4 \rho_0 c_0} A \left(1 + \frac{S_T \lambda_0}{8V}\right)}{\rho_0 c_0 S_T v^2} \quad (6)$$

where $\rho_0 c_0$ is the air impedance, A is the absorption area retrieved from the reverberation time [m^2], S_T is the floor area [m^2], V is the volume of the receiving room [V], and v is the vibration velocity [m/s].

For the floating floor, the Cremer's equation is available [34], according to Equation (7):

$$\Delta L'_{n,w,floating,Cremer} = 30 \log \frac{f}{f_0} \text{ (dB)} \quad (7)$$

where f_0 is the resonance frequency [Hz] of the floating floor composed by the resilient layer and the screed and expressed by Equation (8):

$$f_0 = \frac{1}{2\pi} \sqrt{\frac{s'}{m'_{screed}}} \text{ [Hz]} \quad (8)$$

where s' is the dynamic stiffness of resilient layer [MN/m^3] and m'_{screed} is the mass per square meter [kg/m^2] of the screed.

Finally, some models are present for sound insulation prediction of lightweight partitions. Anyway, most of them are related only to the weighted index and do not provide a frequency trend. The only available approach could be the Sharp's one [35,36], providing a frequency domain formulation, reported in Equation (9):

$$R = 20 \log \left(m'_{partition} f\right) - 47.2 \text{ (dB)} \quad (9)$$

where $m'_{partition}$ is the mass per square meter [kg/m^2] of the wall or floor.

3. Results and Discussion

3.1. Impact Noise–Tapping Machine

The impact sound pressure level results in 1/3 octave bands for bare CLT floors are shown in Figure 8.

Interestingly, the impact sound pressure levels of the weighted index measured using the tapping machine as the generator provide very similar results for all the different horizontal partitions. This is very important since it demonstrates that all the further studies and noise reduction actions will have very similar influence on all bare floors. The retrieved differences depend on floor dimensions, receiving room shapes and volumes [37]. Accordingly, in the low frequency range, some differences are evidenced. In the middle frequencies (1000–2000 Hz), they tend to offer very similar results, while at higher ranges, again, some diversities are present.

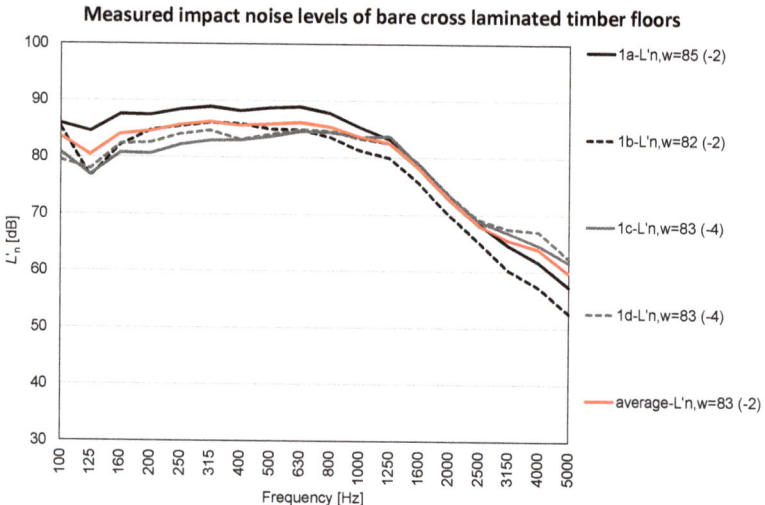

Figure 8. In situ measurements of normalized impact sound pressure level (tapping machine) for four bare CLT floors (configuration 1).

In Table 3, the 1/3 octave band average trend and the standard deviation are reported. It is evident how for most 1/3 octave frequency bands, the standard deviation falls within the ±3 dB range. This permit to consider the average data reliable and thus a reference.

Table 3. Average trend and standard deviation of averaged impact sound pressure levels (tapping machine).

Frequency [Hz]	IMPACT Noise Average (dB)	Standard Deviation (dB)
100	83.7	3.2
125	80.4	3.7
160	84.1	3.0
200	84.6	2.9
250	85.7	2.6
315	86.2	2.5
400	85.6	2.5
500	85.8	2.3
630	86.2	2.1
800	85.4	1.8
1000	83.6	1.7
1250	82.6	1.7
1600	78.2	1.6
2000	72.7	1.7
2500	68.1	1.9
3150	65.5	3.3
4000	64.0	4.2
5000	59.9	4.4

When using Equation (4), the predicted trend is not similar to the measured one, as depicted in Figure 9.

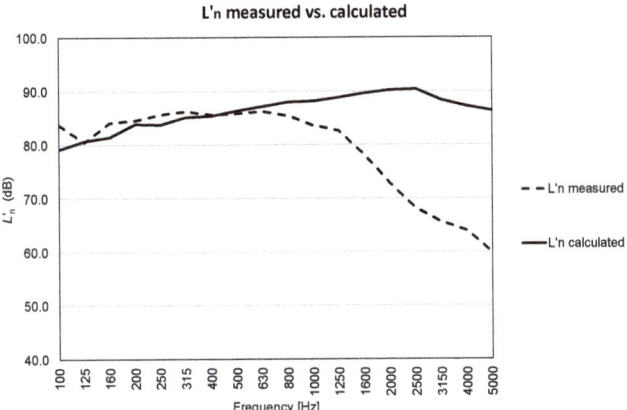

Figure 9. Measured vs. predicted impact noise.

It is possible to highlight that for middle-low frequencies, the model more or less fits the measured values. In Table 4, the difference between measured (average) and calculated values are reported. It could be noticed that low and middle frequencies (125–800 Hz) present very good agreement. Accordingly, the prediction falls within a range of ±3 dB. In contrast, from 1000 Hz on, the model is not able to correctly fit middle-high and high frequencies, mostly because the measurement of the structural reverberation time is measured using hard-surface sources (hammer). When the head of the hammer impinges the wood, it tends to present a resilient behavior (compared to concrete) on middle and high frequencies. For this reason, the measurement could not accurately determine this parameter, thus affecting acoustic performance predictions.

Table 4. Average trend and difference between measured and calculated values (Δ).

Frequency [Hz]	Impact Noise Average (dB)	Δ (dB)
100	83.7	4.6
125	80.4	−0.3
160	84.1	2.7
200	84.6	0.7
250	85.7	1.9
315	86.2	1.1
400	85.6	0.2
500	85.8	−0.5
630	86.2	−0.9
800	85.4	−2.5
1000	83.6	−4.5
1250	82.6	−6.2
1600	78.2	−11.4
2000	72.7	−17.4
2500	68.1	−22.2
3150	65.5	−22.8
4000	64.0	−23.2
5000	59.9	−26.5

When considering a suspended ceiling addition, no analytical model is present in literature or in standards.

In Figure 10, the results are reported when the exciting source is the tapping machine. It can be seen how different configurations can act on the impact noise reduction when compared to the average impact noise of the bare CLT floor (configuration 1). Accordingly, when at the bare floor a suspended ceiling is added (configuration 2), a significant noise reduction both in frequency and weighted index is verified. In particular, this reduction follows the trend of the average bare floor almost constantly.

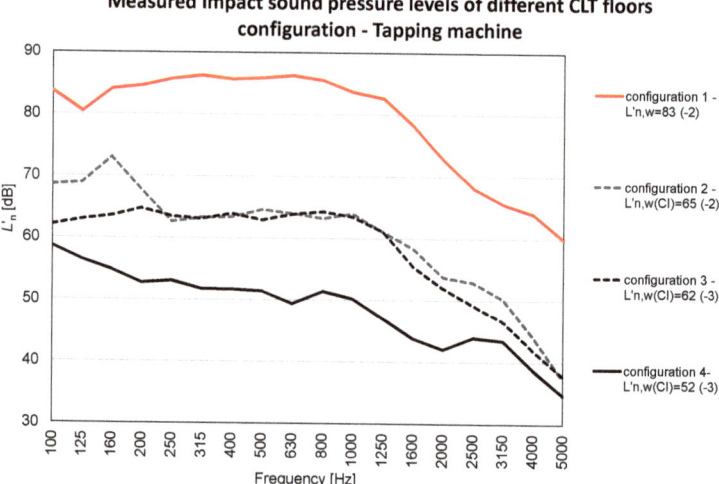

Figure 10. Impact sound pressure level for CLT floors (configurations 1, 2, 3, and 4). Source: tapping machine.

When considering the range of 250–3150 Hz, we can also easily derive a regressive equation (Equation (10)):

$$\Delta L'_{n,w,ceiling} = -0.028 \, (f) + 23.8 \; (dB) \tag{10}$$

where f is the frequency [Hz].

The results could be fitted, with a regression coefficient of $R^2 = 0.89$. By means of this equation, it could be possible to estimate the effect of this kind of suspended ceiling on a generic CLT floor of 20 cm thickness.

Moving onto configuration 3 (only floating floor and bare CLT floor), it could be acknowledged that a similar reduction is proposed, compared to configuration 2. Here, low frequencies (100–200 Hz) are reduced more efficiently, as well as high frequencies (1600–4000 Hz). However, this technology could not work properly, because its performance requires a heavy mass as bare floor. In this case, a cross laminated plate could not represent this element, because of its lightweight structure.

When applying Equation (7) to configuration 3, a different resulting trend is produced. In Figure 11, the frequency tendencies of the two impact noise reductions are depicted. Clearly, Cremer's model cannot be applied to this kind of wooden partitions, since it fails by a large amount.

The main reason is that Cremer's model considers the bare floor as completely rigid, featuring an ideally infinite mass in comparison to the floating floor. In the case of CLT floors, this does not happen. Accordingly, the density of a CLT floor is 90 kg/m^2, very similar to the floating floor. It is evident that the bare timber floor cannot be considered neither more rigid nor more massive than the floating floor, thus significantly affecting the application of Cremer's model.

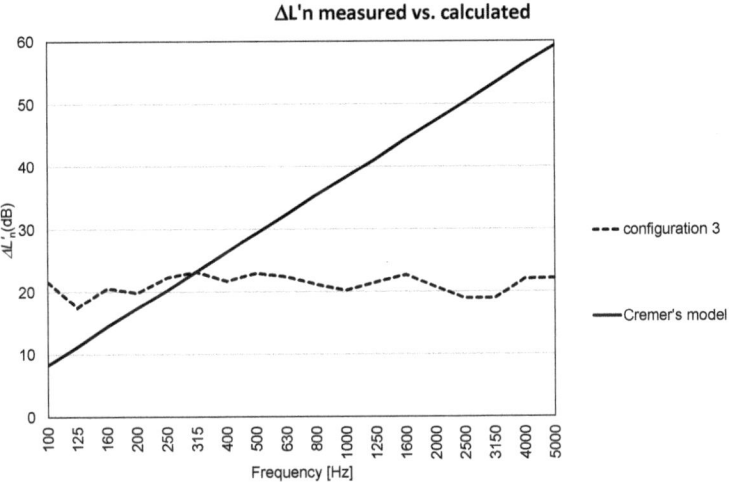

Figure 11. Comparison between Cremer's and measured $\Delta L'_{n,w}$ for configuration 3.

When investigating the frequency influence on the measured noise reduction index reported in Figure 11, in the range 250–3150 Hz, a relation can be found, as expressed in Equation (11), with a regression coefficient of $R^2 = 0.70$. However, a poor influence of frequency on impact noise reduction is highlighted:

$$\Delta L'_{n,w,\text{floating,CLT model}} = -0.012\,f + 22.9 \text{ (dB)} \tag{11}$$

when combining the two technologies in the bare floor (configuration 4), a significant reduction is verified, in comparison to configuration 1 (bare CLT floor) and to both configuration 2 and 3. Anyway, when combining Equations (10) and (11), the obtained result is not reliable (Figure 12).

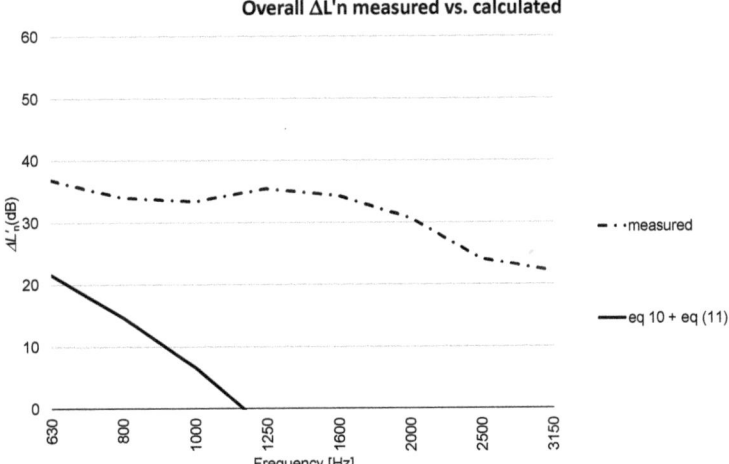

Figure 12. Measured vs. calculated $\Delta L'_{n,w}$.

The retrieved equation from measured values is reported below, with a regression coefficient of $R^2 = 0.81$ (Equation (12)).

$$\Delta L'_{n,w,overall} = -1.9\,f + 40.1 \text{ (dB)} \tag{12}$$

Here, we can see that frequency affects more significantly impact sound reduction, in comparison to configuration 2 and 3. It is thus evident that we have to avoid the combination of the two equations related to single actions, as the merging would lead to a significant underestimation of the final results.

3.2. Impact Noise–Rubber Ball

When using the impact ball as noise source, we have to consider that the excitation is different from the traditional tapping machine. As reported above, this methodology injects into the structures an impulse which is poor of middle-high frequencies (800–5000 Hz) and focuses its action in the range 100–630 Hz. The results of the standardized maximum impact sound pressure relate to bare and lined CLT floors are shown in Figure 13. As demonstrated above, bare CLT floors mostly present the same frequency trends when excited. Therefore, for the sake of brevity, only average bare floor trends are presented hereafter.

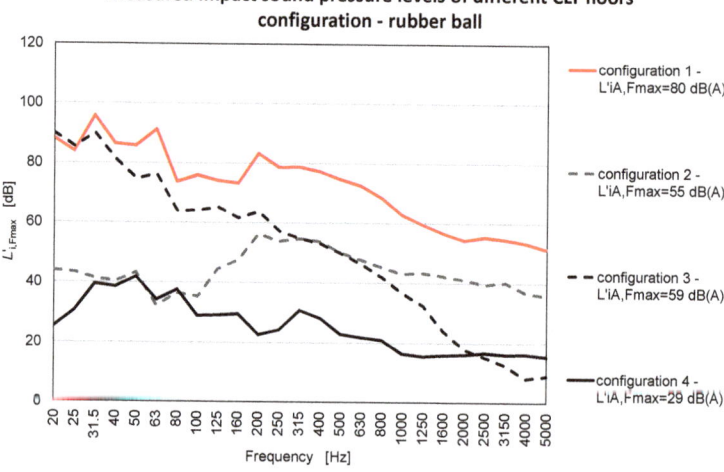

Figure 13. Impact sound pressure level for CLT floors (configurations 1, 2, 3, and 4). Source: rubber ball.

From Figure 13, it is evident that configuration 2 acts efficiently in noise reduction especially at low (20–100 Hz) and high frequencies (1600–5000 Hz). The presence of the fibrous material within the ceiling air gap could influence the impact noise propagation. However, when the resonance frequency is overcome (over 80 Hz), its efficiency significantly decreases. Since the measured trend is composed by three different zones, showing three different behaviors, it is not worthy to infer a regressive equation.

When only floating floor is considered (configuration 3), it is evident how the provided noise reduction is significantly lower. This is mainly due to the fact that the floating floor works at a different frequency range. It was previously demonstrated [38] that this technology reduces significantly the transmission on middle-high frequency ranges (1000–5000 Hz). When using the rubber ball, this range is not injected in the floor, as reported in Table 2. For this reason, a smaller reduction is found, compared to configuration 2. In this case, the trend presents a homogeneous behavior and therefore a regressive approach may be used. The result is presented in Equation (13), with a regression coefficient of $R^2 = 0.97$:

$$\Delta L'_{iA,Fmax,floating} = 35.1 \log(f) - 49.5 \text{ (dB)} \tag{13}$$

It is interesting to note that, in comparison to tapping machine excitation, the equation is not linear anymore, but it follows a logarithmic trend, based on the exciting frequency.

When considering suspended ceiling and floating floor together (configuration 4), a significant overall reduction is verified. Accordingly, in some frequencies, the background noise could have influenced the results, since they are comparable to it.

In this case too, the trend presents a homogeneous behavior and therefore a regressive approach can be used. The result is presented in Equation (14), with a regression coefficient of $R^2 = 0.74$.

$$\Delta L'_{iA,Fmax,floating} = 10 \log(f) - 38.1 \text{ (dB)} \tag{14}$$

In this case, the frequency contribution is less significant than the configuration 3 represented by Equation (13) and a logarithmic trend is evidenced.

3.3. Airborne Sound Insulation

The investigation of the sound insulation to airborne noise is useful in order to understand if the actions of the floating floor and of the suspended ceiling, applied for impact noise reduction, can influence also soundwaves propagation in air. For this reason, in Figure 14, the measured trends are reported.

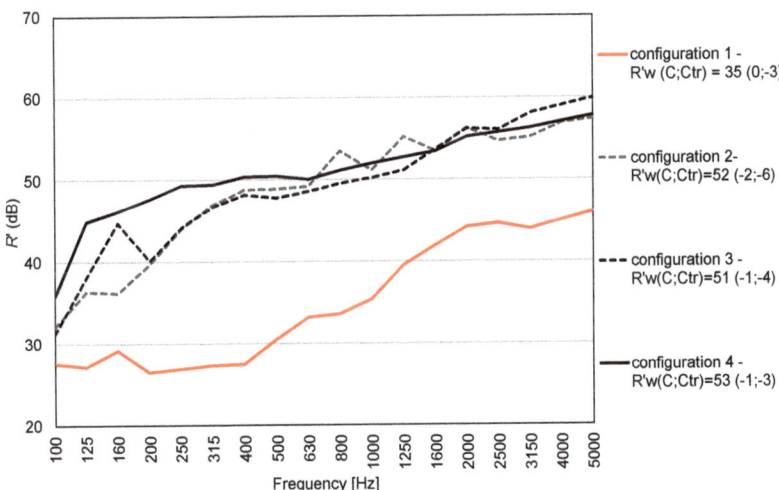

Figure 14. Airborne sound insulation for CLT floors (configurations 1, 2, 3, and 4).

It is evident how the bare floor provides very poor frequency performances, while the addition of a suspended ceiling (configuration 2) positively affects sound insulation. In this case, also floating floor (configuration 3) positively affects sound insulation, showing a very similar trend compared to configuration 2. When combining the two solutions, some significant improvements can be seen at middle-low frequencies, until 1600 Hz.

In Table 5, the results of the calculated frequency sound insulation are reported. In addition, the difference Δ_n between the measured and the calculated values (using Equation (9) are included after each configuration. It is interesting to notice that configuration 1 (bare floor) is not fitted robustly. Accordingly, differences up to -19.8 dB are verified, with a mean value of -13.9 dB. When considering the suspended ceiling addition (configuration 2), we can verify a significant improvement of the sound insulation prediction. A maximum of 9.8 dB difference is provided, featuring a mean value of −1.6 dB. It is worthy to highlight that from 100 to 2000 Hz, the prediction falls within a range of ± 3 dB, with the exception of 315 Hz (3.7 dB) and 400 Hz (3.5 dB). This fact demonstrates how low, middle, and middle-high frequencies can be successfully calculated using Sharp's theory.

Table 5. Calculated sound insulation values, using Sharp's theory. Δ_n represents the difference between the measured and calculated results.

Frequency [Hz]	1	Δ_1	2	Δ_2	3	Δ_3	4	Δ_4
100	31.9	−4.3	33.2	−1.2	38.4	−7.2	38.8	−3.0
125	33.8	−6.6	35.2	1.2	40.3	−2.2	40.8	4.1
160	36.0	−6.8	37.3	−1.1	42.5	2.3	42.9	3.2
200	37.9	−11.4	39.2	0.5	44.4	−4.3	44.8	2.8
250	39.8	−13.0	41.2	2.8	46.3	−2.2	46.8	2.5
315	41.9	−14.6	43.2	3.7	48.3	−1.6	48.8	0.6
400	43.9	−16.5	45.3	3.5	50.4	−2.3	50.9	−0.5
500	45.9	−15.3	47.2	1.7	52.4	−4.6	52.8	−2.4
630	47.9	−14.7	49.2	0.0	54.4	−5.8	54.8	−4.8
800	49.9	−16.4	51.3	2.2	56.4	−6.9	56.9	−5.8
1000	51.9	−16.5	53.2	−2.1	58.4	−8.2	58.8	−6.8
1250	53.8	−14.3	55.2	0.0	60.3	−9.2	60.8	−8.0
1600	56.0	−14.0	57.3	−3.8	62.5	−8.8	62.9	−9.5
2000	57.9	−13.7	59.2	−3.0	64.4	−8.2	64.8	−9.6
2500	59.8	−15.2	61.2	−6.5	66.3	−10.3	66.8	−11.1
3150	61.9	−17.9	63.2	−8.1	68.3	−10.3	68.8	−12.5
4000	63.9	−18.9	65.3	−8.4	70.4	−11.4	70.9	−13.8
5000	65.9	−19.8	67.2	−9.8	72.4	−12.4	72.8	−15.0

When considering only floating floor addition to the bare floor (configuration 3), the prediction is not to be considered robust and reliable. Differences are significant (up to −12.4 dB) with a mean value of −6.3 dB. A different trend is verified for the complete layering (configuration 4). For low frequencies (100 Hz–500 Hz), a good prediction is provided, falling within the ± 3 dB range, with the exception of 125 Hz (4.2 dB) and 160 Hz (3.2 dB). From 630 Hz, a constant increase in the difference is verified, reaching its maximum at 5000 Hz (−15.0 dB) and a mean value of −5 dB.

As an overall result, we can say that the Sharp's model provides a reliable prediction only for configuration 2 up to middle frequencies, while for the other configurations, no consistent trends are found. For all configurations, the Sharp's model tends to overestimate the sound insulation and the worst range is represented by high frequencies (>1600 Hz).

3.4. Weighted Indexes Results

Even if weighted indexes do not provide frequency information, thus eliminating some of the interesting results, it is evident how it is easier to compare measurements using just the single index instead of 18 different values (1/3 octave bands). For this reason, results in terms of weighted index are reported in Table 6.

It is possible to notice that, for impact noise reduction using the tapping machine, the significant variation is caused by the use of whether a suspend ceiling or a floating floor is similar. Anyway, when applying the second configuration, it is possible to notice that the reduction is different if measured with the rubber ball or with the tapping machine. According to the standard, $L'_{iA,Fmax,50-630}$ is the parameter representing the subjective evaluation of the noise disturbance produced by floor impact sound. Conversely, according to literature [20], $L'_{iA,Fmax,20-2500}$ is more accurate. In this case, we can see no significant difference comparing the two parameters.

Table 6. Impact noise and airborne sound insulation weighted index results for each configuration.

Configuration	$L'_{n,w}$ (dB)	$L'_{iA,Fmax,50-630}$ (dB)	$L'_{iA,Fmax,20-2500}$ (dB)	R' (dB)
1	83	80	80	35
2	65	55	56	52
Δ_2	18	25	24	17
3	62	59	60	51
Δ_3	21	21	20	16
4	52	29	31	53
Δ_4	31	51	49	18

Considering configuration 3, we can see that almost the same impact reduction is measured with both tapping machine and rubber ball and that no significant difference is found between $L'_{iA,Fmax,50-630}$ and $L'_{iA,Fmax,20-2500}$.

Moving to configuration 4, a significant difference can be reported between tapping machine and rubber ball test, evidencing how, for the latter, a significant improvement in performance is assessed in comparison with the bare floor.

From the sound insulation point of view, when adding a technology of impact noise reduction, we can see a substantial increment of the performances. Anyway, (i) changing the configurations or (ii) merging them do not vary importantly final results.

Another overall finding is that configuration 3 (floating floor) and 4, where the combination of the two technologies ensures a more insulated partition, are capable to respect the law requirements of most European countries [39].

4. Conclusions

In this work, airborne and impact noise insulation measurements were carried out on a building featuring Cross Laminated Timber floors. In particular, the apparent sound reduction index and the impact sound pressure level measured with a normalized generator and rubber ball impulses were measured step-by-step during the construction phase. In particular, the application of floating floor, suspended ceiling, and the merging of these two technologies applied to the bare Cross Laminated Timber floor was investigated.

Findings highlighted how this lightweight sustainable timber structures do not present the same performances of heavyweight ones. We can then resume our main conclusions as follows:

- the bare Cross Laminated Timber floors present similar acoustic performances, thus an average trend can be considered;
- the impact noise reduction offered by suspended ceiling or floating floor excited by a tapping machine is very similar. Regression equations demonstrate that frequencies do not play a significant role; the same consideration is possible even when considering both these techniques at the same time.
- the Cremer's equation does not work with this structure. In particular, for middle-low frequency, Cremer's law fails by a large amount.
- when excited by a rubber ball, a suspended ceiling acts better than the floating floor, especially at low frequencies. The floating floor presents a linear-decreasing trend, which anyway is not able to reduce efficiently the impulse injected by the rubber ball;
- in the case of airborne sound insulation, both floating floor and suspended ceiling offer similar improvements. When merging the two technologies, no significant performance increasing is assessed. In this case, no analytical model was found to correctly predict the final results.

Author Contributions: F.B. and M.C. developed the research. F.B. and M.C. defined the methods and comparisons. F.B and M.C. studied and analyzed typical wooden structure. F.B. and M.C. performed acoustic measurements. M.C. and F.B. collected data and analyses results. M.C. and A.G. overviewed and supervised the research. M.C. and F.B. wrote the paper. All authors edited and proofread the paper. All authors have read and agreed to the published version of the manuscript.

Funding: This work was developed within the Interreg Project BIGWOOD, Interreg V-A Italy-Austria 2014–2020 (code ITAT 1081 CUP: I54I18000300006), which is gratefully acknowledged. This work was supported by the Open Access Publishing Fund of the Free University of Bozen-Bolzano.

Acknowledgments: Authors would like to really thank Ater Trieste for their precious help in this research and specifically Andrea Zeriali.

Conflicts of Interest: The authors declare that they have no known competing financial interests or personal relationships that could have appeared to influence the work reported in this paper.

References

1. Ramage, M.H.; Burridge, H.; Busse-Wicher, M.; Fereday, G.; Reynolds, T.; Shah, D.U.; Wu, G.; Yu, L.; Fleming, P.; Densley-Tingley, D.; et al. The Wood from the Trees: The Use of Timber in Construction. *Renew. Sustain. Energy Rev.* **2017**, *68*, 333–359. [CrossRef]
2. Frangi, A.; Fontana, M.; Knobloch, M. Fire Design Concepts for Tall Timber Buildings. *Struct. Eng. Int.* **2008**, *18*, 148–155. [CrossRef]
3. Kuzman, M.K.; Sandberg, D. *A New Era for Multi-Storey Timber Buildings in Europe*; Forest Products Society: Portlan, OR, USA, 2016.
4. Smith, I.; Frangi, A. Overview of Design Issues for Tall Timber Buildings. *Struct. Eng. Int.* **2008**, *18*, 141–147. [CrossRef]
5. Kaiser, A.; Larsson, M.; Girhammar, U.A. From File to Factory: Innovative Design Solutions for Multi-Storey Timber Buildings Applied to Project Zembla in Kalmar, Sweden. *Front. Archit. Res.* **2019**, *8*, 1–16. [CrossRef]
6. Kuzmanovska, I.; Gasparri, E.; Monné, D.T.; Aitchison, M. Tall Timber Buildings: Emerging Trends and Typologies. In Proceedings of the WTCE 2018, Seoul, Korea, 20–23 August 2018.
7. Mayo, J. *Solid Wood: Case Studies in Mass Timber Architecture, Technology and Design*; Routledge: England, UK, 2015; ISBN 978-1-317-58749-1.
8. Asiz, A.; Smith, I. Connection System of Massive Timber Elements Used in Horizontal Slabs of Hybrid Tall Buildings. *J. Struct. Eng.* **2011**, *137*, 1390–1393. [CrossRef]
9. Bolvardi, V.; Pei, S.; van de Lindt, J.W.; Dolan, J.D. Direct Displacement Design of Tall Cross Laminated Timber Platform Buildings with Inter-Story Isolation. *Eng. Struct.* **2018**, *167*, 740–749. [CrossRef]
10. Di Bella, A.; Mitrovic, M. Acoustic Characteristics of Cross-Laminated Timber Systems. *Sustainability* **2020**, *12*, 5612. [CrossRef]
11. Pérez, M.; Fuente, M. Acoustic Design through Predictive Methods in Cross Laminated Timber (CLT) Panel Structures for Buildings. In Proceedings of the Internoise, Innsbruck, Austria, 15–18 September 2013.
12. Pagnoncelli, L.; Fuente, M. Cross-Laminated Timber System (CLT): Laboratory and in Situ Measurements of Airborne and Impact Sound Insulation. In Proceedings of the EuroRegio Conference, Porto, Portugal, 13–15 June 2016.
13. Öqvist, R.; Ljunggren, F.; Ågren, A. On the Uncertainty of Building Acoustic Measurements—Case Study of a Cross-Laminated Timber Construction. *Appl. Acoust.* **2012**, *73*, 904–912. [CrossRef]
14. Ljunggren, F.; Simmons, C.; Hagberg, K. Findings from the AkuLite Project: Correlation between Measured Vibro-Acoustic Parameters and Subjective Perception in Lightweight Buildings. In Proceedings of the Internoise, Innsbruck, Austria, 15–18 September 2013.
15. Zhang, X.; Hu, X.; Gong, H.; Zhang, J.; Lv, Z.; Hong, W. Experimental Study on the Impact Sound Insulation of Cross Laminated Timber and Timber-Concrete Composite Floors. *Appl. Acoust.* **2020**, *161*, 107173. [CrossRef]
16. Kim, K.-W.; Jeong, G.-C.; Yang, K.-S.; Sohn, J. Correlation between Dynamic Stiffness of Resilient Materials and Heavyweight Impact Sound Reduction Level. *Build. Environ.* **2009**, *44*, 1589–1600. [CrossRef]
17. Fortini, M.; Granzotto, N.; Piana, E.A. Vibro-Acoustic Characterization of a Composite Structure Featuring an Innovative Phenolic Foam Core. *Appl. Sci.* **2019**, *9*, 1276. [CrossRef]
18. Vardaxis, N.-G.; Bard, D.; Persson Waye, K. Review of Acoustic Comfort Evaluation in Dwellings—Part I: Associations of Acoustic Field Data to Subjective Responses from Building Surveys. *Build. Acoust.* **2018**, *25*, 151–170. [CrossRef]
19. Vardaxis, N.-G.; Bard, D. Review of Acoustic Comfort Evaluation in Dwellings: Part II—Impact Sound Data Associated with Subjective Responses in Laboratory Tests. *Build. Acoust.* **2018**, *25*, 171–192. [CrossRef]
20. Späh, M.; Hagberg, K.; Bartlomé, O.; Weber, L.; Leistner, P.; Liebl, A. Subjective and Objective Evaluation of Impact Noise Sources in Wooden Buildings. *Build. Acoust.* **2013**, *20*, 193–213. [CrossRef]
21. Ågren, A.; Ljunggren, F.; Jarnerö, K.; Bolmsvik, Å. Flanking Transmission in Light Weight Timber Houses with Elastic Flanking Isolators. In Proceedings of the Internoise, New York, NY, USA, 19–22 September 2012.
22. Mahn, J.; Müller-Trapet, M. Characterization of Laminated Timber Building Elements to Estimate Flanking Transmission. INTER-NOISE and NOISE-CON Congress and Conference Proceedings. *Inst. Noise Control Eng.* **2019**, *259*, 4170–4178.
23. Ågren, A.; Ljunggren, F. In Situ Measured Flanking Transmission in Light Weight Timber Houses with Elastic Flanking Isolators: Part II. In Proceedings of the Internoise, Innsbruck, Austria, 15–18 September 2013.
24. Rabold, A.; Hessinger, J. Flanking Transmission at Impact Sound Excitation—Calculation According to DIN 4109 and PrEN ISO 12354-2—INTER-NOISE and NOISE-CON Congress and Conference Proceedings. *Inst. Noise Control Eng.* **2016**, *253*, 4308–4317.
25. Tronchin, L. Variability of Room Acoustic Parameters with Thermo-Hygrometric Conditions. *Appl. Acoust.* **2021**, *177*, 107933. [CrossRef]

26. Herzog, T.; Natterer, J.; Schweitzer, R.; Volz, M.; Winter, W. *Timber Construction Manual*; Birkhäuser: Basel, Switzerland, 2012; ISBN 978-3-0346-1463-4.
27. Östman, B.; Brandon, D.; Frantzich, H. Fire Safety Engineering in Timber Buildings. *Fire Saf. J.* **2017**, *91*, 11–20. [CrossRef]
28. Cho, T. Vibro-Acoustic Characteristics of Floating Floor System: The Influence of Frequency-Matched Resonance on Low Frequency Impact Sound. *J. Sound Vib.* **2013**, *332*, 33–42. [CrossRef]
29. Schiavi, A. Improvement of Impact Sound Insulation: A Constitutive Model for Floating Floors. *Appl. Acoust.* **2018**, *129*, 64–71. [CrossRef]
30. ISO 16283-1:2014. *Acoustics—Field Measurement of Sound Insulation in Buildings and of Building Elements—Part 1: Airborne Sound Insulation*; ISO: Geneva, Switzerland, 2014.
31. ISO 16283-2:2020. *Acoustics—Field Measurement of Sound Insulation in Buildings and of Building Elements—Part 2: Impact Sound Insulation*; ISO: Geneva, Switzerland, 2020.
32. ISO 12354-2. *Building Acoustics—Estimation of Acoustic Performance of Buildings from the Performance of Elements—Part 2: Impact Sound Insulation between Rooms*; ISO: Geneva, Switzerland, 2017.
33. Carl, H. *Sound Insulation*; Butterworth-Heinemann: Oxford, UK, 2007; 648p, ISBN 978-0-7506-6526-1. £55.99, [PDF Document]. Available online: https://fdocuments.in/document/sound-insulation-carl-hopkins-butterworth-heinemann-oxford-uk-2007-648.html (accessed on 18 May 2021).
34. Cremer, L. Theorie Der Schalldämmung Dünner Wände Bei Schrägem Einfall. *Akust Z* **1942**, *7*, 81–104.
35. Bies, D.A.; Hansen, C.H. *Engineering Noise Control: Theory and Practice*; Spon: London, UK, 1995; p. 745.
36. Woo, S.-H.A. The Measurement of Transmission Loss and Absorption Coefficient of the Rat and Porcine Skin: Synthesizing Artificial Material for an Implantable Microphone Test. *Appl. Acoust.* **2013**, *74*, 1388–1393. [CrossRef]
37. Hagberg, K.G. Evaluating Field Measurements of Impact Sound. *Build. Acoust.* **2010**, *17*, 105–128. [CrossRef]
38. Hui, C.K.; Ng, C.F. New Floating Floor Design with Optimum Isolator Location. *J. Sound Vib.* **2007**, *303*, 221–238. [CrossRef]
39. Rasmussen, B. Sound Insulation between Dwellings. Comparison of National Requirements in Europe and Interaction with Acoustic Classification Schemes. In *Proc 23rd International Congress on Acoustics*; Deutsche Gesellschaft für Akustik: Aachen, Germany, 2019.

A Perforated Plate with Stepwise Apertures for Low Frequency Sound Absorption

Xin Li, Bilong Liu * and Chong Qin

School of Mechanical & Automobile Engineering, Qingdao University of Technology, No. 777 Jialingjiang Road, Qingdao 266520, China; jz03-4lx@163.com (X.L.); qinchong95@163.com (C.Q.)
* Correspondence: liubilong@qut.edu.cn

Abstract: A perforated plate with stepwise apertures (PPSA) is proposed to improve sound absorption for low frequencies. In contrast with an ordinary perforated plate with insufficient acoustic resistance and small acoustic mass, the perforated plate with stepped holes could match the acoustic resistance of air characteristic impedance and also moderately increase acoustic mass especially at low frequencies. Prototypes made by 3D printing technology are tested in an impedance tube. The measured results agree well with that of prediction through theoretical and numerical models. In addition, an absorber array of perforated plates with stepwise apertures is presented to extend the sound absorption bandwidth due to the introduced multiple local resonances.

Keywords: perforated plate; stepwise apertures; sound absorption; low frequency

1. Introduction

Porous materials and resonant structures are widely used for sound absorption [1,2]. Typical resonant structures for sound absorption are perforated plates, micro-perforated plates, Helmholtz resonators and thin plate resonators. One of the conditions for effective sound absorption in resonant structures is that their acoustic resistance should match the characteristic impedance of the air. Usually, the acoustic resistances of an ordinary perforated plate with apertures in the range of a few millimeters to centimeters are insufficient and therefore the absorption coefficients are very small. In building acoustics, perforated plates with large perforation ratio are often used as protective plates over porous layers for sound absorption [3–5]. To replace porous materials, Maa proposed a well-known micro-perforated plate (MPP) for sound absorption in the 1970s [6]. For MPP, the apertures are reduced to submillimeter and thus sufficient acoustic resistances can be provided when the perforation ratio is specified. Additionally, in contrast with Helmholtz resonators, when the frequency is away from the resonance frequency, the acoustical reactance of MPP increases slowly to ensure the value is smaller than that of the acoustical resistance in a wide bandwidth, and this characteristic guarantees the broadband absorption of MPP.

When the perforation ratio is constant, MPP with smaller aperture has better sound absorption performance, while in the meantime, the number of holes is increased and the thickness shall be thinner [7]. The increase of hole numbers will increase the cost for the perforation and thinner plates may result in insufficient strength in application. In contrast, a thick MPP with small apertures will lead to excessive acoustic resistance and a decrease in sound absorption performance. To reduce the acoustic resistance of a thick MPP, MPP with variable section have been proposed in recent years [8–11]. Randeberg [8] proposed a micro-horn shaped MPP and the numerical results showed that micro-horn perforation has the potential to improve the sound absorption bandwidth. Sakagami et al. [9] conducted a pilot study to improve the absorption of a 10 mm thick MPP using a tapered perforation, and the measured results exhibited the shift of the resonant frequency to lower frequencies, but the absorption peak decreases. Lu et al. [10] studied the acoustic properties of MPP with variable cross-section, and showed that the absorption performance of such MPP mainly depends on the part of small holes, and the part of large holes is only to increase the plate thickness. He et al. [11] experimentally analyzed the effects of tapered and stepped holes on the sound absorption performance of thick MPP, and the results showed that large tapered holes can broaden the absorption bandwidth in the higher frequency domain. Based on the MPP model, Ma [12] performed an equivalent simulation of the experimental results for a tapered MPP, and the equivalent aperture obtained is between the large part and the small part of the tapered hole. Qian et al. [13] developed a numerical model of MPP with a tapered hole in the acoustic module of COMSOL Multiphysics, and the simulation results showed that the absorption performance of MPP with tapered holes was mainly influenced by the inlet diameter and outlet diameter. In addition, Jiang et al. [14] gave an empirical impedance correction model related to the cross-sectional ratio based on 176 sets of numerical simulations. These aforementioned literatures concern with reducing the excess acoustic resistance of large-thick MPPs by replacing straight-through holes with sub-millimeter variable cross-section holes.

In comparison with MPP, perforated plates with large apertures have the advantage of less perforation holes if the acoustic resistance can be improved sufficiently through some ways. Recently, various perforated structures for low to medium sound absorption, such as perforated panel with extended tubes (PPET) [15], composite honeycomb sandwich panels (CHSPs) [16], perforated composite Helmholtz-resonator (PCHR) [17], coiled space resonators (CSRs) [18], parallel-arranged perforated panel absorbers (PPAs) [19], panel containing coiled Helmholtz resonators [20] and inhomogeneous multi-layer Helmholtz resonators with extended necks (HRENs) [21], have been investigated. However, perforated plates with stepwise apertures for low frequency sound absorption have not been reported. For this motivation, a perforated plate with stepwise apertures (PPSA) larger than 1.5 mm is proposed for low-frequency (100–300 Hz) sound absorption in a compact space.

Additionally, the array structures consisting of multiple sub-absorbers in parallel arrangement have been studied to improve the sound absorption. Cha et al. [22] designed a MPP absorber array with two different cavities and gave the measured normal absorption coefficients by impedance tube. Wang et al. [23] established a numerical model to study the sound absorption mechanism of a MPP absorbers array with different cavity depths in detail. Uenishi et al. [24,25] studied a permeable membranes absorber array (PMAR) numerically and experimentally, and the results showed that PMAR is an effective absorbing structure due to the influence of multiple locally reacting air cavities at different depths. Furthermore, Wu et al. [26] proposed a profiled structure using perforated plates in some wells, thus adjusting the depths of the wells to improve low frequency absorption. In this paper, based on the local resonance effect, without changing the structure parameters, a simple PPSA absorbers array is initially designed to extend the sound absorption bandwidth only by inserting one rigid partition plate in the air cavity.

This paper is organized as follows. In Section 2, theoretical and numerical models are developed to predict the absorption coefficients of PPSA sound absorbers, and the predictions are verified by impedance tube measurements. In Section 3, the sound absorption performances of PPSA absorber and single perforated panel (PP) absorber are compared and discussed, and a simple array structure of two PPSA absorbers in parallel is presented to improve low frequency sound absorption. Finally, conclusions are drawn in Section 4.

2. Models and Methods

2.1. Theoretical Calculation

Figure 1a shows the structure of a PPSA absorber, which consists of a PPSA and an air cavity supported by a rigid wall. The PPSA is perforated with a series of stepped holes, which are composed of two unequal circular apertures in the coaxial line. For each circular aperture, the ratio of diameter to depth is greater than 1 and the diameter is not less than 1.5 mm. The diameter, thickness and perforation ratio of the small aperture are d_1, t_1, σ_1, those of the large aperture are d_2, t_2, σ_2, respectively, and the air cavity depth is D.

Structurally, PPSA can be viewed as a serial combination of two perforated panels PP1 and PP2 without spacing.

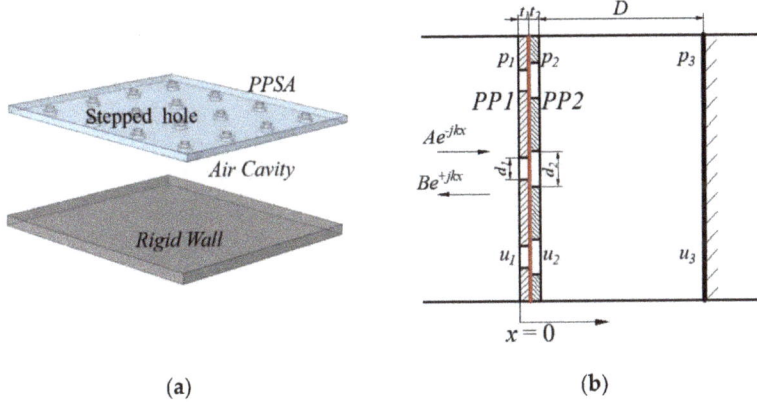

Figure 1. A perforated plate with stepwise apertures (PPSA) absorber. (a) Structure diagram; (b) One-dimensional acoustical system.

Based on the transfer matrix method [27], for the one-dimensional acoustical system element of PPSA absorber, as shown in Figure 1b, the sound pressure p_1 and particle velocity u_1 on the left side and the sound pressure p_3 and particle velocity u_3 on the right side can be expressed as:

$$\begin{bmatrix} p_1 \\ u_1 \end{bmatrix} = \begin{bmatrix} T_{11} & T_{12} \\ T_{21} & T_{22} \end{bmatrix} \begin{bmatrix} p_3 \\ u_3 \end{bmatrix}, \quad (1)$$

where T_{11}, T_{12}, T_{21} and T_{22} are the four pole parameters of the total transfer matrix $[T]$. The total transfer matrix $[T]$ is obtained by multiplying the unit transfer matrix of PP1, PP2 and air cavity, written as:

$$[T] = [T_{PP1}][T_{PP2}][T_{Air}], \quad (2)$$

For PP1 and PP2, the transfer matrix $[T_{pp}]$ can be given as:

$$[T_{PP1,2}] = \begin{bmatrix} 1 & Z_{P1,2} \\ 0 & 1 \end{bmatrix}, \quad (3)$$

The acoustic energy loss of the perforated panel mainly includes the air viscous dissipation inside the hole and the end correction caused by viscous friction and sound radiation. Therefore, the acoustic impedance of perforated panel is the sum of the acoustic impedance inside the hole and the end correction outside the hole. According to the viscous motion theory in the tube derived by Rayleigh and simplified by Crandall [28], the acoustic impedance in the circular hole is expressed as:

$$z_{hole} = j\omega\rho_0 t \left[1 - \frac{2}{k\sqrt{-j}} \frac{J_1(k\sqrt{-j})}{J_0(k\sqrt{-j})} \right]^{-1}, \quad (4)$$

According to Ingard and Rayleigh theory [29], the corrections of acoustic resistance and reactance at both ends of the hole are $\sqrt{2\omega\rho_0\eta}/2$ and $0.85d$, respectively. Due to the continuity of the surfaces of PP1 and PP2, the corrections of acoustic impedance at one end is considered. Thus, the acoustic impedance of PP1 and PP2 is written as:

For the air cavity, the transfer matrix $[T_{Air}]$ can be written as:

$$Z_{P1,2} = \frac{1}{\sigma_{1,2}} \left(j\omega\rho_0 t_{1,2} \left(1 - \frac{2}{k_{1,2}\sqrt{-j}} \frac{J_1(k_{1,2}\sqrt{-j})}{J_0(k_{1,2}\sqrt{-j})}\right)^{-1} + j\omega 0.425 d_{1,2} + \frac{\sqrt{2\omega\rho_0\eta}}{4} \right), \quad (5)$$

$$[T_{Air}] = \begin{bmatrix} \cos(k_0 D) & j\rho_0 c_0 \sin(k_0 D) \\ j\sin(k_0 D)/\rho_0 c_0 & \cos(k_0 D) \end{bmatrix}, \quad (6)$$

where $\omega = 2\pi f$ is the angular frequency, η is the dynamic viscosity coefficient of the air, $k = d\sqrt{\omega\rho_0\eta}/2$ is the ratio of the inner radius to the viscous boundary layer thickness inside the tube, for square arrangement, perforation ratio $\sigma = 0.785d^2/b^2$, d and b are the diameter of holes and the spacing between holes, J_0 and J_1 are the Bessel functions of the zero order and the first order, respectively. ρ_0 is the air density, c_0 is the sound speed in the air, $k_0 = \omega/c_0$ is the air wave number.

Since the air cavity is supported by a rigid wall, the particle velocity on the rigid wall is $u_3 = 0$. Therefore, it can be obtained from Equation (1):

$$p_1 = T_{11} p_3, \quad u_1 = T_{21} p_3, \quad (7)$$

Then, the surface impedance of the PPSA absorber at normal incidence is expressed as:

$$Z = \frac{p_1}{u_1} = \frac{T_{11}}{T_{21}} \quad (8)$$

Therefore, the surface reflection coefficient of the PPSA absorber is given by:

$$R = \frac{Z - \rho_0 c_0}{Z + \rho_0 c_0} \quad (9)$$

Thus, the absorption coefficient of the PPSA absorber for normal incident wave is written as:

$$\alpha = 1 - |R|^2 = \frac{4\text{Re}(Z/\rho_0 c_0)}{[1 + \text{Re}(Z/\rho_0 c_0)]^2 + [\text{Im}(Z/\rho_0 c_0)]^2} \quad (10)$$

2.2. FEM Simulation

In the thermo-viscous and pressure acoustics frequency domain interface of COMSOL Multi-physics, 3D finite element models are performed to simulate the acoustic behavior of the PPSA absorber under normal incidence. Considering viscosity and thermal loss, the acoustic field of single PPSA is built up in the thermo-viscous-acoustics, frequency domain interface, as shown in Figure 2a. Due to the stepped hole is a symmetric structure, to reduce the simulation time, 1/4 unit of the stepped hole is constructed. This numerical element model is composed of a stepped hole domain, two air domains and two perfectly matched layers (PML) at the ends. Moreover, the background pressure field is defined in an air domain, and PML acts as an infinite air field. The domains marked by the yellow and red line are the inlet and outlet surfaces of acoustic wave, respectively. In the simulation, the maximum frequency is chosen as 1000 Hz, the calculated frequency range is 100–500 Hz and the frequency interval is 5 Hz. For the stepped hole domain, the maximum element size of free tetrahedral meshes is set as the viscous boundary layer thickness size, and for the background sound field and air domain, the maximum element size of free tetrahedral meshes are equal to 1/3 of the small hole radius. In addition, the distribution of mesh elements for PML is at least six layer using the swept node. The mechanical and thermal boundary conditions for the sidewalls of the steppe hole are no slip and isothermal, respectively. For a stepped hole with $d_1 = 1.5$ mm, $d_2 = 4$ mm, $t = 2$ mm and hole spacing of 5 mm, the 3D finite model is meshed with a total of 72,269 tetrahedral meshes and the maximum element for the stepped hole domain is 0.07 mm.

The transfer impedance Z_{trans} of the PPSA is defined as [6]:

$$Z_{trans} = \frac{\Delta p}{\bar{u}} \tag{11}$$

where Δp is the pressure drop between the inlet and outlet surfaces, and $\bar{u}$ is the mean velocity in the stepped hole. Then, define the numerical value of Z_{trans} as a global variable using derived values.

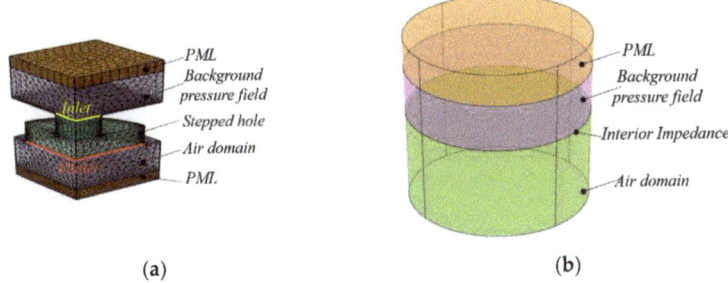

Figure 2. Finite element simulation. (**a**) Thermos-viscous model of PPSA; (**b**) Pressure acoustic model of PPSA absorber.

After that, a finite element model of the PPSA absorber is established in the pressure acoustics frequency domain interface. The upper PML acts as an infinite air domain, the sound incident is placed in background pressure field and the air cavity behind the PPSA is set as air domain, as shown in Figure 2b. The values of the transfer impedance Z_{trans} are then imported using the Interpolation function command in the Definitions toolbar, thus the acoustic impedance of the PPSA can be defined by the built-in impedance. Thus, the sound pressure reflection coefficient R is expressed as:

$$R = \frac{p_{sc}}{p_{in}} \tag{12}$$

where p_{sc} and p_{in} are the scattered and incident sound pressure, respectively. Finally, the sound absorption coefficient of the PPSA absorber can be obtained from Equation (10).

Figure 3 plots the theoretical and simulated sound absorption of PPSA absorbers with different perforation ratio and cavity depth. The parameters for three PPSA absorbers are listed in Table 1, for PPSA1 and PPSA2 absorbers, the theoretical sound absorption coefficient curves are the same as that of the numerical simulation. In addition, for PPSA3 there is an offset of about 2 Hz between the theoretical and the numerical resonances. In addition, in Figure 3b, there exists a difference between the theoretical and simulated acoustic resistance at frequencies far from resonance, which may be further modified by model mesh refinement and considering the thermal effects of air in the calculations, but its acoustic reactance is almost identical. Overall, the finite element simulation is in agreement with the theoretical calculation.

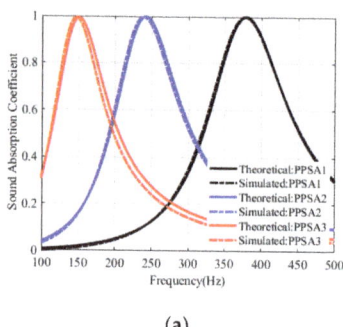
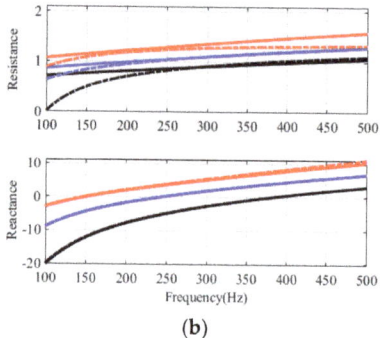

(a) (b)

Figure 3. The theoretical and simulated results for PPSA absorbers. (**a**) Sound absorption coefficients; (**b**) Specific acoustic impedance.

Table 1. Parameters for three PPSA absorbers in the theoretical and simulated comparison.

Parameters	PPSA1	PPSA2	PPSA3
$d(d_1/d_2)$ (mm)	1.5/4	1.5/4	1.5/4
$t(t_1/t_2)$ (mm)	1/1	1/1	1/1
$\sigma(\sigma_1/\sigma_2)$ (%)	0.27/1.92	0.23/1.60	0.18/1.28
D (mm)	25	50	100

2.3. Experiment Measurements

To further verify the feasibility of the theoretical and numerical models, the sound absorption coefficients of PPSA absorber at normal incidence are measured by SW422 impedance tube with diameter of 100 mm, as shown in Figure 4a, and PPSA samples are made of resin materials by 3D printing using SLA (light curing molding) equipment. The outer diameter of the specimen is about 99 mm, so the sample is placed in the specimen tube with sealing strips or tape to ensure the tightness.

The sound absorption measurement in impedance tube follows the two-microphone transfer function method [30], and the principle is described below. The sound pressure p_1 and p_2 of two microphones located at position 1 and position 2 are expressed as:

$$p_1 = P_I e^{jk_0 x_1} + P_R e^{-jk_0 x_1}, p_2 = P_I e^{jk_0 x_2} + P_R e^{-jk_0 x_2} \tag{13}$$

The transfer function of the incident wave and the reflected wave are written as:

$$H_I = \frac{p_{2I}}{p_{1I}} = e^{-jk_0(x_1-x_2)} = e^{-jk_0 s}, H_R = \frac{p_{2R}}{p_{1R}} = e^{jk_0(x_1-x_2)} = e^{jk_0 s} \tag{14}$$

According to Equation (13), the transfer function of the total sound field is denoted as:

$$H_{12} = \frac{p_2}{p_1} = \frac{e^{jk_0 x_2} + re^{-jk_0 x_2}}{e^{jk_0 x_1} + re^{-jk_0 x_1}} \tag{15}$$

Substituting Equation (14) into Equation (15), the reflection coefficient is expressed as:

$$r = \frac{H_{12} - H_I}{H_R - H_{12}} e^{j2k_0 x_1} \tag{16}$$

where x_1 and x_2 are the distances between microphone position 1 or position 2 and the front surface of the test sample, respectively, and s is the distance between two microphone position 1 and position 2. Once the reflection coefficient is determined, the sound absorption coefficient of the test sample can be calculated.

The sound absorption coefficients of a PPSA absorber in the frequency range of 100–300 Hz from theoretical, numerical and experimental results are plotted in Figure 4b. The parameters of the PPSA are d_1 =1.5 mm, d_1 =3 mm, t_1 = 1 mm, t_2 = 1 mm, p_1 = 0.24%, p_2 = 1.08% and the air cavity depth is D = 80 mm. The peak frequencies of three absorption coefficient curves are almost at 190 Hz, and the peaks are 0.999, 0.999 and 0.992, and the frequency ranges of absorption coefficients greater than 0.6 are 152–244 Hz, 153–242 Hz and 154–239 Hz, respectively. The results showed that there are tiny errors between the measured and predicted results. These unavoidable deviations may be due to factors such as machining accuracy and inaccurate mounting. In conclusion, the proposed theoretical and numerical models are feasible for predicting the sound absorption of the PPSA absorber. Meanwhile, it implies that the expected sound absorption is also relied on the accuracy of the sample processing.

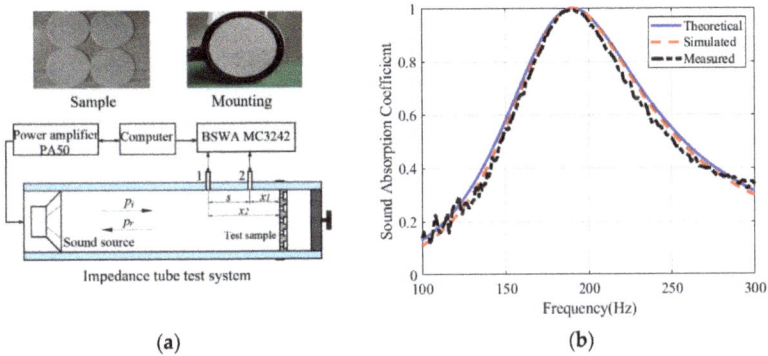

Figure 4. Experimental setup and results. (a) Impedance tube system and test sample; (b) Absorption coefficients of PPSA absorber from three models: theoretical, FEM and experimental.

3. Results and Discuss

3.1. Sound Absorption of PPSA and Single Perforated Panle(PP) Absorber

To explain the feasibility of the proposed PPSA structure for low frequency sound absorption, comparisons of the sound absorption of PPSA absorber with that of single PP absorber are given here, with a depth of 80 mm for each air cavity. Figure 5 displays the theoretical sound absorption coefficients and acoustic impedance of PPSA and single PP absorbers with the same perforation ratio. The relevant parameters of PPSA and PP are listed in Table 2. In Figure 5a, the resonance peaks of PPSA, PP1 and PP2 absorber are located at 168 Hz, 195 Hz and 219 Hz, and the bandwidth of the sound absorption coefficient well above 0.6 are 76 Hz, 40 Hz and 110 Hz, respectively. In Figure 5b, PPSA has a relatively matched acoustic resistance from 1 to 1.41 in the range of 100–300 Hz. In contrast, the acoustic resistance of PP is extremely inadequate, especially the maximum acoustic resistance of PP1 with a large aperture is below 0.5. In addition, compared to the PP absorbers, the zero acoustic reactance of the PPSA absorber is shifted to a lower frequency. Even though, PP2 has a relatively large absorption bandwidth, its resonant frequency occurs at higher frequency, and a large number of perforations will increase the manufacturing costs. Thus, PPSA is more suitable for low-frequency sound absorption.

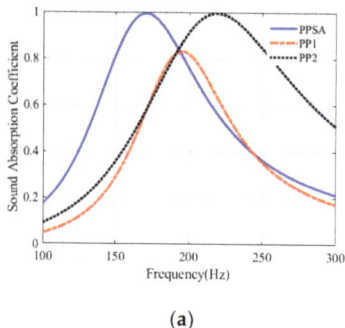
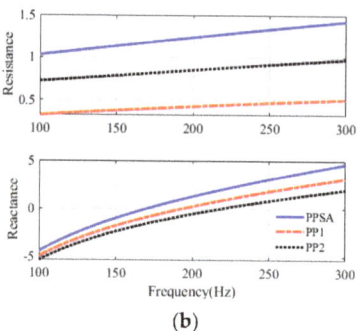

Figure 5. Sound absorption of PPSA and single PP absorbers with the same perforation ratio. (a) Sound absorption coefficients; (b) Specific acoustic impedance.

Table 2. Parameters for PPSA and single PP absorbers with the same perforation ratio.

Parameters	PPSA	Single PP1	Single PP2
$d(d_1/d_2)$ (mm)	1.5/3	3	1.5
$t(t_1/t_2)$ (mm)	1/1	2	2
$\sigma(\sigma_1/\sigma_2)$ (%)	0.21/0.81	1.02	1.02

Figure 6 illustrated the theoretical sound absorption coefficients and acoustic impedance of PPSA and single PP absorbers with the same hole spacing. The parameters of PPSA and PP are given in Table 3. First, comparing PPSA and PP1, their resonant frequencies are close to 153 Hz and their sound reactance curves are almost overlapping as shown in Figure 6b. For PPSA with $d_1 = 2$ mm and $d_2 = 4$ mm, its thickness is $t = 2$ mm, while for PP1 with $d = 4$ mm, its thickness is 6.5 mm, thus the panel thickness of PPSA is about 3.25 times that of PP1. That is, for the same cavity depth and hole spacing, when PPSA and PP absorbers are resonating at the same frequency, PP with the large hole diameter requires a larger thickness. Meanwhile, the resonance peak of PPSA is close to 1, and that of PP1 is 0.88. The sound absorption coefficient of PPSA is greater than 0.6 from 135 Hz–196 Hz, and that of PP1 is greater than 0.6 from 143 Hz–182 Hz. Obviously, the sound absorption of PPSA is better than that of PP1. Furthermore, for PP2 of the thickness $t = 2$ mm, its resonance occurs at a higher frequency of 226 Hz with a peak of only 0.6. This is due to its inadequate acoustic resistance and high acoustic reactance. Therefore, the introduction of stepped holes not only effectively increase the acoustic resistance, but also shift the zero acoustic reactance of the PPSA absorber to lower frequencies.

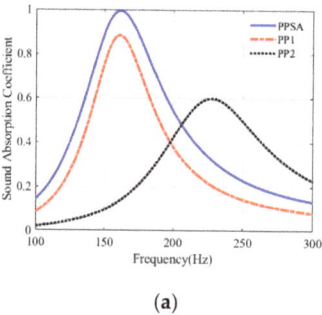
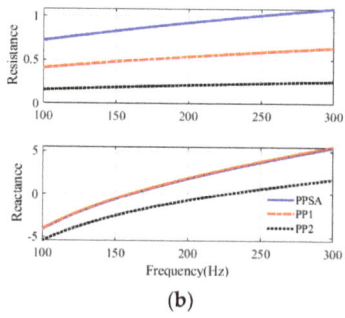

Figure 6. Sound absorption of PPSA and single PP absorbers with the same hole spacing. (a) Sound absorption coefficients; (b) Specific acoustic impedance.

Table 3. Parameters for PPSA and single PP absorbers with the same hole spacing.

Parameters	PPSA	Single PP1	Single PP2
$d(d_1/d_2)$ (mm)	2/4	4	4
$t(t_1/t_2)$ (mm)	2	7	2
b (mm)	39.6	39.6	39.6

3.2. Sound Absorption of PPSA Absorber with Varied Hole Spacing, Aperture and Plate Thickness

The theoretical absorption coefficients of the single PPSA absorber with varied hole spacing, aperture and plate thickness are marked with the color bar in Figure 7a–d. The parameters of PPSA are listed in Table 2 and hole spacing b = 30 mm, air cavity D = 80 mm. In Figure 7a, when other parameters remain unchanged, with the increase of hole spacing b, the effective sound absorption is distributed in the lower frequency range, and the maximum sound absorption coefficient reaches 1 and then decreases. In Figure 7b, when aperture d_1 increases, the resonance shifts to higher frequencies and becomes weak, and the maximum sound absorption coefficient is significantly reduced. That is, when the perforation ratio is constant, the PPSA with a smaller aperture d_1 is more conducive to sound absorption in the low frequency range. The effect of aperture d_2 on the sound absorption is similar to that of aperture d_1, so no explanation is given here. In Figure 7c, as the thickness t_1 increases, the resonance occurs in the lower frequency, but the maximum sound absorption coefficient becomes lower. This is because the small aperture with a large thickness causes excessive damping. In Figure 7d, when the thickness t_2 increases, the resonance also moves to lower frequencies, however, the maximum absorption coefficient of almost 1 is perfect in the whole range of t_2. This is because for the large aperture, the sound mass changes obviously as the thickness increases, while the sound resistance changes relatively slightly. Therefore, proper parameters should be considered to obtain an effective PPSA absorber for low frequency sound absorption.

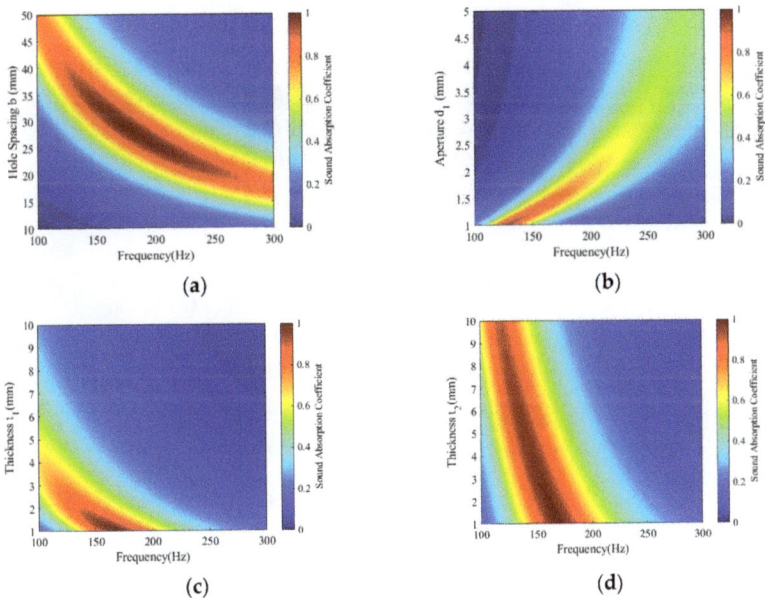

Figure 7. The sound absorption coefficients of PPSA absorber with varied structure parameters. (**a**) Hole spacing b; (**b**) Hole aperture d_1; (**c**) Plate thickness t_1 of the small aperture; (**d**) Plate thickness t_2 of the large aperture.

3.3. Sound Absorption of PPSA Absorber Array

Due to its Helmholtz resonance nature, PPSA absorber exhibits good sound absorption in the vicinity of the resonance. To further improve the sound absorption of PPSA absorber, only one rigid plate is inserted to separate the air cavities, thus introducing additional resonances to expand the absorption bandwidth, while the structural parameters of the PPSA remain unchanged.

Without loss of simplicity, a PPSA absorber array consisting of two sub-PPSA absorbers arranged in parallel is shown in Figure 8a. According to the electroacoustic analogy method, the surface impedance of the PPSA absorber array is expressed as:

$$Z = \left(\frac{\varphi_1}{Z_1} + \frac{\varphi_2}{Z_2}\right)^{-1} \tag{17}$$

where φ_1 and φ_2 are the area ratios of sub-PPSA1 and sub-PPSA2 to the PPSA absorber array, Z_1 and Z_2 are the surface impedance of sub-PPSA1 and sub-PPSA2 absorbers, respectively.

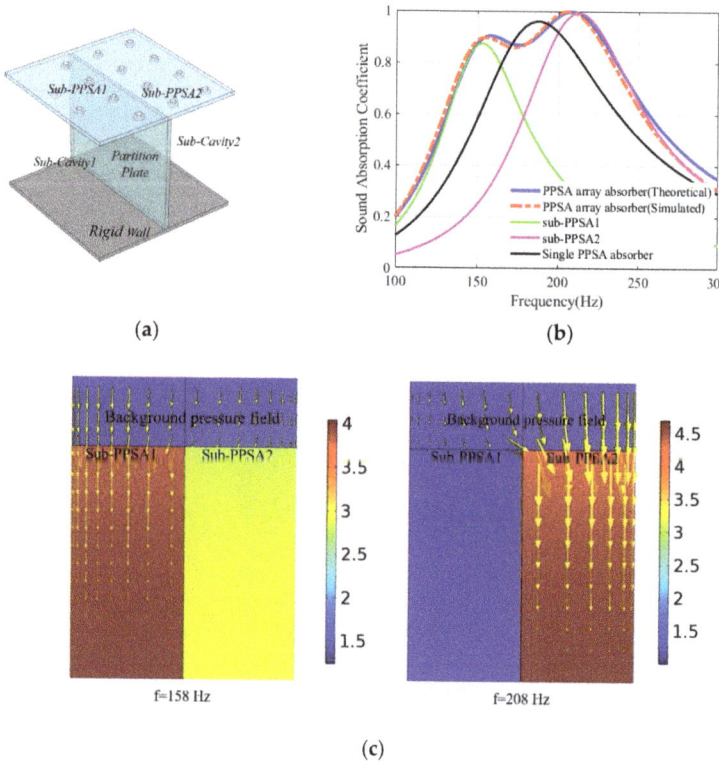

Figure 8. PPSA absorber array. (**a**) Structure diagram; (**b**) Sound absorption coefficients; (**c**) The acoustic pressure field (color map) and velocity distribution (yellow arrow).

Next, we will discuss the sound absorption performance of PPSA absorber array. As an example, a PPSA absorber array with panel thickness t = 2 mm, air cavity D = 100 mm, diameters of stepped hole d_1 =1.5 mm and d_2 = 4 mm, and its relevant parameters are listed in Table 4. The sound absorption coefficients of PPSA absorber array, sub-PPSA absorber and single PPSA absorber are demonstrated in Figure 8b. It can be observed that, the two peak of the PPSA absorber array are located at 158 Hz and 208 Hz, and the peaks of sub-

PPSA1 and sub-PPSA2 absorber are positioned at 154 Hz and 213 Hz, respectively. That is, the two peaks of the PPSA absorber array are corresponding to those of sub-PPSA1 and sub-PPSA2 absorber, and the apparent frequency shift can be attributed to the interaction of sub-PPSA1 and sub-PPSA2. In addition, the PPSA absorber array has a sound absorption coefficient greater than 0.6 from 129 Hz to 257 Hz, and its sound absorption bandwidth is about 128 Hz. In contrast, the single PPSA absorber has a sound absorption coefficient greater than 0.6 from 150 Hz to 237 Hz, and its sound absorption bandwidth is about 87 Hz. Consequently, an array of PPSA absorbers can expand absorption bandwidth for low frequency under the common coupling effect of multi-local resonances.

Table 4. Parameters for PPSA absorber array and single PPSA absorber.

Parameters	PPSA Absorber Array		Single PPSA Absorber
	Sub-PPSA1	Sub-PPSA2	
$d(d_1/d_2)$ (mm)	1.5/4	4	1.5/4
$t(t_1/t_2)$ (mm)	1/1	1/1	1/1
$\sigma(\sigma_1/\sigma_2)$ (%)	0.095/0.67	0.185/1.315	0.28/1.98

Intuitively, Figure 8c shows the distribution of the normalized sound pressure and particle velocity at two absorption peak frequencies $f = 158$ Hz and $f = 208$ Hz. As observed, at $f = 158$ Hz, the sound pressure in the air cavity of sub-PPSA1 is approximately four times higher than that of the incident sound field, and most of the particle velocity flow is distributed in sub-PPSA1 absorber. Similarly, at $f = 208$ Hz, due to strong local resonance, the maximum sound pressure and particle velocity flow are mostly concentrated in the sub-PPSA2 absorber, and even the sound pressure does not change in the Sub-PPSA1. Thus, it is confirmed that acoustic energy is mainly dissipated by the local resonances of the PPSA absorber array.

For PPSA absorber array and single PPSA absorber, the measured and theoretical sound absorption of sample 1 and sample 2 are shown in Figures 9 and 10, respectively. The air cavity depth of two samples is 80 mm, and the approximate parameters for samples are given in Table 5. There are some differences between the measured and the theoretical absorption coefficients, as well as the acoustic impedance, but their sound absorption characteristics are almost identical. For PPSA absorber array1, as shown in Figure 9a, the measured sound absorption coefficient is higher than 0.5 from 141 Hz to 280 Hz, and its effective sound absorption bandwidth is about 105 Hz. While for single PPSA absorber1, the measured sound absorption coefficient is above 0.5 from 153 Hz to 247 Hz, and its effective sound absorption bandwidth is about 59 Hz. Moreover, compared to a single PPSA absorber without partition, as observed in Figure 9b, the specific reactance of the PPSA absorber array changes relatively slowly and tends to 0, and its specific acoustic resistance is close to 1 except for the non-strong coupling domain of the sub-PPSA absorber.

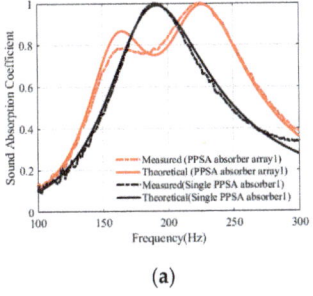

(a)

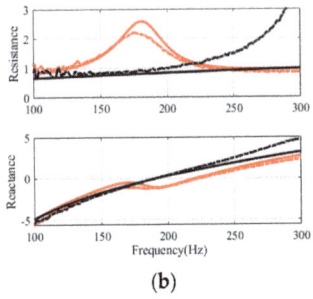

(b)

Figure 9. The sound absorption of Sample 1. (a) The measured and theoretical sound absorption coefficients; (b) The measured and theoretical specific acoustic impedance.

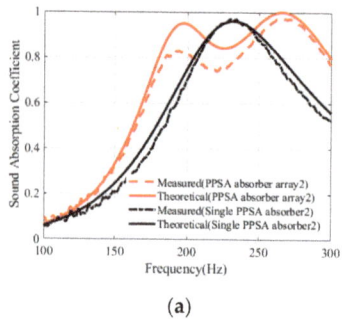
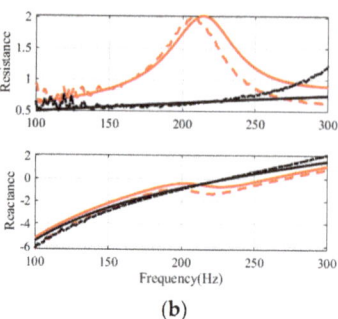

Figure 10. The sound absorption of Sample 2. (**a**) The measured and theoretical sound absorption coefficients; (**b**) The measured and theoretical specific acoustic impedance.

Table 5. Parameters of Samples of PPSA absorber array and single PPSA absorber.

Sample 1 Parameters	PPSA Absorber Array1		Single PPSA Absorber1
	Sub-PPSA1	Sub-PPSA2	
$d(d_1/d_2)$ (mm)	1.8/3	1.8/3	1.8/3
$t(t_1/t_2)$ (mm)	1/1	1/1	1/1
$\sigma(\sigma_1/\sigma_2)$ (%)	0.095/0.27	0.195/0.54	0.29/0.81
Sample 2 Parameters	PPSA absorber array2		Single PPSA Absorber2
	Sub-PPSA1	Sub-PPSA2	
$d(d_1/d_2)$ (mm)	1.8/3.8	1.8/3.8	1.8/3.8
$t(t_1/t_2)$ (mm)	1/1	1/1	1/1
$\sigma(\sigma_1/\sigma_2)$ (%)	0.14/0.615	0.275/1.23	0.415/1.845

Similarly, for PPSA absorber array2, as shown in Figure 10a, the measured sound absorption coefficient is higher than 0.5 from 165 Hz to 334 Hz, and its effective sound absorption bandwidth is about 129 Hz. While for single PPSA absorber2, the measured sound absorption coefficient is above 0.5 from 186 Hz to 302 Hz, and its effective sound absorption bandwidth is about 72 Hz. In addition, Figure 10b exhibits that the acoustic impedance characteristics of PPSA absorber array2 are the same as that of PPSA absorber array1. In summary, it is also demonstrated that the PPSA absorber array has the potential to enhance sound absorption compared to a single PPSA absorber. In addition, the overall dimensions of the fabricated specimens are 82 mm, which are only about 1/30th and 1/27th of the maximum wavelength of the semi-absorption coefficient, indicating that the PPSA absorber array is a compact structure for low frequency sound absorption.

4. Conclusions

In this paper, a PPSA absorber is studied to improve sound absorption for low frequencies. The advantages of the PPSA are that it matches acoustic resistance of air characteristic impedance and moderately increase acoustic mass by introducing stepped hole. The theoretical and numerical predictions agree well with the experimental results. In addition, an array consisting of two PPSA absorbers arranged in parallel is explored, and PPSA absorber array exhibits an effective broadband sound absorption due to the coupling effect of local resonances. The measured results also show that PPSA absorber array as a compact structure has the potential to control large wavelength noise in a limit space. Consequently, the proposed PPSA provides a meaningful method for the application of perforated plates in low frequency sound absorption. Moreover, in the subsequent work, we will investigate the sound absorption characteristics of the array structure of multiple inhomogeneous PPSA absorbers with different cavities.

Author Contributions: Conceptualization, X.L. and B.L.; methodology, data curation and investigation, X.L.; validation and software, C.Q.; resources and supervision, B.L.; writing—original draft preparation, X.L.; writing—review and editing, X.L. and C.Q. All authors have read and agreed to the published version of the manuscript.

Funding: The financial support given by NSFC with Grant No. 11874034 and Taishan Scholar Program of Shandong (No. ts201712054) are highly appreciated for this research.

Institutional Review Board Statement: Not applicable.

Informed Consent Statement: Not applicable.

Data Availability Statement: Not applicable.

Conflicts of Interest: The authors declare no conflict of interest.

References

1. Yang, M.; Sheng, P. Sound Absorption Structures: From Porous Media to Acoustic Metamaterials. *Annu. Rev. Mater. Res.* **2017**, *47*, 83–114. [CrossRef]
2. Liu, B.; Li, X. Noise transmission and absorption of lightweight structures: An overview and experience. In Proceedings of the 26th International Congress on Sound and Vibration, Montreal, QC, Canada, 7–13 July 2019.
3. Callaway, D.B. The Use of Perforated Facings in Designing Low Frequency Resonant Absorbers. *J. Acoust. Soc. Am.* **1952**, *24*, 309–312. [CrossRef]
4. Davern, W. Perforated facings backed with porous materials as sound absorbers—An experimental study. *Appl. Acoust.* **1977**, *10*, 85–112. [CrossRef]
5. Allard, J.F.; Atalla, N. *Porous Materials with Perforated Facings*; Wiley: Hoboken, NJ, USA, 2009; pp. 187–212.
6. Maa, D.Y. Theory and design of microperforated panel sound absorbing constructions. *Science* **1975**, *xviii*, 55–71.
7. Maa, D.-Y. Potential of microperforated panel absorber. *J. Acoust. Soc. Am.* **1998**, *104*, 2861–2866. [CrossRef]
8. Randeberg, R.T. Perforated Panel Absorbers with Viscous Energy Dissipation Enhanced by Orifice Design. Ph.D. Thesis, NTNU, Trondheim, Norway, 2000.
9. Sakagami, K.; Morimoto, M.; Yairi, M.; Minemura, A. A pilot study on improving the absorptivity of a thick microperforated panel absorber. *Appl. Acoust.* **2008**, *69*, 179–182. [CrossRef]
10. Lu, W.; Zhang, B.; Li, X. Study on Acoustic Characteristic of Micro-Perforated Panel with Variable Cross-Section. *Noise Vib. Control* **2009**. [CrossRef]
11. Li-Yan, H.E.; Xi-Zhi, H.U.; Chen, T. The Influence of Variable Section of Orifice on Sound Absorption Characteristics of Thick Microperforated Panel. *Noise Vib. Control* **2011**, *30*, 141–144.
12. Zhihui, M.A. Pilot Study on Simulations of Micro-Perforated Panel with Variable Cross-Section. *Audio Eng.* **2014**, 3811–3813.
13. Qian, Y.J.; Cui, K.; Liu, S.M.; Li, Z.B.; Kong, D.Y.; Sun, S.M. Numerical study of the acoustic properties of micro-perforated panels with tapered hole. *Noise Control Eng. J.* **2014**, *62*, 152–159. [CrossRef]
14. Jiang, C.-S.; Li, X.-H.; Cheng, W.-Y.; Luo, Y.; Xing, T. Acoustic impedance of microperforated plates with stepwise apertures. *Appl. Acoust.* **2020**, *157*, 106998. [CrossRef]
15. Li, D.; Chang, D.; Liu, B. Enhancing the low frequency sound absorption of a perforated panel by parallel-arranged extended tubes. *Appl. Acoust.* **2016**, *102*, 126–132. [CrossRef]
16. Peng, X.; Ji, J.; Jing, Y. Composite honeycomb metasurface panel for broadband sound absorption. *J. Acoust. Soc. Am.* **2018**, *144*, EL255–EL261. [CrossRef]
17. Liu, C.R.; Wu, J.H.; Chen, X.; Ma, F. A thin low-frequency broadband metasurface with multi-order sound absorption. *J. Phys. D Appl. Phys.* **2019**, *52*, 105302. [CrossRef]
18. Long, H.; Shao, C.; Liu, C.; Cheng, Y.; Liu, X. Broadband near-perfect absorption of low-frequency sound by subwavelength metasurface. *Appl. Phys. Lett.* **2019**, *115*, 103503. [CrossRef]
19. Li, X.; Wu, Q.; Kang, L.; Liu, B. Design of Multiple Parallel-Arranged Perforated Panel Absorbers for Low Frequency Sound Absorption. *Materials* **2019**, *12*, 2099. [CrossRef]
20. Chen, J.-S.; Chen, Y.-B.; Cheng, Y.-H.; Chou, L.-C. A sound absorption panel containing coiled Helmholtz resonators. *Phys. Lett. A* **2020**, *384*, 126887. [CrossRef]
21. Guo, J.; Zhang, X.; Fang, Y.; Jiang, Z. Wideband low-frequency sound absorption by inhomogeneous multi-layer resonators with extended necks. *Compos. Struct.* **2021**, *260*, 113538. [CrossRef]
22. Cha, X.; Jian, K.; Zhang, T.; Zhou, X.; Fuchs, H. Application approach for microperforated panel sound absorbers. *Acta Acustica* **1994**, *19*, 258–265.
23. Wang, C.; Huang, L. On the acoustic properties of parallel arrangement of multiple micro-perforated panel absorbers with different cavity depths. *J. Acoust. Soc. Am.* **2011**, *130*, 208–218. [CrossRef]
24. Uenishi, K.; Okuzono, T.; Sakagami, K. Finite element analysis of absorption characteristics of permeable membrane absorbers array. *Acoust. Sci. Technol.* **2017**, *38*, 322–325. [CrossRef]

25. Okuzono, T.; Uenishi, K.; Sakagami, K. Experimental comparison of absorption characteristics of single-leaf permeable membrane absorbers with different backing air cavity designs. *Noise Control Eng. J.* **2020**, *68*, 237–245. [CrossRef]
26. Wu, T.; Cox, T.J.; Lam, Y.W. A profiled structure with improved low frequency absorption. *J. Acoust. Soc. Am.* **2001**, *110*, 3064–3070. [CrossRef]
27. Lee, D.; Kwon, Y. Estimation of the absorption performance of multiple layer perforated panel systems by transfer matrix method. *J. Sound Vib.* **2004**, *278*, 847–860. [CrossRef]
28. Crandall, I.B. *Theory of Vibrating Systems and Sound*, 2nd ed.; D. Van Nostrand Company: New York, NY, USA, 1927.
29. Ingard, U. On the Design of Acoustic Resonators. *J. Acoust. Soc. Am.* **1953**, *25*, 830. [CrossRef]
30. ISO (10534-2). *Acoustics–Determination of Sound Absorption Coefficient and Impedance in Impedance Tubes–Part 2: Transfer-Function Method*; 2001.

Article

On the Determination of Acoustic Properties of Membrane Type Structural Skin Elements by Means of Surface Displacements

Daniel Urbán [1,2,*], N. B. Roozen [3], Vojtech Jandák [1], Marek Brothánek [1] and Ondřej Jiříček [1]

[1] Department of Physics, Faculty of Electrical Engineering, Czech Technical University in Prague, Technicka 2, 166 27 Prague, Czech Republic; jandav1@fel.cvut.cz (V.J.); brothan@fel.cvut.cz (M.B.); jiricek@fel.cvut.cz (O.J.)
[2] Department of Materials Engineering and Physics, Faculty of Civil Engineering, Slovak University of Technology in Bratislava, Radlinského 11, 810 05 Bratislava, Slovakia
[3] Department of Physics and Astronomy, Soft Matter and Biophysics, Laboratory of Acoustics, KU Leuven, Celestijnenlaan 200D, 3001 Leuven, Belgium; bert.roozen@kuleuven.be
* Correspondence: daniel.urban@stuba.sk

Abstract: The article focuses on the determination of the acoustic properties (sound transmission loss, sound absorption and transmission coefficient under acoustic plane wave excitation) of membrane-type of specimens by means of a combination of incident plane wave sound pressure and membrane surface displacement information, measuring the sound pressure with a microphone and the membrane displacement by means of a laser Doppler vibrometer. An overview of known measurement methods and the theoretical background of the proposed so-called mobility-based method (MM) is presented. The proposed method was compared with the conventional methods for sound transmission loss and absorption measurement in the impedance tube, both numerically and experimentally. Finite element model (FEM) simulation results of two single layer membrane samples of different shape configurations were compared, amongst which six different variations of the backing wall termination. Four different approaches to determine the sound transmission loss and two methods to determine sound absorption properties of the membranes were compared. Subsequently, the proposed method was tested in a laboratory environment. The proposed MM method can be possibly used to measure the vibro-acoustic properties of building parts in situ.

Keywords: membranes; acoustics; measurement method; transmission loss; simulations; experiment

Citation: Urbán, D.; Roozen, N.B.; Jandák, V.; Brothánek, M.; Jiříček, O. On the Determination of Acoustic Properties of Membrane Type Structural Skin Elements by Means of Surface Displacements. *Appl. Sci.* **2021**, *11*, 10357. https://doi.org/10.3390/app112110357

Academic Editor: Alessandro Ruggiero

Received: 29 September 2021
Accepted: 2 November 2021
Published: 4 November 2021

Publisher's Note: MDPI stays neutral with regard to jurisdictional claims in published maps and institutional affiliations.

Copyright: © 2021 by the authors. Licensee MDPI, Basel, Switzerland. This article is an open access article distributed under the terms and conditions of the Creative Commons Attribution (CC BY) license (https://creativecommons.org/licenses/by/4.0/).

1. Introduction

The membranes of variable shape are used both indoors and outdoors where membranes have become part of roofing and shielding elements as well as of facades. A wide range of solutions for structural skins exists, whether for single, second skin or double skin facades, atria coating or exterior environment covering [1]. Moreover, lightweight solutions such as membrane-based constructions are considered as a sustainable solution in architecture [2]. From an acoustic point of view, every new construction solution brings specific pitfalls associated with it. For example, the impact of the frequently used double transparent facades (DTF) on administrative buildings for sound insulation improves the sound reduction index, but has possible negative effects in the low frequency range caused by standing wave resonances occurring in the air cavity inside the DTF. DTFs can also cause problems related to speech privacy in the interior caused by flanking transmission paths between attached offices, which can be problematic mainly in cases of low background noise level in the DTF cavity [3,4]. Nowadays, when the influence of facades on environmental noise is increasingly being discussed, adaptive facade (or smart façade-facades that adapt to the climate and environment through their skin) solutions with implemented membrane structures are a topic of growing interest. The properties of membrane structures are very dependent on their mass, dimensions and mechanical stresses. The present work was motivated by the idea of Martens et al. [5], where authors investigated in the determination of the sound energy absorbed by the plant leaves based on the measured surface velocity and sound pressure. The goal was to verify it that would be possible to apply the proposed theory in an experimental way.

The theory of circular and annular membranes was described by Rayleigh [6]. For more complex shapes, several approximate methods have been proposed by Mazumdar [7]. Later, the impact of the circular core fixed to the membrane was investigated [8]. A number of previous works were published with a focus on the variations of the membrane boundary conditions. For example, Wang investigated the impact of a pinned large axisymmetric mass at the centre of the membrane on its natural frequency [9,10]. These kinds of membranes were also called membrane-type metamaterial (MAMs) with so-called negative dynamic mass [11–14].

By stacking together membrane panels with attached mass (circular shaped weights) in the centre of membrane surfaces, the sound transmission loss of the membrane composition can be increased in a broad band frequency range from 50 to 1000 [15]. The effect of the mass of the membrane and the membrane tension on the transmission loss was investigated by a number of researchers [15,16]. Normally, the bending stiffness of membranes can safely be ignored. The restoring force arises entirely from the applied tension, not from bending stiffness as is the case for plates.

Relatively popular MAMs or locally resonant sonic materials (LRSMs) contain arrays of elastic resonators composed of a heavy core surrounded by a soft coating layer. In principle, by loading the membrane by a relatively heavy object the so-called dipole resonance occurs. The dipole resonance enhances the acoustic performance [17,18]. These resonant materials are able to control low-frequency sound reflection and transmission very effectively. The negative dynamic mass causes the subwavelength attenuation of sound in the audible frequency band and breaks the mass density law. In the frequency range from 100 to 1000 Hz, a significant increase of the normal incidence sound transmission loss (nTL) can be achieved [19]. Spatially averaged force and acceleration are opposite in phase, which leads to near-total reflection (anti-resonance) at the frequency between two eigenmodes. In this region, the in-plane average of normal displacement is close to zero [19]. This finding is usually visible in the sound transmission loss TL (dB) spectra as a peak in the spectrum. Dips in TL and peaks in the sound absorption spectra are caused by symmetrical eigenmodes.

An analytical vibroacoustic membrane model as a tool for the design of MAMs was developed in [20]. Another analytical model was developed to compute the sound transmission loss of a mass loaded rectangular membrane in a fast manner. It was shown that the mass of the membrane is especially affecting the first normal incidence transmission loss (nTL) peak and the resonance frequency, while the second resonance frequency strongly depends on the membrane properties [21]. In the publication, the effects of the membrane tension and the membrane surface density on transmission and characteristic frequencies were investigated as well. Zhang later focused on the low-frequency sound attenuation by MAMs carrying different masses at adjacent cells [22]. However, the most universal tool to predict MAMs behaviour is still the Finite Element Analysis (FEA) approach (with a commonly accepted uncertainty of about 20 dB peaks and dips of transmission loss spectra. Additionally, the MAMs with coaxial ring masses were experimentally and numerically analysed. The multiple coaxial arranged rings resulted in multi-peak profile (uniform mass) or broadband TL peak (non-uniform mass) [19].

In later works, Naify investigated the scaling of LRSMs [23] by multi-celled structure analysis. The impact of two parallel cells with mass and air cavity was analysed. It appeared that the cavity thickness difference (from 2–4 mm) had a negligible effect on its normal incidence sound transmission loss (nTL (dB)) spectra in the frequency region below 1 kHz. It must be mentioned at this point, the applications based on MAMs principle can find the application not just in the membrane type constructions. By application the dynamic vibration absorbers the significant local control of low-frequency noise can be achieved [24–27].

Overview of Measuring Methods

Most of the investigations were performed under the acoustic plane wave incidence conditions, by means of the Impedance Tube Method (ITM), also called the Standing Wave or Kundt's Tube Method. This measurement approach typically determines the nTL and sound absorption (α(-)) (or reflection r(-)) coefficient. The impedance tube apparatus is commonly used for the characterization of locally reacting material samples. The sound absorption determination by ITM can be done by measuring maximum and minimum pressure amplitude in the tube by means of the moving microphone probe (the method using the standing wave ratio, as described in [28]), or by determination of the pressure transfer function between wave components at two or more microphone positions at a given distance from the specimen along the tube [29]. The disadvantage is that the ITM does not allow for oblique incidence measurement. Another standardized laboratory method which is used very often is to determine the statistical sound absorption coefficient α_S(-) in a diffuse field in a reverberant room, according to ISO 354 [30]. The test results obtained by this method are often considered the more realistic for characterizing specimen absorption properties in situ, as compared to the ITM approach. However, this method requires a reverberant room and a flat specimen with a total surface of 10–12 m^2. From this expensive measurement procedure "just" the absorption coefficient is obtained (and not a complex valued reflection coefficient, as is the case in the ITM) and the measurement uncertainty is relatively high. The absorption coefficient is determined based on Eyring's formula and is dependent on the reverberation time measured in the reverberation room with and without the specimen, the room volume and the surface area of the specimen. There are several microphone or p-u probe free-field methods. The basic principles are explained in, e.g., Cox and d'Antonio [31]. Methods differ regarding the required sample size, wave decomposition methods, measurement setup composition and procedure (number of microphones—from two to array, distance of microphones from specimen, angle of incidence, distance of source, etc.). Free-field methods consider the incident sound wave as a plane wave (implying that a well-defined acoustic field is required, demanding the absence of spurious reflections and edge-diffracted waves [32]). A good accuracy can be achieved by means of free-field methods in the frequency range above 290 Hz (for oblique incidence above 400 Hz [33]). Champoux and L'esoerance [34] found that the measurement does not yield accurate results for low values of kR (for $R = 3$ m and $k < 5.5$ m^{-1}), where k is wave number and R is the distance of the sound source from the specimen surface. They also found that phase mismatch between microphones plays a crucial role, especially in the measurement of low frequencies or highly reflective materials. Assuming the non-standardized, impulse-response based microphone methods, the work of Nocke's [35] can be mentioned, which describes a method to determine the sound absorption from frequency 80 Hz onwards considering Fresnel zones. A different technique for sound absorption determination, by means of a p-u probe where the measured sound pressure and the normal component of the particle velocity determines the absorption, was introduced for the first time by Liu and Jacobsen [36].

Several approaches exist to determine the sound transmission loss. The simplest, which are the same as in the sound absorption case, make use of ITM. For example, the three-microphones method to measure the high nTL (up to 100 dB) acoustic samples was developed by [37] (the usual limit is around 50 dB in the frequency range below 500 Hz [38]). Generally, all ITM methods can be divided into two groups: the first group is based on the wave decomposition (WD) (three or more microphones, one or two acoustic loads) and the second group is based on the transfer matrix (TM) method (one or two acoustic loads). The disadvantage of ITM methods, similarly as in the case of sound absorption determination, is that the size of the test specimen is non-realistically small (which causes problems in relation to the way the test specimen are fitted in the tube) and the TL is determined under normal-incidence acoustic waves only (nTL). There are several standardized methods to test "real-size" specimens. For example, the most often used laboratory methods are in accordance with ISO 10136-2 [39]. The method is intended to determine the airborne sound insulation R of separating structures mounted in the transmission suite. In this approach, it is required that sound transmission via flanking paths is suppressed sufficiently well and the sound field in the source and receiving room are assumed to be diffuse. The spatially averaged sound pressure level in the source and receiving room are measured by a microphone, and the contribution of the reverberant sound field to the total measured sound field in the receiving room is accounted for. The less popular and alternative laboratory technique follows the standard ISO 15186-1 [40] where the intensity sound reduction index R_I is determined based on averaged sound pressure level in the source room, and the sound intensity level radiated from specimen surface in the receiving room. In this approach, the radiated intensity levels are determined by means of a sound intensity probe, and the receiving room is preferably an anechoic room. For in situ measurements, the standards ISO 16283-1 [41] and ISO 16283-3 [42] for airborne sound insulation of walls, small elements and facades, respectively, were established. Similar to the case of laboratory measurement, the intensity method exists for in situ cases [43]. To cope with the high measurement uncertainty of the sound reduction index measurements of building elements in the laboratory according to standards, at low frequencies, two alternative measurement approaches were developed. The first one is a measurement procedure in which a diffuse field is created in the source room through positioning an array of loudspeakers close to the specimen to be excited in the near field [44]. The structural response measurement was done by means of vibrometry (laser Doppler vibrometer, LDV). The second one is a hybrid experimental numerical approach to determine airborne sound insulation by using mobility measurement combined with a numerical procedure [45]. In this approach the device under test is mechanically excited by means of a shaker, and the response is measured by LDV. An alternative approach is to excite the structure by means of a Nd:YAG pump laser [46]. This measurement method has the advantage that the excitation is done contact-less, yielding a contact-less approach for both excitation and response measurement, which would have advantages for application in situ.

The sound absorption coefficient as well as sound transmission loss can be determined by different methods relating to the type of acoustic field and source. The application of the vibrometry technique has already proved its usefulness in building acoustics several times. Vibrometry generally helps for better understanding the structure's behaviour in the low frequency range. In the literature, one can find already the scanning laser Doppler vibrometer application for a normal incidence sound absorption determination (for high frequency range—above 3 kHz) [47]. However, the reflection coefficient was determined based on a number of Doppler frequency shifts measurements at different laser beam angles obtained by scanning the field of the standing wave tube made from glass (during operation with the test specimen), backed by a rigid wall with retroreflective tape, which is very far from the technique numerically investigated in this article.

Despite of the wide range of the measurement approaches briefly mentioned above, in this article, we focus on the determination of the acoustic properties (sound transmission loss nTL transmission coefficient $\tau(-)$ and acoustic absorption $\alpha(-)$) of membrane-type specimens excited by well-defined plane wave excitation by means of surface displacement (in the impedance tube environment). Numerical models were used to simulate the membrane-type specimen being mounted in an impedance tube. Both properties were determined by means of incident pressure and specimen surface mobility information under normal incidence plane wave excitation. The data processing procedure yields both α and τ. However, because these two quantities are related to each other (as will be discussed in Section 2, near Equations (6)–(8)), emphasis is put on the determination of the transmission coefficient τ. Subsequently, the proposed method was experimentally tested.

By combining the known incident sound power and the frequency response of the average surface mobility, both acoustic characteristics can be determined for normal incidence plane waves. The paper is outlined as follows: Section 2 Materials and Methods including the theoretical explanation of the approach used for the determination of nTL, α and τ and the numerical study focused on theoretical verification for two different specimens and six different boundary scenarios. In the Section 3, the laboratory experiment is introduced. Subsequently, numerical simulations and experimental results were analysed (Section 4). This work should be considered as an intermediate step towards a method to measure the acoustic characteristics of membrane structures (e.g., tent structures) in situ.

2. Materials and Methods

2.1. Theory

2.1.1. Determination of Normal Incidence Sound Transmission Loss

The normal incidence sound transmission loss nTL (dB) is defined as the ratio of the incident and transmitted sound power (Watts), or by means the sound transmission coefficient $\tau(-)$ using the ITM. The transmitted and incident sound power (W_t and W_i) need to be derived from measurements in the impedance tube. Generally, the most accurate technique to determine nTL is the measurement approach based on the transfer matrix ™ approach, precisely described in ASTME2611-09 [48] and ISO 10534-2 [29]. An application of the method described in the standard is given in [49]. The method requires the determination of the transfer matrix by means of a measurement of the complex sound pressure (amplitude and relative phase) at four locations, two on either side of the specimen.

$$nTL = 10 log_{10}\left(\frac{W_i}{W_t}\right) = 10 log_{10}\left(\frac{1}{\tau}\right) = 20 log_{10}\left|\frac{T_{11} + \left(\frac{T_{12}}{\rho c}\right) + \rho c T_{25} + T_{22}}{2 e^{jk_0 d}}\right| \quad (1)$$

where W_i, W_t, τ, k_0, c, d, and ρ are incident and transmitted sound power (Watts), transmission coefficient (-), wave number (m^{-1}), speed of sound (m/s), diameter of the tube (m), density of the air (kg/m^3) and T_{11}, T_{12}, T_{21}, T_{26} are transfer matrix elements derived from transfer functions between sound pressure measured at the microphone positions, respectively. Usually, two different terminations (anechoic, open, minimally reflecting, etc.) are used. In specific cases, when the specimen is geometrically symmetrical and is presenting the same physical properties to the sound field on both sides, the one-load method is sufficient for use. When using this method, the effect of reflections from the termination is almost negligible. For more information about the measurement procedure, see standard ASTME2611-09 [48]. Later, a modification of the method was developed for just three microphone measurements (two in the upstream part of the impedance tube, third microphone flush mounted directly on the hard termination) [50].

Another possible method to determine nTL is based on wave decomposition (WD) theory, which deals with complex wavefields upstream and downstream of the element. The goal of the method is to decompose the wavefields in terms of forward and backward propagation waves. The method went by several modifications from three microphones (two flush mounted upstream and one downstream) developed by Seybert and Ross [51] to four microphones (similarly mounted as in the TM approach) developed by Chung and Blaser [52,53]. Later, the WD-TM hybrid method was developed by Bonfiglio and Pompoli [54]. They proposed a one-termination measurement approach based on a transfer matrix formulation, taking into account the reflection contribution from the end termination and the phase shift introduced by the material. The two mentioned WD methods assume a fully anechoic termination. From the WD methods, the best results might be achieved by an approach developed by Salissou [55], whose work was influenced by Ho et al. [37], and Peng et al. [56] as well. The method takes into account the complex reflection coefficient at the surface of the sample on the source side and on the termination side (r_1 and r_2) as well as the complex reflection coefficient at the surface of the termination r_b. As the reflection coefficient r_2 can be derived just by combining two terminations measurement data, this measurement technique requires two terminations (read more about in [55]). The normal incidence transmission loss can be subsequently derived as (Equation (2)).

$$nTL = -20\log_{10}\left|H_{32}\left(1 - r_2 r_b e^{2jk_0 D_2}\right)\frac{e^{jk_0 L_1} + r_1 e^{-jk_0 L_1}}{e^{-jk_0 L_2} + r_b e^{jk_0 L_2}}\right| \quad (2)$$

where H_{32}, D_2, L_1, L_2 and j is the transfer function between microphones 2 and 3, the distance between the termination and the sample, the distance between microphone 2 and the sample on the source side and microphone 3 and the sample on the termination side, respectively, and imaginary unit (Figure 1).

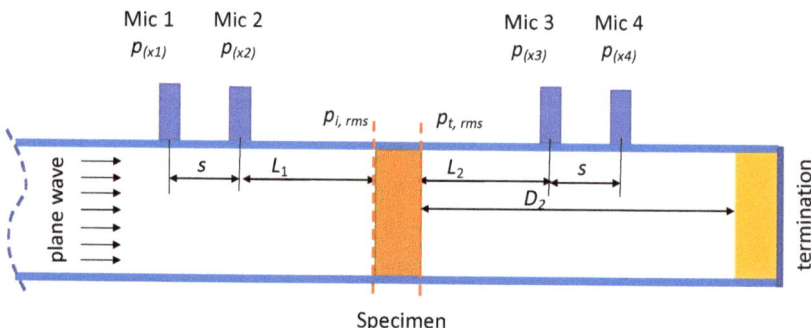

Figure 1. The scheme of the impedance tube with indication of all necessary variables to determine nTL. Upstream tube (Left), downstream tube (Right). Where $p_{(x1-4)}$ and Mic 1–4 denote the microphone positions, where the sound pressure is measured related to the x-coordinate, $p_{i,rms}$ and $p_{t,rms}$ are effective values of the incident and transmitted sound pressure at the surface of the specimen (derived from the measurement data $p_{(x1-4)}$), s is distance between microphone positions and L_1, L_2 are distances from of the microphone to the specimen surface.

An interesting approach was recently developed by Wei [57], who proposed the WD-based nTL method using only two upstream microphones (the so-called upstream tube wave field decomposition UWD).

One of the methods that is used in this paper as a reference for the determination of nTL was derived from the work by Seybert [58]. Unlike other methods, it takes into account the multiple reflection form the back of the impedance tube. The method was developed originally for the sound transmission loss determination in ducts systems (Equation (3)).

$$nTL = 10\log_{10}\frac{S_{11} + S_{22} - 2C_{12}\cos k_0 s + 2Q_{12}\sin k_0 s}{S_{33} + S_{44} - 2C_{34}\cos k_0 s + 2Q_{34}\sin k_0 s} \quad (3)$$

where S_{11}, S_{22}, S_{33}, and S_{44} are auto spectra (Pa^2) of the total acoustic pressure at microphone positions 1, 2, 3 and 4 (Figure 1), Q_{12} and Q_{34} are imaginary parts and C_{12} and C_{34} are the real parts of pressure cross spectra between microphones 1 and 2 or 3 and 4 and s (m) is distance between microphone pairs 1 and 2 or 3 and 4, respectively. The method is precisely described in Reference [58].

Thus far, an overview of several of the most well-known methods for nTL determining has been mentioned. As mentioned earlier, motivated by the idea of Martens et al. [5], the presented work wants to prove the theory that if the incident sound pressure and the vibration vector of membrane measured by means of the chosen vibrometry technique is known, the sound transmission loss as well as absorption can be determined. In the case of an impedance tube, the radiated sound power into the downstream part of the tube, or the sound pressure at a specific distance from the vibrating surface (depending on the termination), can be determined from the spatially averaged measured displacement of the vibrating surface. The normal component of the wall velocity is equal to the particle velocity at the wall surface in the case of the perpendicular plane wave excitation [59]. The measured specimen can be considered as a non-baffled piston, assuming a simple $\rho \cdot c$ impedance. Motivated by the work of Chen [20] (hereinafter referred to as the Mobility-based Method—MM), the sound transmission loss can be subsequently determined as (Equation (4)):

$$nTL = 20 log_{10} \frac{p_{i,rms}}{|j \cdot \omega \cdot \rho_0 \cdot c_0 \cdot \langle w \rangle|} \quad (4)$$

where $\langle w \rangle$ is the spatially averaged displacement measured at the specimen surface at the receiving side, $p_{i,rms}$ (Pa) is the rms value of the incident sound pressure at the z-coordinate of the upstream side of the specimen, c_0 is speed of the sound (m/s) and ρ_0 density of the air (kg/m^3). The above described method, which combines measurement data of the membrane displacement as measured by means of a laser Doppler vibrometer and the sound pressure measurement data of two microphones at the source-side of the impedance tube, is referred to as the mobility-based method (MM). The mobility-based measurement method proposed in this paper, was motivated by the work of Tijs [60] as well as Chen [20]. The same principle was used for the sound absorption determination (see Section 2.1.2).

The application of this procedure can be found in membrane analysis, when the specimen is accessible only from the acoustic excitation side (laboratory or in situ) specially in the cases when the surface of investigation in inaccessible places due to location or extreme conditions. In case of access from the receiving side, the application can be applied for planar specimen without limitations. The comparison with methods mentioned above (Seybert, Salissou and ASTM E261109) and below (ISO 10534-2) can be found in Sections 4 and 5.

2.1.2. Determination of the Normal-Incidence Sound Absorption and Transmission Coefficient

As mentioned above, the transfer function method (TFM) in accordance to ISO 10534-2 is the approach most often used for determination of the sound absorption coefficient in practice [29]. The method uses an impedance tube with a sound source connected to the one end of the tube and the test sample fixed in the tube at the other end. The complex sound pressure is measured by means of two flush-mounted fixed microphone positions in front of the specimen. The complex reflection coefficient r can then be determined by means of the acoustic wave field interference decomposition. The sound absorption coefficient (α(-)) (Equation (5)) as well as other quantities like surface impedance (Z (Pa s/m)) and admittance (G(-)) of absorbing materials can be derived subsequently. The acoustic waves generated by the source below the cut-off frequency of the tube may be considered as plane waves.

$$\alpha = \frac{W_a}{W_{in}} = \frac{W_q + W_T}{W_{in}} = 1 - |r \cdot r^*| = 1 - |r|^2 = 1 - \left| \frac{\frac{p_{(x2)}}{p_{(x1)}} - e^{-jk_0 s}}{e^{jk_0 s} - \frac{p_{(x2)}}{p_{(x1)}}} e^{2jk_0 x_1} \right|^2 \quad (5)$$

where r^*(-) and s (m) are complex conjugate of the reflection coefficient and the distance between microphone positions 1 and 2, $p_{(x1)}$, $p_{(x2)}$ and k_0 is sound pressure at coordinate x_1 (m) and x_2 (m) and wave number (m^{-1}) (Figure 2).

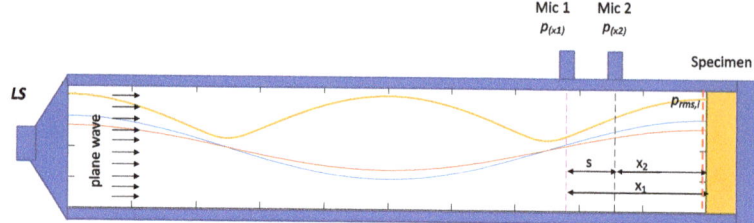

Figure 2. Scheme of determination of the sound absorption by means of an impedance tube. The curves indicates the amplitude of incident (blue curve), reflected (red curve) normal incidence plane wave and the standing wave ratio (yellow curve). Where $p_{(x1-2)}$ and Mic 1–2 denote the microphone positions, where the sound pressure is measured related to the x-coordinate, $p_{rms,I}$ is effective values of the incident sound pressure at the surface of the specimen (derived from measurement), s is distance between microphone positions, x_1, x_2 are distances from of the microphones 1 and 2 to the specimen surface, respectively, and LS is loudspeaker.

The measurement method proposed in this paper combines the laser doppler vibrometer and microphone measurement data (i.e., the surface displacement and known incident pressure $p_{rms,1}$ at the plane at the surface of the specimen—specifically a membrane). The sound transmission and the absorption coefficient of the membrane are closely related. Whilst in Section 2.1.1 it was already detailed how the sound transmission nTL can be determined from sound pressure and vibration measurements, the absorption coefficient α can also be determined in this way, as explained below. The sound absorption coefficient is defined as a ratio of energies (Equation (5)), where W_a, W_{in}, W_q, W_T in (W) are, respectively, the absorbed sound power, incident sound power, dissipated sound power in the membrane and the transmitted sound power. Whereas the sound absorption in porous materials is caused by viscous and relaxation losses, in stretched membrane resonates it depends on the material properties, tension and the geometry of the membrane. If the excitation of the membrane is low (and non-linearities are neglected), the dissipation caused by dissipation of vibration energy (into heat) is also negligibly low. Therefore, in case of nonperforated membranes, the dissipation of energy out of the resonance region can be in most of cases neglected. The observed decrease in the sound reflection spectra is mainly related to the high sound transmission at the membrane resonance frequencies. By neglecting the dissipated energy in the membrane (which is often valid in the case of the single, thin membranes without internal dissipation), the absorption can be approximated by $\tau(-)$, as defined by Equation (6):

$$\tau = \frac{W_T}{W_{in}} \approx \frac{(\omega \cdot \rho_0 \cdot c_0 \cdot \langle w \rangle)^2}{p_i^2} \tag{6}$$

where W_T and W_{in} are the transmitted (obtained from the surface mobility at the receiving side of specimen) and incident sound power in (W) at the specimen surface and p_i is the sound pressure at the surface of incidence and can be expressed as (Equation (7)):

$$p_i = \frac{p_{(x_1)} e^{-jk_0 x_1} - p_{(x_2)} e^{-jk_0 x_2}}{e^{-2jk_0 x_1} - e^{-2jk_0 x_2}} \tag{7}$$

where $p_{(x1)}$, $p_{(x2)}$ and k_0 is sound pressure at coordinate x_1 (m) and x_2 (m) and wave number (m^{-1}), respectively. The pressure data $p_{(x1)}$, $p_{(x2)}$ can be obtained by the two microphones at the source side of the impedance tube.

From the above mentioned the sound absorption can be derived (Equation (8)). The equation is valid only for the perpendicular plane wave excitation of the specimen with negligible low internal losses (ideal membrane).

$$\alpha \approx 1 - \left| \frac{p_{i,rms} - (j \cdot \omega \cdot \rho_0 \cdot c_0 \cdot \langle w \rangle)}{p_{i,rms}} \right|^2 \tag{8}$$

2.2. Description of Numerical Study
2.2.1. Single Layer Membrane Sample

A 3D Finite Element Analysis (FEA) model that includes acoustic-structure interaction was created in the commercial software COMSOL Multiphysics to simulate the surface mobility of a membrane mounted in an impedance tube. Based on the simulation data, the nTL, α and τ were determined using the theory that was presented in the previous chapter. To resemble the real case, the situation of a membrane being mounted in an impedance tube, the FEM model of impedance tube with inner diameter of the cylinder shape tube was $d = 0.1$ m created ($d < 0.586 \cdot c/f_{upper\ frequency\ limit}$, which corresponds to the upper frequency limit, or the cut-off frequency of 2 kHz). The distance between microphones (receiving datapoints) was set to $s = 0.075$ m ($s << c/(2 \cdot f_{upper\ frequency\ limit})$).

The upstream and downstream impedance tube is a cylindrical tube with acoustically hard wall boundary conditions. The model allows for a variation of the surface impedance of the tube termination (backing wall), with the impedance $Z = (1+r)/(1-r) \times (\rho \cdot c_0)$, where r is the desired reflection coefficient of the backing wall. As the testing specimen, a 0.5 mm thin membrane with material properties of PTFE (Polytetrafluoroethylene) foil was chosen. PTFE is widely used in modern architecture to cover open spaces. It is also used as a façade-coating material.

The membrane was clamped at the perimeter. The tension was applied as initial stress in the radial and tangential directions of the membrane as $T_0 = 10$ kN/m². The Young's modulus, Poison's ratio, and density of the PTFE membrane were 4.8125×10^9 Pa, 0.33 and 2175 kg/m³, respectively. The structural loss factor was defined as $\eta_s = 0.02(-)$ (for objective reasons related to the use of linear solvers, it was necessary to enter at least minimal damping into the model). The membrane was surrounded by air ($\rho_0 = 1.29$ kg/m³; $c_0 = 343$ m/s) at both sides of the membrane and was excited in by a 1 Pa plane wave radiated from the upstream end of the tube. Six absorption properties of termination were simulated ($\alpha_1 = 1.0$; $\alpha_2 = 0.9$; $\alpha_3 = 0.7$; $\alpha_4 = 0.5$; $\alpha_5 = 0.2$; $\alpha_6 = 0.1$), to investigate the impact of the termination on the resulting nTL, τ and α, respectively. The generated mesh resulted into 34,547 degrees of freedom (DOF) with a maximum element size ($c_0/f_{upper\ frequency\ limit}/5$) $\cong 0.034$ m (Figure 3a).

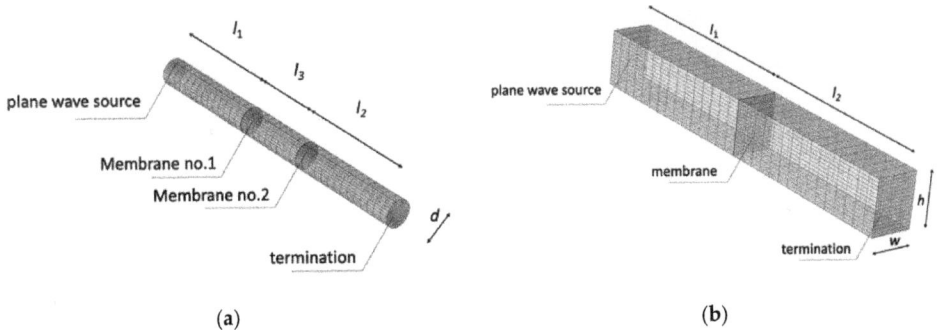

Figure 3. View of 3D FEM model meshing. (a) Single membrane; (b) rectangular shape membrane, where l_1, l_2, h, w, d are length of downstream and upstream part of impedance tube, height, width and diameter of the tube cross section, respectively.

2.2.2. Rectangular Shape Membrane Specimen

Despite the experience that the cross section of the impedance tube is almost always a circle, an additional study with a rectangular shaped membrane was performed. The reason was that in the realization of building structures one seldom encounters circular-shaped membranes. The change in shape should introduce additional resonant areas into the membrane response. For this purpose, a model of an impedance tube with dimensions in the cross section of 100 × 125 mm with a membrane thickness of 0.5 mm (PTFE foil) was created. The tension, Young's modulus, Poison's ratio, structural loss factor and density of the PTFE was set similar to the case with one membrane. Again, six absorption properties of termination were simulated ($\alpha_1 = 1.0$; $\alpha_2 = 0.9$; $\alpha_3 = 0.7$; $\alpha_4 = 0.5$; $\alpha_5 = 0.2$; $\alpha_6 = 0.1$), to see the impact of the termination on the resulting nTL, τ and α, respectively. For this specimen case, only the ASTM, ISO and Mobility based methods were compared. The generated mesh resulted to 106,430 DOF with maximum size of mesh element $\cong 0.049$ m (Figure 3b). It should be mentioned that the upper frequency limit, or the cut-off frequency, is 1372 Hz for this case.

3. Description of Measurements

3.1. Description of Measurement Setup

In this section, the measurement setup and the specimen examined in the study is described. The measurement setup was created based on the impedance tube principle as described in the ASTM or ISO standards [25,44]. The core part of the construction was a set of rigid steel tubes of diameter 0.1 m, which gives us an upper cut-off frequency of about of 2 kHz. To allow an LDV-scan of the vibrating membrane the impedance tube was accessible from one side surface of the chosen specimen. In this paper only the single membrane experiment is presented so the scanning from one side, the muffler side, was sufficient. However, the measurement setup gives opportunity to perform scanning measurements from both sides of the sample (also from the source side). This would find the application in cases of more complex specimen (which were not investigated here). Therefore, the loudspeaker (on the source side) was mounted on the (cylindrical) wall of the impedance tube as shown in Figure 4b.

(a)　　　　　　　　　　　　　　　　　　(b)

Figure 4. The measurement setup modification description. (**a**) Photo of full setup; and (**b**) the axis perpendicular side connection of LS.

The 6 speaker type "Eminence ME6-7586408 ohm" was mounted on a rigid plate. The speaker was driven by a Mono Power Amplifier (Vincent SP-996). On the other side of the impedance tube apparatus, a low frequency muffler with an open end was mounted. The muffler consisted of a sheet-steel wall-based hollowed cone (upstream diameter = 0.75 m; downstream diameter = 0.1 m; length = 0.97 m), filled with mineral wool (see Figure 4a—

right end). The muffler was designed in accordance to the standards ISO 5136 and ISO 7235 [61,62]. The measured sound absorption of the muffler is shown in Figure 5a. One can see that the sound absorption has a straight tendency as the function of the frequency in the range from 200 to 1100 Hz.

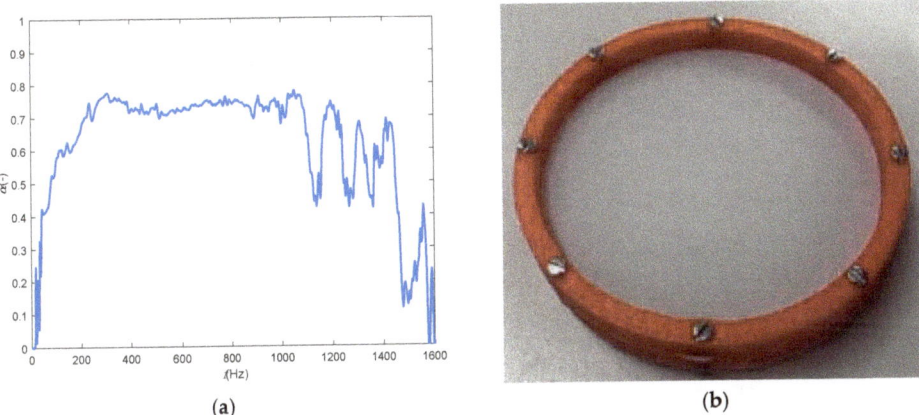

Figure 5. (a) The sound absorption coefficient spectra of the muffler measured in accordance to ISO 10534-2; and (b) test specimens—a single-leaf 0.5 mm PTFE membrane.

Due to this, the presented measurement results were also evaluated only in this frequency region. Several holes were available in the tube apparatus for flush mounting the measurement microphones. The chosen pair distance (for the upstream and downstream part for nTL as well as τ and α determination) was 75 mm in both cases. A scheme of the total setup is shown in Figure 6. The microphones that were used for the measurements were a pair of $\frac{1}{2}$" ICCP pre-polarized microphones (BSWA MA231), conditioned by the multichannel measurement system (Soft db—Tenor 24 bits, 8—channel data-logger). The ASTM and ISO based results were obtained by means of the impulse response measurement. As the excitation signal, for microphone measurement-based methods, a sine sweep was used. The Matlab™ postprocessing routines were created for the data processing.

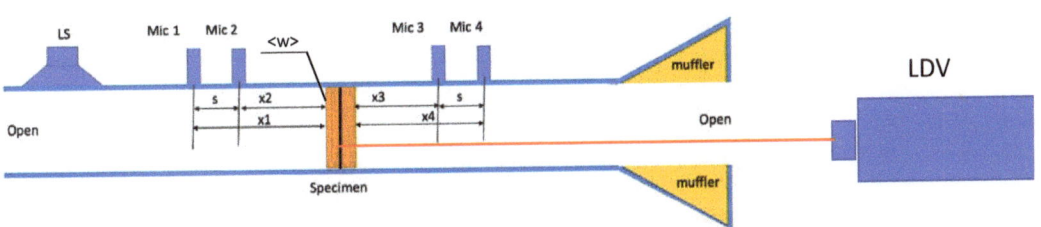

Figure 6. Scheme of measurement setup with LDV scanning head. Where Mic 1–4 denote the microphone positions, s is distance between microphone positions, x_1–x_4 are distance of the microphones to the specimen surface, <w> is the spatially averaged displacement measured at the specimen surface, LS is loudspeaker, LDV is laser doppler vibrometer.

To determine the mobility-based sound transmission loss, a scanning laser Doppler vibrometer Polytec PSV 400 controlled by PSV Acquisitions SW was used. The measuring perpendicular mesh of 253 points was generated by SW tool and scanned. The reference excitation signal for the mobility-based method was pink noise generated by means of portable signal generator type Minirator-MR1 (NTI). The scanning grid used for spatially averaged velocity (or displacement data) consisted of 305 points.

3.2. Specimen Description

The test specimen was a stretched PTFE membrane with a thickness of 0.5 mm and density of 2175 kg/m^3 (Figure 5b). Other material properties were derived from the numerical parametric study and measurements (Young's modulus and Poison's ratio were 4.8125×10^9 Pa, 0.33). The membrane was stretched on a stretching ring made from PLA material precisely printed by means of a 3D printer (Prusa i3 (Anet a8)) and was fixed inside of the impedance tube apparatus by mastic. The stretching ring consisted of two rings connected by means of eight screws. In this way, the rings' perimeter was divided into eight parts with specific stiffness. After mounting the specimen into the impedance tube, the rings were slightly bended, which caused the variation of the stiffness at the perimeter. Specifically, two of the sixteen perimeter parts were significantly affected (the effect on the measured result is discussed in the Section 4). The tension in the membrane was $T_0 = 850$ N/m^2. The value of tension was derived from the numerical parametric study.

4. Results

4.1. The Normal Incidence Sound Transmission Loss (Simulations)

The nTL, τ and α as determined by the different methods (for nTL-Seybert, Salissou, ASTM and the Mobility-Based method, for α-ISO and for τ-Mobility-Based method) were compared. All the methods were compared for the circular shaped single layer membrane. For the rectangular shaped membrane, the Seybert and Salissou methods were considered for reasons of brevity.

Measuring the acoustic properties (nTL, τ and α) in an impedance tube environment serious artefacts can be caused by standing waves in the impedance tube. Obviously, these effects are unwanted in the measurement of the acoustic properties of the sample. As these artefacts are known to be strongly dependent up the acoustic termination of the impedance tube, terminations were considered having six different values of the sound absorption coefficient α of: $\alpha_1 = 1.0$; $\alpha_2 = 0.9$; $\alpha_3 = 0.7$; $\alpha_4 = 0.5$; $\alpha_5 = 0.2$; $\alpha_6 = 0.1$. In a number of cases, a negative nTL was obtained at some frequencies, which is obviously non-physical, and also related to standing waves in the impedance tube. These negative areas are marked by a pale red colour (see figures below). The most accurate method, which does not show a large dependency on the amount of reflection of the backing, was the ASTM method. For this reason the ASTM method with 100% absorption backing wall has been considered as the reference.

Seybert's method, as mentioned above, is a one-load method and its results are dependent on the termination sound absorption (Figure 7a). By increasing the reflection coefficient of the back termination, the spectra of nTL are strongly affected by multiple reflection between the sample and the termination. Due to these effects, this method requires an anechoic termination. The frequency location of "unwanted" dips in the spectra can be predicted from the relation $f_x = n \cdot c_0 / (2 \cdot l_2)$, where n, c_0 and l_2 are an arbitrary natural number, the speed of sound in the air, and the length of the downstream tube, respectively. Beside the dips and peaks related to the standing wave modes in the downstream tube, also the dips which are related to the membrane resonances and the peaks which are related to the anti-resonances, are affected. The worst highest and lowest backing absorption are compared to the ASTM method in Figure 7f. Almost negligible peaks/dips in nTL spectra are occurring in case with the 100% absorptive termination (the thick blue curve), showing the real acoustic properties of the membrane structure under test. By decreasing the termination absorption to 20% the differences increased up to 14 dB. The wave decomposition (WD) by Salissou [55] is a two-load method (Figure 7b). The results that are obtained with this method also strongly dependent on the load termination absorption. In order to obtain reasonable results (less artifacts due to resonances in the impedance tube), at least one of the two loads needs to have an high absorptive termination. Nevertheless, the method of Salissou cannot eliminate the effect of the multiple termination reflections effectively. In the worst case with termination absorption ratio 0.2: 0.1 (very reflective composition), the ΔnTL reaches the differences more than 20 dB in comparison to the anechoic termination.

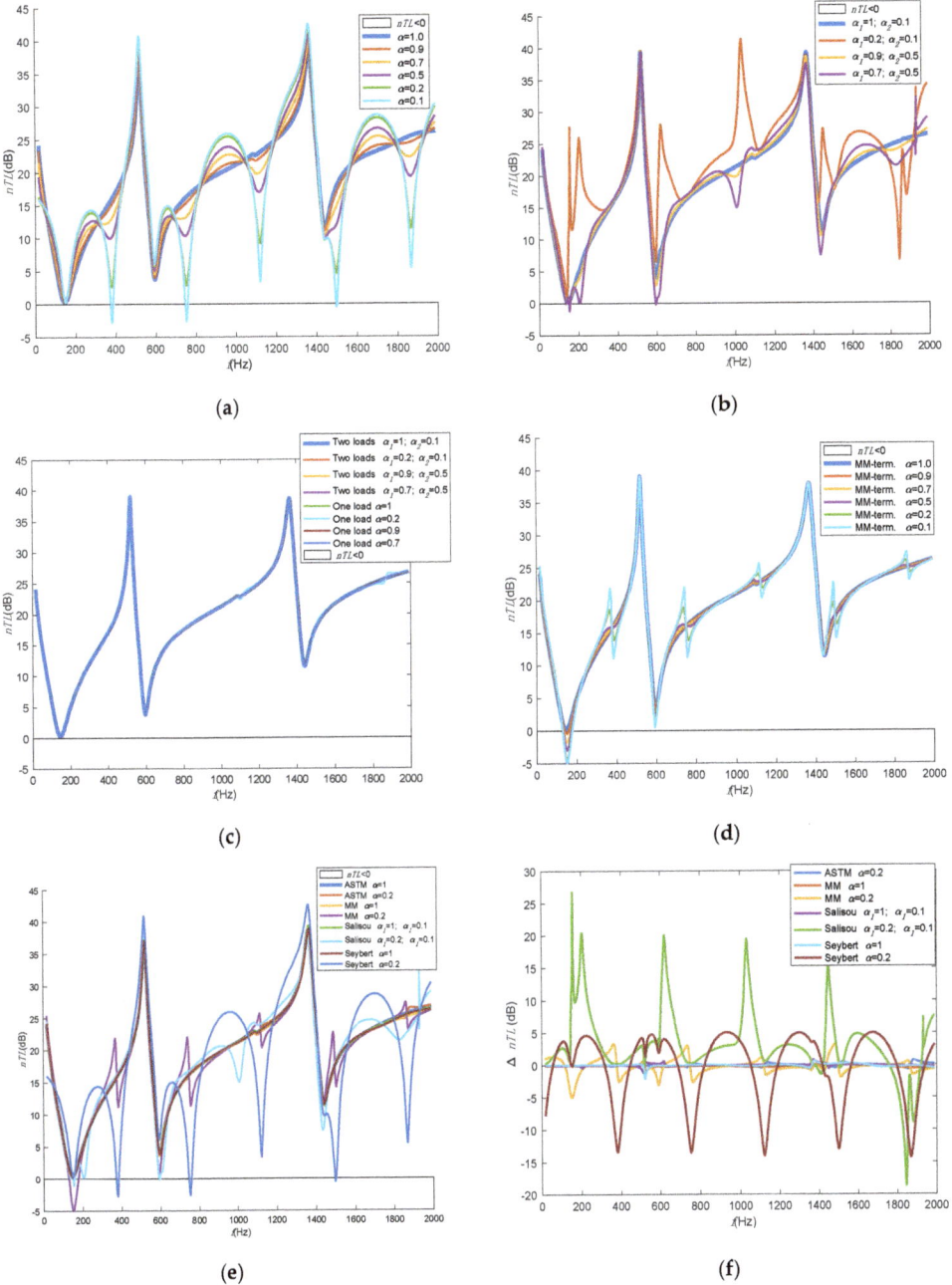

Figure 7. Cont.

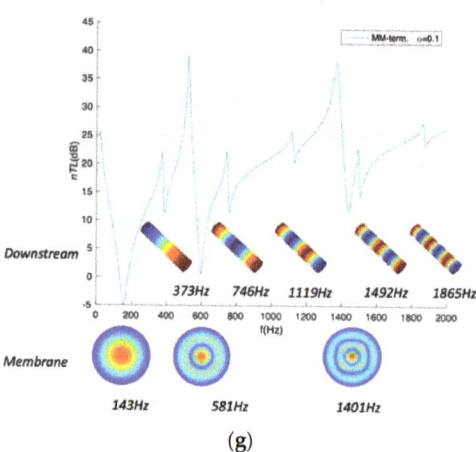

(g)

Figure 7. The nTL of 0.5 mm thin membrane determination by means of different methods from the FEM model for six different backing wall sound-absorption terminations (variation of termination absorption from α=0.1 to 1). (**a**) Seybert (Wave field decomposition method (WD)—one load); (**b**) Salissou (WD-TM hybrid method—two loads variations with termination ("term." in the legend) absorptions denoted as α_1, α_2 for first load and second load); (**c**) ASTM E261109 ("ASTM" in the legend, Transfer matrix method—single or two-load variations with different termination absorptions denoted as α_1, α_2 for first load and second load variations); (**d**) mobility based method (MM—single load); (**e**) comparison of methods; (**f**) comparison of chosen cases by the difference in the frequency spectra ($\Delta nTL = nTL_i - nTL_{ASTM\ \alpha=1}$); and (**g**) nTL spectra of calculated based MM, with termination α = 0.1. The figure also includes structural modes of the membrane as well as the acoustic modes of downstream tube causing the resonant phenomena in the spectrum.

The most accurate method (independent on the termination) for the determination of nTL is the method in accordance to ASTM E2611-09 [48] (Figure 7c). Two transfer matrix (TM) methods (single or two loads method) are described in the standard. In the case of a phase synchronized and amplitude calibrated system, the two-loads method can properly and accurately determine nTL while effectively neglecting the influence of the backing wall termination on the sound absorption. The single-load method, for the numerical case when the model was perfectly geometrically symmetric, gave reasonably accurate data (comparable with the two-load method). The single-load method can be slightly affected by a high reflection of the termination (Figure 7f). In the worst case for the single layer membrane, the effect was not more than 0.7 dB at specific frequencies.

The results obtained by means of the mobility-based method (MM) are presented in Figure 7d and a comparison with the ASTM method is shown in Figure 7e,f. In this comparison, the ASTM method with an absorption factor α = 1 was chosen as a reference as this method gives most accurate results. As expected, the results obtained with the MM method are also affected by the multiple back/front reflections in the impedance tube. In case of an absorption of 20% at the impedance tube backing wall, differences up to 4 dB were observed compared to the ASTM (α = 1)-reference method.

Figure 7g present the structural and acoustic modes which influence the dips in the nTL spectra. In case of the circular (symmetrical) shaped specimens, only the symmetrical modes are influencing the resulting spectra. The acoustic modes are dependent on the length of the downstream. In order to demonstrate the applicability of the MM method to the modally slightly more complicated shape of membranes, the response of a rectangular membrane was numerically assessed. As in the previous case, a comparison of the results was made only between the ASTM and MM methods (Figure 8). The sound transmission loss and absorption of the rectangular membrane are most affected by the modes that have an odd number of half-wavelengths in the transverse direction of the membrane patch (Figure 8c). As in the previous cases, for the anechoic termination, the spectrum determined on the basis of both methods correlates well with each other in a global sense. Exceptions occur at specific frequencies which are related to resonances and anti-resonances. Here, visible deviations up to 3 dB occur from the second mode having an odd number of half wavelengths (Figure 8c). Paradoxically, this deviation, as in previous cases of anechoic terminations of the MM method, is due to the fineness of the datapoint mesh on the membrane surface. This can distort the attenuation in the resonant phenomenon. By increasing the reflectivity of the backing wall termination, the front-back reflection in the form of additional peaks in the spectrum is more pronounced.

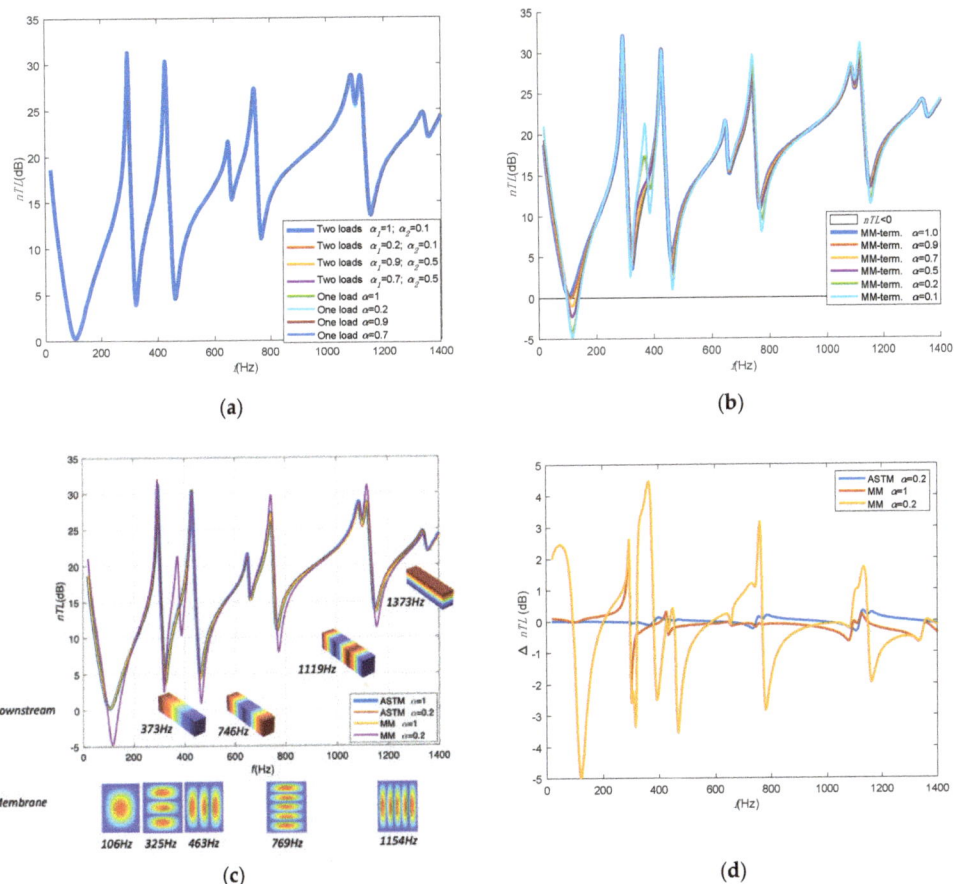

Figure 8. The nTL of 0.5 mm thin membrane determination by means of different methods from the FEM model for six different backing wall sound-absorption terminations (variation of termination ("term." in the legend) absorption from $\alpha = 0.1$ to 1) (**a**) ASTM E261109 ("ASTM" in the legend, Transfer matrix method—single or two-load variations with different termination absorptions denoted as α_1,α_2 for first load and second load variations); (**b**) mobility based method (MM—single load); (**c**) comparison of methods including graphical representation of resonant phenomena causing decreases in the spectrum.; and (**d**) comparison of chosen cases by the difference in the frequency spectra($\Delta nTL = nTL_i - nTL_{ASTM\ \alpha=1}$).

4.2. The Normal-Incidence Sound Absorption and Transmission Coefficients (Simulations)

The normal incidence sound absorption and transmission coefficients were determined by means of two techniques. The first one, the reference method, was the TFM in accordance with ISO 10534-2. The second method, the mobility method, included the surface spatial averaged displacement in the normal direction to the surface (in figures denoted as the mobility-based method—MM). The comparison of results is shown in Figures 9 and 10. One can see that the results are in both cases dependent on the sound absorption of the impedance tube termination (as expected). For a fully anechoic termination, almost the same results were obtained for both methods. However, reducing the absorption coefficient of the downstream termination the difference of the resulting absorption has increased up to $\Delta \alpha = 1(\%)$ to $1.5(\%)$, respectively, where $\Delta \alpha = (\alpha - \tau) \cdot 100\%$, at frequencies of the membrane symmetrical mode resonances. By using the parametric study, one can simply distinguish between the membrane resonance caused absorption/transmission coefficient peaks, the downstream tube termination cased resonances (strong effect in case of single membrane—the increasing effect is visible by increasing the reflection of the termination) (Figure 9a,b).

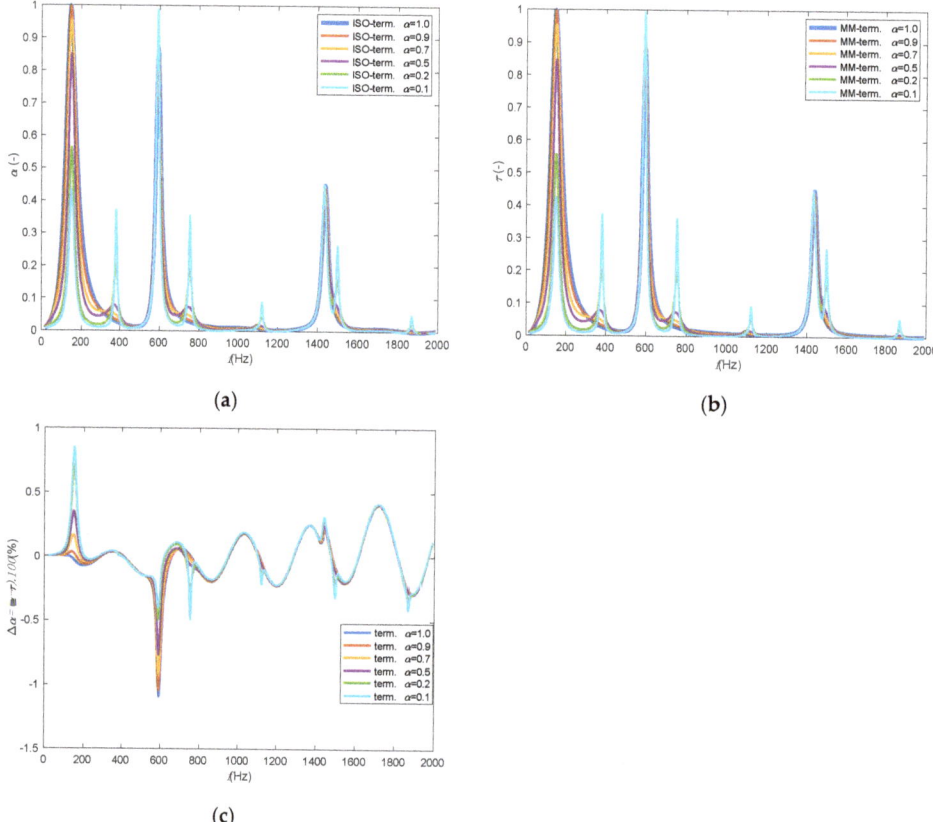

Figure 9. Normal-incidence sound absorption of a single leaf PTFE membrane determined for six different terminations (variation of termination ("term." in the legend) absorption from $\alpha = 0.1$ to 1, data were obtained from FEM). (a) TFM-ISO 10534-2 ("ISO" in the legend); (b) mobility-based method ("MM" in the legend); and (c) difference between sound absorption obtained by means two methods expressed in percentage.

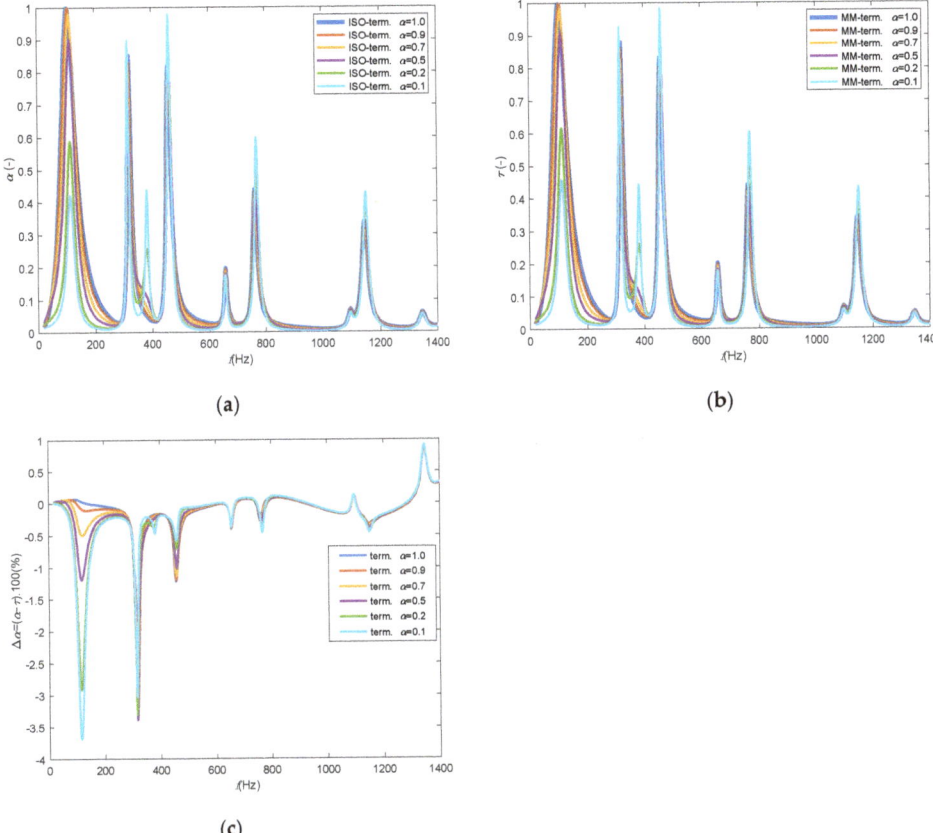

Figure 10. Normal-incidence sound absorption of a single leaf PTFE rectangular shape membrane determined for six different terminations (variation of termination ("term." in the legend) absorption from α = 0.1 to 1, data were obtained from FEM). (**a**) TFM-ISO 10534-2 ("ISO" in the legend); (**b**) mobility-based method ("MM" in the legend); and (**c**) difference between sound absorption obtained by means two methods expressed in percentage.

For a rectangular membrane (Figure 10), resonances caused by downstream front-back reflection are strongly suppressed except for the first mode of the tube, as it occurs near the 3rd and 6th odd membrane modes. The difference in spectra between the individual methods is, unlike the transmission loss (logarithmic expression), expressed as a percentage. Here, again, depending on the type of tube termination, the resonant response manifested in the peak/dip spectrum increases. The deviation with anechoic termination in comparison with MM with the ISO method reaches a deviation of up to 3.5% for the second odd mode and below 1% for other modes, what is acceptable. Interestingly, by changing the shape of the membrane and the associated distribution of resonant modes, an increase in the sound absorption of the sample was achieved.

4.3. Measurement Results

The sound transmission and the sound absorption and transmission coefficient were determined in the impedance tube for the one PTFE foil-based membrane specimens under a plane-wave excitation environment. The mobility method results (nTL, α and τ) explained above were compared with results determined in accordance to the ASTM E2611 –09 approach (for nTL—single load) and in accordance with the ISO 10534-2 (α). Additionally, the FEM model was created taking in the account the membrane material properties (see Section 3.1) as well as the measured boundary condition (the tension was $T_0 = 850$ N/m²). The resulting comparisons are shown in Figure 11. Additionally, the operation deflection shapes (ODS) of a vibrating membrane related to the chosen frequencies, measured by means of the LDV, are also presented in Figure 11. With focusing to identify the mode shapes, the ODSs are the spatial surface plot of the imaginary part of displacement (the excitation signal was used as the reference signal to acquire information of the phase surface phase).

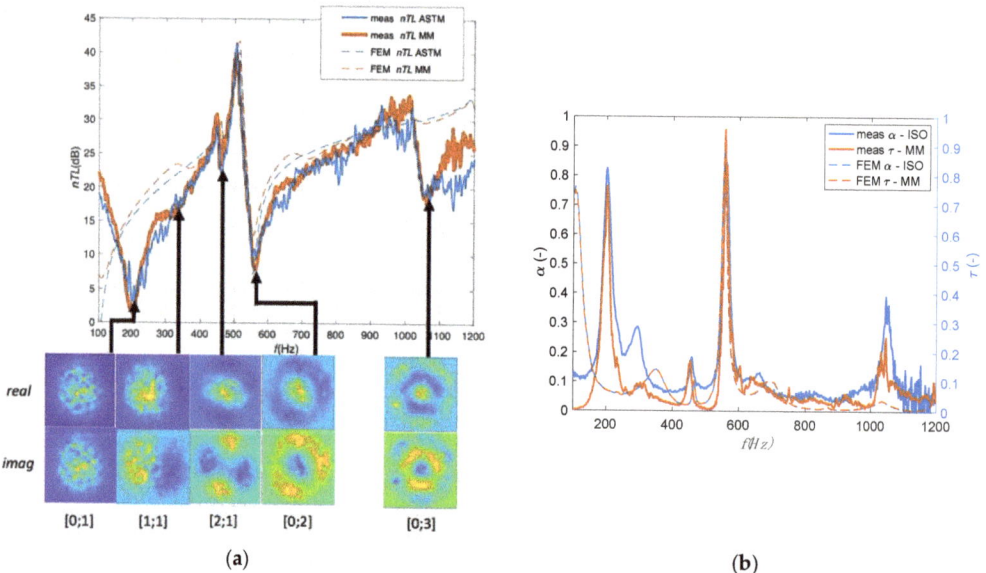

Figure 11. (a) Sound transmission loss spectra of the single layer 0.5 mm PTFE membrane. (b) Measured sound absorption and transmission coefficient s of the single layer 0.5 mm PTFE membrane. Abbreviation describing the measurements based on: ASTM—ASTM E261109; MM—mobility based method; ISO-ISO 10534-2.

The measured nTL spectra corresponds to each other rather well. The highest peak of single-membrane nTL spectra at a frequency of about 510 Hz is caused by anti-resonance phenomena (the displacement of membrane surface is too low). On the other hand, the dips of nTL and peaks of α τ spectra at a frequencies of approximately 205 Hz, 562 Hz and 1078 Hz are caused by structural resonances caused by 1st mode (0.1—the first axisymmetric mode), 4th mode (0.2—the second axisymmetric mode) and the 9th mode (0.3—3rd axisymmetric mode) of the membrane system. Two unexpected dips (that are missing in the idealised simulation cases, e.g., presented in chapter 5.1) in the nTL spectra occurs at frequencies 296 Hz and 464 Hz. The dips are related to the 2nd and 3rd structural mode (1.1 and 2.1) of the membrane. Normally, if the membrane edge boundaries would be uniform, the influence of the 2nd and 3rd mode would not be visible. In the experimental case, the stretching ring from PLA material was slightly bent, which affected the stiffness at the membrane edges. The stretching ring consisted of two rings connected by means of eight screws. In this way, the rings' perimeter was divided into eight parts with specific stiffness. After mounting the specimen into the impedance tube, the rings were slightly bended, which caused the variation of the stiffness at the perimeter. Specifically, two of the sixteen perimeter parts were significantly affected. This has been verified also in the FEM tuning process where the significantly lower stiffness (the spring constant k_L was lower by factor 10^4) was needed to set in the boundary system of the membrane clamping. Caused by the already mentioned nonuniformities in the tension in the stretching ring and its bending, that not possible perfectly fit all the investigated frequency spectra. Nevertheless, the FEM and measurement based obtained results obtained for both discussed methods correspond reasonably well with each other.

Despite the fact that the absorption of the muffler is relatively balanced only in the frequency range from 200 Hz to 1100 Hz, the data from 100 to 1200 Hz were presented in Figure 11. The reason was to demonstrate the effect of the change in the absorption of the termination on the differences in the results. Results comparison of nTL spectra is giving similar results in the range from 200 to 1100 Hz. Outside this frequency range, the results differ, which is possibly caused by a high reflection of the muffler that causes unwanted acoustic resonances in the system. The measured and predicted sound absorption spectra show good similarities. The peaks caused by axisymmetric resonance modes have been identified well by both methods. However, the absorption in spectra between first and fourth peak (1st and 3rd axisymmetric mode) differ significantly. In this region the nonsymmetric modes 1.12 and 2.1 are present. The effect of the bending and non-uniform stretching of the membrane possibly increases the interaction between membrane and the ring that causes the resonant interaction and internal loses that were not recognised well by the LDV. This caused the difference between the sound absorption and transmission coefficients.

5. Conclusions

In this article, we focus on the determination of the acoustic properties (sound transmission loss, sound absorption and transmission coefficient) of membrane type of specimens under acoustic plane wave excitation. An overview of the measurement methods to extract the acoustic properties from impedance tube measurement data was given. It was noted that the determination of the acoustic properties (nTL, τ) in an impedance tube environment can be hampered by serious artefacts related to standing waves in the impedance tube. Many measurement methods suffer from this, obstructing the extraction of the real acoustic properties of the test specimen. The nTL measurement method least sensitive on possible backing wall reflection caused by a non-perfectly anechoic termination is the ASTM method (in accordance to standard ASTM E2611-09 [48]). In the case of the membrane sound absorption coefficient measurement, the backing wall impedance is directly influencing the resulting sound absorption. The method recommended by ISO 10534-2 [29] was used as a reference throughout the paper. Subsequently, the theoretical background of the proposed so-called mobility-based method (MM), which combines laser doppler vibrometer measurement data and microphone measurement data, was presented. The proposed MM method was compared with the conventional methods for sound transmission loss and absorption measurement.

The methods were compared using numerically generated data from a finite element model. The FEM models included six different variations of the backing wall termination ($\alpha_1 = 1.0$; $\alpha_2 = 0.9$; $\alpha_3 = 0.7$; $\alpha_4 = 0.5$; $\alpha_5 = 0.2$; $\alpha_6 = 0.1$). The numerical investigation focused on the assessment of the influence of the termination on the resulting values of sound absorption and transmission loss spectra of two differently shaped membranes (single layer circular shaped membrane and rectangular shaped membrane). The proposed mobility-based method was compared with the standardized ASTM (nTL measurement) and ISO (α determination) methods, as well as with two other chosen methods, and the effect of the termination on the sound reflection was assessed. The ASTM method describes a measurement method that uses four microphones and one or two loads (different terminations). When dealing with symmetrical test specimen, only one load suffices.

In the case if two loads method is applied almost no difference in results could be observed. Based on the FEM results, the MM gave similar results for anechoic backing wall termination as the results obtained in accordance to the ASTM E2611-09 with the local deviation up to 3 dB. This is a common phenomenon in numerical modelling, where no or very little damping is defined in the model. In the area of resonance, the results obtained from different domains may be overestimated (in this particular case, the results from the acoustic and the structural domain were compared). In absorption assessment, the deviation is up to 3% for the first membrane resonance frequencies.

At other frequencies the deviation is not more than 1%, for both the absorption factor and the transmission loss. By increasing the reflection of the backing termination, the deviations increases and the effect of the front-back reflection can be recognised. The effect usually did not reach a deviation in the absorption of more than 3% and in the transmission loss no more than 5 dB (excluding the 1st mode resonance effect).

In the experimental part the circular shaped single layer PTFE foil specimen was tested and compared with the FE model fitted to the experiment. The MM was compared with the ASTM (nTL) and ISO (α) measurement methods. The results were presented in narrow band spectra, to see more precisely the differences in the results. The MM method gave reasonable results for nTL spectra. Although the measurement results were affected by the specimen bending caused by mounting in the measurement apparatus, which caused unexpected dips in the spectra, the resulting spectra are comparable. Specifically, the resulting nTL spectra determined in accordance to ASTM and MM correspond to each other rather well. The membrane asymmetrical resonances and anti-resonances (which normally have a dominant effect on the nTL, α and τ spectra) were nicely recognised. LDV gave us the opportunity also to identify other modes of the vibrating membranes. Specifically, in the presented case, when the membrane was not stretched symmetrically (caused by soft bending of the stretching ring—something that would occur often in practice), it was able to determine the reason of occurrence of the additional peaks (dips) in the spectra.

The MM would clearly find application in membranes analysis even for more complicated elements, with higher energy dissipation in the structure and possible internal resonances, the α cannot replace the τ. For practical applications, the advantage of MM is that the nTL as well as α can be determined from a single-sided scan. In case of more complex samples the measurement procedure will be needed to perform from both sides of the specimen.

The method may be extended by a single microphone based incident sound pressure determination approach known from standards. The presented work can be considered as an intermediate step for method development applicable in practice. Main disadvantage of the proposed method has only the limited application and is time consuming in comparison to the conventional methods. The absorption measurement approach can be applied only for membrane-based constructions, specially, with membranes with negligible internal losses. Method is also sensitive on the amount of excitation energy (sensitivity of LDV, respectively). Further investigation in the MM is expected. Future experiments in the anechoic laboratory environment and the in situ free field are essential to prove the wider application of the method. The goal is to have a method appropriate for the determination of membrane-based structures acoustic/structural properties from larger distances. Mainly in the cases when the surface of investigation in inaccessible places due to location or extreme conditions.

Author Contributions: Conceptualization, methodology, software, investigation, resources, writing—original draft preparation, visualization, D.U.; formal analysis, writing—review and editing, D.U., N.B.R. and O.J.; validation D.U., V.J., M.B. All authors have read and agreed to the published version of the manuscript.

Funding: This research was supported by the International Mobility of Researchers in CTU CZ.02.2.69/0.0/0.0/16_027/0008465, CTU project SGS19/166/OHK3/3T/13 Development of modern acoustic measurements and was funded by European Union, grant number H2020-MSCA-RISE-2015 project 690970.

Institutional Review Board Statement: Not applicable.

Informed Consent Statement: Not applicable.

Data Availability Statement: All data included in this work are available upon request by contact with the author Daniel Urbán.

Conflicts of Interest: The authors declare no conflict of interest.

References

1. Paech, C. Structural membranes used in modern building facades. *Procedia Eng.* **2016**, *155*, 61–70. [CrossRef]
2. John, G.; Clements-Croome, D.; Jeronimidis, G. Sustainable building solutions: A review of lessons from the natural world. *Build. Environ.* **2005**, *40*, 319–328. [CrossRef]
3. Urbán, D.; Roozen, N.B.; Zaťko, P.; Rychtáriková, M.; Tomašovič, P.; Glorieux, C. Assessment of sound insulation of naturally ventilated double skin facades. *Build. Environ.* **2016**, *110*, 148–160. [CrossRef]
4. Urbán, D.; Tomašovič, P.; Rychtáriková, M.; Roozen, N.B.; Glorieux, C.H. Sound propagation within a double skin facade and its influence on the speech Privacy in offices. In Proceedings of the Euronoise 2015, Maastrich, The Netherlands, 31 May–3 June 2015; pp. 2543–2548.
5. Martens, M.J.; Michelsen, A. Absorption of acoustic energy by plant leaves. *J. Acoust. Soc. Am.* **1981**, *69*, 303–306. [CrossRef]
6. Strutt, J.W.; Rayleigh, B. *The Theory of Sound*; Macmillan and Co.: London, UK, 1877.
7. Mazumdar, J. A Review of Approximate Methods for Determining the Vibrational Modes of Membranes. *Shock. Vib. Dig.* **1984**, *16*, 9. [CrossRef]
8. Laura, P.A.; Romanelli, E.; Maurizi, M.J. On the analysis of waveguides of doubly-connected cross-section by the method of conformal mapping. *J. Sound Vib.* **1972**, *20*, 27–38. [CrossRef]
9. Wang, C.Y. On thepolygonal membrane with a circular core. *J. Sound Vib.* **1998**, *215*, 195–199. [CrossRef]
10. Wang, C.Y. Vibration of an annular membrane attached to a free, rigid core. *J. Sound Vib.* **2003**, *4*, 776–782. [CrossRef]
11. Ho, K.M.; Cheng, C.K.; Yang, Z.; Zhang, X.X.; Sheng, P. Broadband locally resonant sonic shields. *Appl. Phys. Lett.* **2003**, *83*, 5566–5568. [CrossRef]
12. Huang, T.Y.; Shen, C.; Jing, Y. Membrane-and plate-type acoustic metamaterials. *J. Acoust. Soc. Am.* **2016**, *139*, 3240–3250. [CrossRef] [PubMed]
13. Ciaburro, G.; Iannace, G. Modeling acoustic metamaterials based on reused buttons using data fitting with neural network. *J. Acoust. Soc. Am.* **2021**, *150*, 51–63. [CrossRef]
14. Naify, C.J.; Chang, C.M.; McKnight, G.; Nutt, S. Transmission loss of membrane-type acoustic metamaterials with coaxial ring masses. *J. Appl. Phys.* **2011**, *110*, 124903. [CrossRef]
15. Yang, Z.; Dai, H.M.; Chan, N.H.; Ma, G.C.; Sheng, P. Acoustic metamaterial panels for sound attenuation in the 50–1000 Hz regime. *Appl. Phys. Lett.* **2010**, *96*, 041906. [CrossRef]
16. Naify, C.J.; Chang, C.M.; McKnight, G.; Scheulen, F.; Nutt, S. Membrane-type metamaterials: Transmission loss of multi-celled arrays. *J. Appl. Phys.* **2011**, *109*, 104902. [CrossRef]
17. Yang, M.; Ma, G.; Yang, Z.; Sheng, P. Coupled membranes with doubly negative mass density and bulk modulus. *Phys. Rev. Lett.* **2013**, *110*, 134301. [CrossRef]
18. Sharma, G.S.; Skvortsov, A.; MacGillivray, I.; Kessissoglou, N. Sound scattering by a bubble metasurface. *Phys. Rev. B* **2020**, *102*, 214308. [CrossRef]
19. Yang, Z.; Mei, J.; Yang, M.; Chan, N.H.; Sheng, P. Membrane-type acoustic metamaterial with negative dynamic mass. *Phys. Rev. Lett.* **2008**, *101*, 204301. [CrossRef]
20. Chen, Y.; Huang, G.; Zhou, X.; Hu, G.; Sun, C.T. Analytical coupled vibroacoustic modeling of membrane-type acoustic metamaterials: Membrane model. *J. Acoust. Soc. Am.* **2014**, *136*, 969–979. [CrossRef] [PubMed]
21. Zhang, Y.; Wen, J.; Xiao, Y.; Wen, X.; Wang, J. Theoretical investigation of the sound attenuation of membrane-type acoustic metamaterials. *Phys. Lett. A* **2012**, *376*, 1489–1494. [CrossRef]
22. Zhang, Y.; Wen, J.; Zhao, H.; Yu, D.; Cai, L.; Wen, X. Sound insulation property of membrane-type acoustic metamaterials carrying different masses at adjacent cells. *J. Appl. Phys.* **2013**, *114*, 063515. [CrossRef]
23. Naify, C.J.; Chang, C.M.; McKnight, G.; Nutt, S.R. Scaling of membrane-type locally resonant acoustic metamaterial arrays. *J. Acoust. Soc. Am.* **2012**, *132*, 2784–2792. [CrossRef]
24. Roozen, N.B.; Urban, D.; Piana, E.A.; Glorieux, C. On the use of dynamic vibration absorbers to counteract the loss of sound insulation due to mass-spring-mass resonance effects in external thermal insulation composite systems. *Appl. Acoust.* **2021**, *178*, 107999. [CrossRef]
25. Sharma, G.S.; Sarkar, A. Directivity-based passive barrier for local control of low-frequency noise. *J. Theor. Comput. Acoust.* **2018**, *26*, 1850012. [CrossRef]
26. Fuller, C.R. Active control of sound transmission/radiation from elastic plates by vibration inputs: I. Analysis. *J. Sound Vib.* **1990**, *136*, 1–15. [CrossRef]
27. Sharma, G.S.; Sarkar, A. Directivity based control of acoustic radiation. *Appl. Acoust.* **2019**, *154*, 226–235. [CrossRef]
28. ISO 10534-1. *Acoustics—Determination of Sound Absorption Coefficient and Impedance in Impedance Tubes—Part 1: Method Using Standing Wave Ratio*; International Standards Organization: Geneva, Switzerland, 1996.
29. ISO 10534-2. *Acoustics—Determination of Sound Absorption Coefficient and Impedance in Impedance Tubes—Part 2: Transfer-Function Method*; International Standards Organization: Geneva, Switzerland, 1998.
30. ISO 354. *Acoustics—Measurement of Sound Absorption in a Reverberation Room*; International Standards Organization: Geneva, Switzerland, 2003.
31. Cox, T.; d'Antonio, P. *Acoustic Absorbers and Diffusers: Theory, Design and Application*; CRC Press: Boca Raton, FL, USA, 2016.
32. Kuipers, E.R. *Measuring Sound Absorption Using Local Field Assumptions*; University of Twente: Enschede, The Netherlands, 2013.

33. Kimura, K.; Yamamoto, K. The required sample size in measuring oblique incidence absorption coefficient experimental study. *Appl. Acoust.* **2002**, *63*, 567–578. [CrossRef]
34. Champoux, Y.; L'espérance, A. Numerical evaluation of errors associated with the measurement of acoustic impedance in a free field using two microphones and a spectrum analyzer. *J. Acoust. Soc. Am.* **1988**, *84*, 30–38. [CrossRef]
35. Nocke, C. In-situ acoustic impedance measurement using a free-field transfer function method. *Appl. Acoust.* **2000**, *59*, 253–264. [CrossRef]
36. Liu, Y.; Jacobsen, F. Measurement of absorption with ap-u sound intensity probe in an impedance tube. *J. Acoust. Soc. Am.* **2005**, *118*, 2117–2120. [CrossRef]
37. Ho, K.M.; Yang, Z.; Zhang, X.X.; Sheng, P. Measurements of sound transmission through panels of locally resonant materials between impedance tubes. *Appl. Acoust.* **2005**, *66*, 751–765. [CrossRef]
38. Selamet, A.; Ji, Z.L. Acoustic attenuation performance of circular expansion chambers with extended inlet/outlet. *J. Sound Vib.* **1999**, *223*, 197–212. [CrossRef]
39. ISO 10140-2. *Acoustics—Laboratory Measurement of Sound Insulation of Building Elements—Part 2: Measurement of Airborne Sound Insulation*; International Standards Organization: Geneva, Switzerland, 2010.
40. ISO 15186-1. *Acoustics—Measurement of Sound Insulation in Buildings and of Building Elements Using Sound Intensity—Part 1: Laboratory Measurements*; International Standards Organization: Geneva, Switzerland, 2000.
41. ISO 16283-1. *Acoustics—Field Measurement of Sound Insulation in Buildings and of Building Elements—Part 1: Airborne Sound Insulation*; International Standards Organization: Geneva, Switzerland, 2014.
42. ISO 16283-3. *Acoustics—Field Measurement of Sound Insulation in Buildings and of Building Elements—Part 3: Façade Sound Insulation*; International Standards Organization: Geneva, Switzerland, 2016.
43. ISO 15186-2. *Acoustics—Measurement of Sound Insulation in Buildings and of Building Elements Using Sound Intensity—Part 2: Field Measurements*; International Standards Organization: Geneva, Switzerland, 2003.
44. Roozen, N.B.; Leclere, Q.; Urbán, D.; Kritly, L.; Glorieux, C. Assessment of the sound reduction index of building elements by near field excitation through an array of loudspeakers and structural response measurements by laser Doppler vibrometry. *Appl. Acoust.* **2018**, *140*, 225–235. [CrossRef]
45. Roozen, N.B.; Leclère, Q.; Urbán, D.; Echenagucia, T.M.; Block, P.; Rychtáriková, M.; Glorieux, C. Assessment of the airborne sound insulation from mobility vibration measurements; a hybrid experimental numerical approach. *J. Sound Vib.* **2018**, *432*, 680–698. [CrossRef]
46. Roozen, N.B.; Labelle, L.; Leclere, Q.; Ege, K.; Alvarado, S. Non-contact experimental assessment of apparent dynamic stiffness of constrained-layer damping sandwich plates in a broad frequency range using a Nd: YAG pump laser and a laser Doppler vibrometer. *J. Sound Vib.* **2017**, *395*, 90–101. [CrossRef]
47. Vanlanduit, S.; Vanherzeele, J.; Guillaume, P.; De Sitter, G. Absorption measurement of acoustic materials using a scanning laser Doppler vibrometer. *J. Acoust. Soc. Am.* **2005**, *117*, 1168–1172. [CrossRef]
48. ASTM E2571-09. *Standard Test Method for Measurement of Normal Incidence Sound Transmission of Acoustical Materials Based on the Transfer Matrix Method*; ASTM International: Conshohocken, PA, USA, 2011.
49. Piana, E.A.; Roozen, N.B.; Scrosati, C. Transmission tube measurements on the DENORMS round robin test material samples. In *Proceedings of the 26th International Congress on Sound and Vibration*, Montréal, QC, Canada, 7–11 July 2019.
50. Salissou, Y.; Panneton, R.; Doutres, O. Complement to standard method for measuring normal incidence sound transmission loss with three microphones. *J. Acoust. Soc. Am.* **2012**, *131*, EL216–EL222. [CrossRef]
51. Seybert, A.F.; Ross, D.F. Experimental determination of acoustic properties using a two microphone random-excitation technique. *J. Acoust. Soc. Am.* **1977**, *61*, 1362–1370. [CrossRef]
52. Chung, J.Y.; Blaser, D.A. Transfer function method of measuring acoustic intensity in a duct system with flow. *J. Acoust. Soc. Am.* **1980**, *68*, 1570–1577. [CrossRef]
53. Chung, J.Y.; Blaser, D.A. Transfer function method of measuring in-duct acoustic properties. II. Experiment. *J. Acoust. Soc. Am.* **1980**, *68*, 914–921. [CrossRef]
54. Bonfiglio, P.; Pompoli, F. A single measurement approach for the determination of the normal incidence Transmission Loss. *J. Acoust. Soc. Am.* **2008**, *124*, 1577–1583. [CrossRef]
55. Salissou, Y.; Panneton, R. A general wave decomposition formula for the measurement of normal incidence sound transmission loss in impedance tube. *J. Acoust. Soc. Am.* **2009**, *125*, 2083–2090. [CrossRef]
56. Peng, D.L.; Hu, P.; Zhu, B.L. The modified method of measuring the complex transmission coefficient of multilayer acoustical panel in impedance tube. *Appl. Acoust.* **2008**, *69*, 1240–1248. [CrossRef]
57. Wei, Z.; Hou, H.; Gao, N.; Huang, Y.; Yang, J. Normal incidence sound transmission loss evaluation with a general upstream tube wave decomposition formula. *J. Acoust. Soc. Am.* **2018**, *144*, 2344–2353. [CrossRef] [PubMed]
58. Seybert, A.F. Two-sensor methods for the measurement of sound intensity and acoustic properties in ducts. *J. Acoust. Soc. Am.* **1988**, *83*, 2233–2239. [CrossRef]
59. Rindel, J.H. *Sound Insulation in Buildings*; CRC Press: Boca Raton, FL, USA, 2017.
60. Tijs, E.; Druyvesteyn, E. An intensity method for measuring absorption properties in situ. *Acta Acust. United Acust.* **2012**, *98*, 342–353. [CrossRef]

61. ISO 5136. *Acoustics—Determination of Sound Power Radiated into a Duct By Fans and Other Air-Moving Devices—In-Duct Method*; International Standards Organization: Geneva, Switzerland, 2003.
62. ISO 7235. *Acoustics—Laboratory Measurement Procedures for Ducted Silencers and Air-Terminal Units—Insertion LOSS, Flow Noise and Total Pressure Loss*; International Standards Organization: Geneva, Switzerland, 2003.

Article

Comparison Failure and Successful Methodologies for Diffusion Measurements Undertaken inside Two Different Testing Rooms

Lamberto Tronchin [1,*], Angelo Farina [2], Antonella Bevilacqua [2], Francesca Merli [3] and Pietro Fiumana [4]

1. Department of Architecture, University of Bologna, 47521 Cesena, Italy
2. Department of Industrial Engineering, University of Parma, 43124 Parma, Italy; angelo.farina@unipr.it (A.F.); antonella.bevilacqua@unipr.it (A.B.)
3. CIRI-Interdepartmental Centre for Industrial Research in Building and Construction, University of Bologna, 40132 Bologna, Italy; francesca.merli8@unibo.it
4. Techno Srl, Via Pirano 7, 48122 Ravenna, Italy; pietro.fiumana@gmail.com
* Correspondence: lamberto.tronchin@unibo.it

Citation: Tronchin, L.; Farina, A.; Bevilacqua, A.; Merli, F.; Fiumana, P. Comparison Failure and Successful Methodologies for Diffusion Measurements Undertaken inside Two Different Testing Rooms. *Appl. Sci.* 2021, *11*, 10523. https://doi.org/10.3390/app112210523

Academic Editor: Theodore E. Matikas

Received: 22 September 2021
Accepted: 4 November 2021
Published: 9 November 2021

Publisher's Note: MDPI stays neutral with regard to jurisdictional claims in published maps and institutional affiliations.

Copyright: © 2021 by the authors. Licensee MDPI, Basel, Switzerland. This article is an open access article distributed under the terms and conditions of the Creative Commons Attribution (CC BY) license (https://creativecommons.org/licenses/by/4.0/).

Abstract: The scattering phenomenon is known to be of great importance for the acoustic quality of a performance arts space. The scattering of sound can be achieved in different ways: it can be obtained by the presence of architectural and/or decorating elements inside a room (e.g., columns, statues), by the geometry and roughness of a surface (e.g., Quadratic Residue Diffuser (QRD)) and by the diffraction effect occurring when a sound wave hits the edges of an obstacle. This article deals with the surface scattering effects and the diffusion phenomenon only related to MDF and plywood panels tested by disposing the wells both horizontally and vertically. The test results undertaken inside a semi-reverberant room and inside a large reverberant room have been compared to highlight the success and the failure of the measuring methodologies. In detail, according to the existing standards and regulations (i.e., ISO 17497—Part 2), diffusion measurements have been undertaken on a few selected types of panel: two QRD panels (made of Medium Density Fiberboard (MDF) and plywood) with and without a smooth painted solid wood placed behind the QRD. The panels have been tested inside two rooms of different characteristics: a semi-anechoic chamber (Room A) and a large reverberant room (Room B). The volume size influenced the results that have been analyzed for both chambers, showing an overlap of reflections on panels tested inside Room A and a clear diffusion response for the panels tested inside Room B. In terms of the diffusion coefficient in all the octave bands between 125 Hz and 8 kHz, results should not be considered valid for panels tested in Room A because they were negatively impacted by extraneous reflections, while they are reliable for panels tested in Room B.

Keywords: scattering effect; diffusion coefficient; reflecting panels; QRD; ISO 17497

1. Introduction

The acoustic properties of surfaces are essential to estimate and calculate sound propagation within an enclosed space [1,2]. The acoustic scattering from surfaces and sound absorption characteristics are very important in all aspects of room acoustics, e.g., in opera houses, concert halls, industrial workplaces and reverberation chambers.

The sound scattering mechanism is activated by the corrugations of the walls with a sufficiently rough structure or by single elements such as columns, statues, etc., or by diffraction effects along the edges of panels. For example, concert halls or theatres could present focalization of the sound, so diffusing panels are inserted to solve this problem [3,4]. Many measurement methods have been developed to quantify the various types of sound scattering coefficients and to determine the sound diffusion mechanisms. For many years, acoustical surface scattering has been deeply studied by researchers worldwide [5–7], and its standard definition is the ratio of the energy reflected outside the specular zone to the total reflected energy.

Cox suggested quantifying the diffusion by means of the standard deviation of the reflected energy distribution [8,9]. A similar approach was proposed using a new diffusion uniformity coefficient based on the circular autocorrelation function of the polar reflected energy diagram [10,11]. Moreover, different techniques depending on the type of incident sound field (free field or diffuse field) were proposed to measure the sound scattering coefficient [12,13]. Contrastingly, the Audio Engineering Society (AES) proposed a measuring technique of the diffusion uniformity coefficient [14].

Continuous studies in this field [15,16] brought the introduction of the standards ISO 17497-1:2004 [17], which refers to the measurement of the random-incidence scattering coefficient, and ISO 17947-2:2012 [18], which refers to the measurement of the directional diffusion coefficient.

In this paper, two diffusion measures are introduced with somewhat different applications. One measure was performed in a semi-anechoic chamber (Room A) and the second in a large reverberant room (Room B). To determine the sound diffusion coefficient, two QRD panels made of different materials were tested following ISO 17947-2:2012 regulation. The success and the failure of the measuring methodologies being used are highlighted by the contribution of extraneous reflections recorded inside Room A that compromised the scattering results, which have been discarded because they were considered to not be affordable values. The results of the panels tested inside Room B instead have been compared with the reference curves of a theoretical model based on the principle of free field sound propagation, while data analysis consisted of a polar distribution of the scattered field through the use of the Fast Fourier Transform (FFT).

This concept could be extended to the correct architectural design of a room with regard to the purpose of its appropriate use that sometimes, in the context of cost reduction, is wrongly used for other types of sound tests by facing unexpected objectives.

Literature Review

Summarizing the two parts of the reference standard, the method detailed in part 1 of ISO 17497 is focused on measuring the random-incidence scattering coefficient based on the degree of roughness of the tested surface, while the method described in part 2 of the same standard is focused on measuring the diffusion coefficient of a surface based on the angle of the incident ray. For the panels selected for this paper, the method described in ISO 17497.2012 part 2 has been adopted, specifically in two non-anechoic rooms of different volume sizes.

The methodologies of ISO 17497 have been revised firstly by Mommertz and Vorlander, who developed the free-field scattering measurements [15]. Outcomes of this research were the assessment of the absorption coefficient for each frequency band, after an FFT post-processing of the measured RIR obtained by rotating the panel at 5° steps on 72 angles, and thereafter the evaluation of the scattering coefficient of the reflected sound.

Other practice experimentations were identified in the wave field synthesis (WFS) approach by Farina [19], who characterized the scattering properties of a generic, finite-size object by a large number of RIR measurements taken by moving the microphone at small steps along a straight line instead of following the trajectory of a hemi-circumference. Since the scattered wavefronts have more curvature than the specularly reflected ones, the WFS has been adopted because it can easily separate the two types of wavefronts. With this technique, the estimation of the scattering coefficient is obtained by minimizing the difference between the numerical calculations and the measured results.

2. Technical Description of the Two Types of Diffusers

In acoustics, different types of material and geometry applied to the diffusers have been exploited and developed since the pioneering studies and research conducted by Schroeder in the 1970s [8]. A common purpose of all the diffusers is to spread the sound waves into all directions, trying to reduce the strength of the undesired specular reflections or echoes, while the sound energy remains preserved in the space [20].

Among the wide variety of panels (differing by material, shape, geometry, etc.), the selected types of diffusers treated in this article are the following:

- Two Quadratic Residue Diffusers (QRD), varying in material component (i.e., MDF, plywood) and used in the horizontal and vertical configuration of the grooves;
- A smooth painted reflecting panel was used as the backing of the QRDs.

2.1. The Quadratic Residue Diffusers (QRD)

The spatially dependent reflectivity for the QRD follows the numerical sequences with a uniform spatial Fourier transform of their reflection coefficient.

The phenomenon of diffusion started to be studied extensively in 1975 by Schroeder [8], who provided a way of designing highly diffusing surfaces based on binary maximum-length sequences showing that these periodic sequences have equal harmonic amplitudes.

Later on, he extended his method and proposed surface structures that give excellent sound diffusion over larger bandwidths. Specifically, this kind of diffuser is composed of a periodic sequence of grooves having the same length and different widths. The maximum width is given by the maximum wavelength to be diffused, while the width of every groove is determined by the dimension of half-wavelength to be diffused. The depth of the sequence is determined by Equation (1).

$$d = n^2 \cdot mod(p) \tag{1}$$

In this case, n is an integer number, p is an odd prime number and $mod()$ is the operator modulus. By the input of these two variables, it is possible to determine the depth of the diffusing panel by the relationship of the maximum depth (d_{max}) and the maximum number of the sequence (n_{max}), as summarized in Equation (2).

$$d = \frac{d_{max}}{n_{max}} \tag{2}$$

Scientific studies [8] confirm that the limits for the effectiveness of the quadratic residue diffusers are in function of the wavelength and, thus, of the frequency. Below the lowest effective frequency, the diffuser works as a flat panel because the sequences are too small to be influencing the incident sound wave, having no scattering effect. In fact, the typical thickness of the QRD is half of the wavelength, corresponding to the low cut-off frequency.

In a similar way, above the highest effective frequency, the wave propagation becomes irregular and it cannot be considered a plane wave. The lower and upper limits are defined by Equations (3) and (4).

$$\lambda_{max} = 2p\frac{d_{max}}{n} \tag{3}$$

$$\lambda_{min} = 2w \tag{4}$$

The input data for the measurements presented in this paper are as follows:

- $p = 17$ for the horizontal sequences;
- $p = 13$ for the vertical sequences.

The dimensions of the panels tested are 900 × 600 mm [L × H], as shown in Figure 1. The same dimensions are valid for both MDF and plywood materials.

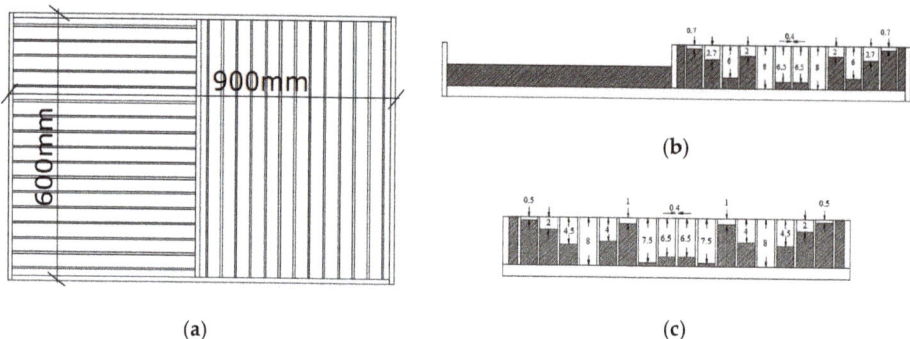

Figure 1. Quadratic residue diffuser (QRD) used during the experimental measurements: (**a**) elevation; (**b**) horizontal section; (**c**) vertical section. All the numbers are in mm.

The choice of the p numbers falls on the maximum efficiency of the panel to be comprised between 250 Hz and 2 kHz.

2.2. Reflecting Panel

A painted solid wood panel has been used as the backing of the QRDs during the measurements. It is not perforated and presents a smooth surface having dimensions of 900 × 900 mm [L × H]. Measurements were undertaken with and without this reflecting panel, in order to obtain absolute values of the QRDs in their configuration and to simulate the applications of the QRDs in specific environments such as auditoria, theatres, recording studios, or conference rooms.

3. Measurements and Methodology

3.1. Standards and Regulations

3.1.1. Methodology in Line with ISO 17497: 2004+A1:2014, Part 1—Measurement of Random-Incidence Scattering Coefficient in a Reverberant Room

Part 1 of the ISO 17497 deals with the method for measuring a random-incident scattering coefficient by describing the number of reflections deviating specularly from a surface. The frequency range of the measurements is comprised between 100 Hz and 5 kHz, in third-octave bands. The test should be undertaken in a reverberant room (as fully described in ISO 354:2003 [21]) such that the absorption (A) inside the testing room should not exceed $A \leq 0.3 \times V^{2/3}$.

The test sample fixed to a rigid base/plate is rotated by a turntable mechanized system. The plate where the sample is fixed should be symmetrical with respect to the axis of rotation and should have a size corresponding to the maximum dimension of the test sample.

The test sample should be circular or flush-mounted, having a surface area as large as possible in order to obtain a good measurement accuracy. It is recommended that the sample structural depth should be small compared to the size of the surface to be tested, it should be $h \leq d/16$, where d is the diameter of the turntable. Another condition to be considered for the test sample is that the random-incidence absorption coefficient should not exceed $\alpha_s = 0.50$.

Procedures for the measurement methodology should follow the ISO 18233:2006 [22]. The room impulse response (RIRs) should be measured without and with the test sample accordingly with the ISO 354, with two source positions and three microphone positions at least. The duration of the measurement should be equal to the time that the turntable employs to make a complete revolution. Measurement should be taken with and without the test sample, in static and rotating turntable conditions, for a total of four different settings.

3.1.2. Methodology in Line with ISO 17497:2012, Part 2—Measurement of the Directional Diffusion Coefficient in a Free Field

Part 2 of the ISO 17497 deals with the method for measuring the directional diffusion coefficient by describing the uniformity of the reflected polar distribution, best known as the quality of the diffusing surface.

The diffusion coefficient describes the energy reflected by a surface, which is spatially distributed by the description of a polar response. For this methodology, the microphones are positioned radially in front of the test sample. The frequency range is the same used for the turntable method, comprised between 100 Hz and 5 kHz in third-octave bands.

The environment of the measurements should be an anechoic chamber or a large semi-reverberant room simulating the reflection-free environment. It is recommended that the RIR should be taken in the far-field for monitoring the achievement of the amount of diffusion and use the near field for any aberration or focusing effect.

In relation to the measurement procedures, at least 80% of the receiving positions should be outside of the specular zone in order to meet the far-field conditions and the distance between the source and the test sample should be 10 m, while the receivers' radius should be 5 m. The receiver angular resolution should be of a maximum of 5°. Regarding the equipment, the sound source should be omnidirectional, emitting the sound signal as described in ISO 18233:2006, while the microphones should have the same sensitivity to all the conceivable reflection paths.

The measurements should be undertaken without and with the test sample. The polar response processing is based on the isolation of the reflections given by the test sample from other types of reflections (e.g., room boundaries). The influence of background reflections shall be removed through windowing the RIR. If the window is set with a unity gain where the reflections are present and zero elsewhere, the residual reflections will be removed. The windowed RIR shall then undergo the Fourier transformation in each frequency band of interest.

3.2. Real-Scale Room Models and Instrumentation

Two measurement campaigns were conducted in two real-scale rooms selected for testing the diffusers and described as follows:

- A semi-anechoic room having dimensions 9 × 10 × 4.5 m [L × W × H] (Room A), one of the facilities of the SCM Group located in Rimini. This room has a hard finish floor and absorbing panels applied on walls and ceiling.

A reverberant room having dimensions 16 × 20 × 7 m [L × W × H] (Room B), one of the laboratory facilities of the University of Parma. This room has hard material as a finished floor, plastered bricks on walls and an exposed concrete slab. Volume size is considered big enough to ensure the condition of a free field. The equipment used for the acoustic measurements is composed of the following items:

- An equalized loudspeaker (Genelec 8351 SAM), Finland;
- 25 microphones pre-polarized for free field conditions (B&K 4188), Denmark;
- 8 converters for data acquisition (Behringer ADA-8000), Germany;
- Firewire interface M-Audio (Profire Lightbridge), USA.

MacBook Pro 15". Because the diffusion coefficient indicates how the quantity of the reflected energy is distributed in space, both sound source and receivers were placed in a certain way to determine the spatial distribution of the polar response of the reflected sound. In particular, 25 microphones were positioned at a constant radial distance from the sound source, recording the one-third-octave bands between 100 and 5 kHz. The anechoic conditions for investigating the panels' early reflections were obtained by setting the microphones at floor level to prevent receivers picking up waves reflected from the floor, which would distort the measurements.

The conditions of the experimental measurements followed the rules of the far-field, by having 80% of the receivers out of the specular zone. In this research, the sound source was located only in front of the sample. The methodology for measuring the diffusion coefficient used during the two campaigns followed ISO 17497, part 2.

The disposition of the instrumentation was different between Room A and B. In particular, inside Room A, given the limited dimension of the space, the 25 microphones were installed at a radius of 4 m from the test sample, which was located at the center of a virtual semi-circumference, and the sound source was at a radius of 8 m distant from the test sample, as indicated in Figure 2.

 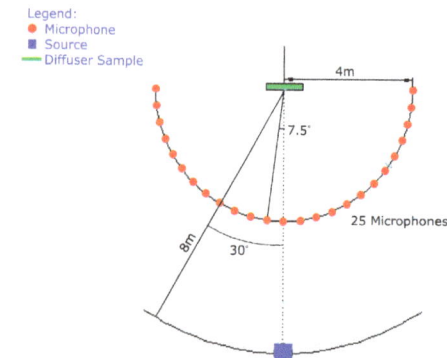

Figure 2. Equipment disposition inside the semi-anechoic chamber available at SCM Group in Rimini (Room A).

Differently, in Room B the 25 microphones were installed at a radius of 5 m from the test sample, always located at the center of the semi-circumference, and the sound source was at a radius of 10 m distant from the test sample, as indicated in Figure 3.

 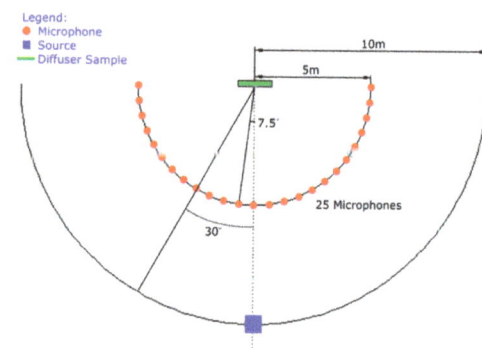

Figure 3. Equipment disposition inside the reverberant laboratory of the University of Parma (Room B).

The excitation signal employed for the RIR was an exponential sine sweep (ESS), having a frequency range set between 40 Hz and 20 kHz. In each room and for each panel configuration, the measurements were repeated three times with a silence gap of 5 s in between.

The size of the speaker was big enough to cover the diffuser dimensions, while all the microphones were set to have the same sensibility for any reflection going from the diffuser to the receivers, with a drift of ± 1 dB.

The sets of measurements were undertaken to capture the 25 RIRs with and without the test sample.

The type of diffuser utilized for this experiment was a single plane, having an acoustic impedance constant along the x-axis. On this basis, the diffusion coefficient can be measured on a plane orthogonal to the direction x, calculating the maximum diffusion.

3.3. Tests Performance

In each room, different configurations of the QRDs have been tested, with and without the backing reflecting panel. Table 1 summarizes the test configurations.

Table 1. Test performance organized in Room A and B.

Configuration	Room A	Room B
Empty Room	Tested	Tested
Only reflecting panel	-	Tested
Only MDF QRD—Vertical	-	-
Only MDF QRD—Horizontal	-	-
MDF QRD with backing refl. Panel—Vertical	Tested	-
MDF QRD with backing refl. Panel—Horizontal	Tested	-
Only Plywood QRD—Vertical	-	Tested
Only Plywood QRD—Horizontal	-	Tested
Plywood QRD with backing refl. Panel—Vertical	Tested	Tested
Plywood QRD with backing refl. Panel—Horizontal	Tested	Tested

4. Data Analysis and Post-Processing

Data analysis has been realized by using the software Adobe Audition CC, which illustrates contemporarily all the RIRs given by the 25 microphones, as reported in Figures 4 and 5.

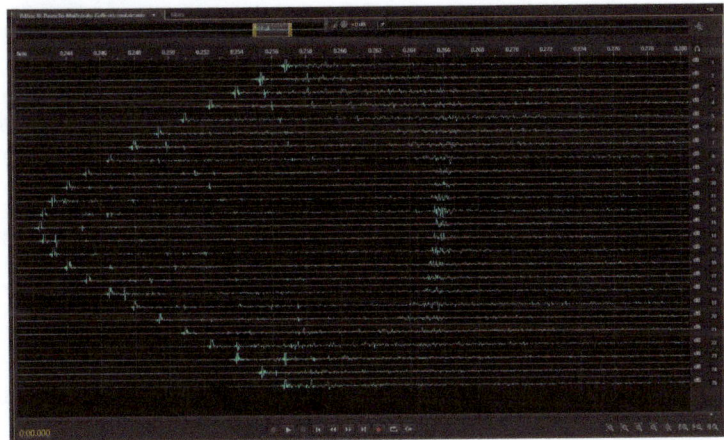

Figure 4. Example of a polar plot of RIR data measured inside Room A: direct sound on the left and reflected sound in the center.

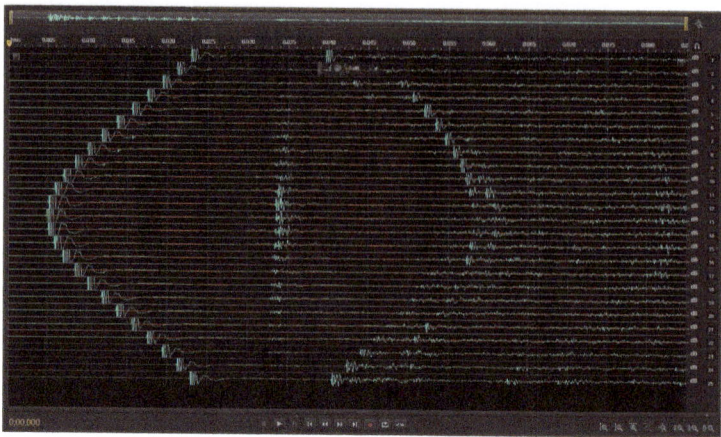

Figure 5. Example of a polar plot of RIR data measured inside Room B: direct sound on the left, early reflections in the center and late reflections on the right.

Both Figures 4 and 5 illustrate the direct sound recorded by all the microphones, as shown in a hyperbolic shape on the left of the screen. Based on the geometrical organization of the microphones, channel 13 is the closest to the sound source and hence it represents the first receiver recording the signal. As long as the other microphones are equidistant from the source (located symmetrically with respect to the main axis crossing the sound source, microphone 13 and the sample), the direct sound is recorded with a variable time delay, slightly increasing towards the extreme microphones (i.e., channel 1 and 25).

The main characterization factor between the analysis undertaken for Room A and B is the reflected signals. In particular, for Room A the early reflections result was confused with that of the late reflections, while for Room B the early reflections are clearly identified at the center of the screen, with different energy intensities. This phenomenon is mainly due to the volume sizes of the rooms where the surveys have been performed: the small dimensions of Room A create an overlap of the early and late reflections, causing the windowing process as difficult to be carried out; in Room B the volume size was large enough to make a distinction between all types of reflections, in line with the standard. Section 5 shows and comments on how the results in Room A have been compromised by the vertical walls, albeit minimally—an outcome that is considered successful for the tests performed in Room B.

Following the standard requirements, time windowing is a necessary process undertaken to select the early reflections related to each channel and discard the late or reverberant sound coming at a second stage. The windowing operation was implemented by using the software Adobe Audition 3.0. The plugin Aurora, suitable for all the versions of Adobe Audition, has been utilized to convert the sound wave from a time domain to a frequency domain through an FFT, in order to obtain all the sound levels at different frequencies and, hence, to calculate the diffusion coefficient.

To estimate the values of the absorption (α) and scattering (s) coefficients, a numerical model was required to compare the results. One of the assumptions applied to the model consists of the theoretical behavior that the digital entities should assume, to be considered ideal surfaces. This assumption is important to acquire an exhaustive comparison between the model and the curves obtained experimentally.

The construction of the theoretical model follows the rules described by literature in previous studies [19]. Given the sound levels at each band of frequency, as recorded by the 25 microphones, the absorption (α) and scattering (s) coefficients have been calculated by assuming the following:

- The direct sound was calculated by following the theory of sound propagation in free field conditions, as indicated in Equation (5);

$$L_p = L_w - 10Log\left(4\pi r^2\right) = L_w - 20Log(r) - 11 \ [dB] \quad (5)$$

- The reflected soundwave in the specular zone is obtained by the contribution of the specular reflected wave and the diffused reflected wave, as indicated in Equation (6);

$$L_{diff+spec} = L_w - 10Log\left(\left(\frac{S_{panel}}{4\pi r_1^2}\right)\frac{(1-\alpha)s}{2\pi r_2^2}\right) + 10Log(\frac{(1-s)(1-\alpha)}{4\pi\left(r_1^2+r_2^2\right)^2}) \quad (6)$$

- The reflected soundwave out of the specular zone is given by the contribution of the diffuse energy only, as indicated in Equation (7).

$$L_{diff+spec} = L_w - 10Log\left(\left(\frac{S_{panel}}{4\pi r_1^2}\right)\frac{(1-\alpha)s}{2\pi r_2^2}\right) \quad (7)$$

For the equations above, clarifications on nomenclature are required, in particular:

- r_1 is the distance between the sample and the central microphone;
- r_2 is the distance between the sample and the sound source.

S_{panel} is the surface area of the sample, in square meters. Equations (5)–(7) describe a theoretical model in function of α and s. This result allows for the construction of the reference curves at each band of frequency, based on the theoretical model explained above. Figure 6 shows the reference curve trend at 500 Hz based on the disposition of the microphones around the test sample.

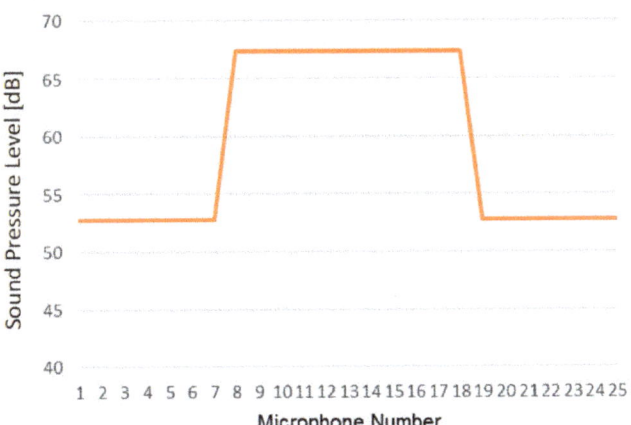

Figure 6. Curve trend of the theoretical model at 500 Hz.

The values of α and s have been considered when their results, describing a curve along all the 25 microphones, indicate little variations with respect to the theoretical model. It should be noticed that the reference curve is different for each frequency band, becoming narrower at high frequencies related to the noise levels centered on the microphones close to the sound source. Making the theoretical model as a reference curve, it is possible also to calculate the directional diffusion coefficient as one of the essential requirements of the standard ISO 17947-2: 2004. The procedure to obtain the directional diffusion coefficient (d_θ) is described in Formula (8).

$$d_\theta = \left(\frac{\left(\Sigma_{i=1}^{n} 10^{L_i/10}\right)^2 - \Sigma_{i=1}^{n} \left(10^{L_i/10}\right)^2}{(n-1) \Sigma_{i=1}^{n} \left(10^{L_i/10}\right)^2} \right) \qquad (8)$$

where n is the number of microphones.

5. Results and Discussion

The test samples have been measured with the methodology described above. The following sections show the results relative to the diffusers tested inside Room A and Room B.

5.1. Measurement Results Undertaken inside Room A—Semi-Anechoic Room Facility at the SCM Group of Rimini

Diffusing panels made of two different materials (MDF and plywood) and reflecting panels are illustrated in Figure 7. The measurements of diffusing panels were repeated for different configurations, considering the panel in the horizontal and vertical orientation with a reflecting panel as the back. The analysis was carried out to evaluate the acoustic behavior and differences between diffusing panels made of MDF and plywood.

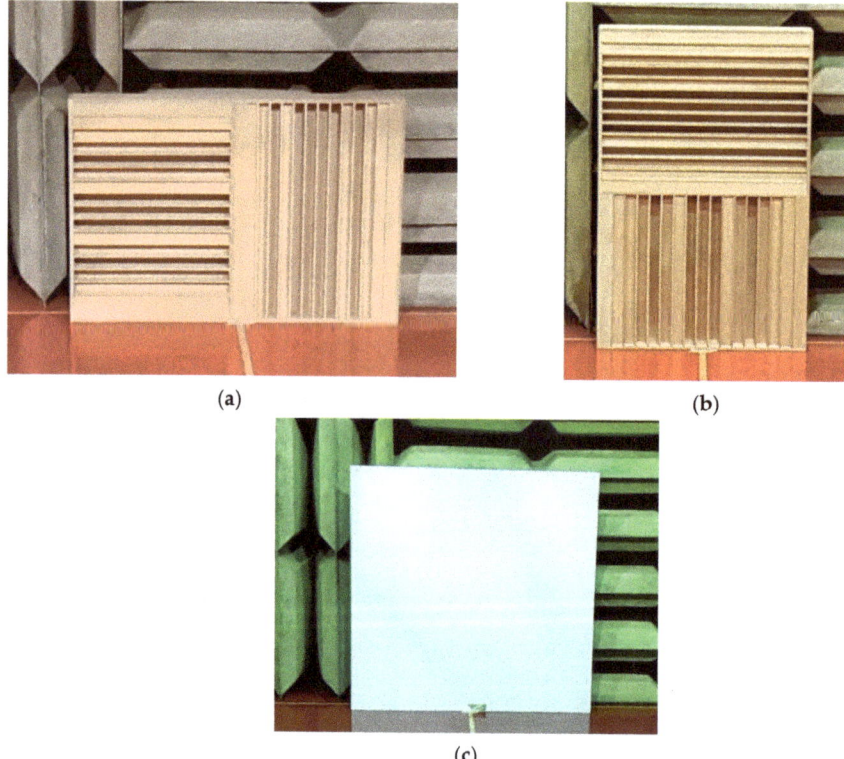

Figure 7. Diffusing panels made of MDF (**a**), plywood (**b**), and reflecting panel (**c**) tested inside the semi-anechoic chamber in SCM company in Rimini (Room A).

The graphs shown in Figure 8 represent the variation at the mid-frequencies range of sound pressure levels measured for the four panel's configurations. From the results, it is possible to see that there is a slight difference between diffusing panels made of MDF and plywood and between the vertical and horizontal orientations.

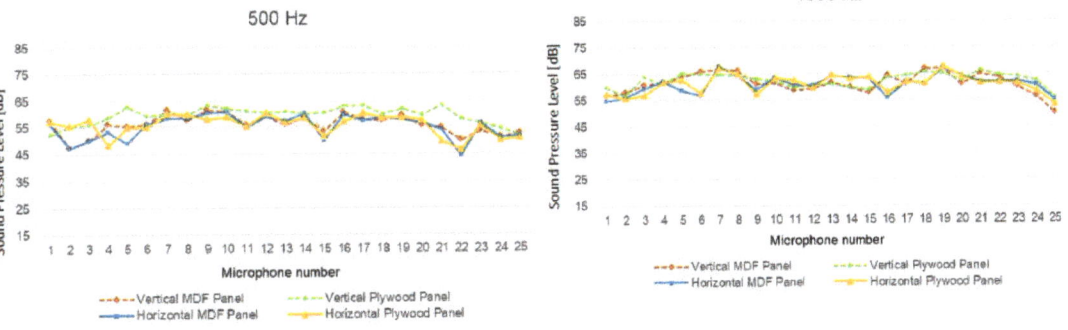

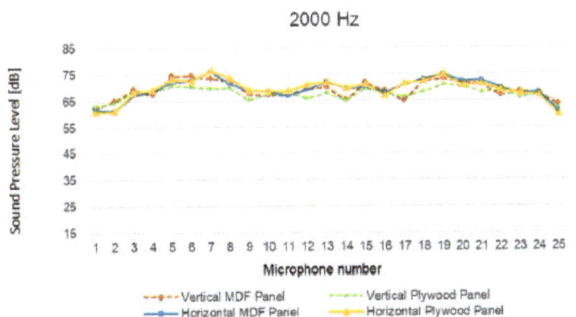

Figure 8. Results for the four panel's configurations tested inside Room A at mid-frequencies.

Figure 9 reports the matching between numerical and experimental data for the Horizontal plywood and MDF panels. From the graphs, it is possible to note that the reflected energy captured by the side microphones (microphone 1 and 25) is far more than expected. Indeed, there is a slight difference between the sound pressure levels recorded by the central microphones and the lateral ones. This is not due to the ability of the panel to reflect a lot of lateral energy, but it might be caused by the small dimensions of Room A that have influenced the measurements, causing reflections able to slant the results. Therefore, we have verified that the semi-anechoic chamber in Rimini is not suitable for detecting the diffusion measurements and ensuring the free field conditions.

Figure 9. Matching between numerical and experimental data for the horizontal plywood and MDF panels inside Room A at mid-frequencies.

5.2. Measurement Results Undertaken inside Room B—Reverberant Room Facility at the University of Parma

Another set of measurements was performed inside Room B, a reverberant chamber that represents one of the laboratory facilities at the University of Parma. From the results in Section 5.1, the difference of the scattering coefficients between the QRD composed of plywood and MDF is minimal; as such, the authors for this campaign preferred to test the plywood QRD only, with and without the backing panel, in both horizontal and vertical configurations. As anticipated in Table 1, this campaign also consists of measuring the RIRs with the presence of the backing reflecting panel. This latest one has been introduced as a totally reflecting surface, representing a reference for making any comparison with the other configurations.

Figure 10 shows the plywood QRD that has been tested inside Room B, with and without the backing reflecting panel.

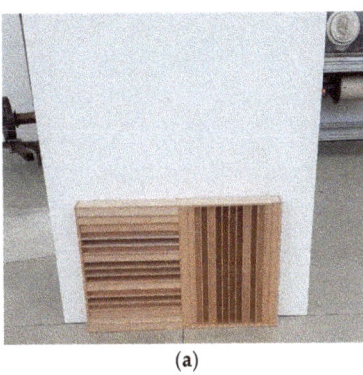

(a)   (b)

Figure 10. Plywood QRD tested in Room B, with (a) and without (b) the backing reflecting panel, in the horizontal configuration.

The graphs in Figure 11 report the scattering coefficient obtained for each band of frequency between 125 Hz and 8 kHz, and for the configurations of the plywood QRD described above. These results were compared to those obtained by testing the reflecting panel only. The results of the acoustical coefficients are obtained by considering the average values of all the measuring points related to each microphone.

At 125 Hz, all the configurations are similar and comparable, with a broad diffusion between channels 8 and 20. At the extremities, the peaks appear at channels 4 and 22, having a symmetrical trend with respect to channel 13 that is placed at the center.

The graph relative to 250 Hz shows an increase in sound levels at channels 11 and 16, with the best performance equal to 71 dB registered by measuring the plywood QRD with the backing reflecting panel. Other peaks are found at channels 4 and 22, with comparable sound levels recorded at 125 Hz. The downward peaks belong to channels 2, 7, 13, 19 and 24.

At 500 Hz, the sound level of channel 13, relative to the presence of the reflecting panel only, reaches 76 dB, equal to 5 dB above the plywood QRD in the horizontal configuration and with the backing reflecting panel. Other peaks are revealed at channels 9 and 17 with minor energy floating between 65 and 70 dB for all the configurations. The downward peaks recorded at 250 Hz, are herein increased up to 15 dB at the same channels.

The graph relative to 1 kHz shows a flatter trend of the results across all the microphones, with the elimination of the fluctuations registered at side channels. In particular, since the performance of the horizontal configuration with the backing reflecting panel resulted, in the best case, between 125 and 500 Hz, in this frequency band the vertical configuration with the backing reflecting panel gives higher sound levels, especially at channels 8 and 15, while at channel 13 the result is equal to the horizontal configuration having the backing panel.

From 2 kHz onwards, the performance of the only reflecting panel is the best only relative to channel 13, while it results lower than all the other configurations at the other microphone positions. The best performance across all the channels is given by the vertical configuration having the backing panel, especially at channel 13, but with small peaks registered at channels 7 and 20, recording 76 dB at these two positions.

The results at 4 and 8 kHz are very similar in trend line and maximum scattering sound energy, the only difference consists of the peaks registered at channels 7, 10, 12, 14, 16 and 18, resulting in the more accentuated at 8 kHz.

Other than the scattering coefficient, the directional diffusion coefficient has been calculated by the results obtained inside Room B. Figure 12 shows the values of the diffusion coefficient, correlated to the frequency range between 125 Hz and 8 kHz.

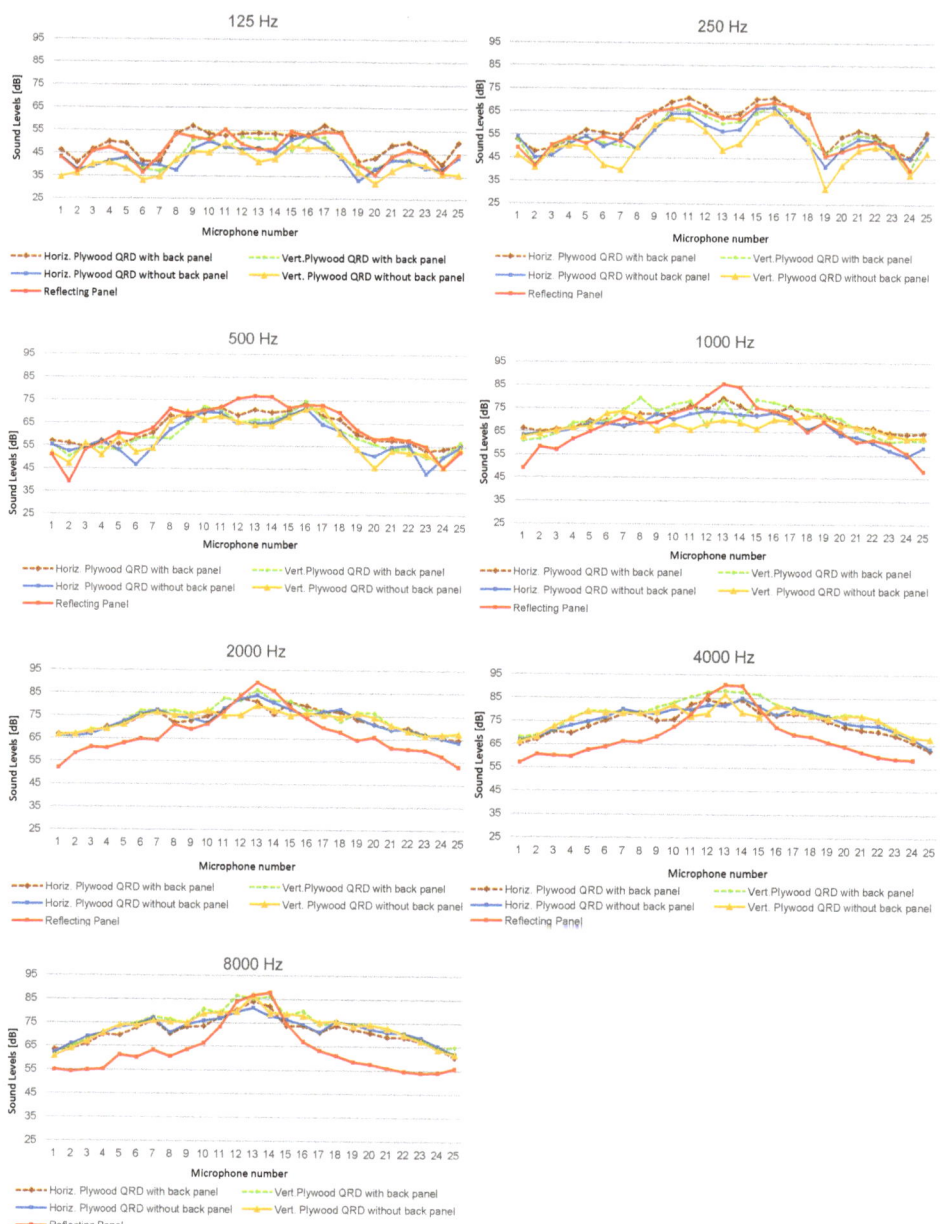

Figure 11. Plywood QRD tested with and without the backing reflecting panel, in horizontal and vertical configurations.

Among all the test samples and relative configurations tested in Room B, the specimen indicating the best performance of the diffusion coefficient is the plywood QRD in the vertical configuration, without any reflecting panel behind. In particular, the results indicate that the performance of $d = 0.63$ has been achieved at 1 and 2 kHz. The worst performance is given at 250 Hz and 8 kHz, with values of d floating between 0.23 and 0.22, respectively.

A second diffusion performance has been achieved by the plywood QRD in the horizontal configuration, without any reflecting panel behind. For this specific case, the highest value has been achieved with $d = 0.55$ at 1 kHz. A different trend line is obtained for this sample because a downward pick has been recorded at 2 kHz with $d = 0.34$.

The trend line similar to the latest sample has been registered for the plywood QRD in the vertical configuration, having the backing reflecting panel with slightly lower performance. The specimen that follows a different trend line is the reflecting panel tested by itself, having values around $d = 0.10$ from 1 kHz onwards.

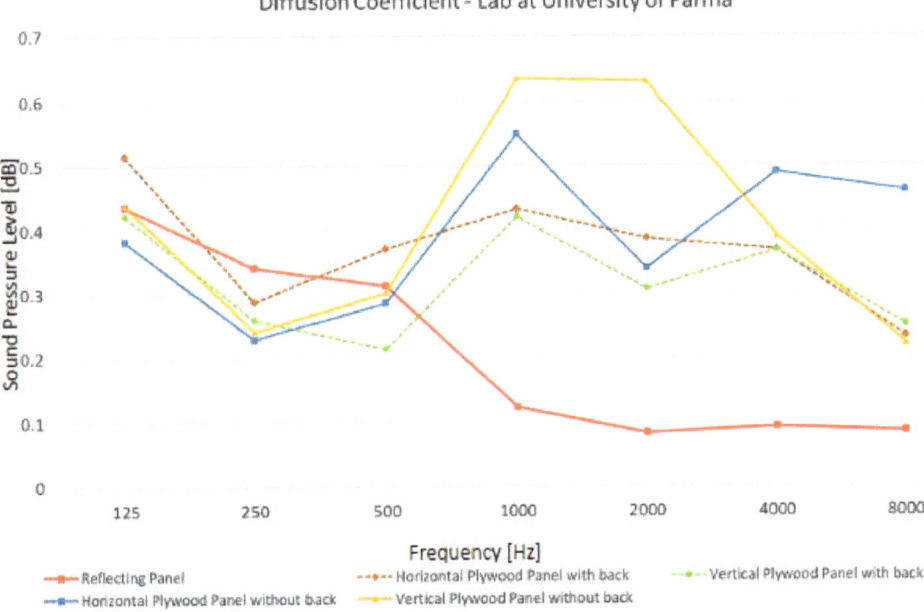

Figure 12. Directional diffusion coefficient related to the samples tested inside Room B.

5.3. Considerations upon Measurements' Results Undertaken inside Room A and B

By the results, as commented in Sections 5.1 and 5.2, it has been shown that the values of the scattering coefficient, related to the measurements undertaken inside Room A, are consistently high. This is due to the microphones that have recorded much more reflected sound energy than what was expected. This phenomenon has been created by the small distance between the microphones and the vertical walls of the room, whose reflected energy has been overlapped with the sound energy scattered by the QRD. This statement is confirmed by the concentration of sound energy in the corners of the room, related to microphone positions 1 and 25.

In summary, the values registered by the tests performed inside Room A should not be subject to consideration, because they were impacted by extraneous factors not related to the samples.

The results obtained by testing the panels inside Room B are considered valid because the samples were tested in an appropriate environment in accordance with the guidelines. The differences between the measurements undertaken in Room A and B are shown by the graphs in Figure 13, related to the same sample (i.e., plywood QRD in the horizontal configuration, without any backing reflecting panel).

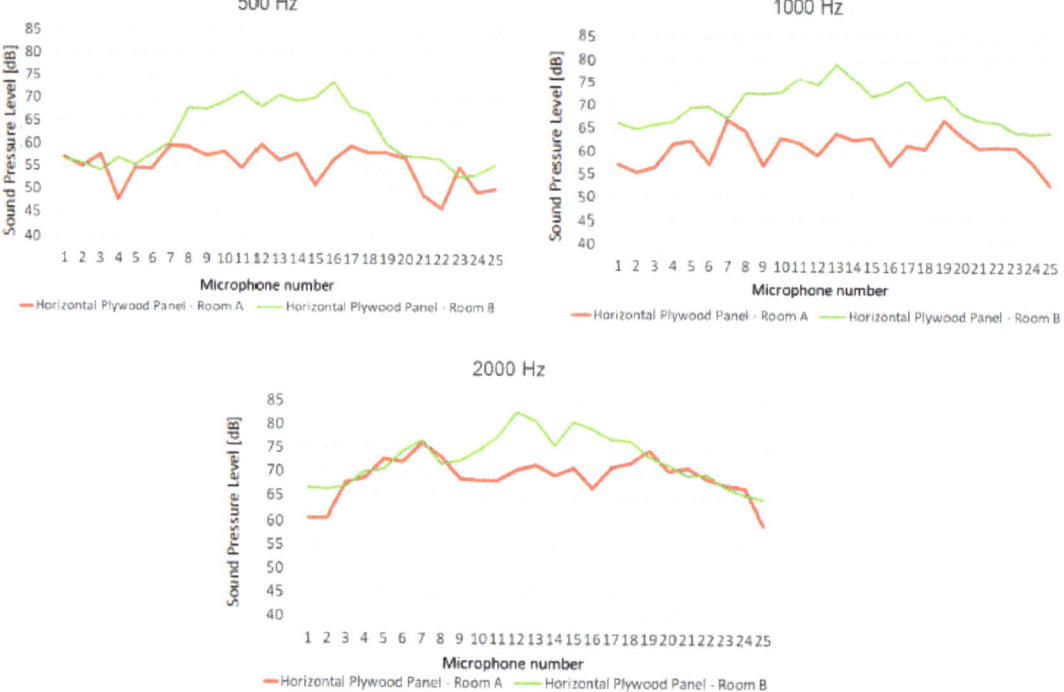

Figure 13. Comparison of the scattering coefficient based on measurements undertaken inside Room A and B.

Figure 13 shows that the scattering coefficients in Room A have comparable levels at 500 Hz across all the microphones, with downward peaks up to 10 dB, related to channel 4 and 22. Results obtained in Room B indicate a noticeable difference of up to 15 dB between the central channels (8 to 19) and the laterals, approximating the reference curve of the theoretical model introduced in Section 6. A similar trend has been found in the graph related to 2 kHz, where the central channels of Room B revealed higher sound energy than that tested in Room A, while the values obtained at the lateral channels (i.e., 1 to 7, and 19 to 25) are very comparable.

Curves indicated in the graph related to 1 kHz accentuate the difference between the results obtained in Room A and B, including the lateral channels for a level difference comprised between 10 and 15 dB.

The graph in Figure 14 reports the comparison among the Horizontal Plywood Panel with back, tested in Room A and Room B. The light blue line reports the values of the reflecting panel (alone), whilst the dotted line reports the scattering coefficient values of the Horizontal Plywood Panel without reflecting panel tested in Room B. From the graph, the Horizontal Plywood Panel—Room B scattering coefficient (dotted line) resulted higher than 0.4 for all the frequencies, except for 250 and 125 Hz, while for the other frequencies the scattering coefficient increases with increasing frequency. The values obtained for the Horizontal Plywood Panel with back—Room A gave inconsistent results due to the size of Room A.

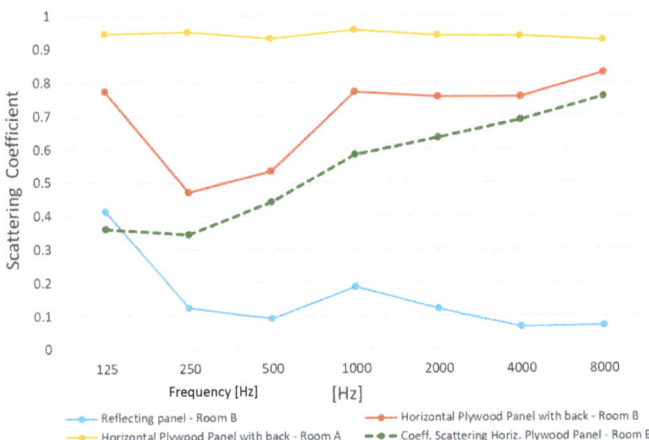

Figure 14. Comparison of the scattering coefficient based on measurements undertaken inside Room A and B ("Coeff. Scattering Horizontal Plywood Panel–Room B" = "Horizontal plywood panel with back-room B"–"Refecting panel").

6. Conclusions

Measurements were undertaken on the popular QRD in two specific configurations: horizontal and vertical disposition of the wells, placed with a rigidly backed smooth panel. Following part 2 of the reference standard (ISO 17497), the measurements consisted of placing the samples at the center of a virtual concentric arch of evenly spaced 25 microphones. The microphones' positions ranged from $\theta = 0°$ to $\theta = 90°$ with a spacing of $7.5°$ between each other and along a semicircle. This configuration has been employed in two rooms of different volume sizes and characteristics of wall finishes: a semi-anechoic chamber available at SCM Group in Rimini (Room A) and a reverberant laboratory available at the University of Parma (Room B).

Other than the physical features of the two testing rooms, the measurements differed in the radius dimension of the virtual semicircle, where the samples were placed at the center: $r = 4$ m for Room A, $r = 5$ m for Room B. The choice of testing inside a semi-anechoic chamber, although considered too narrow for carrying this type of test, fell by keeping unwanted acoustical contributions from the vertical walls, while the concern of the floor reflections was solved by disposing of microphones on the floor. Although very minimal, the contribution of extraneous reflections inside Room A compromised the results of the scattered sound from the panels, which should be discarded because they cannot be compared with the affordable values obtained in Room B. This outcome would be considered a challenge when trying to undertake a data analysis where the conditions are not favorable. On this basis, the best solution was to discard the results not in line with the procedure, as outlined by the standard requirements.

The results of panels tested inside Room B instead were compared with the reference curves of a theoretical model based on the theory of sound propagation in free field conditions, and data analysis consisted of a polar distribution of the scattered field through the use of the Fast Fourier Transform (FFT). A final calculation related to the diffusion coefficients of the selected panels in the specific configurations has been carried out for the frequency range comprised between 125 Hz and 8 kHz.

This paper would like to highlight the attention given to the correct procedure outlined by the regulations to be followed for a successful data output, which, instead, would be compromised by extraneous factors that should not be in place.

Author Contributions: Conceptualization, L.T. and A.F.; methodology, L.T. and A.F.; software, F.M.; validation, A.B.; formal analysis, L.T. and A.F.; investigation, P.F.; resources, L.T.; data curation, F.M.

and P.F.; writing original draft preparation, A.B.; visualization, A.B. and P.F. All authors have read and agreed to the published version of the manuscript.

Funding: This work was carried on within the project "SIPARIO-Il Suono: Arte Intangibile delle Performing Arts—Ricerca su teatri italiani per l'Opera POR-FESR 2014-20", n. PG/2018/632038, funded by the Regione Emilia Romagna under EU Commission.

Institutional Review Board Statement: Not applicable.

Informed Consent Statement: Not applicable.

Conflicts of Interest: The authors declare no conflict of interest.

References

1. Hodgson, M. Evidence of diffuse surface reflections in rooms. *J. Acoust. Soc. Am.* **1991**, *88*, S185. [CrossRef]
2. Embrechts, J.-J. A geometrical acoustics approach linking surface scattering and reverberation in room acoustics. *Acta Acust. United Acust.* **2014**, *100*, 864–879. [CrossRef]
3. Embrechts, J.-J. An analytical model for reverberation energy decays in rooms with specular and diffuse reflections. *J. Acoust. Soc. Am.* **2019**, *145*, 2724–2732. [CrossRef] [PubMed]
4. Tronchin, L.; Merli, F.; Manfren, M.; Nastasi, B. The sound diffusion in Italian Opera Houses: Some examples. *Build. Acost.* **2020**, *27*, 333–355. [CrossRef]
5. Bibby, C.; Hodgson, M. Characterization and improvement of absorption and scattering by profiled architectural surfaces without specialized test facilities. *Appl. Acoust.* **2011**, *72*, 889–898. [CrossRef]
6. Cox, T.J.; D'Antonio, P. *Acoustic Absorbers and Diffusers: Theory, Design and Application*, 2nd ed.; CRC Press: New York, NY, USA, 2009.
7. Kuttruff, H. *Room Acoustics*, 3rd ed.; CRC Press: London, UK, 2016.
8. Schroeder, M.R. Binaural dissimilarity and optimum ceilings for concert halls: More lateral sound diffusion. *J. Acoust. Soc. Am.* **1979**, *65*, 958–963. [CrossRef]
9. Cox, T.J. The optimization of profiled diffusers. *J. Acoust. Soc. Am.* **1995**, *97*, 2928–2936. [CrossRef]
10. Takahashi, D. Development of optimum acoustic diffusers. *J. Acoust. Soc. Jpn.* **1995**, *16*, 51–58. [CrossRef]
11. Cox, T.J.; Dalenback, B.-I.L.; D'Antonio, P.; Embrechts, J.J.; Jeon, J.Y.; Mommertz, E.; Vorländer, M. A tutorial on scattering and diffusion coefficients for room acoustic surfaces. *Acta Acust. United Acust.* **2006**, *92*, 1–15.
12. Hargreaves, T.J.; Cox, J.T.; Lam, Y.W.; D'Antonio, P. Surface diffusion coefficients for room acoustics: Free-field measures. *J. Acoust. Soc. Am.* **2000**, *108*, 1710–1720. [CrossRef] [PubMed]
13. Choi, Y.-J.; Jeong, D.-U. Some issues in measurement of the random-incidence scattering coefficients in a reverberation room. *Acta Acust. United Acust.* **2008**, *94*, 769–773. [CrossRef]
14. AES-4id-2001. AES information document for room acoustics and sound reinforcement systems—Characterization and measurement of surface scattering uniformity. *J. Audio Eng. Soc.* **2001**, *49*, 148–165.
15. Vorländer, M.; Mommertz, E. Definition and measurement of random incidence scattering coefficients. *Appl. Acoust.* **2000**, *60*, 187–199. [CrossRef]
16. Vorländer, M.; Embrechts, J.-J.; De Geetere, L.; Vermeir, G.; De Avelar Gomes, M.H. Case studies in measurement of random incidence scattering coefficients. *Acta Acust. United Acust.* **2004**, *90*, 858–867.
17. ISO 17497-1:2004. *Acoustics—Sound-Scattering Properties of Surfaces—Part 1: Measurement of the Random-Incidence Scattering Coefficient in a Reverberation Room*; Organisation Internationale de Normalization: Geneva, Switzerland, 2004.
18. ISO 17497. *Acoustics—Sound-Scattering Properties of Surfaces—Part 2: Measurement of the Directional Diffusion Coefficient in a Free Field*; Organisation Internationale de Normalization: Geneva, Switzerland, 2012.
19. Farina, A. A new method for measuring the scattering coefficient and the diffusion coefficient of panels. *Acta Acust. United Acust.* **2000**, *86*, 928–942.
20. Ballestero, E.; Jimenez, N.; Groby, J.P.; Dance, S.; Ayugun, H.; Romero-Garcia, V. Experimental validation of deep-subwavelength difusión by acoustic metadiffusers. *Appl. Phys. Lett.* **2019**, *115*, 081901. [CrossRef]
21. ISO 354. *Acoustics—Measurement of Sound Absorption in a Reverberation Room*; Organisation Internationale de Normalization: Geneva, Switzerland, 2003.
22. ISO 18233. *Acoustics—Application of New Measurement Methods in Building and Room Acoustics*; Organisation Internationale de Normalization: Geneva, Switzerland, 2006.

Correction

Correction: Begum, H.; Horoshenkov, K.V. Acoustical Properties of Fiberglass Blankets Impregnated with Silica Aerogel. *Appl. Sci.* 2021, *11*, 4593

Hasina Begum * and Kirill V. Horoshenkov

Department of Mechanical Engineering, The University of Sheffield, Sheffield S1 3JD, UK; k.horoshenkov@sheffield.ac.uk
* Correspondence: hbegum3@sheffield.ac.uk; Tel.: +44-75-2157-0011

The authors wish to make the following corrections to the published paper [1]. They should be as follows:

Change in main body paragraphs

There are three mistakes in this article [1]:

1. Page 9, in the Table 1 heading, the unit of "Pore Size, $\bar{s}^{(i)}$, mm" will be corrected to "Pore Size, $\bar{s}^{(i)}$, μm".
2. Page 9, in the sixth line of the fifth paragraph in Section 4.2. Acoustical Properties, the unit of "99.4 to 20.5 mm" will be corrected to "99.4 to 20.5 μm".
3. Page 10, in the 11th line of the 2nd paragraph in Section 5. Conclusions, the unit of "mm" will be corrected to "μm".

Change in Tables

The authors wish to make the following correction to this paper [1] due to an error in Table 1 headings. It should be as follows:

Table 1. Values of the non-acoustical parameters inverted from fitting the model [28] to the measured complex reflection coefficient data for the five types of fiberglass blankets.

Filling Ratio, %	Layer Thickness, d, mm	Pore Size, $\bar{s}^{(i)}$, μm	Porosity, $\phi^{(i)}$	Standard Deviation in Pore Size, $\sigma_s^{(i)}$	Calculated Porosity, ϕ	RMS Error, %
0	8.12 ± 0.77	99.4 ± 4.15	0.994 ± 0.0098	0	0.965 ± 0.0041	1.4
25	9.33 ± 1.60	48.0 ± 20.2	0.938 ± 0.018	0.160 ± 0.213	0.960 ± 0.0044	1.7
50	9.26 ± 0.47	32.8 ± 2.00	0.929 ± 0.011	0	0.952 ± 0.0026	1.8
75	10.35 ± 0.85	20.5 ± 1.35	0.959 ± 0.032	0	0.951 ± 0.0036	3.6
100	9.34 ± 0.84	83.0 ± 2.04	0.505 ± 0.091	0.55 ± 0.015	0.94 ± 0.0067	2.5

These were inadvertent errors; we apologize for any inconvenience caused to the readers and authors by this change. The changes do not affect the scientific results.

Reference

1. Begum, H.; Horoshenkov, K.V. Acoustical Properties of Fiberglass Blankets Impregnated with Silica Aerogel. *Appl. Sci.* **2021**, *11*, 4593. [CrossRef]

MDPI
St. Alban-Anlage 66
4052 Basel
Switzerland
Tel. +41 61 683 77 34
Fax +41 61 302 89 18
www.mdpi.com

Applied Sciences Editorial Office
E-mail: applsci@mdpi.com
www.mdpi.com/journal/applsci

www.ingramcontent.com/pod-product-compliance
Lightning Source LLC
LaVergne TN
LVHW070726100526
838202LV00013B/1180